AT HOME WITH
Muhammad Ali

Also by Hana Ali

More than a Hero
The Soul of a Butterfly
Ali on Ali

AT HOME WITH
Muhammad Ali

A memoir of love, loss and forgiveness

BANTAM PRESS

LONDON · NEW YORK · TORONTO · SYDNEY · AUCKLAND

TRANSWORLD PUBLISHERS
61–63 Uxbridge Road, London W5 5SA
www.penguin.co.uk

Transworld is part of the Penguin Random House group of companies
whose addresses can be found at global.penguinrandomhouse.com

Penguin
Random House
UK

First published in Great Britain in 2018 by Bantam Press
an imprint of Transworld Publishers

All photographs have been kindly supplied by the author with the following
exceptions: pp. 8 (top), 26, 35, 87 (both), 100, 270, 342, 417 © Howard
Bingham; p. 59 © Guy Crowder; pp. vi, 242 (bottom) © Michael Gaffney;
p. 379 © Jean Kilroy; p. 423 (bottom) © Adrees Latif; p. 92 © Tim Shanahan;
p. 430 © John Stewart; p. 423 (top) © John Summers; p. 29 USA Today Sports.

Every effort has been made to obtain the necessary permissions with
reference to copyright material, both illustrative and quoted. We apologize
for any omissions in this respect and will be pleased to make the
appropriate acknowledgements in any future edition.

A CIP catalogue record for this book
is available from the British Library.

ISBNs 9780593078341 (cased)
9780593078358 (tpb)

Typeset in 10.5/15 pt Avenir
by Integra Software Services Pvt. Ltd, Pondicherry

Printed and bound in Great Britain by Clays Ltd, Elcograf S.p.A.

Penguin Random House is committed to a sustainable future for our
business, our readers and our planet. This book is made from
Forest Stewardship Council® certified paper.

1 3 5 7 9 10 8 6 4 2

CONTENTS

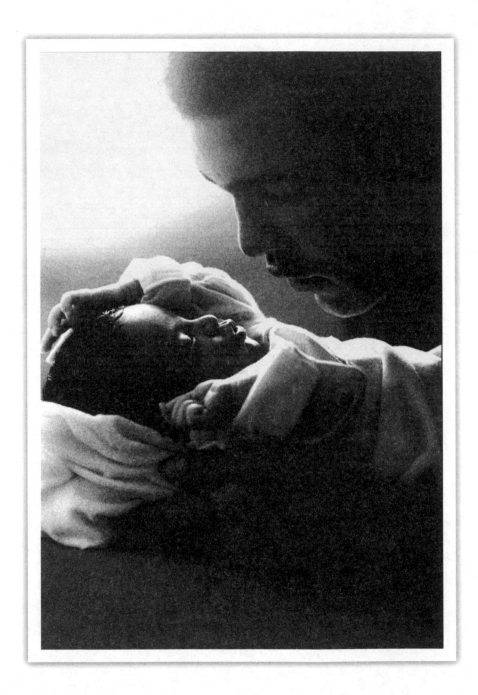

For my ineffable father, the love of my life.
"If tears could build a stairway and memories were a lane,
I would walk right up to heaven and bring you back again ..."

INTRODUCTION

NOTHING INSPIRES LIKE love: love for life, love for our family and friends, love for our husbands or wives, and love for our parents and our children. It is love that makes the pain worth bearing, the heart worth chancing, and *love* that saves us after we've risen and fallen, only to rise and fall again. As the great romances of our time—*A Farewell to Arms, Doctor Zhivago, The Notebook, The Great Gatsby, The Bridges of Madison County*—eternally express, *love* is all-consuming.

It's been said that my father is one of the most written-about people in the world. As the chronicles continue to grow, the deepest, and most essential, essence of his spirit is still largely unknown.

My father once said: *"I've been an actor my entire life. I wrote my own lines. I directed my own scenes. I starred in my own plays. I sold my own legend!"* Have you ever wondered what happened after the curtain fell, the final song, and the last bow? Have you ever wondered what went on behind the scenes, in the everyday private life of, arguably, the world's most famous man? What dreams he planned, what fears he endured, or the kind of parent he was to his nine children?

This is a love story. About a husband and the wife he lost, a father and the children he adored, and a man and the world that admires him. It is also the tale of a little girl and her adventures with her beloved father—the joy and laughter, the pain and sorrow—and the memories of her childhood home. Brought together here, through a confluence of audio recordings, love letters, diaries, and family

1

photos, this memoir paints a candid portrait of Muhammad Ali's *untold* family legacy.

We all know about the eighteen-year-old Olympic gold medalist who went on to become the world's greatest champion, winning the heavyweight title for the first time at the age of twenty-two. With his quick wit, remarkable confidence and dazzling speed, he danced rings around his opponents while rhyming and predicting the rounds in which they would fall.

You've probably read about his religious conversion, when he changed his name to Muhammad Ali, and the stand he took refusing to fight in the Vietnam War on religious and moral grounds. Before entering the induction room on the morning of April 28, 1967, he was offered deals—told that he could perform boxing exhibitions and never see the battlefield—but he refused to compromise his principles. When the hour of truth arrived, and the name Cassius Marcellus Clay Jr was called at the induction center, Muhammad Ali stood perfectly still. He knew in advance there would be consequences, and he was ready to pay the price of freedom.

Never wavering in his resolve, he would be unjustly stripped of his heavyweight title, banned from boxing, fined thousands of dollars, sentenced to five years in prison, and have his passport revoked. He lost three and a half of his prime fighting years, then on June 28, 1971, the Supreme Court unanimously overturned his conviction. And we all know about his return to glory and the legendary fights that followed.

In the late 1970s my father began making a series of audiotapes, mostly in our Los Angeles home. He chronicled nearly a hundred hours of memories and conversations on various topics and issues. My father always had his own way of doing things. His audio diaries are his unique efforts at recording his own legacy.

"If anyone is wondering why I, Muhammad Ali, am making these tapes, it's because history is so beautiful. And, at the time we're living, we don't always realize it ..."

Someone once told me my father is like an impressionist painting—a beautiful, complex work of art. Up close, you can see the brush strokes, the fine details, but you need to step back to see the whole canvas.

In these pages, which link the golden and sometimes shadowy barriers between the past and present, I offer you this unique gift: a glimpse deep into my father's heart. When observing him closely, you may find that sometimes his colors clash and contradict one another, but they never overshadow his natural light—his *true* nature.

To know the spirit of *the Man*, Muhammad Ali, and understand his heart and mind, you must walk the path he traveled and experience the overwhelming responsibilities he felt. While no book can recapture the magic, nor the inspiration, of his entire life, I hope *At Home with Muhammad Ali* will personify and extend his spirit—and show my father as he truly was: a remarkable human being with extraordinary *qualities* and human *flaws*. More importantly, a gentle father, patient and caring, with a heart purer than most will ever know.

Many athletes, and men in general, have reputations for being absent fathers. They have children they've never seen or taken financial responsibility for. It's important to my father's legacy that the world knows how much his children meant to him and how hard he worked to keep us united. How he remained friendly with all his ex-wives and was exceptionally generous when the relationships ended. You learn a lot about a person's character by observing the way they handle their mistakes. My father wasn't perfect, nobody is, but he owned up to his responsibilities. He never pointed fingers or made excuses for himself. He always provided for his children and our mothers. He is a father who adored his kids. Everything he did was for the livelihood of his family.

The prevailing questions asked of my siblings and me over the years are "How does it feel having Muhammad Ali as a father?" and "What was he like at home?"

I was born on August 6, 1976, the eldest of two daughters from my father's third marriage to Veronica Porche. It's been an incredible and adventurous experience, but, as you will see, growing up Muhammad Ali's child wasn't always pain-free.

Like any family, we've had ups and downs, sorrows and regrets, happy and unpleasant memories. The difference is we had to share our dad with one another, and the world.

My father had Maryum (May May), Rasheda, Jamillah, and Muhammad Jr with his second wife, Belinda Boyd. He had Laila and me with his third wife, Veronica Porche, and two children, Miya and Khaliah, with women he was never married to, Pat and Aaisha. In 1989, he and his widow, Lonnie, adopted a son. Asaad was born long after my father made his recordings, so he isn't mentioned often in this book, but Asaad is an important part of his heart and legacy.

Dad never had children with his first wife, Sonji Roi, who once said to his eldest daughter, Maryum, "You should have been mine."

Although, as his children, our stories differ, and each of our experiences is unique, we share this in common: throughout our lives, our father showered us with unconditional love and affection. I often told my dad he was the eighth wonder of the world. He was complicated in so many ways, yet simple in others. In his ability to show both compassion and forgiveness, he stood uniquely alone. As writer Steven Leckart once said to me, he witnessed the worst in people and still somehow retained the best in himself. In my eyes, he will always be the measure of greatness.

He was an Olympic gold medalist, a three-time World Heavyweight Champion, a conscientious objector, an Ambassador of Peace, and a hostage negotiator. He has ignited the Olympic cauldron and received the Presidential Medal of Freedom; now loved and admired for the same reasons he was once despised and scorned, he's lived the life of a hundred men. Yet the role he cherished most was being a father.

"Khaliah," he said to my sister when she was six years old, "*when you were a little girl you would never talk to me, you would just hang up the phone ... How old are you now, Khaliah?*"

"*I'm in the first grade ... Daddy, I saw your picture in the store window.*"

"*What kind of picture was it?*"

"*You were smiling ...*"

5

When people achieve great success, something in their lives has to suffer. For Dad, it was him and his children. The demands of his career often kept him away from home. He missed out on a lot of the special little moments, like first steps, first words, and first days of school. With eight children from four different relationships, living in four different states, he could not be physically present for us all. Some of my siblings saw him more often on television than in person and spoke to him mostly over the telephone.

"Daddy, guess what?" continued Khaliah, "There was a boy at school and he said you were ugly and I said, 'My daddy's BEAUTIFUL!' And he said he can beat you up, and I said, 'No, you can't!' And guess what I did?"

"What did you do?"

She pauses, as if considering. "Nah, I can't tell."

"Did you slap him?"

"How did you know?!"

"I was just guessing—you didn't slap that boy?"

"Yes, I did!"

"No, you didn't!"

"Yes, I did!"

"Then what did you say to him?"

"I told him my daddy's 'The Greatest'!"

We each had a unique relationship with our dad—though we all felt the sting of missing him when he was away, and the ache of having to say goodbye when our parents separated. The happy memories outweigh the unpleasant by far, and we're left only with an incredible feeling of gratitude and appreciation for our remarkable father.

I've edited the recordings in this book for readability, not content. And I have changed some names for anonymity. I hope people will enjoy and recognize this document for what it is: an honest and intimate glimpse into the daily life of an imperfect, yet remarkable, human being. It reveals the life of a man who loved using his fame for good and making people smile. A man who lived his life openly, welcoming and friendly to everyone. A man who had the foresight to know his invaluable tape recordings would be cherished. And a man who, as his voice began to diminish, recorded every word for his family and posterity. As with all great portraits, to fully appreciate its depth and beauty both the light and shade are necessary.

When I started this book, my father was living, but he is no longer of this world. To hear his old, familiar voice, to experience him in his everyday *home life*, is an invaluable gift I wish to share, in written word, with the world to which he has always partly belonged.

In life, we all have parts to play. As this book will show, my father had many roles. The legend of his love will carry on for generations without end, and his voice will become a *living* memory. Like the enduring words of the world's greatest writer William Shakespeare, "So long as men can breathe and eyes can see, so long lives this, and this gives life to thee."

Top: Dad and Asaad.

"Time is somewhat of a mystery;
we often get caught up in its history."

– Muhammad Ali, letter to Veronica, 1985

PROLOGUE

THERE ARE LOVE stories that get lost in the sphere of time, that can be seen through the looking glass of a thousand stars. This is one of them. It began with a gift, a gift that was safely tucked away in an old weathered briefcase, collecting dust in the corner of a basement. In the company of old trophies, awards, and boxing memorabilia, its golden messages whispered in the dark, waiting patiently for the years to pass so they may fulfill their purpose. Then, one quiet evening, a trembling yet steady hand reached for the case, dusted it off, and carried it upstairs. Beneath a soft light, Muhammad Ali carefully opened it. He took out an old audio recording and put it into the tape player. Then he closed his eyes, leaned back in his chair, and listened to his old, familiar voice and the sound of his children's laughter ...

"This is Muhammad Ali at 55 Fremont Place, January 5, 1980. The time is 11 a.m., in Los Angeles. I'm chasing Hana and Laila ..."
    At eleven o'clock in the morning, around the corner from a guarded entrance to an exclusive residential enclave stood a beautiful white, rococo mansion. A tan-and-brown Rolls-Royce Corniche convertible sat in the driveway. To the left was a furnished patio, to the right a flight of steps leading to the swimming pool. Butterflies fluttered in the back garden as two regal Doberman pinschers, Sheba and Samson, paced the tailored lawn.

Within the ornate stone walls of this thirty-room house, my father, wrapped in a brown terry bathrobe, worked eagerly in his first-floor mahogany-paneled den, as if in a race against time. His feet stuck out from under his gold-trimmed Louis XVI desk. Collections of exotic birds, the passion of my mother, Veronica, screeched from the adjoining conservatory.

Upstairs, our antique-filled home swarmed with young life. As two little girls, my sister Laila and I ran downstairs, love and laughter echoed through the halls. When he heard us, our father put down his pen. Contemplating our fleeting youth, he grabbed the tape recorder from his desk drawer and rushed after us ...

"This is Muhammad Ali at the house on Fremont Place ..." His breathing heavy. His voice shaky from running. *"I'm chasing Hana and Laila ... I'm Bigfoot!"* He growled, stomping down the hall behind us. *"I'm the Incredible Hulk!"* Stomp! Stomp! Stomp!

We ran into his office, screaming with unbridled laughter. *"Aaaaaahh!"*

"Now they're on the couch, cuddling up together. I'm coming after them! Hana's four, Laila's three ... I'm coming!"

"Aaaaaahh!" we screamed, then jumped off the sofa and ran out of the room.

"Chase me again, Daddy ..." I called, running up the stairs into my mother's room.

"Me, too!" said Laila, following behind me.

"Now they're grabbing their mother's coat-tail, trying to hide—I'm coming for them!"

I jumped out from behind my mother: *"I'm The Big Bad Wolf! Roooaarr!"*

"Hana's making a scary face," he whispered in the recorder. *"Aaaaaahh!"* He mock-screamed.

"Roooaarrr!" I roared again, dangling my arms above my head, as I ran towards him. *"I'm Dracula!"* I shouted, as Laila mimicked me.

"Aaaaaahh! Now they're both coming after me!" he hollered, as we chased him back down the hall. Our voices trailed off with the sound of love and laughter ...

Top: Me on the right, Laila on the left, at Dad's training camp in 1980.

After the noise settled my father spoke into the recorder again, addressing posterity and our future selves: *"Now we're going to listen to this tape, so Hana and Laila can hear how they sound. I wish that I had tapes of myself when I was this small—I'm sure most people do. I'm thankful to almighty God that I appreciate life and realize how great life is. Once we get old, we'll never be back at this age again, and I know it's nice to have a record of all these things. This is Muhammad Ali at 55 Fremont Place, January 5, 1980. The time is 11:05 a.m. in Los Angeles. This is for you, Hana and Laila and Veronica, to hear years from now. You will thank me for this one day."*

Eighteen Years Later, 1998

ONE FATED AFTERNOON IN Los Angeles, my father and I were watching a classic Clint Eastwood film in his hotel room when, without warning, he pulled an old briefcase from behind his chair and dumped its contents on the rug in front of me. I was nineteen by then and had already received so many gifts from him—monetary gifts, boxing memorabilia, priceless manuscripts by the scholar and teacher Hazrat Inayat Khan, about love, life, and the human condition, which he referred to as "the wisest books in the world". I'm grateful for everything, but nothing prepared me for what I was about to receive in that room, and nothing would *ever* compare.

I stared curiously at a pile of micro tape cassettes. I didn't know yet that soon my life would change forever, that I'd discover things about my dad I never knew. All that would come later.

When I was in junior high, my father had casually mentioned the recordings he'd made when I was a little girl. He said, "One day, when you're a big lady, I'm going to play them for you, so you can hear how you used to sound." But the moments he'd captured would remain elusive—a phantom I'd heard of but had yet to see. And over the years their existence faded into the shadows of my distant memories.

14

I wondered again why he'd never mentioned the recordings of love, his plans, fears, and adventures, waiting to share their secrets with his children and the world. If he had told me, if I had known what was on the tapes, waiting to be discovered, there's no way I would have forgotten them—not a chance. But, like their enduring messages, frozen in time, he waited patiently for the years to pass.

Carefully examining the tapes, I struggled to make out the scratchy writing labeling each cassette. Apart from his signature, which he wanted to be large and clear so people could read his name, my father's penmanship was never legible. When we were writing his auto-biography, *The Soul of a Butterfly*, in 2003, I watched as he worked in the leather-bound journals I'd bought him for one of his birthdays. He sat peacefully at his desk, beneath a soft light, copying his favorite quotes and poems from lined yellow paper onto the crisp cream pages of the journals. Just as he did when I was a little girl sitting on his lap in his office at Fremont Place as he read and wrote. He always kept a list of his favorite passages and anecdotes. I never noticed as a child—perhaps it was a habit he acquired later in life—his compulsion to rip out the pages he had written on. He was unsatisfied with his imperfect handwriting. An inclination I would also acquire. Like in my father's office, dozens of beautiful journals line my bookshelf—all with torn-out pages. The apple landed faithfully beside the tree.

With a raised brow, I picked up one of the cassettes. "What's on these tapes, Dad?"

His eyes brightened as he waved his hand slowly across the lot. His voice had a mystical tenor, as though he was about to reveal a sacred truth. *Ha*, I thought, *how typical of my father to reel me in with the theatrics.* As usual, it was working. The moment his eyes widened, I was hooked.

"There are tapes here of you and Laila, and your other sisters and brother, talking to me when you were young." He paused and leaned forward. "One day, when you have children of your own, you'll be able to play these for them, so they can hear their mother talking to her father when she was a little girl." He settled back in his chair beaming, unable to conceal his tremendous pride in this fact.

As I stared at the tapes, a cloudy memory resurfaced. The echo of my father and me singing, laughing and playing rings softly in my ear.

"Up in the morning off to school, the teachers teach the golden rule ..."

Singing together, *"American history and practical math ... hoping and hoping and hoping to pass ..."*

Did he really record all these moments—my childhood memories? Hairs began to quiver on the back of my neck and an odd sixth sense overcame me. I saw a vague image of him chasing Laila and me down the hall, past the large Tiffany glass screen that dominated the second floor. We were laughing uncontrollably. *"Now they're on the couch, cuddling up together. I'm coming after them! Hana's four, Laila's three ... I'm coming!"*

Suddenly, I felt an overwhelming urge to hear the recordings and slid one of the tapes into the tiny machine. My father smiled as I pressed play and the past sprang to life.

***

"MUHAMMAD, THE PRESIDENT'S wife, Mrs Carter, has been calling for you for three days; can I give her your telephone number in Los Angeles?"

"Yeah, I spoke to her. I told her I'd be there in DC when she needs me. Hold on, Mr Lomax, my other line is ringing ..."

I played another recording. *"Muhammad, where have you been lately? I saw your picture in the newspaper."* An Israeli reporter is calling from overseas. *"You were in Hong Kong and Cambodia, and some other places."*

"I've just come back from Peking. They made me their official boxing trainer and boxing promoter—to help bring boxing back to China ..."

I played another recording. *"Tell me, Champ, you are NOT going back to the ring!"*

"I've had so many offers and, naturally, I went out on top. I went out supreme. I went out three-time champion, still dancing and moving fast—good reflexes, good coordination, good timing ..."

"Sting like a bee!"

"*Yeah! So naturally people would like to see me. I think I might. I've been tempted, but I don't know ...*"

I played another recording. "*Muhammad, what do you think about the peace treaty between Israel and Egypt—do you find it a good one?*"

"*I know nothing about the politics of Israel and Egypt. Although I am a Muslim, I don't understand the problems the two countries have been having over the years. But I know all people are God's people regardless of race, religion or color, and I know that God, Allah, is not for war. I know God, Allah, is not for violence, and I know he is for peace ...*"

As I sorted through the tapes, I felt like I was handling a pile of gold. All the love and adventures of my childhood, days gone by, moments lived long ago, were reaching out to me in the present. And I heard my father's voice—loud, clear and full of life.

"*Mama Bird,*" he says to his mother, "*I want to ask you something—make me laugh one more time. Do you remember that day Cash, Daddy, came home to get some money or something, and you followed him out and chased him down the street?*"

With a sweet Southern accent, "*Yeah, I remember! And he was running down the alley! Sure, I remember ... you were a little boy. Wasn't that funny?*"

"*Yeah, he had a woman in the car ... he ran so fast the dirt flew up!*"

Laughing, "*They were flying down that alley ...*"

As I listened, the memories circled in my mind like a merry-go-round of bygone dreams and adventures. Without ever leaving the comforts of my father's hotel room I lost myself in that time and place, and felt the heart-aching nostalgia of never being able to go back again.

"*Hana, you were a sweet little girl. You are so beautiful, I just kiss your little jaws all the time. I always squeeze you and hug you—and I love you ...*"

Every recording took me back to a different period. "*This is Muhammad Ali making a tape for future reference. We're now in a crisis where the Iranian college students are holding over fifty American hostages. People have been calling me and pleading for* me not to go. They're very frightened when it comes to taking a stand for what is right and for God ..."

My father's voice was like a ghost from the past—the way it sounded when I was a little girl. Before time conveyed the inevitable. Every word he spoke lured me deeper into the fabric of a dream. I went to a grand and melancholy place—*Fremont Place*—where our tongues had a silver lining and our words were laced in gold.

"*I want to go upstairs and see Mommy.*"

"*Mommy is washing her hair. Then she has to roll her hair and dry her hair.*"

"*I want to, Daddy! I want to go upstairs and see Mommy! I want her to hear me talking on that thing.*"

"*You want her to hear you talking on this tape?*"

"*Yeah.*"

"*Hana, can you wait thirty minutes? Mommy told me not to bring you up until she's finished. If I take you up now, I might get in trouble. What if she whoops me?*"

"*I want to, Daddy ... I want to go now!*"

"*Hana, you are three years old, trying to boss me.*"

"*I WANT TO GO NOW!*"

"*Stop hollering, Hana.*"

"*Can I holler a little bit?*"

"*Okay.*"

Now whispering, "*I want to go upstairs and see Mommy ...*"

I played another recording, and another and another. As one memory rolled into the next, I traveled back to that grand old house which so long ago ceased to belong to us; where my most cherished childhood memories still thrived in the annals of my heart and mind, and in dozens of micro tape cassettes—*before the divorce.*

Before the "*For Sale*" signs appeared on our lawn and the movers emptied the house. Before I cried myself to sleep at night, worrying about my father. And before the picture-perfect image of my childhood began fraying at the edges.

***

December 9, 1979

IT'S A LIVELY morning at Fremont Place. The relentless ringing of the telephone, the shuffling of lined yellow paper, and the clicking of the tape recorder have already begun. My father is sitting comfortably behind his grand mahogany desk, as always, ready to tackle the adventures of another bustling day. He smiles at the sight of Laila and me playing on the floor in our pajamas, then he leans back in his huge leather chair and takes another sip of coffee before reaching for the ringing telephone.

"Hello?"

"Hello, Muhammad, this is Jerry Lister calling from the New York Post. Listen, what I want to tell you is in the Star newspaper, which we also own, you've just been voted by their four million readers as the celebrity of the decade—over everybody!"

"No kidding—you jokin', man! Who was in the running with me?"

"Farrah Fawcett, Robert Redford, Paul Newman—everybody!"

"Are you serious? When is it going to come out?"

"In two weeks. They want to know what your reaction is to being voted the Celebrity of the Decade."

"I can't believe it! You mean out of all those movie stars and athletes, too?"

"Yep! You were also voted by the New York Post and the World News Corporation as the Athlete of the Decade. They didn't think it was going to happen, but all of the ballots came in and you were voted the Celebrity of the '70s."

"You mean of ALL the celebrities?"

"Of everybody! The ballots came in yesterday afternoon."

"I can't believe it. I know worldwide that I have a higher rating, but I didn't know that it was the same in America."

"Yep, America's number one celebrity for the '70s—of all the movie stars, politicians, everybody!"

"No kidding! That's hard to believe because there are so many more celebrities and movie stars ... That means movie stars and athletes?"

"Movie stars, athletes, politicians—everybody!"

19

"No kidding—of ALL the '70s!"

"Of ALL the '70s!"

"I have a trophy room here at my new house in Los Angeles. I'm putting up photos of great moments in my career and plaques and awards and trophies. And this, what you're telling me about, they don't give no trophy or nothing, do they?"

"Yes, they're going to give you a special award."

"Yeah, because I want to put that with the rest of my awards. Who voted?"

"All the Star readers. They sell almost four million copies a week . . ."

He looks down at the telephone. All three lines are flashing. "My other line is ringing—hold on . . . Hello?"

"Champ, would you do me a personal favor? I'm one of your greatest admirers." Another journalist is calling from across the sea. "When I heard that somebody offered you to come back to the ring I was going to write you to say, 'NO, Champ!'"

"I appreciate it. I'm very glad you felt like that. This is one reason I haven't returned, because people want to see me go out a winner, and I think it would be a sin and a shame—a crime—for me to continue and jeopardize what I've built, which is something I don't think any man will break in our lifetime. They say records are made to be broken, but I don't think any man will ever be four-time World Heavyweight Champion."

"No, Champ. Not in this century ... Maybe not even the next ... Tell me, Champ, what are your plans for the 1980s?"

"I'm real confused. I don't know what it is that I want to do. I have offers to train professional boxers here in America. I don't think that will make me happy. I have offers to have a nationwide television show, speaking to various people on world issues. I don't think that will make me too happy. I have an offer to probably make a couple of movies once a year. That wouldn't make me too happy. I don't know what it is that I want to do, so I'm trying to decide what I want to do with my life ..."

Domestic Affairs

I used to chase women all the time. I won't say it was right—but look at all the temptation I had. I was young, handsome and heavyweight champion of the world. Women were always offering themselves to me. I had two children by women I wasn't married to. I love them. They're my children. I feel just as proud and good about them as my other children. But that wasn't the right thing to do. Running around living that kind of life wasn't good for me. It hurt my wife, offended God and it never really made me happy. Ask any man who is forty years old—if he knew at twenty what he knows now, would he do things different? Most people would. Sometimes things you do early in life, you feel embarrassed about later. So, I did wrong, I'm sorry. And all I'll say, as far as running around and chasing women is concerned, is that's all in the past.

    – Muhammad Ali in *Muhammad Ali: His Life and Times*,
Thomas Hauser, 1991

1

Summer of 2012

FOURTEEN YEARS AFTER my father's tape recordings were revealed to me there was the unearthing of his old love letters—letters that had been lost for a long time, waiting out nearly three decades in a crowded storage room in Los Angeles. I still think about it sometimes: my mother's storage, full of old newspaper clippings, family photos, diaries, paintings, and antique furnishings from my childhood home, all neatly stacked together in labeled cardboard boxes collecting dust. My father's words whispering in the dark; swelling and sighing with yesterday's hopes and dreams. His heart, etched on lined yellow paper, a hidden treasure waiting to be discovered.

I wonder what was on his mind when he left the envelope of letters on his office floor. Was it too painful for him to place them in my mother's hands? Did he hope she would find them, or that they would somehow find their way to her? Perhaps he simply forgot them, over-looking them in the distress of gathering the last of his belongings from our newly sold home. Knowing Dad, I'd say he left the letters there on purpose, thinking that Marge, the executive secretary, would discover them in his otherwise empty office and deliver them to Mom after he was gone. Or maybe he wrote them only for himself—to tuck away with all the other things left unsaid and undone between them.

I guess I will never know. I'm okay with that. Some questions are best left unasked. They cause too much pain. But it saddens me to

Laila on Dad's lap and me on my mother's. Taken at Fremont Place.

think that, if my father had handed my mother the letters, if he had at least told her about them, if the envelope hadn't been thrown in a random box and then stored away until she discovered them some thirty years later, it all might have turned out differently for my father, for me, my sister Laila—and for their marriage.

Like old ghosts, the memories of my childhood home haunt the annals of my mind and leave me wondering about days gone by: the constant ringing of my father's telephone, the crackling of the evening fire, the screeching of my mother's exotic birds, the smell of Dad's freshly brewed coffee, the clicking of his tape recorder capturing fleeting moments in time, the image of my father's Rolls-Royce returning home, and the haunting sound of his once lively voice echoing in the halls. I still think about them sometimes.

Damn ghosts!

2

"Hana, it's 10:30 p.m. You just woke me up asking for a popsicle. I went downstairs to get you one, but there were no popsicles left. Now you sent me back down to get you a pickle. This is December 24, 1979, at the house on 55 Fremont Place—Signing off."

I REMEMBER THE house on Fremont clearly. A shining memory, impervious to time, perfectly captured and protected—an image that will never fade. I can describe my childhood adventures, but a description will fail to capture the grandeur and exhilaration those moments held for me then, and still hold for me now. One day stands out in my memory because my father was coming home.

I close my eyes and see the gray-blue of the early-morning sky. The subtle scent of flowers that line the driveway washes over me and I feel a cool breeze caress my cheek. When I remember with my heart, more details materialize: the song of the birds whispering their melody in the wind, the echo of the barking Dobermans, the soothing rhythm of water rippling in the swimming pool. The familiar sounds of my childhood home reach across the barriers of time and take me back to a long-ago place. When I open my eyes, I'm six years old again.

It's quiet this morning, an almost eerie silence, and I'm standing on my tiptoes in the driveway beneath the balcony. I shouldn't be outside alone, barefoot in my pajamas, as Cruella De Vil aka the Big Bad Wolf (our new governess) would say. But Daddy is coming home

27

today, so here I wait with my forehead pressed against the cold iron gates, watching the clouds roll by, with a half-eaten carrot in my hand.

I had reached for the popsicles first, of course. But they were too high up. When Daddy left town, Cruella rearranged the freezer. One morning I had tried to get Cruella to give me a popsicle but she had handed me a carrot instead.

"If I am in charge, young lady," she said, with her thick Jamaican accent, "NO popsicles in the morning."

I wanted to punch her in the nose. By the time I was two years old my right hook was legendary—a side effect of watching my father train and our playful sparring lessons on weekend afternoons. "Show your strength, Hana," he'd say and I, his devoted clone, would raise both arms, flex my tiny muscles, clench my teeth and "Geeeer!"

People never paid heed to my mother's warnings. "Careful," she'd caution, as they pinched my chubby cheeks. "She hits." They must have assumed she was kidding. What harm could a toddler do? They learned the hard way.

With a few bruised noses under my belt, I fantasized about adding Cruella to my record. I imagined the look on her face when she caught a glimpse of my mighty little fist soaring up at her doomed nose. But then a list of possible punishments came to mind: *a week without cartoons, a week without swimming, a week confined to my room after preschool, a week with NO POPSICLES!* Nah, it wasn't worth it. I pouted and ate the carrot.

It's getting chilly outside. I've been up since 5 a.m., waiting for Daddy. The winter sun is shy and my little toes are beginning to feel as frozen as the popsicles I covet. I was in such a hurry to sneak out, crawling quietly through Cruella's adjoining bedroom, down the stairs, past the kitchen, and out the back patio door that I hadn't realized I was barefoot. I wasn't going back for my shoes. I'd learned from my last mistake. Getting caught buck naked under the coffee table the week before was an unforgettable experience, but I'll tell you about that one later.

The sound of an engine wakes me. I had fallen asleep on the patio steps waiting for Daddy.

Dad and me at home in 1979.

"Three tomorrows," he'd promised. "I'll be home in three tomorrows." My father had a way of explaining things. He could speak the secret language of children.

"You'll be home tomorrow?" I questioned, wide-eyed, as he prepared to leave.

"Not tomorrow. I'll be home in three days."

"When I go to bed and wake up again, then you'll be back?"

"After you go to bed and wake up THREE TIMES, then I'll be back. I'll be home in three tomorrows."

I rush down the steps as his brown Rolls purrs up the driveway. Daddy is HOME! *I know what that means ...*

3

I GREW UP inside a fairy tale. A family of four, living in a beautiful mansion, complete with a trellis and floral vine balcony. My father was the most famous man in the world, and my mother one of the most beautiful women in the world. Celebrities visited often: Michael Jackson, John Travolta, Sylvester Stallone, Clint Eastwood, Tom Jones, Cary Grant, Mr T, Kris Kristofferson, Lionel Richie, etc.

The house was always full of people. There was Marge, the executive secretary, Edith, the cook, Howard, the photographer, Abdel, the assistant, friends, fans and hangers-on, housekeepers, babysitters, governesses, grandparents, aunts and uncles. Life at Fremont Place was an endless adventure, and everyone wanted my father's time and attention.

There were pool parties and magic shows. Birthday celebrations with dancing clowns sculpting animals out of red and yellow balloons, children laughing on the lawn, riding rented ponies, eating cotton candy, sipping lemonade from peppermint straws. Life was good. And the feeling I remember most as a child is *love*.

Then, one day when I was ten years old, the fairy tale ended. The climbing plants growing slowly up the walls, beautiful and steadfast as they were, threatened the façade. The leafy vine began twining up roof shingles, pushing little rootlets into the sheathing and creeping into tiny cracks and crevices, fracturing the mortar and destroying the picture-perfect image of my childhood.

I blamed my mother. Laila was neutral. All my sister knew was that we were moving to a new house and Daddy wasn't coming. As long as she was with our mother her world was intact. It was my life that turned upside down—my heart that shattered into a trillion pieces.

As far as I was concerned, it was all my mother's fault. In my eyes, my father could do no wrong. He was the reason the sun rose in the morning: the first thing on my mind when I woke up and my last thought before going to sleep. He was and always would be the most wonderful thing in the world to me. So I appointed my mother the villain. After all, she was the one who left him, the one who destroyed our happy home … wasn't she?

***

WE ALL THINK we know our parents. Some of us may, but in most cases only half of what we think we know is true. If we're lucky, a fragment of the remaining portion is revealed to us later in life. In my case, through lost love letters, old audio recordings and forgotten interviews.

But where do I begin? It's impossible to recount all my childhood memories; everything seen and said at the house I grew up in at 55 Fremont Place. So much happened in the ten years we lived together as a family. I will share, then, the memories and stories that are most vivid, and those events which my father chose to immortalize for his children, himself, and posterity. Things he planned, concerns he fretted over; the decisions that brought him immeasurable joy and sometimes immense sorrow. The daily events of which the world never knew, and of course the special moments we shared that will never fade from my memory.

But first, I'll tell you a little about my mother and the letters.

I always thought my mother was impervious to tears. Love stories, family photos, happy and sad memories never made her weep like my father would. But that's not saying much—Dad teared up at the sight of Laila and me coming home from our first day of school. He was rather disposed to tears, and all things concerning the heart. My mother wasn't, or so I thought.

But that wasn't true. She wept in private. I know because I used to hear her crying at night, after the divorce. Her desolate sobs muffled in the dim light, creeping through the cracks of the bathroom door. And I was there when she discovered the letters—thirty years later during the summer of 2012. I saw her reaction to them, and it was more than overwhelming.

"I always thought he never fought for me," she said, her eyes damp. But, after all these years, it turns out she was wrong.

July of 2012

IT WAS A warm afternoon in mid-July, the sun was blinding, and the flowers were in full bloom, which meant my allergies were at full throttle. I stopped at a corner drug store, grabbed a bottle of Benadryl and a box of tissues, and went to the counter to pay. I was meeting my mother at her storage in downtown Los Angeles and I knew the dust and pollen would only make my allergies worse. I was looking forward to another afternoon of helping Mom sort through the old containers and files from my childhood home on Fremont Place.

When I walked into the storage unit, I could see Mom had already started. Three dozen or so boxes were stacked against the walls with their lists of contents written on the lids and sides—thirty years of memories, still housed in their original packaging. I love digging through her aged belongings. To the average person, they might smell of dust and mildew, but for me, they carry a nostalgic aroma of brewed coffee and Chanel perfume.

"Hey, Mom," I said as I walked into the storage unit. "I'm here."

"Hi," she called from the back of the room. "Be careful. I broke a glass in the front corner."

"Okay."

"I got most of it up, but there still might be a few broken pieces."

"Mom, I'm going to look through some of these boxes along the wall."

"All right—the ones on the right are mostly from the Malibu and Venice houses, but I saw a few boxes marked Fremont."

"Okay."

Malibu and Venice represented her two marriages after my father. She knew I was only concerned with boxes and items from Fremont Place. Most of them were stored in my grandmother's garage, but occasionally Mom would call me after she stumbled upon an old box from my childhood home in one of her storage units.

"Watch out for the spiders," she warned.

"I will." I put my purse down on a portable chair, next to my mother's, and started reading the labels. When I found the first box marked "Fremont Place", I couldn't resist ripping it open. Inside lay a host of forgotten items. Strange, how the contents in an old tattered box—French lace, crystal cologne bottles, books, my mother's diaries, newspaper clippings, old clothes—contents seemingly insignificant to anyone else, were so priceless to me, conjuring my happiest childhood memories.

"Time for our singing lessons, Hana, ready?"

"Yeah ..."

"This is dedicated to the one I love ..."

Each box triggered a wave of sneezes.

"Put your mask on, Hana!" my mother shouted from the opposite end of the storage.

She does that often these days—raises her voice. In my formative years, she spoke in gentle whispers, mostly. Her voice, light and airy, like a floating feather. But lately it sounded slightly elevated—and rather heavy. I'm not sure why, really. Maybe she metamorphosed when she left my father. Or maybe it was the strain of her second marriage, or the death of her third husband that changed her.

"Hana ... your mask!"

I was too enthralled to respond. I stood there sniffling and coughing, fumbling through my father's trophies and awards, old photo albums and enchanting gifts he and Mom had received from princes, queens, and heads of state from around the world. I leaned against the storage room wall and let my mind travel back to my majestic childhood home. To a time when my father was still healthy, before the letters and the divorce. A time when I was a happy little girl running barefoot in my pajamas around my father's office—wild, innocent and free. Blissfully unaware of what would become of us.

***

IT'S CHRISTMAS MORNING, 1979. I'm in my father's office playing on the floor in my pajamas. Daddy is sitting at his desk flipping through the crisp, ivory pages of his phone book, contemplating who to call first: *Johnny Carson, Joe Frazier, Mayor Bradley, John Travolta, Clint Eastwood, Sidney Poitier, Richard Pryor, Kris Kristofferson, Tom Jones, Michael Jackson* ... He decides on Mike Douglas, a popular television talk-show personality who ruled afternoon TV for twenty-one years as the singing host of *The Mike Douglas Show.*

"Hello ..."

"Merry Christmas, Mr Douglas!"

"Who is this?"

"The Greatest of All Times!"

"Oh, Muhammad Ali! How are you doin', Champ?"

"I had to surprise you."

"I thought you were overseas."

"No, I just got back from Peking."

"Yeah, I saw your picture in the paper. You were in China."

"They made me their official coach for the '84 Olympics. They want me to train their boys."

"That's great."

"So, I'm looking through my phone book and saw your name and I said, let me call and wish you a Happy Holidays."

"Well, aren't you a nice man. Thank you, that's awfully nice, Champ."

"Don't cost nothin'. Know something I do ... I pick up the phone and dial whatever number comes to mind and the people come on and say, 'Hello,' and I say, 'Merry Christmas! How are you doing? What's going on?' And they ask, 'Who is this?' I say, 'I don't want to tell you who it is because if I tell you right away, you'll think I'm lying, but I want you to guess who it is ...' They say, 'This sounds like Ali.' I say, 'It's Muhammad Ali! Merry Christmas!' They say, 'I can't believe it! Why are you calling me? How did you get my phone

34

Dad at the White House with Jimmy Carter.

number?' I say, 'I just picked up the phone and I just dialed ...' So, I've been doing this for the last hour."

"Isn't that wonderful," said Mike.

"Yeah, I have a lot of fun out of people."

"That's wonderful, Champ. Listen, let me ask you something, on January 7th I'm having a show for my 18th year on television ..."

"I'm in the White House on the 7th."

"You're where?"

"The White House. President Carter wants to be briefed on my trip to Peking, China."

"Oh, shoot! I was looking forward to having you."

"Louis Martin, the black guy in the White House, called me today— we just arranged it. As a matter of fact, I'm in the White House at 12:30 noon."

"Isn't that wild ... well, I think that's great anyway."

"I wish I could have been on your show."

"Poor kid from Louisville, Kentucky, at the White House talking about being in China."

35

"*It's a big Nigga!*" my father said, jokingly.

"*The head man!*" Mike shot back.

They both laughed.

"*That's a good one,*" said Dad. "*Poor kid from Louisville, Kentucky, at the White House talking about being in China. That's a good one, Mike ...*" He laughed again. "*So just take your time and be good. I just called to say hello.*"

"*Champ, you're wonderful. Thank you very much. The best to you and your family ...*"

The phone dials as my father speaks into the recorder. "*Now I'm calling Joe Frazier ...*" The one fighter in history he said brought out the best in him.

"*Hello ...*" A young woman answers.

Disguising his voice, "*Hello, may I speak to Mr Joe Frazier ...*"

"*Who's calling?*"

"*I want to surprise him.*"

"*Okay, hold on ...*"

After a moment, she comes back to the phone. "*He's not here, may I ask who's calling, please?*"

"*This is a good friend of his. He will be very shocked if he doesn't get this call.*"

"*Oh, well—he's not here.*"

In his own voice now. "*Tell him Muhammad Ali called!*"

"*Are you serious?*"

"*That's me. How ya doin'? Who am I talking to?*"

"*You're talking to one of his daughters. I don't believe this.*"

"*Yeah, this is me. I'm in California. You don't recognize my voice?*"

"*Now I do—I'm flattered!*"

"*Good! Is this the big one?*"

"*No, I'm the next one down.*"

"*Okay, let me talk to the big one.*"

"*Okay, hold on ... [in the background] Muhammad Ali is on the phone!*"

"*What's up, Muhammad?*"

"Hey, girl, what's happenin'?"

"Not much. Merry Christmas!"

"Same to you. I was just calling to wish Joe a Merry Christmas. I'm in Los Angeles."

"Oh, you sound so good. Do you remember me?"

"Yeah, that's why I asked to speak to you. You're getting so big and fine. How old are you now?"

"I just turned eighteen on December 2nd. You can send me a birthday present if you want and be one of ..."

"One of your secret men?" my father jokes.

"Yeah!" She laughs. "What are you doing these days?"

"I just came back from Peking, China."

"Oh, really!"

"Yeah, I was over there. They want me to teach their boys how to box."

"Check you out! I'm quite sure you can do that ... Okay, well, he should be back pretty soon."

"Tell Joe when he comes home he can just call back."

"Okay, bye-bye."

"Take care ..."

Dad speaks into the recorder: "I'm calling Mayor Tom Bradley in Los Angeles ..."

"Hello, Merry Christmas."

"Merry Christmas! This is Muhammad Ali calling for the mayor!"

"All right, just a moment, hold on."

"Hello ...? Hello, great mayor. Muhammad Ali!"

"Hey! How are you doing?"

"Oh, calling to wish you Merry Christmas and Happy New Year."

"How was your trip to China?"

"Oh man, I'd like to tell you about that. We got over there and I was surprised most of the people recognized me. And Deng Xiaoping, one of the leaders, he made me their official trainer for boxing."

"No kidding?"

"Yeah, they want me to bring over boxing gloves and all kinds of equipment. They'll send a plane for it. They want me to train their boys for the '84 Olympics."

"That's great!"

"So, I was just wondering—accepting a little task like that, can you consider that bettering relationships between the two nations?"

"Oh, absolutely."

"So, they can't call me a traitor for training the Chinese?"

"No, that would really go over well in Washington. When I spoke to the Vice Premier of China, when he was over here asking about your trip, he said, 'Oh yeah, they know Muhammad Ali over there.'"

"So, are you still working hard?" Dad asks. "Got a lot on your mind?"

"I don't worry about it. You know, take it day by day."

"When your term is over, would you like to do it again?"

"I haven't made up my mind. I'm going to really think about it really hard and decide whether I'm going to run for re-election, or run for Governor, or run for US Senator."

"Senator is a bigger job. What would we have to do to make a pitch to get a black president?"

"Well, I think that's some time off, Muhammad, but if you're ready to run, then it's four years from now."

Laughing, "No, I'm trying to say, a man like you, if you seriously wanted to, what would your first step be?"

"Well, you have to get a lot of financial backing because it's really expensive, and you have to get them in all of the states."

"So that's what you mean, when you say it's hard for a black to come in, it might be hard to find people to back him."

"That's right."

"So even if the people would vote for you," says Dad, "if you got the position, it would be tough getting the money together."

"Right, you have to get the money together first."

"Do you know roughly how much money it would take? Would ten million do it?"

"That would probably do it in the primary, then if you win the primary you have to get financing from the federal government.

Some people can do it for less than ten million. I think Connally is shooting for ten million."

"Right, I want to ask you something, then I'll let you go. Of all the people that we have in office that are qualified, if any of the black politicians tried, including yourself, who do you think would have the best chance?"

"Brooks was in a good position to get on ticket—as vice presidential candidate—but now that he's out of the Senate, I really don't know anybody now who can get that kind of financial support all over the country."

"If you could get the support, do you think you would have a better chance? The reason I'm asking you all this is I think it would be you. I was talking to General Gaddafi of Libya, and Sheikh Zayed of Abu Dhabi, and King Khalid of Saudi Arabia, and they mentioned that they would back a worthy cause and that was one of the causes."

"Is that right, Muhammad?"

"If I got somebody like you, somebody that would make a play for it, and if you need fifty million, they talk like they will do it. So, if not yourself, who will take a chance, if they did get the money?"

Mayor Bradley considers it.

"Well ..." says Dad, "when you're ready let me know. I'll walk with you."

I remember Tom Bradley, Los Angeles' first black mayor, visiting the house when I was a little girl. He was a nice man—quiet and dignified. I think my father was always ahead of his time; instead of letting the wrongs of the world weigh his spirit with the burdens of his era's prejudice, he set goals, held fast to his vision, and lived into his future. But I don't think my father ever imagined that America would see a black president in his lifetime.

Dad supported President Obama and what he stood for. Not just because he was black but because my father could see that he was a caring, decent, intelligent, charismatic, and exceptional human being. The fact that he was black was the icing on the cake.

One morning, sometime during Obama's first term, I walked into my father's bedroom at his home in Scottsdale, Arizona, and handed him a bowl of freshly rinsed grapes. When I was a little girl, Dad would fill his bowl with water and shake the fruit clean. He did this at home and in hotel bathrooms when visiting in Los Angeles after my parents' divorce. If we were in a restaurant he'd pour his water into his fruit bowl and rinse it himself—to make sure it was clean.

"Here you go, Daddy," I said, handing him the bowl. "Freshly rinsed grapes, the way you like them."

Dad usually ate grapes and green apples as a morning appetizer, while Lonnie and her sister Marilyn, whom she hired to help with my father, cooked his breakfast: steak, eggs, oatmeal, and a tall glass of orange juice. They always prepared a large meal for him. Sometimes they added buttermilk pancakes and cheese grits to the menu. It was easier for Dad to get the food down in the morning. As the day progressed, the symptoms of Parkinson's were more challenging. I'm not sure why that is, really. But as the hours passed, it was more diffi- cult for him to do even the simplest of tasks. Like to button his shirt, tie his shoes, hold his spoon without shaking, chew and swallow his food, speak or stand up on his own and walk across the room. Even in the face of his illness and its challenges, there were exceptional days—magical moments when my father was his old self again. Bright- eyed and speaking clearly.

Whatever the situation on any given day, Dad would want the world to know he wasn't in pain. He was happy. Through the ups and downs he always enjoyed being Muhammad Ali.

As I lay beside my father that morning, watching him pop grapes into his mouth as we watched old westerns—his morning ritual—I asked Dad if he wanted a glass of water.

"Yeah," he said, popping another grape into his mouth.

As I stood he asked, "What do we have, sweet?"

"Daddy, it's 8 a.m., Lonnie's cooking your breakfast."

"What's she cooking?"

"Steak and eggs, and oatmeal with bananas and brown sugar," I said.

"How much longer?" he asked. With all his patience, he never liked waiting for food.

"I'll go check," I said, walking out the room.

I returned in a few minutes with a full tray. He ate breakfast in bed that day, but he usually was dressed and sitting at the kitchen table next to the living room, with Boston and Fenway, Lonnie and Asaad's two Yorkshire terriers, waiting by his feet. Dad would toss a spoon of his oatmeal and pieces of bread, steak and eggs on the floor for them when she wasn't looking.

"Don't we have a black president?" he asked, as I helped him with his food.

"Yeah, Obama, remember? You were at his inauguration."

"Yeah, that's right," he said, chewing his food. "Tell Lonnie to get him on the phone and see if there's anything I can do to help with public relations ..."

I lived for moments like those. Now, I cherish the memories.

***

I CONTINUED RUMMAGING through the boxes. There were old files and folders; my parents' prenuptial agreement, Dad's original will, dated June 8, 1977; old passports and credit cards, the script of *Freedom Road* and *The Greatest* (two movies Dad starred in). I piled everything into a neat stack. A framed certificate stamped with a gold seal and signed by Tom Bradley caught my eye. I wiped off the dust and read the inscription.

CITY OF LOS ANGELES PROCLAMATION
MUHAMMAD ALI DAY

WHEREAS, MUHAMMAD ALI will be honored with the World Boxing Council's "Lifetime Achievement Award" on May 22, 1985, AND

WHEREAS, MUHAMMAD ALI'S professional boxing record consists of 56 wins and 5 losses. He won the Gold Medal in boxing at the 1960 Olympic games in Rome, Italy; Amateur

41

Athletic Union (AAU) Championship in the United States in 1960; USA Golden Gloves Championship in 1960; AND

WHEREAS, HE made his professional boxing debut on October 29, 1960 in Louisville Kentucky VS. Tunney Hunsaker. He won the heavyweight title in 1964 at the age of 22 by defeating Sonny Liston, after only 20 professional bouts; AND

WHEREAS, HIS GREATEST FIGHTS OF ALL TIME include "The Rumble in the Jungle"—ALI VS. FOREMAN, 1974 in Kinshasa, Zaire; "THE THRILLA IN MANILA"—ALI VS. FRAZIER, 1975 in Manila, The Philippines; AND

WHEREAS, MUHAMMAD ALI risked his position in boxing, sports, and society because of his principles and respect for his religion; AND

WHEREAS, MUHAMMAD ALI is the only boxer in history to win the World Heavyweight Championship THREE TIMES. He is the most charismatic and popular athlete of ALL TIME; has been welcomed and received by the Pope, Kings, Queens and Presidents all over the world and is highly respected for his love and philanthropic achievements on behalf of the children of the world:

NOW THEREFORE, I, TOM BRADLEY, MAYOR OF THE CITY OF LOS ANGELES, JOINED BY THE LOS ANGELES CITY COUNCIL, DO HEREBY PROCLAIM MAY 22, 1985 "MUHAMMAD ALI DAY" IN LOS ANGELES IN RECOGNITION OF HIS RECEIVING THE WORLD BOXING COUNCIL "LIFETIME ACHIEVEMENT AWARD" FOR HIS TREMENDOUS CONTRIBUTION TO THE SPORT OF BOXING, AND IN DEEP APPRECIATION FOR BEING THE GREATEST SPORTS HERO AND SETTING AN OUTSTANDING EXAMPLE TO THE YOUTH OF THE WORLD.

May 22, 1985
Tom Bradley
Mayor
Pat Russell
Councilwoman 6th District
President, Los Angeles City Council

I set the proclamation aside, imagining it framed in gold on my office wall beside my father's boxing ring drawings, a portrait of him smiling, and my favorite image—a memory frozen in time of Dad sitting on the patio steps at Fremont Place with all his children around him.

I was reading one of my father's old training journals when my mother found the letters. From the corner of my eye I saw her sit on the floor. It's not normal for her to sit down in the middle of a filthy storage-room floor, so that should have tipped me off, but it didn't. I was too preoccupied, reading my father's notes about his bills and finances. The endless list of names of people he was taking care of—how he gave up sex and salt and only ate fish for three months before the Foreman fight.

His scratchy, handwritten notes and inspirational quotes on random loose pages: *Love is the net where hearts are caught like fish; If fate throws a knife your way, you can catch it in two ways: by the handle or by the blade; Life would be unbearable if we couldn't dream; Your happiness, your health, and your success depends on the way you think; Death is so near, and the time for friendly action is so limited; Enjoy life, it's later than you think.* And his impressive penciled sketches of my mother's face drawn on lined yellow paper: *In Africa, Zaire, Veronica: By Muhammad Ali, October 3, 1974.*

I reached deeper into the box and pulled out a small framed photo of a modest log cabin nestled amongst pine trees and rolling hills, surrounded by snow. It looked familiar, as though I had been there before. I turned it over and read the inscription. "Fighters' Heaven, 1975". It was my father's log cabin at his training camp in Deer Lake, Pennsylvania. As I stare at the image a faint memory resurfaces.

I'm four years old watching my father put on his gray jogging suit, lace up his black army boots and set out into the biting cold for his jog up "Agony Hill", the name he gave the mountain he climbed every morning before the first glimmers of light poured over the horizon. Dad always jogged in big black army boots (instead of tennis shoes), so that his feet would feel light in the ring.

As I stared at the photo, remembering my father training for his last fight, I could feel the chill of the mountain air brushing against my cheek, as my little head hung out the window of the heated car following behind him in case he tired. No matter how steep the hill, or trying his course, he always kept going.

"The real training begins when the pain sets in," he once said. *"Those are the only miles I count—they're the only ones that matter. It's what you can do after you're tired that counts in the ring."* Watching my father in his later years, from a different vantage point, I could see the same was true of life.

I put the photo in the pile of keepsakes I was taking home and continued rummaging through the boxes. There were old airline tickets, receipts, date books, invitations to White House dinners, our drawings and scribbles, signed in my father's handwriting at the bottom: *By Hana at the LA home on 55 Fremont Place, 8PM, December 4, 1979, by Muhammad Ali.* Neither of my parents threw anything away. I was grateful for that. Perhaps my most amusing discovery was a small bundle of letters with my name on them— addressed to my parents from my nursery-school teachers. I pulled the first from the bunch and read:

> The staff and director of Pilgrim Foundation are quite concerned with the continual misbehavior of Hana. If improvement does not take place soon, it has been suggested that a different atmosphere and or school be sought! Any questions? Please see Mrs Beckel. Thank you for your cooperation.
>
> — Nursery Staff

It wasn't the first or last letter home to my parents. I was kicked out of two nurseries and a couple of kindergartens. The result of all my weekend sparring lessons with my father, no doubt. I was a handful at best, and I always acted out when Daddy was away. When he was around, I was perfectly fine. But when he left the letters followed me home. The days seemed longer when he was gone, and the nights were lonely. I used to sit on the edge of my bed staring out the window, waiting for his headlights to appear in the driveway, watching our Dobermans, Sheba and Samson, lying on the steps leading up to the swimming pool. I think they were waiting for him too.

I worried that my father might lose his keys, get lost, or drive his car off the road. Dad had a difficult time staying in his own lane. He swerved a little when he drove, especially at night. He once went in the wrong way on an off-ramp. The police would stop him, but they'd usually just get an autograph and then point him in the right direction. But there was one occasion when Dad was asked to get out the car and walk a straight line. The officer, noticing him swerving in the lane, mistakenly assumed he'd been drinking. Laila and I were in the back seat and Mom was up front. I watched my father from the window as he tried to walk a straight line, but he couldn't. Dad was noticeably irritable and the officer, realizing he hadn't been drinking, let us go. No one understood it at the time, but it was one of the first signs of his Parkinson's. And he still had two fights ahead of him: Larry Holmes and Trevor Berbick.

I worried about him all the time, but he always made it home; his headlights always appeared in the driveway at Fremont Place.

"Hana," he said on a recording after reading the note, "say, I'm a good girl."

"I'm a good girrrrl."

"Say, I'm a pretty girl."

"I'm a pretty girrrrl."

"Say, I won't bite the boys no more."

"I won't bite the boys no more."

"Say, I won't scratch the boys no more."

"I won't scratch the boys no more."

I was a little terror—a mini tornado passing through unexpectedly, leaving everything in my path in disarray. When Laila started boxing, people who knew us when we were young assumed the press had got it wrong, that it was me who had become a fighter.

"No," they said, watching the evening news. "That can't be right … they must be talking about Hana."

My sister was sweet, shy and quiet. No one could fathom the thought of her in the ring. Even my father had a hard time accepting it in the beginning. At first he tried to reason with her, talk her out of it. "Women shouldn't box," he said. "You bear children, you have breasts. Your body wasn't made to get hit." But when he saw that she was serious, and good, he was proud and supportive. When Muhammad Jr was a little boy, a reporter once asked my father, "What would you do if your son wants to become a boxer?"

"First, I would do everything I could to try and change his mind," he said. "Then I'd do everything in my power to help him." Years later he made good on his statement, only it wasn't his son but his youngest daughter who followed him into the ring.

After Laila won her first fight, Dad walked into her dressing room. She was surrounded by friends and family, who parted like the Red Sea when they saw him. Laila stood as he made his way across the room. He hugged her, kissed her, then looked at her proudly.

"You get it from me," he said. "Hana writes books, Laila throws hooks."

Whenever we did something impressive, like write a poem, help a friend in need, or give a homeless person money or food, Dad would smile at us and say, "That's me in you."

I opened another box, overjoyed with the prospect of unearthing further buried treasures. And, deep down, in the corner, among assorted newspaper clippings and photographs, my eyes widened: a micro audiotape labeled *"For my Veronica, 1976"*.

"Mom! Look what I found!"

She didn't answer.

I was overjoyed. The tape recordings my father had given me had changed my life. I had listened to them countless times, laughing, crying—remembering. I couldn't wait to get home and see what was on this tape. The fact that it was addressed to my mother—dated the year I was born—fascinated me. I dug through nearby containers hoping to discover more audiotapes, but instead I found a handful of my mother's old diaries. Agendas from 1982 to 1987. I opened the one from 1986—the last year we lived together as a family. I skimmed the wilted pages cautiously. A small sheet of paper was attached at the top with a rusty paperclip. In flawless handwriting it read:

46

11/29/1985 New address as of December 6, 1985
Hana Ali
841 Longwood Los Angeles, California 90035
213–934-4001
Mail to:
P.O. Box 36121
Los Angeles, California 90036
Veronica Porche Ali

I browsed the yellowing pages and found a folded set of papers wedged into the back pocket of the book. I opened them. As I read, it became clear what I had found. In my hands was an original copy of the listing agreement to Fremont Place, signed by both of my parents. Attached at the top was a photo advertisement of the house: *Behind the Gates—55 Fremont Place.* I opened it and looked at the collection of photos of the house and grounds. At the top left corner was a picture of my bedroom. My heart sank. Tears swelled in my eyes. I couldn't understand how, after all these years, images of my childhood home affected me so deeply. I took a long breath and read the sales description beneath the photos:

Like its owner, Muhammad Ali, this magnificent estate is world class. Behind the gates in prestigious Fremont Place, a private gated park-like residential community near Hancock Park, this stunning home stands supreme. Elegant fixtures surround the home including a large mahogany paneled entry, richly uphol-stered walls, carved African striped mahogany, gold leafed fixtures, newly finished hardwood floors, lovely cast and carved moldings, and fine polished woods. The library [Dad's office], paneled in oak, has a massive fireplace, and a half circle solarium features Ernest Batchelder's gothic period tiles as lustrous as the day it was installed.

Beautiful craftsmanship is part of everyday life. A large Tiffany glass screen dominates the second floor, which has five large bedrooms, including a master suite with fireplace, a sleeping porch, solarium, linen room, five bathrooms, and servants' quarters. There is a billiard room, ballroom, laundry room, dark room, wine room, a tremendous amount of storage area, and a five-room garage apartment. Spacious yards, a swimming pool, and decking, arbors, fountains, flower beds, and ornamental gates make this home a royal paradise.

As I read, memory stirred and Fremont Place came rushing back to me.

4

IN THE EARLY hours of the morning, when Mom and Laila were still asleep, Dad used to carry me downstairs in my pajamas. I'd watch wide-eyed as he tore out a few pages of lined yellow paper from the notepad on his desk, crumpling and rolling them into a long cone shape. Then I'd follow him down the hall to the kitchen, where he lit the tip of the paper on the stove.

My heart beat rapidly as we rushed back down the hallway to his office, Dad's attention fixed tensely on the paper, his eyes widening with every step as the tiny flame burned swiftly toward his fingers. My eyes were glued on him. He was so theatrical. More entertaining than any of my favorite cartoons: *Scooby Doo, Tom and Jerry, Casper, Bugs Bunny, Yogi Bear, The Road Runner, Felix the Cat*—even *Wonder Woman* had nothing on my father.

When I close my eyes and remember with my heart, I can still feel the rush of excitement and anticipation I felt as we made the long trip from the kitchen to his office, sometimes two or three times on the occasions when the flame burned too quickly.

When we finally arrived, Dad would toss the burning paper into the fireplace. We watched as the flames crackled, growing high and bright. Then he'd sit at his desk and drink his coffee. As always, I sat on his lap trying to emulate him, writing in cursive while he made random phone calls or spoke into his recorder, practicing his speeches:

"Where is love? Where is charity? Where is mercy? Where is God? We can answer each of these questions by saying in the heart of man ... If you were to look at what gives us courage to stand firm in the struggle on the battlefield of life, that which gives us the patience to endure all that comes, that which gives us will and power ... it is your heart ..."

We repeated the fireplace ritual every morning. Looking back, I wonder why he didn't just use a match to light the paper right there in his office. It would have been much easier and far less dramatic, and it would have saved him the time and trouble of running back and forth from his office to the kitchen. But if he had done things conventionally I wouldn't have my adventurous memories to share, and his tape recordings may have never existed.

Not all of my memories are pleasant. I spent a lot of time worrying about my father. But the chronic worrying didn't begin until I was seven or eight years old. One morning I woke up and ran down to his office to watch him light the fire, but he wasn't there. There was no coffee on his desk. His briefcase was beside the sofa, unopened, and his papers were still neatly stacked—the way he had left them the night before.

Daddy's been kidnapped! It was my first thought. I searched for him all morning. But he was nowhere to be found. I pressed my cold little nose against the large picture window in his office. His Rolls-Royce was in the driveway, parked in its usual spot near the swimming pool, but where was he? I had already checked the guest rooms twice; he wasn't there. I searched the bathrooms next—nothing. I ran into the living room, where he said his morning prayers. No sign of him. The kitchen was empty, too.

I ran down to the basement and checked the far corner room where the large freezer housing all the popsicles was. Our governess, Cruella De Vil, had no idea that I knew they were there. I'd discovered them the week before, when Daddy was looking for sweets and had carried me down with him. We did that often, staying up late together watching television while eating popsicles and bean pie. He bought them from the clean-shaven Muslim men selling their newspapers and pies at every corner on Crenshaw Blvd.

I scanned the large, cold room. No sign of him. I opened the freezer. No popsicles left either. I ran back up the steps, looking hastily over my shoulder. The basement was spooky. I often felt as if someone was following behind me.

When Laila and I were little girls, my father worried that we'd get kidnapped. Cruella De Vil used to tell him he had nothing to worry about because anyone crazy enough to snatch me would return me immediately. I was a little wildling. I drove adults bananas and my father was the only grown-up in the world that had patience with me. He used to sit Laila and me down on the sofa in his office and educate us on the dangers of the world. He'd warn passionately, "*Be very careful riding your bikes and playing around the neighborhood. God protects you but some people are crazy. They might try to kidnap you because you're my daughters ...*" At four and six years old, we'd nod our heads, eyes wide, unable to fully grasp the concept or understand his concern.

Finally, I checked the third-floor media room, where I'd once found my father sleeping on the sofa. I'd figured he had fallen asleep watching his favorite actor, Christopher Lee, in *Dracula*, or an old western on the large television screen next to his trophy display.

I rushed up the steps, hoping to find him stretched out on the leather-tufted sofa, bright-eyed, sipping his coffee and talking on the telephone. But he wasn't there either. Aside from the faint sound of water trickling from the fish tanks in the far corner, the room was cold and silent.

I had literally searched high and low. Daddy was always in his office when I woke, but that morning he was nowhere to be found.

Someone must have taken him, I assumed. I always noticed the way people looked at him—how they lit up whenever he entered a room, hugging and kissing him as if he was *their* father, brother, husband or friend. I recognized the look in their eyes, the overwhelming and complete awe and pleasure of simply being near him. Oh, I recognized it all right, it was the same look I had on my face every day of my young life. Everyone wanted something from him—his time, attention, money, friendship, love. And he accommodated them all. Now, one of these people had taken him.

51

"Someone stole Daddy! Someone stole Daddy!" I shouted repeatedly, running down from the third floor to my mother's bedroom. By the time I reached her, I was out of breath.

Mom rose calmly from her slumber. "What is it, Hana?" she asked, yawning and stretching her long graceful arms, like a beautiful swan, never losing composure.

There came a stirring in the morning stillness. Sheba and Samson, the Dobermans, were barking in the background. This should have tipped me off, but it didn't. I never thought to check outdoors.

"Mommy! Daddy's gone—someone kidnapped him!" I cried. I was a dramatic child.

"What do you mean, Hana?" she asked, with one arm around my shoulder, trying to soothe and calm my overactive imagination. My father would have thrown both arms around me. He would have carried me downstairs for a popsicle, offered me money, put on my favorite cartoon—anything to get me to stop crying. Tears were his kryptonite.

In a few minutes, my mother will put on her silk robe. We'll walk downstairs together and find my father sleeping outside on the patio sofa, fully clothed. He'll explain how he'd lost his keys and didn't want to wake anyone, knocking on the door. He'll scoop me up in his arms and give me a big bear hug—no one hugged like my father.

When he sits me down in the kitchen chair and pours a glass of milk, he'll notice the fretful look in my eyes and tell me not to worry—that he's fine. That God always watches over him and me because I'm his daughter. But it's too late. The distress is already etched in my heart. In the months to come, my mother will drop me off at my first counseling session. At six years old my overwhelming anxiety about my father's well-being worried them both. Especially by my ninth birthday, knowing what was coming: the end of their marriage.

Once it was the four of us, with all our laughter and adventures; then, one day, we were moving to a new house and Daddy wasn't coming.

5

IT WAS THE sound of my mother's gasp that brought me back. I turned as she slowly rose to her feet. "What is it?" I asked. She didn't respond. She stood there leaning against the storage room wall, as if to release a weighty burden. Tears streaming slowly down her cheeks, she pressed a handful of pages hard against her chest. Then she walked out the storage unit and disappeared down the hall.

I stood in the doorway and called her name a few times, but I didn't go after her. Laila might have. She always needed to help resolve a situation—bring closure to it immediately. But I knew better. I learned early in life; our mother preferred to cry alone.

Some things don't bear much telling. I think my mother knew this—how words have a way of flattening the deepest emotions. I piled a stack of my findings, along with old newspaper and magazine articles, into an empty box and prepared to leave. It was getting late, Mom had been gone for half an hour. I was about to go looking for her.

I was closing the storage door when she reappeared. I held the audiotape—my most precious discovery—in my hand. I could see she'd been crying. Puffy eyes, red nose, her shaky expression as she struggled to regain her composure.

"What's wrong, Mom?" I asked.

She said nothing.

Again, I asked, "Mom? What's the matter?"

She double-checked the lock, then slowly turned to face me. "I always thought he never fought for me." And she handed me a thick manila envelope full of letters.

April 28, 1983
Dear Veronica, Love Always
When I bow before Allah, I think of him and his relation to little me. I become aware that God has created this vast universe for the benefit of us. My mind is filled with respect towards the great power that has been responsible for the universe. By me now praying every day in devotion and submission, something has developed in me. And now I am coming closer to God. I am more conscious of the fact that I should not commit sins. By praying five times a day, I see this, and it is helping me to be a better person. You will like me, and even love me, now. (Smile)

If you give me one more chance, I love you so much, and it hurts me so much now that I cannot sleep with you. I am so sorry for the way I used to treat you. If you don't forgive, I pray that God will.

I write to you because it is hard to talk to you. I am having a hard time being without you. I guess this is the weakness of the human mind. The Quran teaches that the righteous parents and children will be reunited in heaven. Me, you, Hana, and Laila, in the hereafter. I want to continue to have a good acquaintance with you there. The prayer has been prescribed to keep in constant memory of God. That's why I pray five times a day. I wish you would pray with me sometimes, before you leave me. God can do anything if we ask his help ...
Love Muhammad

I was seized by a sudden urge to cry as I imagined my father sitting behind his desk at Fremont Place, imagined light falling through the clouds into the window as he poured his heart onto the page. How could this have happened? How could these letters have remained undiscovered for so long? I read the yellowing pages, cautiously, overwhelmed with conflicting emotions: curiosity, amazement, gratitude, sorrow, and anger.

How could my mom have overlooked his letters? The note written across the envelope was addressed to her: "Veronica, Muhammad left these behind—Marge."

Why didn't she open it, or at least deliver the envelope back to him? There were plenty of opportunities. Dad visited regularly after the divorce. If she had opened the envelope, said something to him, maybe he would have told her that he left them there for her. Maybe she would have read them in time. Maybe she would have given him another chance.

A dozen what-ifs and maybes ran through my mind. Mostly, I wondered if he was waiting for her to say something—for a sign that she had received them, read them. Or maybe he had given up hope long ago, when the house on Fremont sold.

I had just discovered my father's letters and, already, they haunted me. My dad wore his heart on his sleeve. Love was his first language— he spoke it well from the letter's first words to its closing declaration, in which he expressed his humility, his heart open, vulnerable, and bare on the page. His pleas for another chance, his promise to be a better husband; his perpetual sadness to be losing his wife and family; his poetic attempts to recapture her heart; his ultimate awareness and acceptance that the marriage was over.

In total, there were twenty-eight pages—twenty-eight pages spanning three years, immortalizing his enduring hope and unwavering love. His thoughts pinned to the page like butterflies stunned out of magnificent flight, forever engraved on the folios of time.

Dear Veronica,
As your husband, I applaud and affirm all that you are, even if not always all that you do ... I have found that you are your own person ... I want you to have the freedom that you want ... I am all for you, in all ways, and I am with you, always. Living with you or not, though we may be continents apart, as you put in your words, about us being two different people. Never will I leave

55

you. Nor do you, in any way, have to earn my love. You have these, everything I have, because you are you and because, after living with you, I have found that Veronica is such a wonderful, special someone to know. For what it's worth, I still love you.

My mother has always been a quiet, graceful being. As a child, I never threw myself into her arms to hug her the way I did with my father. She reminded me of a delicate flower, soft and fragile. I would hug her as if her petals might bruise. But that afternoon at the storage facility I couldn't help myself. I threw my arms around her and she hugged me back. I had never seen her rendered so helpless.

I held the audiotape I had discovered in my hand. I looked at it, wondering how it had escaped my father's collection—my collection. Its inscription intrigued me: *"For my Veronica, 1976"*, the year I was born. He must have given it to her then, I thought. Because the briefcase of recordings he gave to me began in 1978.

I remembered how hearing his long-ago voice, speaking to my future self, made me feel. *"Hana, you were a sweet little girl. You are so beautiful ..."* His tender declarations, the love in his words, *"I just kiss your little jaws all the time. I always squeeze you and hug you—and I love you ..."*

He captured the moments we shared, the play and laughter—an everlasting wave of affection, floating through every room in the house. Preserved on micro tape cassettes and in my heart with the infallible memory of his love.

God knows what's on this tape, I thought, slipping it into my back pocket. *Mom's had enough for one afternoon. I'll give it to her tomorrow.*

6

I WENT STRAIGHT home from the storage. I wanted answers about the love letters. But my mother was too befuddled for an interrogation. I'd have to do a little of my own research, revisiting times long past. If the day had taught me anything, it was that history has a unique way of telling its own story, of revealing its mysteries when it wants to. I placed the envelope of letters on my nightstand. Mom let me bring them home, so I could finish reading them.

I played my favorite classical music, "Clair de Lune", went to relax in a hot bath, and let the melancholy soak away. I heard my fiancé, Kevin, come home. It was just after 6 p.m. so he was coming from one of his training sessions at the gym and would be heading back out for his 7 p.m. jog soon. In a few months I was marrying a mixed-martial-arts fighter who had a lot of wonderful qualities that reminded me of my father.

"How did it go with your mom?" he asked. "At the storage."

"You won't believe what we found," I said. "A stack of love letters my father wrote my mother thirty years ago, that she never knew about."

"Really? That's crazy. How did that happen?"

"That's what I want to know. I'm trying to decide if I'm going to ask Dad about them."

He walked into the bathroom to change into his jogging suit. "Do you want to talk about it? I can go to the gym later."

"Not right now, honey," I said. "I feel emotionally drained."

"Okay, babe, I'm heading back out. I'll be home in an hour. Call if you need me."

"Okay, honey. Love you."

Kevin kissed me goodbye. Then, with a heavy heart, I put on my bathrobe and went to the kitchen to make some ginger mint tea. I was usually a decaf coffee drinker, but after a recent trip to London tea was my new favorite thing. I took my drink into the living room and bundled up beneath a blanket in a cozy armchair. I wasn't ready to read any more of my father's love letters—to be reminded of his pain—so I picked up one of the old newspaper clippings I'd found, from the *Midnight Globe*. It featured one of my parents' first interviews together, its yellowing pages carrying the faint scent of dust and mildew. I noted the date: July 1, 1978. I'm two years old. Dad's training for his third championship—the fight against Leon Spinks that he'll win, becoming the first man in history to gain the heavyweight title three times. I welcome the memory. When I read the first line—"They met four years ago in Salt Lake City …"—the ghosts begin to stir.

***

WHEN MY MOTHER packed her bags for Salt Lake City, she had no idea her life would change forever, that her name and face would headline newspapers around the world—that she'd have a secret wedding ceremony under the African moon with the most famous man on earth.

It was 1974. Nixon was on the verge of resigning, the Dolphins won the Super Bowl, and George Foreman was the new World Heavyweight Champion. My mother, an eighteen-year-old pre-med student moonlighting as a cheerleader, was waiting with a group of girls wearing colorful bikinis to escort my father down the aisle for a charity exposition bout. Dad began their courtship by giving Mom and the other girls one of his stern lectures about clothing, or her lack of it: "I told her she shouldn't be walking around half-nude. She was so tall and pretty. I was scared of her beneath it all. Oh, I was scared all right. But I knew that she was just what I was looking for. I don't know what she was thinking about me."

The day my parents met. Salt Lake City, 1974.

Mom obligingly told the reporter, "What he said made sense to me. A lot of us didn't want to wear swimsuits in front of everyone. We wanted to wear some nice dress or trousers. So, when he gave us that lecture, he was telling me what I already wanted to do."

I knew the lecture well. He'd given it to me once when I was twelve. My father had a unique way of expressing himself. He liked to paint vibrant pictures with his words and plant seeds of wisdom that would sprout throughout our lifetimes. He took all the knowledge, love, and faith he received from the world and cultivated us with it.

"Everything that God made valuable in the world is covered, protected, and hard to get to. Where do you find diamonds? Deep in the ground covered by the earth. Where do you find pearls? Deep in the bottom of the ocean covered and protected in a beautiful shell. Where do you find gold? Way down in the mine, covered under layers of rock. Where do you find oil? Deep in the ground beneath

the earth. You have to work hard to get to it, and half the time you don't strike." His brows would furrow. *"Your body is sacred. You're far more precious than gold, diamonds, and pearls. You should be covered, too."*

It was the first and last time I wore a short skirt. I imagine the speech had a similar effect on my mother; she went to her room and put on a dress.

After leaving Salt Lake City, my father flew to Kinshasa, Zaire (now the Democratic Republic of the Congo), to fight a much younger— much stronger—George Foreman in "The Rumble in the Jungle", perhaps the most important, most infamous bout of his career.

Mom slipped him a note the night before the fight: *Win or lose, I love you.* He later told her, "You helped me win."

"So, what happened after the fight?" the reporter asked my father, referring to his blossoming affair with my mother.

"We stayed in contact."

"Stayed in contact!" Mom exploded with laughter. "He wouldn't let me go home for six months."

"All right, it's true," he admitted, joining her laughter affectionately. "I had to brainwash her. I knew if she went back to college she'd find another fellow. I didn't want that. I knew if I kept her with me she wouldn't want another fellow. And that's what happened ..." He told the reporter how proud he was of her and how intelligent she was—how he can talk to her about anything. He can—and does— go on and on about her. "In these four years, she has never used profanity, she doesn't want to go to nightclubs, or parties. Not like most beautiful women, they want to show off. She doesn't, not at all. She doesn't want to go out without me, and that's good." He said this proudly, adding, "Me and Veronica don't argue. We never fall out."

"Not ever?" the reporter asks.

"We have our arguments, over silly things," he clarified. "Like, you know, we have to go out in an hour and she isn't ready."

"That's because you wake me up late," my mother objected. "And you want to be punctual, on time, right up to the minute."

They both laughed. It was true. Dad was always on time, early mostly—sometimes waiting to welcome guests coming to meet him. I can still see him standing in the doorway, anticipating their arrival, waving, as they pulled up the drive.

Unlike most celebrities, who make a show of concern for the public but really feel people are intruding on their lives, my father never resented the intrusion; he welcomed it. He regularly turned down security detail and interacted freely with the crowds that approached him. He was the same with the media and reporters. As sports writer Michael Katz said, "He liked attention; he knew how to get it; and he accepted writers as part of his world."

Perhaps one of the most endearing aspects of my father's character was his unshakeable faith – his belief that God was his bodyguard. "*Allah watches over me,*" he once said. "*If I walk into a stadium with thousands of people, no man can keep somebody from shooting me ... I can't be worrying about things like that. A man filled with fear doesn't live and enjoy life.*"

My father's love for people was extraordinary. I would come home from school to find homeless families sleeping in our guest bedrooms. He'd see them on the street, pile them into the back of his Rolls-Royce and bring them home with him. He'd buy them clothes, take them to hotels and pay the bills for months in advance.

"*I'm going to help you clean up and find a good job,*" he'd say.

Some people accosted him for money—and whatever he had in his pockets he'd give to them. "*Service to others is the rent we pay for our room in heaven,*" he'd tell me.

His generosity was legendary. At the house on Woodlawn in Chicago, homeless women showed up at 2 a.m. with babies in their arms. People would ring the bell and burst into tears when he answered the door, and he cried right back at them. He used to sit me on his lap, look into my eyes and quote the great poets: "*Hana, if you can stop one heart from breaking, you shall not live in vain; If you can ease one life the aching, or cool one pain, or help one fainting robin into his nest again, you shall not live in vain.*" His words will forever echo in my conscience.

It's also true that my parents rarely argued. They got along well. Dad feared that if a couple quarreled they'd end up divorced. He never liked confrontation; elevated voices made him uncomfortable. You could see it in his expression. I've always suspected it had something to do with his parents, Papa Cash and Mama Bird, witnessing their arguments when he was a child. But I'll get to them later.

The only time I remember my father raising his voice at my mother was after she'd gently slapped my hand for doing something she'd repeatedly asked me not to do: rummaging through her make-up drawer, breaking the head off her designer Yves Saint Laurent red lipstick after pressing it too hard against my puckered little lips, or spilling her Chanel perfume on her silk negligée. Maybe I had rubbed styling grease on my hair, then laid my oily head on her French lace pillows. Whatever my mischief that day, my father's loud roar of *"Don't ever hit her!"* startled us both.

Neither of my parents were disciplinarians. Whenever my mother tried to give us a spanking, Laila and I would grab the opposite end of the belt in her hand and end up in a tug of war that resulted with the three of us sprawled out on her bedroom floor laughing uncontrollably.

When my father reached his limit, he'd take off his belt and shout "Aaaaaaaaaaaahh," as he pretended to whoop us but hit the seat of the sofa we were sitting on instead. Dad always had a flair for the dramatic. My mother would hear us screaming from his office and run down the stairs. "Stop it, Muhammad," she would say. "You're scaring them."

It's funny, how the things we worry about never happen—or cause our greatest pain. It's the events we never see coming that turn our world upside down.

"No, we never fight." He smiled at the reporter and my mother.

"Since I've known him, he's always been traveling," my mother said, sighing. "I have a dream that one day Muhammad will hang up his gloves for good so we can live at home like ordinary people."

"Yeah, I want that," my father added meekly. "Being at home, cutting the grass. Maybe go out and do some fishing, huh. Just living an ordinary life together ... I want that."

But it was a dream that would never come true, and our life was far from ordinary.

We lived in a four-story mansion with a full staff of rotating nannies, housekeepers, and cooks. Laila was always threatening to run away from home. At four years old, she'd toss her belongings into plastic garbage bags and drag them down the hall, pouting.

"I'm going now!" she'd say. "I'm running far, far away from here!" She made it past the front door once—all the way down the street— before my mother caught up with her, running after her in mulberry silk and high heels, her long hair sailing behind her.

"Where are you going, Laila?"

My sister felt like she was living in a glasshouse—a beautiful doll on display—with no escape. I was a daddy's girl; Laila wasn't. She was sweet, quiet, and shy, and at times she could be excessively dramatic. She once locked herself in her bedroom and threatened to jump off the balcony. I don't know why, really. But she always calmed down after getting what she needed most—our mother's attention. Laila was never that close to our father. She never felt as comfortable with him as she did with our mother. Daddy was always in his office entertaining, on the sofa performing magic tricks, or sitting behind his grand desk talking on the telephone or telling jokes, enjoying being the center of attention. Laila dreaded being called into the middle of it all. But I loved it. I used to sit at his feet beaming up at him, watching, listening, soaking it all in.

"*I'M BIG BUSINESS!*" he'd say, going over his many offers, leafing through a stack of loose papers on his desk. "*I'm writing lectures, I've got to train for fights, I've got causes, I've got television appearances, I've got to meet the Ambassador of France, I've got to go on* Face the Nation ... *I've got problems like everybody else. I've got a lot on my mind ... Yeah, I get tired. Ford does, too. The Pope of Rome does, too. But they got to keep going just like I do ...*"

He was always inviting the outside world in. All anyone had to do was tell the guard at the gatehouse, "I'm here to see Muhammad Ali." He never turned anyone away. He'd talk to them for hours and give them a tour of the house. He even invited a fan from the United Kingdom, a stranger named Russ Routledge, who became a friend, to stay with us in our home for two weeks, driving the lucky man around town with him every day.

"Bring your camera with you," he'd remind Russ as he prepared for the trip. *"We'll take pictures so everyone will see you were really here, with Muhammad Ali."*

The house was always full of guests, friends, fans, and hangers-on. Like Laila, my mother didn't like it and would retreat to a quiet sunroom in a far corner of the house. She had created a private sanctuary where she could be alone. Laila's escape was her bedroom. Neither of them felt safe in the open atmosphere at Fremont Place. For them, it was like living in a glass castle, and the feeling my little sister remembers most as a child is loneliness. She knew our father was a big-hearted man who loved and adored her, but she didn't enjoy being smothered with excessive hugs and kisses, especially in front of strangers.

"Hana never complains about my kisses," he said to her one evening after dinner.

"Then give her all your kisses." She shoved him and ran to her room.

"I've had 150 fights," my father continues in the interview with my mother. "I've been fighting since I was twelve ... I've got one more coming up. It should be my last one."

But it was never *the last one*; there was always *one more fight*. He talks about a new movie, *Freedom Road*, in which he plays a former slave who rises to a seat in the US Senate. "I'm a black Clark Gable," he jokes with the reporter, then moves in close, as if to whisper a secret but instead shouts in her ear. *"I'm still 'The Greatest'!"*

7

IN EARLY OCTOBER of 1978, when the leaves began to turn in Natchez, Mississippi, at the old Belmont Manor plantation, the cast and crew braced themselves as my father walked onto the set. He practiced his lines as he passed the wooden slave shacks erected for filming. Dad played Gideon Jackson, an ex-slave turned Union soldier who fought his way into the US Senate. The drama was a six-hour mini-series for NBC called *Freedom Road*. My father considered the mythical character a kindred spirit.

"He's not afraid," Dad said to Dick Russell, a journalist on the set with *People* magazine. "He stood up [for what he believed], like I did with the draft board and by becoming a Muslim. And he's got an idea for freedom and justice for all people ... He's the kind of man I would have been if I was living then. Actually, it's good I wasn't," he added with a smile, "'cause I'd probably have been dead quick!"

As a fighter, my father had always been a supreme "actor", but he had never attempted to play another character. Before Dad played Gideon Jackson, the most excited he'd been about a film role was in 1977 when he'd played himself in a screen version of his auto-biography, *The Greatest*.

"I'm going to be the greatest movie star of them all," he announced to the press, as he embarked on his new career. "Charlton Heston, John Wayne, Steve McQueen, and Paul Newman—yeah, they're all in trouble with me around."

His acting method had always been exaggeration. Now he had to learn a much subtler approach. According to my mother, he started preparing for the role while training to fight Leon Spinks.

"It's a serious film," said the producer, Zev Braun, in the same issue of *People*. "But it took a guy like Ali to really make it work. It's almost as if it had to wait for Muhammad Ali to be created."

Zev Braun lived around the corner from us in Fremont Place. I used to run to his house after school to play with his daughter, Sue, and beg him for ice cream. He always let me search his freezer for popsicles and eat whatever sweets I could find in the pantry. He was a kind and patient man, and is still married today to the same woman, Mayling.

The production of *Freedom Road* was based on the 1944 best-selling book by Howard Fast. Throughout the filming, Daddy wanted to know exactly what was happening at all times. He thought acting was boring and had no problem expressing it.

"I memorized three pages of dialogue," he said to Mom one night after filming. "But it took seven days to shoot it ..." While my father was a natural actor, and his co-stars marveled at his ease on the set, he wasn't built to do it professionally. He didn't like the punishing film schedule; all of the rehearsing and waiting around in between takes and having to reshoot the same scenes, again and again, standing in one place.

"This is boring! I don't know how you do it," he said to his friend and co-star Kris Kristofferson one day after taping. But, as usual, Dad found a way to keep things interesting. Between scenes he held center stage, performing his magic tricks for the cast and crew.

"Watch this, watch this, it's gonna shock you," he said, wide-eyed, whipping out a deck of cards. "Maaaaan, did you see that?" he gushed after the trick. "I studied that one for six months. I got my little show together. My ropes and cards. When I travel the world, I'm gonna show all the people ..."

When he was really bored, he messed with the guards on set who happened to be white. Shaking his script at them, he furrowed his brows, biting his lower lip. "They call me a Nigga in this script!"

he said through clenched teeth, raising his fist. "Did you call me a Nigga?"

"No! No!" said the guards, unaware he was joking.

I think it was my father's way of dealing with the discomfort and pain he'd grown up with. He never understood how a word could hold so much power. This was his way of dethroning it. The NAACP didn't approve, and in the years to come he'd receive a letter from them asking him to refrain from telling sensitive jokes in public. Especially in the White House. He liked to tell presidents one of his favorites. I can picture him sitting in the Oval Office with Presidents Ford, Carter, Reagan, Bush, Clinton, and Obama.

"What did Abraham Lincoln say after a four-day drunk?"

"I freed the who!?"

My father meant no harm. I think he was using humor to cope with the sting of prejudice he experienced throughout his life. That and he simply liked to make people laugh. After receiving the NAACP's letter my father refrained from telling his jokes in most places. But in 2005, when we were at the grand opening of the Muhammad Ali Center in his hometown of Louisville, Kentucky, I noticed that whenever Dad was around President Clinton, with whom he shared a special bond, he was often smiling and whispering in his ear.

Ironically, the actor George Hamilton invited Dad to dinner one night after filming. I'm not sure how it came about. I think the connection was through the director, Zev. George's son told us the story a couple years ago, when we were on *Celebrity Family Feud* together. He casually walked over and told us about the time his father had my parents over for dinner and made a pork roast, unaware that Muslims don't eat pork.

"To make matters worse," he said, "after your father left, someone burned a cross on our lawn."

I was only two years old at the time—too young to remember— but I spent a lot of time on the set of *Freedom Road*, riding around on Kris Kristofferson's shoulders, tugging on his shirt and hair. I still have the photos of us together. Dad wanted Kris to advise him, so he was always around—even on his days off. One afternoon, when

Kris was innocently getting his hair cut outside his trailer, Dad snuck over, then he dropped to his knees and gathered Kris's shorn hair from the ground and put it in his shirt pocket. Then he walked over to a group of teenage fans and distributed the pieces as Kris pleaded in the background.

"I like to see common people happy," Dad told the reporter on set. "When I was a kid, I always wanted to meet celebrities."

"I knew he was going to do something to embarrass me," Kris said when he was back in his trailer. "Muhammad is an amazing man. In some ways, he is as simple as a child. But in other ways, to me, he's inscrutable. Like a sphinx."

There was never a dull moment with my father around. Another time, when everyone was hanging out around the set, Dad rushed over to the telephone. "I'll show you another nice guy," he told the reporter, then he dialed a long-distance call.

"Kris! Kris! I got somebody here I want you to talk to," said Dad. On the other end of the line was one of my father's favorite actors, Count Dracula himself. Dad smiled with delight as Kris took the phone shyly and asked, "Is this Christopher Lee? Oh God, it is! I'm knocked out just listening to you … Hey, great to meet you, over the phone even."

Daddy took back the receiver and said, "You've got Kris Kristofferson blushing!"

Then he made another call to *Freedom Road*'s executive producer, careful to disguise his voice. "You shall die tomorrow if you don't get that Nigga out of that top role," he said theatrically. He allowed a moment of stunned silence, then he laughed and said, "This is Ali!"

Kris, seated on the sofa, shook his head at the reporter. "Zev will have a coronary before this is over." In the background, Dad was asking about the day's work. "Was it good? I really acted good, huh?" When he hung up the phone, he announced to the room, "They're going crazy over the rushes!"

My father was having the time of his life. Especially when John Travolta flew down in his customized DC-3 to help my father with his lines. John was sitting ring-side with my mother when Dad whooped

Leon Spinks and won back his title for an unprecedented third time. He gave Dad dancing lessons during breaks in shooting and joked about how no one would believe that Muhammad Ali couldn't dance.

"I didn't know it would be this hard," said John.

"I only dance in the ring," said Dad.

It was true. In the ring he was elegance personified, but in real life he had two left feet.

"Go back out and walk in like you did in *Saturday Night Fever*, John!" Dad told him once.

And so he did. As reporter Dick Russell observed, John kicked up dirt, treading charmingly as Dad cried: "Go, John! Dance, John! Look at that! Maaaan! Maaaan! Veronica, come over here, show her, too, John!"

"People say John doesn't usually act like that," Mom later told the reporter. "But he was really excited. Jumping up and down. Around Muhammad, he's like a little kid."

Later that night, Dad had John dancing with the people in the lobby of his Natchez motel. Life was always a little outrageous when my father was around; he had fun with his fame and the fame of his friends, but he never took it for granted and he didn't make any demands on set—other than allowing my mother and me, an administrative assistant, and his photographer, Howard, to be there with him. The usual fight entourage was absent.

I'm told our family quarters in Mississippi had a palm-shaded pool I liked to splash around in. Dad would put his hands beneath me, keeping me afloat, as I lay flat on my belly in the water, kicking and spattering, thinking I was swimming on my own.

"*That's it, Hana!*" he said. "*You're a good swimmer! The greatest swimmer of ALLLL time!*"

I was pictured in *People* magazine handing him his boots one morning as he dressed in a seventeenth-century military uniform for his role.

"I see they finally got you into an army uniform," someone joked, as he walked on set.

"Yeah," he grinned back. "But only from a hundred years ago."

He complained to my mother once. He had waited all afternoon to shoot a scene with her. Mom had a cameo in the film, where she would pour him a cup of tea.

"I don't like this acting!" he said, again. "It's too time-consuming." He also didn't like the fact that the films he was making weren't blockbusters.

"You have to go to school for this. You have to study," he said on one of his recordings. *"I got out of acting because it's silly making movies that aren't big hits ..."*

So, quitting acting was a forgone conclusion. Dad enjoyed being himself far too much, anyway, to pretend to be anybody else. "I like being me!" he once said. "I enjoy living my life, as Muhammad Ali!"

He didn't have the patience for acting in any form. When he was to film his third D-Con Roach Spray commercial, he got frustrated and walked off the set.

"That's it! I'm through for the day!" he said after dozens and dozens of takes. "We can finish this tomorrow!" And, with that, he was gone.

Like his father, Dad was restless. He could never stand still for long.

A friend of my father, Tim Shanahan, once told me the story of how in 1977 Warren Beatty rewrote the screenplay *Heaven Can Wait* with my father in mind for the leading role. The original 1940s version had a boxer as the main character. According to Tim, Warren thought Dad was a natural actor and perfect for the part. Sometime before moving to Los Angeles, Warren came to the house on Woodlawn in Chicago and offered him the part. I'm told Dad was excited about the film and loved the storyline about a young athlete who dies suddenly when an overanxious angel takes him to heaven—only to discover he wasn't supposed to die. But his body is cremated before the angel's mistake can be rectified, so he returns to earth to live in another man's body. Dad was all in until Herbert Muhammad, Dad's manager and advisor, told him it was a bad idea because Muslims don't believe in reincarnation. My father always put his religion first. He didn't want to advertise anything that would contradict the teachings of Islam. So he turned down the role.

Warren and Dad kept in touch and became friends of a sort. And on June 19, 1977 he was at my parents' wedding.

"My main thing now is to try and serve God," said my father in the same interview with *People* magazine. "So what if I make a movie? The odds are, forty years from now, we won't be here. Forty years ain't nothing to eternity. How many movies did Charlton Heston or Elizabeth Taylor make? They're old now, life went by ..."

He went on to tell the interviewer about his greatest project. An organization called WORLD—the World Organization for Rights, Liberty, and Dignity—an international service foundation.

"Everything has a purpose," he said. "Trees have a purpose. Pigs have a purpose. Termites have a purpose. Surely God's highest form of life has a purpose, too."

The interviewer asked if Dad was ready to hang up his gloves.

"I really don't know right now," he said. "I'm not worried about leaving boxing. I'm established now. Boxing wasn't nothing. It held me back, kept me in training camp for six months. Six damn months of my life in a training camp. I'm free now ..."

***

WHEN HE WASN'T traveling the world making films or training for fights, my father spent most of his "home time" padding around his office with bare feet, sipping coffee and talking on the telephone—dreaming his dreams aloud—trying to generate world peace.

"There's an organization I want to form called 'WORLD'," said Dad in a recorded interview. *"It stands for World Organization for Rights, Liberty, and Dignity. I'm a little reluctant about pursuing it because it's going to take a lot of work, but I have a lot of plans. I talked to Brezhnev when I was in Russia, and he gave me a spot inside the Kremlin if I want it. I'm not Russian; I'm just trying to make things better.*

"I'd like to set up office in about sixty countries. The sole purpose of the organization is to better relationships between people on a social, civilian level. For example, the common Russian doesn't hate Americans and the common American doesn't hate Russians. It's

just the politics of leaders that cause the titles and the labels, which cause the prejudice or hate ... Like Catholics don't like Protestants, or Muslims aren't with the Germans, or the Buddhist is not with the Hindus, or the Republican is not with the Democrat. God never named anything Catholic. He never named anything Baptist, Jehovah's Witness, Muslim or Judaism.

"Man gave the title and that's what separates and divides people. I'd like to get something started where there is no title involved. All people, all races, all religions fighting for one cause—the human cause. This is what I think I want to do because nothing can surpass what I've already done. I've been so popular and I've done so much in boxing that if I went out and just found one occupation or made movies or whatever I wouldn't be satisfied. I've got to do something big—something that will change lives ..."

8

I REMEMBER KRIS Kristofferson and John Travolta coming to the training camp and the house on Fremont several times to visit my father. On one occasion Kris brought his daughter, Casey, with him. She was two years older than me (I was probably four or five at the time). What I remember most was the two-inch platform shoes she was wearing. It was the first time I'd seen high heels made for little girls. I asked her if I could try them on. Once the shoes were on my feet, there was no getting them off. I ran into the bathroom and locked the door behind me. If memory serves, she went home barefoot that night.

Over the years Kris and my father remained friends. He was at the opening of the Ali Center in 2005, Dad's museum in Louisville, Kentucky, and he and his wife Lisa spent Thanksgiving with us a few years back.

John Travolta was a different story. By the mid-1980s, he'd disappeared. When Mom and Dad were in Texas, at the invitation of Adnan Khashoggi, a wealthy Saudi Arabian businessman, they found out John was staying in the same hotel. They left a message for him, but he never returned the call. They never knew why exactly, but they later discovered that John had cut off his close friends and associates, and fired all of his long-time employees.

A couple years earlier, John was at our house celebrating my mother's birthday, asking my parents to fly to Las Vegas with him on his new airplane. Dad wasn't comfortable flying in little planes, so he didn't want to go.

"Come on, Muhammad," said Auntie Diane. "It's Veronica's birthday. You're always complaining that she doesn't want to go anywhere. Now she finally wants to do something and you don't want to go ..."

Her speech worked. After a few slices of cake, the four of them flew to Las Vegas for the evening. Before they left, John came up to our rooms with my father to tuck us in. It was the last time I remember seeing him.

***

I PICK UP another article and my jaw drops. My father is on the front page of the *Detroit News*, standing on the ledge of a nine-story building. In the photo it's Monday, January 19, 1981, two days after his birthday. The same time next year, one week after Dad's last fight, Mom will throw a small surprise dinner party for him. A vague memory resurfaces.

I'm seven years old. Laila and I are peeking through the stair rails in our pajamas as my father and his guests—Carey Grant, John Travolta, Mayor Tom Bradley, Kris Kristofferson, Lou Rawls, Zev Braun, and friends—are gathered around a belly dancer. Mom and Aunt Diane were in black cocktail dresses, complete with ruffled white aprons. The evening was all jingles, cheers, and laughter. Glasses were raised, toasts were made, jokes were told, all in celebration of Dad's fortieth year. "*I'm getting old,*" he told them. "*It all goes by so fast.*"

I exhale slowly, lean back in my chair and read the story. The photo is overwhelming. Dad is leaning over a balcony, his arms wrapped around a stranger, pulling him over the railing to safety.

> Muhammad Ali reaches for a distraught man who was threatening to jump from the ninth floor of a Los Angeles building yesterday. The former heavyweight champion happened to be driving by the building while police were trying to talk the man out of jumping and asked if he could help. He leans out the window to speak to the man threatening to jump, then helps him back onto the balcony.

The man he talked out of plunging to his death was a twenty-one year old from Michigan who was convinced he was a "nobody". At 2:20 p.m. the man climbed out on a fire escape balcony of a building at 5410 Wilshire Blvd. He locked the door behind him and screamed that he was going to jump.

"He said he couldn't find a job, that he was depressed," Dad told the reporter. "He said his mother and father don't love him, that nobody loves him. He asked, 'Why do you worry about me? I'm nobody.' I told him he wasn't a 'nobody'. He saw me weeping and he couldn't believe I was crying, that I cared that much about him … I'm going to help him go to school and find a job, buy him some clothes. I'm going to go to Michigan with him to meet his mother and father. They called him nobody, so I'm going home with him. I'll walk the streets with him and they'll see he's BIG."

He did the same thing for my sister, Miya. She called him crying one day after school. A few of her classmates had been teasing her. They didn't believe her father was really Muhammad Ali because she didn't look like Dad and they never saw them together. My father was on the next flight to New Jersey. He drove her to school and called an assembly. When all of the kids were in the auditorium, he told them all he was her father. Then he took her home and walked up and down the streets of her neighborhood holding her hand, so everyone could see them together.

Dad escorted the man to the police station in his Rolls-Royce. Then he rode with him in the police car that took him to the hospital for a seventy-two-hour psychiatric observation.

Saving the man was neither a quick nor an easy task. As my dad's involvement began, he went to the nearest window on the ninth floor and began to talk to the man.

"You're my brother," he said. "I love you, and I couldn't lie to you. You got to listen. I want you to come home with me, meet some friends of mine …" A few breathless minutes later, the man opened the door and my father walked out onto the fire escape with him.

He put his arm around the man, then took it away when he became apprehensive. They talked for a while longer and, with a suddenness no one had expected, it was over. The man relaxed, hugged my father, and wept as he led him to safety.

I don't know what became of the young man or his troubled soul, but my father kept his promise.

"What did you say to get him off the ledge?" Mom asked later that evening.

"He thought nobody loved him," said Dad. "I told him I loved him, or I wouldn't be there."

As I stared at the image of my father pulling the man to safety, a story he liked to tell came to mind. There was once a hunter who was walking through the forest. He saw two birds sitting on the branch of a tree. He shot one and it dropped to the ground. It took a few minutes for him to arrive at the spot where the bird fell. While he was walking, the other bird had come down to look at his fallen mate. The bird touched his companion with his beak and realized he was dead. When the man arrived, he found both birds dead.

"One was such a friend to the other," said Dad, "that when it discovered there was no life in its mate's body, it died on the spot. From that day on, the huntsman gave up shooting birds. He said, 'I found a friendship among birds and animals which cannot be found among mankind.'

"This is a simple lesson that we all must learn. Today when nations are against nations, races against races, one community against the other, one religious group bombing the other, now is the time when friendship is most needed. For someone who learns the lesson of friendship in this world, this lesson, in the end, develops into a friendship with God himself."

I thought about another story—one my mother had told me.

One morning in 1979, when she and my father were staying at my grandmother's house near downtown Los Angeles, they were jogging together up Beverly Blvd when a homeless man approached them.

"I must be losing my mind," he said. "You look like Muhammad Ali."

"You're not losing your mind—it's me!"

"Will you sign your autograph for me?"

Dad reached into his pocket for his black marker—he was always ready for occasions like these. Sometimes he stood for hours signing autographs, telling jokes. It was the common everyday people that he enjoyed most. He knew the effect his presence had on them and he seized every opportunity to connect with people. Sometimes in the most unusual places—places you would never dream of bumping into Muhammad Ali, like an abandoned alley or street corner in the slums of Chicago or New York City. He'd walk down the street shaking hands with all who crossed his path.

"I've made so many mistakes," he once said. "I'm just trying to get to heaven."

The homeless man handed my father a crumbled piece of paper.

"What's your name?" he asked. Knowing Dad, he probably drew a smiley face and heart next to one of his favorite inscriptions: "Love is a net where hearts are caught like fish."

The man watched in awe as he signed. "I can't believe it's really you ..." he said.

Before Dad could look up, a clenched brown fist hit him in the face. And, with that, the homeless man took off running, shouting all the way up the street, "I hit Muhammad Ali! I hit Muhammad Ali!"

After the initial shock wore off, both my parents laughed.

"I guess that's a better story than an autograph," said Dad, rubbing his chin. "He never would have got me in my prime."

"No one will even believe him," said Mom.

"Probably not," said Dad. "But he'll know—and that's all that matters."

Someone once said that my father was what God meant people to be. Kind, loving, generous, and good. He was 100 percent sincere in what he said and what he believed. He used to say, "You can't serve God, because he doesn't need you. You serve him by serving people. When you reject and turn people away, you're rejecting the one who created you."

As much as my father loved his faith, he raised us to respect all religions, all people, and to judge no one. He always used his wisdom and fame to help as many people as he could. His whole life was a prayer for peace, justice, and human dignity. He gave so much and asked for nothing in return—only love.

"*Everyone is trying to live the best they can with the hand they've been dealt,*" he once told me. "*It's not always easy. Life is not equally kind to us all. Remember to treat everyone with respect and equality, and God will always bless you.*"

"Muhammad Ali is an international treasure," said Thomas Hauser in his book *The Lost Legacy of Muhammad Ali.* "More than anyone else of his generation, he belonged to the people of the world and is loved by them. No matter what happens in the years ahead, he has already made us better. He encouraged millions of people to believe in themselves, raise their aspirations and accomplish things that may not have been done without him. He wasn't just a standard-bearer for black Americans. He stood up for everyone. And that's the importance of Muhammad Ali."

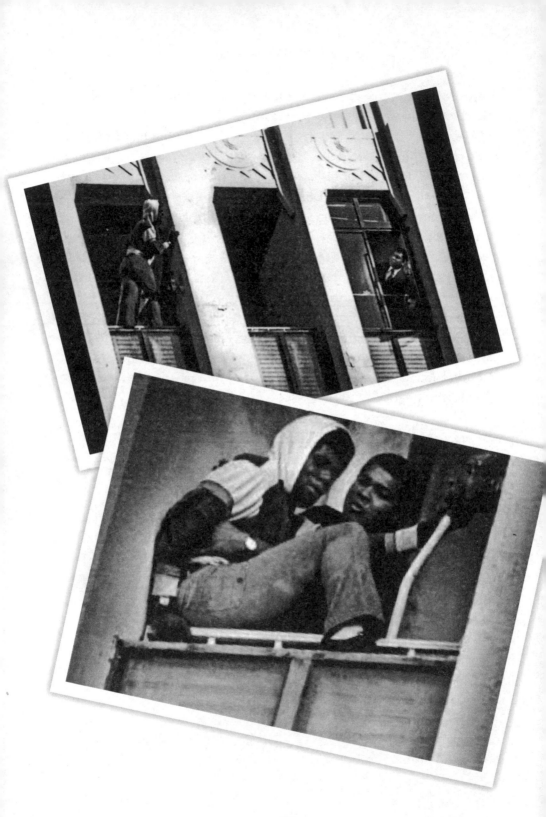

9

I PICKED UP the *Afro Caribbean Post*. My father is pictured in the Kremlin, shaking hands with Brezhnev. It's June of 1978, Dad had just lost his world title to Leon Spinks, but he would regain it in their second meeting, three months later.

I read the headline: "Ali the Ambassador".

MOSCOW: Muhammad Ali, the former world heavyweight champion, hugged and kissed Leonid Brezhnev in the Kremlin last week and said the "quiet and meek" Soviet president invited him to be his Ambassador for Peace to the United States.

"It's hard to believe he is a warmonger," Dad said at a press conference after the meeting. "All he spoke about was peace and love for humanity. He made me an unofficial Ambassador for Peace to the United States. Don't be surprised if you see me in the White House."

"He's so stately and dignified," continued my father. "He received me for thirty-five minutes, sitting there looking at me in the eyes like I was the president. He made me feel good to be a little black boy from Louisville, Kentucky, who couldn't meet the mayor of the city a few years ago."

My father was impressed by Brezhnev's desire for peace, and he told the Soviet leader, "President Carter and the American government want nothing but peace."

"Our country is too beautiful to be destroyed by bombs and killing people," said Dad. "Nobody wants war. Nobody can win. I used to worry about the Russians attacking America. And I am convinced now that there will be no war because America is too intelligent and now I see the Soviet Union is intelligent, too ... So many races and people are living here in peace."

As I read I thought about my father's plan of starting a world organization, how he wanted to gather children of all ages, one from every nationality, culture and race, and fly around the world together on a jumbo jet, meeting with various world leaders, hoping to inspire world peace. It was an improbable but beautiful dream—a dream he spent a lot of time trying to realize until something out of his control altered his course.

***

MY FATHER WOKE up every morning, put on his suit and tie, and opened his black briefcase full of his notes, speeches, and ideas. Then he'd set out to realize his dreams, searching for his new purpose in life. "I'm confused," he admitted to numerous reporters in 1979. "I don't know what to do in life now. I don't know what the purpose of it all is. But I know there's something waiting for me. I haven't heard no voice. A lot of preachers say God called them; well, I haven't heard it, but I want to figure out something that's never been done before in the world of religion. Just like I've done something that's never been done before in the world of boxing ... I enjoy ministering."

My father was always thinking about what to do after he retired. He had been boxing since he was twelve; it was all he knew. Dad didn't do well in school. He barely graduated. He taught himself how to read and write by studying life and the Quran, and he had an extraordinary memory. But he was a terrible speller. He used to have my mother correct his writing. I'm not sure who helped him when he wrote her letters, as he stated in one: "*I had someone help me with the big words ...*" There was a smiley face at the end of this sentence.

"In terms of reading and writing, I may be considered illiterate," he once told a reporter. "But when it comes to matters of the heart, [or] worldly and spiritual knowledge, I'm rich ... When you look at history, all of God's prophets were considered illiterate by today's standards, God took them empty and filled them up with his knowledge so no one else could take credit for it."

My father was dyslexic, as am I, so I know how challenging school was for him. In sixth grade, my favorite subjects were history and English, but I hated reading aloud. You know how the teacher goes around the class having each student read a paragraph? Well, I used to count the students ahead of me, then I'd run my finger down the page trying to find my passage ahead of time so I could familiarize myself with the words. If I didn't, I'd stagger on the big words, trying to sound out the syllables.

"Pro-cra-sti ..."

"Procrastinate!" another student would blurt out, impatient.

In third grade, I didn't even try. I just raised my hand and asked to use the bathroom before it was my turn to read. I'm not sure how my father dealt with reading aloud in school, but he had a friend named Ronnie who let him copy his homework and gave him answers to test questions. Dad said Ronnie was always a little smarter than him and could read and spell good.

Ronnie King was my father's best friend from grade school to his second Sonny Liston fight. They first met when he was walking to school to enroll in classes at Duvalle Junior High, down on the west end of Louisville, Kentucky, on 34th Street, fourteen blocks from his house.

"Will you walk with my little grandson?" asked a heavy-set woman with gray hair. Dad agreed, she introduced my father to Ronnie, and they became fast friends.

"This is my lunch," said Ronnie, noticing Dad staring at the brown paper bag in his hand. "You want it?"

"What is it?"

"An ole hamburger," he frowned.

According to my father, Ronnie's grandmother always made him hamburger sandwiches on homemade wheat bread with mustard and onions and pickles. But he wanted a peanut butter bun and some cookies and milk. Dad said, "I thought to myself, this boy must be crazy. He has a juicy hamburger with mustard, onions and a pickle, and he's talking about some cookies and a peanut butter bun."

"How much do you want for it?" asked Dad.

"Gimme a nickel," said Ronnie.

At lunch, Ronnie got his peanut butter bun with milk and cookies, and my father ate the burger. Every morning for the next couple years Dad was on the corner waiting to get that hamburger. As they walked to school together, Ronnie was always talking about his uncle, Tootie: "Tootie gonna take me fishing ..."

"Tootie goin' huntin' ..."

"Tootie got a motorcycle ..."

"He was always talking about Tootie," said Dad, "so I started calling him Tootie."

It was a good thing he was sitting beside Ronnie in class. Whenever he had trouble with his test questions, Dad would lean over and ask, *"What's the answer to question number two?"*

Ronnie always knew the answer. Dad often said that if it wasn't for his friend Tootie he might not have passed. He wished he had paid closer attention in school and had a better education. His mind was so wrapped up in boxing that he didn't work as hard as he should have. All he could think about was getting home and going to the gym. He shadow-boxed every morning on his way to a little drugstore, where he'd buy a carton of milk and two raw eggs because someone told him it would build his wind and lungs.

The only time I've ever heard my father refer to anyone as his best friend was when he spoke of Ronnie King. He was with Dad when his bike was stolen at the age of twelve. He was there six years later when Dad came home from Rome with an Olympic Gold medal around his neck. He was standing beside him when he threw his medal into the Ohio river after they were both asked to leave a restaurant where they'd tried to order hamburgers because it *"didn't serve Negros"*.

And Ronnie was watching in 1963 as my father ran across the ring at the age of twenty-two, having won his first heavyweight championship against Sonny Liston, shouting at the top of his lungs, *"I AM THE GREATEST!"*

I don't know how or why they lost contact after the second Liston fight. I guess *life* happened to them both. They had gone down different paths.

In 1977, an old classmate of my father's visited his training camp in Deer Lake and told him that Ronnie King had been killed in the streets of Louisville.

"How did it happen?"

"In a drug deal gone bad ..."

Dad wrote and recorded a beautiful speech once about the importance of friendship. It was a topic of great interest to him. There were so many people around him with their hands out—always needing something from him—he probably never knew who he could really count on. I'm sure his childhood friend, Ronnie King, came to mind when he recited the speech and poem:

Friendship is a priceless gift that cannot be bought nor sold,
but its value is far greater than a mountain made of gold.
For gold is cold and, lifeless, it can neither see nor hear.
In times of trouble it's powerless to cheer.
Gold has no ears to listen, no heart to understand.
It cannot bring you comfort or reach out a helping hand.
So, when you ask God for a gift, be thankful if he sends not
    diamonds, pearls, or riches,
but the love of real true friends.

My father once said that if he hadn't been a boxer, he would have liked to be a businessman. I think he was more in love with the idea of wearing suits and carrying a briefcase—looking intelligent—and receiving a consistent paycheck that wasn't dependent on his fleeting physical talents. Like so many athletes before him, he was running out of time.

After regaining his heavyweight title from George Foreman in Zaire, Harvard University asked my father to deliver a speech to the graduating class of 1975—an honor usually reserved for politicians. Oxford University had asked him to become their professor of poetry a couple years earlier, after his loss to Ken Norton in 1973, but the invitation sparked rumors of the end of his boxing career. To these, Dad replied, "Pay heed, and you will see why this is not the time for your university. It's not the pay, although that's small, but I have to show the world I can still walk tall."

While he gave a number of speeches at leading colleges—*The Purpose of Life, The Real Cause of Man's Distress, The Intoxication of Life, The Art of Personality, The Art of Friendship*, and *The Heart*—he wasn't interested in becoming a professor. He'd always wanted to be seen as more than just a boxer. It was enough for him that Oxford had made the offer.

As he said on one of his recordings: "*I'm trying to be a new man and get into something new. I don't want people to think I'm going to be another old champ hanging around fights all the time ...*"

Dad was approaching the end of one road, and he knew it. He had to decide the new course his life would now take, weather the storm of uncertainty and find a new place in the sun. But my father would soon discover how, sometimes, a path leading away can twist and return you right back to the place where you first began.

And wherever his path led, as I grew I learned how to share him with the world.

At the Vatican with Pope John Paul II, and in the Kremlin with Leonid Brezhnev.

10

BY THE TIME I was four years old, I realized my father did not belong to me. He belonged to the world. I can remember as a little girl looking down from the top of the staircase at his luggage gathered by the front door. He was preparing to leave for Deer Lake to train for the Larry Holmes fight in 1980. According to family friend Tim Shanahan, he and my mother stayed up with my father the night before, trying to convince him not to go. No one wanted Dad to come out of retirement. Even he was reluctant in the beginning. He struggled with the prospect for months, carefully documenting the reasons that led to his inevitable, and habitual, return to the ring.

"I'm going to come back!" he tells an old friend over the telephone. *"Win the title for the fourth time!"*

"What do you need with it, Muhammad?"

"Can you imagine FOUR-TIME CHAMPION?"

"Yeah, but what do you need with it? You've conquered the world already."

"You're right, I don't need it." He comes down from the mountain. *"I'm just talkin' ..."*

Three-time heavyweight champion of the world, at thirty-eight he'd secured his place in boxing history after regaining his title the year before, on September 15, 1978, against Leon Spinks. He was the first African-American fighter to get out clean, "at the top of my game", as he put it. But, as with most great athletes, that old feeling stirring within, the one responsible for making him that champion, accompanied by the irresistible prospect of defying seemingly impossible odds, ran too deep for him to resist. Not even "The Greatest" stood a chance against *himself.*

"*Time Magazine* said you do it for pride," said Barbara Walters in an old interview. "Some said you do it for money, others thought you do it for the glory. But why does Muhammad Ali feel the need to return to the ring, again and again?"

He leaned forward in his seat. "It's not pride," he told her. "If I fought for pride, I'd be a sad person. I'm through fighting, but I love boxing. I've been boxing since I was twelve—it's all I know. I like defending my title. I like the idea of staying the world's greatest fighter—the most popular person. As soon as you quit, that's over. I also like the idea of setting records. I want to set a record that will take someone years to break. I want to go out a winner, too, I really do. Sometimes I wonder myself why I didn't quit sooner. It's too late now ... what's happened has happened ..."

But there was another, more pressing reason—one he didn't mention that day.

"*Let me tell you something you don't know,*" he says to a friend in need. "*My mother calls me all the time with all her problems. My father calls me with his problems. They're both separated, so two houses must be maintained. My brother calls me—he's got a baby and he needs help, so I've got to support him. I take care of all my children and their mothers. Belinda gets me for $10,000 a month. I've got this house here and these children I'm taking care of. When I add all this up ... you won't believe it.*

"*I just came back from a trip. I made $70,000, so I'm squeezing that. I paid taxes on it and kept $35,000. That's got to sustain me for another couple months. That's all it's going to last. Then I've got to get out and go somewhere else to work. I'm getting to a point where I have to sell my farm in Michigan before I lose it to taxes. I've got so much on me, and I know you've got problems too, but mine are so big. If I just took care of myself and my present family, I'd be all right. But everyone will be suffering if I don't help them.*

"So this is what I'm trying to do every day. I listen to people telling me about their problems all the time. But I'm at the point now where I've got all these people to take care of and I don't know what I'm going to do ... Send me your bills," he said. *"I'll have Marge mail you a check ..."*

"It's too bad Muhammad Ali didn't have any real friends around him," NBA player Wilt Chamberlain presumed in an old interview, *"to give him good advice and tell him to stay out of the ring."*

But he did. And they tried.

"Hello, Muhammad," greeted his lawyer, Mike Phenner, on a different night. *"I promised you I'd go over your 1980 income. I was just adding up what I know is coming in from existing contracts and it exceeds one million dollars."*

"If I were a man that just took care of my wife, my baby, and myself, I'd be worth millions."

"Yes, you would."

"But I'm not even worth ten-thousand cash. It would be embarrassing if that ever got out—that Muhammad Ali doesn't even have ten-thousand in the bank. That happened once, remember ... Something in the papers saying I was broke? And they gave a list of all my fights. Joe Louis was known for not being smart because he made four million and wound up broke—four million! Just one million, to an ordinary man, you know, going to work, if you said that man once had one million dollars and now he's broke, you would look at him kind of funny.

"Here's a man who had sixty million dollars and I don't know where it went. I mean, you see how I take care of Aaisha [Khaliah's mother], how I take care of Pat [Miya's mother], how I take care of my brother, my mother, my father, Belinda [his former wife]. Then there's this expense, that insurance, taxes—so much is on me, I see myself falling but I don't know when it's going to be.

"If someone, like my mother, got sick, and the bill was thirty thousand, I'd have to mortgage something or borrow it. Then I would owe the bank. So I'm just thinking ... You tell me we have about one million coming, and that's a lot of running to get that million.

Then after taxes, lawyers' fees, and expenses, that might leave four-hundred thousand ...

"Let's face it, the people are getting used to me, and getting tired of me. I'm not getting any more famous and things are slowing down. Marge gave me $21,000 worth of bills last night and I paid them. That almost broke me. I just laid in bed thinking, it's good I haven't gone crazy. I think some people would have jumped out of windows."

"Well, they have, when they get upset," said Mike.

"I'm not that upset. My faith keeps me going. I'm not jumping out no window. But one thing I know ... I know myself better than anybody. I know what I can do. I know if I got my weight down to 220—Herbert Muhammad negotiated eight million to fight Larry Holmes. I know I can whoop Holmes, I trained him. I know I can beat him.

"Then, after all my taxes, I should have about four million. It's worth the gamble.

"I don't want my wife embarrassed, losing the house. I don't want my children with nothing. If I can get myself four million, keep one million, and put three million in bonds, and become the four-time heavyweight champion—I know I'm going to win. But if I lose, I'll just deal with it. But if I do this fight, people will be asking me if I'm broke."

"I remember Johnny Carson asked you that once," said Mike.

"What did I say to him?"

"You just said, 'Why do you ask me that?'"

"Let me tell you something," said Dad. "Evel Knievel is going to jump out of an airplane with no parachute and land on a haystack. If he can do that, I can fight!"

They both laugh.

"Well, Muhammad, there is just one part of your equation I don't think is correct, and that is the money situation. It's not nearly as bad as you think it is. If you were to liquidate your assets—you've got real estate that's worth three or four million dollars—so you're not broke. The Woodlawn house and the farm and Deer Lake ... if handled correctly they're worth a hell of a lot of money.

91

"So, if you're down to a cash position of ten thousand, I want to tell you, my good friend, I'm down to probably one thousand myself. Lots of people in their lives have periods where they don't have much cash. You have a huge income stream. The million dollars you have coming in, you don't have to do anything for that. It's all under the current endorsement contract, and you know that things are coming along every day.

"I think the one part of the analysis you may be wrong about is this: When you announce you are going to fight again, I think you might get a lot of adverse publicity. You've been through adverse publicity, and it doesn't bother you, but one thing it could affect is . . ."

"My credibility."

"Yes, your credibility, your position of leadership in the world, and your income. That's the part of the analysis I think you're being a pessimist about. In the sense that you worry about money, with good reason, because everybody demands it of you—but it's not nearly as bad as you think. So, my point is, Champ, I wouldn't presume to advise you as to whether you should fight or whether you can beat Larry Holmes—I have no doubt you could—but whether it's the right thing for the man, Muhammad Ali, who has a unique position in this world, particularly, as you know, among the black community, and that's at stake here. You have to think about that."

"You're right," Dad said. "But if I okay the fight—I don't care how bad the news is—it's old in a few days. This fight is not as serious as the Iran hostage crisis and people have taken this unnatural circumstance and they have adjusted to it."

"That's true."

"They say, 'What's going on in Iran today?' First, it's big news. If President Carter died, after a while it would be old news. So, once this thing gets out, they'll criticize, they'll talk, and I'll be in my place hiding, and after a week it will be old news!"

"I think that's right and you had a lot worse publicity than that. Hell, the Vietnam thing was worse. The only thing I'm saying is, don't do it only for the money . . ."

"I hear you. You have a good point. I know myself and I believe I can make money, but I wonder—what will I do?"

"You have a unique image and position in this world ... you're not just a fighter. You're bigger than that."

"You're right. I'll think about it. I haven't made my mind up yet."

The concerns of his friends and family had nothing to do with their belief in him. After all, Daddy was a magical man. He made people believe in miracles. As boxing historian Bert Sugar once said, "If God didn't create him, somebody would have invented him." Daddy was like Superman; he triumphed over obstacles, fought injustice, and persevered when he was down. But, as my father and the world would soon be reminded, even Superman has a weakness.

Time was also my father's kryptonite. It waits for no man. Not even the world's greatest champion attempting his last climb.

"I was just wondering," he said one evening to his manager. *"Just to see what your thoughts are. I believe so, I just want to see what you believe. Do you think that if we take four months of eating right and training—I can get a doctor, exercise, get a dietitian, form a good camp—you think we can come back dancing?"*

"Yes, I believe we can. If you do everything you said, I believe it."

But Daddy's speech was failing. His movements and reflexes were noticeably slower. Occasionally, he lost his balance walking. In the beginning, they were subtle changes, noticeable but presumed to be explainable by fatigue, jet lag or minor brain damage.

"Muhammad," said my grandmother over breakfast in 1979. *"Speak into the recorder, honey, you're slurring your words."*

"I know." He cleared his throat. *"I don't know why, but when I play back the tapes I can't always hear myself good."*

"It's because you're talking too fast. You just have to slow down ..."

If only she'd been right.

In 1984, two years after his last fight, my father admitted himself into the Mayo Clinic for testing and was told he had Parkinson's syndrome. As time passed, the symptoms progressed and, in 1986, he was officially diagnosed with Parkinson's disease.

"We're all going to lose things in life," he said to a room full of reporters. "You can lose a fight, or you can lose a debate, or you can just lose in life, period. We're going to lose our health, lose our mothers, lose our fathers; whatever it is, we've got to keep going ..."

At four or five years old, I remember tugging on the babysitter's coat-tail after Daddy stumbled or slurred his words. "What's wrong with my daddy?" I'd ask, peering up through worried eyes. I needed an answer, any explanation. It was the not knowing—not under-standing—that tortured me.

"Nothing's wrong with your father, Hana," the babysitter answered with care. "He's just tired."

"Then why does he talk that way?"

"It's because of how much he coughed when he was young," she fibbed, unsure of what to say. I wanted to believe her. For months, I walked around trying not to cough. It's funny how the very young believe little untruths so explicitly.

Regardless of the countless attempts to ease my troubled mind, I sensed something was wrong with my father and I worried about him all the time. But the world kept turning and the phone calls kept coming.

"Hey, Champ," said one of his managers on another recording. "I was talking to Don King before he left town. He told me to tell you he had gotten eight million for you, so far, and he's working on ten."

"Eight million—for what?"

"You and Larry Holmes—if you want it."

"Tell him to go to the press. He and Holmes can challenge me."

"I told him you wanted it to look like they were challenging you. He liked that idea."

"Hold on, Jerry," he said. "Hana and Laila are cuttin' up. You all stop it! I'm talkin'!"

"Look, everybody realizes you're still the king, and the big talk now is what are you really going to do ..."

There was an enduring pause.

"Man, I went to see a training camp today and—God is my witness—it's ten times better than Deer Lake! Fifty-five acres of rolling hills with *twenty-five log cabins encircled, all brand new. It has a big stable with horses, a heated swimming pool, a large tennis court on top of a hill and a huge kitchen that seats a hundred people. All the cooking utensils and stoves are there, with old English furniture. I'm telling you, there's nothing in the world like it. It's beautiful. I'll fight just for that! Then, when I'm through fighting, it will be a Triple Crown World Headquarters for ALL fighters ..."*

If only I could go back and warn him. "Don't do it, Daddy," I'd plead. "It doesn't end well for you this time." But I was just a little girl who ate popsicles, unable to alter the course of time. Unable to change her father's mind. Unable to save him from *himself*.

Shakespeare said he wrote to be immortal, but books can be lost and words can be erased. Athletes compete to challenge themselves and set records, but records can be broken and new paths are blazed. With so many variables, how can anyone be sure that they've made an impact? So, he was lured back—to that old familiar place, where he once shined as a beacon of light and hope. The place where he could prove to himself and to the world he was capable of miracles, capable of defying the odds—capable of achieving the impossible.

Atop a steep winding dirt drive, nestled among pine forests and rolling fields, Fighters' Heaven in Deer Lake, Pennsylvania, sits on a modest stretch of land.

Encircled with small, rustic log cabins and huge imposing rocks that bear the names of old boxing greats—Jack Johnson, Joe Louis, Sonny Liston, Archie Moore, Kid Gavilan, Jersey Joe Walcott, Rocky Marciano and his favorite, Sugar Ray Robinson—this is where my father retreated to train for a fight. Where he rose in the dawn, putting on his grey jogging suit, lacing up his old black boots and breathing in the fresh mountain air.

Amid the echo of victories long past, and the melody of morning birds, he set out on his enduring run through the woods and fields— up Agony Hill, into the glory of the rising sun.

"I'm starting to run again," he said on a recording. *"I ran three miles today. You know something: it's part of life. It makes you feel*

96

better. You think, eat, sleep ... I mean, just like you have to breathe, it's something you have to do. You can't just get fat, lay around and not work your body; your mind will go too. If you want to enjoy this life on earth as a human, you have to jog or do something."

At the crack of dawn, the calls came flooding in. Everyone wanted to know if it was true.

"Muhammad," said an old friend, "*incidentally, there's a story in today's* Post *that you're going up to Deer Lake to start training again ... It's an item in Jerry Eisenberg's column—I'll read it to you ... It says: 'This is the one that should really shake you. Yesterday morning a longtime and rarely written about member of the Muhammad Ali retinue, a man named James Anderson, was dispatched at Deer Lake, Pennsylvania, with orders to burn the gas and turn on the electricity and put the camp in order because guess who is coming home to the great woods ... The comeback of which so many have spoken, and so few have known, may indeed be on its way. Ali is being drawn to Deer Lake the way a kamikaze pilot used to hone in on the deck of an American carrier ...'"*

But how could he have known what would happen? He was like the sun: the same light that illuminates the sky blinds those who over-gaze. It was no more his fault than it was the fault of the sun, when his dream inflamed. "*People listen to me because I'm champ of the world,*" he once said. "*That's why I keep fighting—so I can keep doing God's work. I'm on a divine mission. I was born to do what I'm doing. I'll be told when to retire.*"

And he was. It was *time* that finally got his attention—when his mind told his legs to shuffle, but they didn't. It was *time* who reared its face when he threw his infamous right-hand lead but missed. And it was *time* who whispered, "It's over now," after his sixty-first and final fight—when he reached down into the well, and the well was empty.

"*I'm going downhill,*" he said one evening after the fight. "*Eventually we all undergo losses and go downhill. I'm no exception ...*" But it was a lesson that had to be learned in the ring: under the pearly lights that had shone upon him since the age of twelve.

But before the Holmes fight he was still the champion of the world—he still *believed*.

"*If I make a comeback, the theme will be ... just think, champion four times! FOUR TIMES! You all thought three was somethin', you all thought I was through, but I'm going to show you HOW GREAT I AM!*

"*To be the four-time champion, I'm going to come back! I'm free! I've been free all my life. I say what I want to say, I go where I want to go. But I'll tell you this ... I've thought about it. They say records are made to be broken—Jesse Owens' record was broken, Babe Ruth's record was broken—everybody's records are broken. For a man to break my record now, he'll have to be four-time champion. It might be possible, but I just know ... ain't no man gonna win the world title FIVE TIMES!*

"*So that's why I'm back! I want to be immortal! I want to be greater than great! I want to be a real Superman! My manager doesn't want me back, my brother, my mother, my father—my wife's crying—but my name's going down in history, not theirs. My name!*

"*Get ready! Get ready! Tell them all—I'M BACK!*"

***

STANDING FIRM IN his office, Dad told Mom and Tim, "You've got two hours to try to talk me out of leaving to go train for the Holmes fight." Once my father issued a challenge to anyone, you knew who would win.

Early the next morning Dad was trying to sneak out of the house before Laila and I woke up. It was too late. The sound of him trying not to make a sound had already awakened me. I could hear him walking around downstairs in his office. I crawled out of bed and tiptoed over to the staircase. That's when I spotted the luggage. My heart sank. I knew what this meant.

"Daddy is leaving!"

The melodrama he was trying to avoid was about to unfold. I raced down the steps, as though it was the end of the world, shouting, "*I want to go with you, Daddy!*" When I reached the bottom of the stairs, I ran into his office, dove into his arms and hugged him with all my might. "*Please take me with you, Daddy!*"

That was when he softly told me, "You have to stay home, Hana. But you and Laila are flying up to my training camp with your mother in four days—*four tomorrows.*" I pushed him away, crying. He walked over to the corner of the room where I lay sobbing on the floor, picked me up and carried me back over to the sofa. As I sat there, on his lap, he wiped my tears.

"Hana, I'm your daddy, but I am also Muhammad Ali, the Champion of the World. People look up to me. I inspire them. So I have to go to Deer Lake to train for a fight that will help me stay a champion. I'm not just your daddy, Hana ... I'm also a 'Daddy to the World'."

I jumped out of his arms, sobbing as I made my way down the hall into the living room. "Hana ... I have to go soon," he called after me. "But I'll send for you. Give me a kiss goodbye." He walked over and tried to pick me up again. I crossed my arms, pouting, and shouted, "You're not my daddy. You're Muhammad Ali!"

It's strange, the things you remember—the moments in time burned into your heart forever.

11

MY FATHER TRAVELED often, but most of my memories are of him at home. I remember playing on his office floor when he was working at his desk or when he was on the telephone. No matter what was going on, his door was always open. Even when he was busy, he made time for us. My memories are rich because of it.

I remember my father eating with us every night he was home. Occasionally finishing my vegetables for me so I could have a popsicle after dinner. I remember him letting Laila and me stay up late watching television and playing dress-up. He watched lovingly as we circled around him in our mother's oversized clothes. I remember him telling me stories until I fell asleep at night and waking me up with kisses every morning. I remember him trying to braid my hair before school and walking me into my first-grade classroom with two uneven ponytails. I looked like Pippi Longstocking, one of my favorite television characters.

I didn't mind my crooked ponytails; I was proud to wear the braids Dad gave me. Every morning, after the babysitter neatly combed my hair, I snuck out of my room, messed it up again, then ran down to my father's office and asked him to braid it. He always tried.

In first and second grade, I remember him bringing me Pioneer Chicken and strawberry soda for lunch almost every day. I can still see him standing in the doorway of my classroom, holding my lunch in one hand and his tape recorder in the other. He'd ask my teacher and classmates all sorts of questions about me—the kind of student I was and asking what boys I had crushes on.

I remember waking up in the hospital when I was nine years old after falling off the jungle gym at school and hitting my head. My head was so hard I probably caused more damage to the ground than it did to me.

I also remember opening my eyes to find my father's round, loving face beaming down at me. He never left. Day and night, he was there. He watched television with me and charmed the nurses into bringing me extra orange ice cream cups, the same ones they served with dinner. We both loved sweets. Sometimes we'd eat our dessert first.

"We can't do this all the time, Hana," he'd say. "Or we'll get worms in our bellies."

I can still picture my father sitting in the corner of my hospital room, shuffling through the lined yellow pages in his briefcase as I watched cartoons and colored in bed.

At night, I remember resting my head on his chest, listening to the sound of his beating heart, as he told his favorite story, a Sufi tale about a slave named Omar that he shared many times over the years. By the end, he was always in tears. "You've taught me a great lesson, Omar ... I may be the King, but it is you who has a king's heart."

And when my parents were traveling the world, I remember presents and postcards coming in the mail from England, Switzerland, Ireland, etc. The notes my mother sent are in a wooden box on my nightstand. There was only one written by my father's hand. It read, in part, "Dear Hana, I love you so much. You are so sweet and beautiful, just like your mother." But it was lost some time ago.

The card was pinned on my bedroom wall for years. I even brought it with me to Boston when I left for college. I read it often, especially when I was feeling nostalgic, until it was stolen from my locker during Thanksgiving break, along with a box of other tokens and keepsakes.

I was upset for a while. Then I realized my father's words had served their purpose the moment I read them. The postcard brought me joy and filled my heart with love every time I laid eyes on it. And it still does when I think about it today. I am grateful he took the time to write to me.

More than anything, I remember my father making me feel like I was the most special little girl in the world. Like Pippi Longstocking, I was wild, free, and unpredictable. My father never clipped my wings—he let me be a little girl. He was, and always will be, the most wonderful thing in the world to me.

***

I PICKED UP where I'd left off with the articles. *Solo*, 1980: "Muhammad Ali's wife talks about the champ fans don't know. A real softy." I was four years old, Laila was three. I paused before continuing, knowing 1980 was a difficult year for my father—the beginning of the end of his boxing career. I exhaled as I read the opening line: "In the wake of his humiliating defeat at the hands of Larry Holmes—Ali's 24-year-old wife, Veronica, has broken her silence ..." In a candid interview, Mom talked about her hope that Dad would retire for good and revealed a side of him most people didn't know.

"I often thought of how surprised people would be if they saw Muhammad at home. He is warm and affectionate, quiet, serious, and soft-spoken. And he makes me feel special. He is terribly soft with our daughters, Hana and Laila. He likes to get up at dawn and take them off for a walk alone. He loves them to climb into our bed in the morning ... When he is training for a fight and we have separate rooms, he'd keep them in bed with him all night if he had his way. But he has to be talked out of it because he needs rest."

I read my mother's words with a heavy heart, and I asked myself hard questions: When did she know she was leaving him? Did it happen all at once, like a blinding flash of clarity? Or bit by bit, like the changing of the seasons? I guess it doesn't matter now; either way, their love story ended the same: with us moving to a new house without my father.

"Muhammad is so good and gentle with all his children," she continued, "that, when I look at him in the ring, it's like watching a stranger. I have an odd feeling of detachment. It's hard to believe the man I know, so soft and kind, is in there beating up another person."

As I read, I began to see certain images. I began to remember Fighters' Heaven, Dad's home away from home. Nestled among pine forest and rolling fields, on top of a dirt drive up a wooded hill there rests a sign nailed to the trunk of an old oak tree: *Welcome to Ali's Camp.*

He built a boxing gym in the center of the property. And placed a series of log cabins and mess halls around it—eighteen stand-alone buildings in total.

Rising at 5 a.m., my father rang the bell that woke his eleven-man crew, including Howard Bingham, Drew "Bundini" Brown, Angelo Dundee, Jimmy Ellis, Gene Kilroy, Lana Shabazz, James Anderson. Breakfast at 8 a.m. followed by a four-mile run through the woods and fields.

I saw the small white mosque my father had built at the entrance of his camp. I saw the large boulders, made from lumps of coal, on which Papa Cash painted the names of those boxing greats, past and present. Many well-known visitors such as Michael Jackson, Frank Sinatra, The Beatles, Tom Jones and Andy Warhol would sit on the rocks or around the camp's giant firepit listening to Dad brag and boast and recite his speeches and poems. But you didn't have to be famous to visit Fighters' Heaven. Deer Lake was open to all who cared to stop by. Dad would take off an entire afternoon from training to laugh and show off his magic tricks. My father was happiest spending time telling stories and his favorite visitors were children.

I see the playground and the swing set where I used to sit in my father's lap, my little hands wrapped around his, as we soared in the sunset.

I remember a time when my parents were still in love. A time when they rode their horses together. Mom's Missouri Fox Trotter and Dad's Clydesdale. A time when she sat ringside at his training camp, watching him spar. A time when they would lie on the sofa together in my father's log cabin looking out the window at the stars. She's smiling at something he's said or done. Gazing up at him lovingly, as she rested in his arms. This was a look he could count on. A look that said, *I'll always be here for you.* But that was another time. When *happily ever after* was still in their eyes.

May 28, 1979

Dearest Hana & Laila,
We're in Gotenberg,
Sweden today. Late
tonight we fly to
Stockholm. Daddy is
working very hard for
you ladies. We
miss you very much.
Every day away seems
like a week. We cannot
wait to get back home
and be all together
again. Lots of love,
   Mommy & Daddy

TO:
Misses Hana Yasmeen
   & Laila Ali
55 Freemont Place
Los Angeles,
California 90005
U S A

12

FOUR THINGS DEFINE my early life. My father, popsicles, Wonder Woman and my mother's closet. And I was determined to have my way with all four of them, *every day*. Which had everything to do with how well I got along with the adults around me—particularly the governesses.

I never understood the difference between a nanny and a governess. Mom just said they were live-in care providers. According to the dictionary, a governess is a woman employed to teach and train children in a private household. Traditionally, they taught reading, writing, and arithmetic to children under their care. They also taught the "accomplishments" expected of middle-class women, such as French, the piano, and painting.

While we had tap, ballet, and piano lessons, we never learned French and it wasn't the governess or the nannies who taught us decorum. That all came from my mother, and the grooming classes she enrolled Laila and I in during the summer. You know, the type that taught young ladies how to sit up straight, cross their legs, and the difference between a salad and dinner fork. I think my mother was hoping the classes would wash away all the masculine habits I had picked up from hanging out with my father every day—the sorts of things that men get away with but young ladies are judged for, such as wiping my nose without a tissue, eating with my hands, making snorting sounds when trying to clear my throat and nose. Fortunately, Barbizon, a modeling and finishing school for young ladies, had successfully polished my manners, teaching me poise and charm by the age of twelve. But all that would come later.

My first babysitter was an elderly black woman named Gertrude. She was from Louisville but relocated to Chicago, where we lived at the time, to take care of me. Gertrude and my paternal grandmother were friends; she was also the mother of Mama Bird's minister, Reverend Simms. I was too young to remember her. I'm told she was a sweet, grandmotherly woman who always wore a white dress that resembled a nurse's uniform and was very attentive to my needs.

My parents hired Gertrude when I was six months old, a few months before their wedding on June 19, 1977. She bathed me, read me stories, changed my diapers and curled my hair the first year of my life. Mom says she disturbed my sleeping patterns by picking me up every time I made the slightest whimper during the night. Mom had moved out of the condo on Hyde Park and we were living in the Woodlawn house by then, occasionally driving down to the farm in Michigan where Dad sometimes trained for a fight.

Gertrude would pick me up and walk around the house comforting me before taking me back to my crib, where she would sing lullabies as she rocked me to sleep. Before then, I slept in my parents' bedroom. One of my favorite photos is of me sleeping with my father when I was five months old, curled up under his chin.

"Gertrude was a good nanny and she loved you dearly," my mother once said. "The perfect kind of person you'd want to take care of your kids. But she became overly attached to you."

Gertrude wanted to take me everywhere with her, even to church on Sundays. Being my father was a Muslim, taking me to church was out of the question.

"I can't leave the baby," said Gertrude. And she stopped going to Sunday Mass.

"She even stopped going to get her hair done, because we wouldn't let her take you," said Mom. "So she started wearing wigs. Then because of the wigs her hair started to fall out. Her attachment to you was becoming unhealthy. It wasn't good for her and eventually we had to let her go."

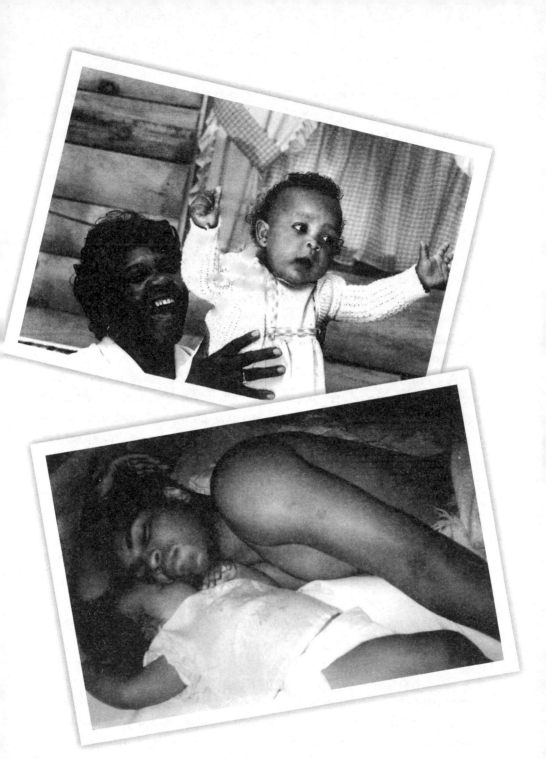

Top: Gertrude and me.

A few months before Gertrude was dismissed, she finally got to bring me to church with her. In May 1977, we all flew into Louisville to visit Mama Bird after Dad's fight against Alfredo Evangelista. Gertrude's son, Reverend Simms, was giving the sermon and out of respect for the woman who'd taken care of his newborn baby Dad accepted her invitation. He even let Gertrude keep me with her in the front row, next to her family and my grandmother, while he and Mom found seats further back in the crowded cathedral.

In the middle of the sermon, Gertrude caught the holy ghost and, along with every other member in the room, threw her hands up in the air, praising Jesus—which was typical of Southern black churches. All my parents could see was me in my yellow ruffled dress raised above the crowd, like baby Simba in *The Lion King*, amid a sea of praising hands.

Around this time Dad had appeared on *The Tonight Show*, starring Johnny Carson, to promote his film, *The Greatest*, in which he played himself. But it was the fight that Johnny seemed to be most interested in. He wanted to know why my father hadn't looked like "the Muhammad Ali of old" in the ring that night.

"Let's be honest," said Mr Carson. "That wasn't your best fight. You've boxed a lot better than that, haven't you?"

"Well," said Dad, "we all look a lot different as time goes by ... We all change." He smiled mischievously at Johnny. "You used to look so nice on television," he said. "You were thinner. The wrinkles weren't there, your hair was black. Now you look like an old man." He reached over and touched Johnny's arm, smiling.

"I know your style," said Johnny, laughing. "I knew you were going to turn this whole thing around on me."

"We all change," Dad said, again.

"You did lay a pretty good one on Howard Cosell [the sports commentator] the other night before the fight," said Johnny. "Cosell said, 'Don't you have a little unnatural wrinkle around your stomach?' And you looked at the top of his head [at his toupee] and said, 'Well, a lot of us carry around things that are unnatural.'"

They both laughed.

"No, but I saw the fight," said Johnny in a more serious tone. "A lot of people think you're the best fighter in the world, but you were covering up a lot during that fight. What was the strategy there?"

"This boy was twenty-two years old, I'm thirty-five, thirteen years older ... I won the title fourteen years ago. It's a miracle just to still be on top right now."

"Did you think he was good?" asked Johnny.

"I know he was. I was in there fifteen rounds with him ... The man was good. He had a lot of energy, he was young ... you can never tell what's going to happen in a heavyweight fight ..."

There was a lot going on for my father in 1977. He fought Alfredo Evangelista on May 16th and Earnie Shavers, who he said was the hardest hitter, on September 19th. He had a movie, *The Greatest*, to promote, and a fast approaching wedding to plan for. He was marrying my mother on June 19th. Having Gertrude around was a tremendous help to them both.

I don't know what became of Gertrude or how my mother letting her go affected her. But in all the photos I have of us together, her arms are wrapped around me and she's smiling. Although I was too young to remember her, I'm grateful for the love she felt and gave me.

Our first live-in caregiver was Janet, but she was only temporary and lacked etiquette, so my mother never referred to her as a governess. But from my third to fourth birthday, she had the same duties as Gertrude. Every morning Janet would dress me and Laila, who had been born eighteen months after me, feed us breakfast, and then put us to bed at night—all the things parents usually did.

Like my father and I, Janet had a sweet tooth. She let me eat as many popsicles as I wanted, but there weren't many left after she opened the box. Other than that, I have no complaints about her. She spent most of her free time in her bedroom on the telephone.

I don't remember much about Janet other than she was a short, heavyset, jolly lady who was always smiling and talking to her boyfriend, and occasionally calling down to my father on the intercom offering to come collect me if I became too distracting: "Muhammad, if Hana gets in your way let me know and I'll come get her."

"Okay ..."

A tempting offer, I'm sure. I was high-spirited, and always up to something: jumping on the sofa; tugging at my father's arm as he wrote; getting ink stains on his white shirt, my pajamas and his desk as I climbed on his lap and scribbled on his pages. I was trying to copy his cursive handwriting. He didn't get angry. He just signed and dated the sheets I drew on, then put them in the hand-carved chest next to his desk, the one Mom brought home from Asia. It sits in my office now. I remember Dad looking in that chest every morning before opening his safe. I discovered why a few years ago, after I brought it home with me. It had been stored in Grandma's garage after we left Fremont. When I opened it, the smell of cedar wood and pine surprised me. The chest was so old, yet it looked and smelled so new. If it hadn't been for the large black writing on the edge of the wood, I wouldn't have remembered it belonged to my father: *Left 42, Around 2 times, Right 99, Left 55.* It was the combination to his safe.

Dad was always forgetting such things, so he'd write important dates and telephone numbers on the inside of cabinets and his desk drawer—a habit he never stopped.

"I'm going to show them to you when you're a big girl," he said, putting the pages I scribbled on into his chest. And he did. He never minded my rambunctious behavior or my relentless begging for a sip of his coffee every morning as he worked.

"*I want some toffee, Daddy ...*"

"*Listen to this, Hana,*" he'd say into the recorder, speaking to my future self, as my three-year-old self sat listening beside him. "*You don't say, coffee, Hana—you say, toffee ...*"

On some occasions, he'd be on the phone as his recorder captured me pleading in the background: "*I want some toffee, Daddy ...*"

"*No, you can't have any more,*" he'd say, placing one hand over the bottom receiver and moving the coffee with his other.

No matter how much I harassed him, how much noise I made, or trouble I caused, he never called for help or sent me away.

Mom finally let Janet go in the summer of 1980. She wasn't happy with her poor use of language. My mother feared that, being so young and impressionable, Laila and I would pick up on her lingo. Mom's sisters, my aunties Diane and Michelle, helped as she searched for a governess.

Diane was exuberant, fun and affectionate. She stroked my hair until I fell asleep at night and tickled me awake in the morning. She was also a firm disciplinarian. When people asked me why I gave them such a hard time but always listened to Auntie Diane, I looked at them wide-eyed and said, *"Because she hits!"*

Diane moved into Fremont in 1980, a few months after they all got back from Hong Kong. She had just left her husband after discovering, in the most unusual way, he was unfaithful. Already suspicious of him, she went to see a psychic who confirmed her husband was having an affair with not just one but two women at work.

"Can you believe it?" she said to my mother. "They even have the same name, Becky Lue and Becky Sue ..."

Diane was only supposed to be at Fremont a few months, until she found her own place, but ended up staying two years. She traveled the world with my parents, went to dinners and events with them, and helped with Laila and me in her spare time. Diane was very different from my mother. She was the kind of person who'd get down in the mud and get her hands dirty. She smoked cigarettes and used profanities. She liked to sit up late talking and telling stories and jokes that her grandmother had told her. My father was always eager to listen.

"Mommy, Mommy, Mommy, I'm tired of running around in circles," said Diane. "Shut up before I nail your other foot to the floor."

They both laughed.

"Tell me another one," said Dad.

"Mommy, Mommy, Mommy, what's wrong with Daddy?" said Diane. "Shut up and keep digging!"

"That's a good one," said Dad. "Shut up and keep digging—that's a good one." He laughed again.

While Diane was with us she took a job at the Dorothy Kirby Center in Los Angeles, where therapists rehabilitate kids for their crimes. She asked my father to come to the center's Halloween party to meet the troubled youth. He went and brought Laila and me with him—wearing nothing but our shirts. He did that often, just picked us up in whatever we had on and walked out the house. When Mom arrived, she and Diane found something to wrap around our bare bottoms.

Diane especially loved to tell me the story about the time she flipped my father onto his back. "I came home from work one night," she said. "Your father was laying on the sofa in your mother's office."

"Mom had an office?"

"Yeah," said Diane. "It was on the second floor at the top of the back stairs."

"I don't remember it." I said.

"That's because you were always downstairs in your father's office," she laughed. "But your mother converted the small room that used to be the maid's quarters into her workplace. She used it for organizing bills and reading mostly."

I remember the bathroom across the hall from Mom's office. Dad was always rushing me to the small sink to rinse my hand, knee or chin after I had cut or bruised myself on the floor. Or bumped into a wall, running through the house while playing hide and seek with him and Laila.

"As I was saying," said Diane, "I came home from work one night and your father was in your mother's office stretched out on the sofa, resting his cheek on the palm of his hand—pouting and sighing." He was trying to get my mother's attention. She was sitting at her desk with her back to him, reading a book. When Dad was bored he'd go looking for my mother. If she was busy it would become sort of a game between them, him trying to get her attention as she turned up her chin ignoring him.

"Diane!" Dad said, as she walked past the room. "Where are you coming from?"

"I just got off work."

"Tell me, Diane," he said, "you can't weigh more than 130 pounds. How will you defend yourself if one of those teenage boys tries to attack you?"

"Get up and I'll show you," she said.

She told him to stand behind her, spread his feet and put his arm around her neck. He did as she said. Then she warned him to brace for impact. He laughed. In a split second, she pulled his arm forward using her back as leverage and flipped him over her shoulder back onto the sofa. He laid there in shock, wide-eyed with his legs and arms bent, frozen in the air—in a claw-like position.

"That's how I'd do it," she said.

Mom, still reading her book, was pressing her lips and covering her face, trying not to let him see her laughing.

"I see you, Veronica," he smiled, now sitting upright on the sofa. "I knew I could get your attention."

They all burst into laughter.

Diane was so playful, nurturing and attentive. I don't know why she never had children of her own. She was a fun auntie. And great company for my father. Dad was usually in his office when she got home from work, sitting behind his desk with a coffee in one hand and the phone in his other. He was always calling to check the time, as though he knew he was running out of it, and adjusting his watch by the second.

"At the tone, the time will be 5:35 p.m. in twenty seconds."

Dad liked plain watches with large numbers he could easily read. I remember my father's hands, how he always had ink stains on his fingers from writing long hours in his lined yellow notepad. I wonder if I was in the room—playing on the floor or sitting on his lap—when he was writing his letters to my mother. They weren't all dated, but the first letter was written on January 8, 1983, one year before he was diagnosed with Parkinson's syndrome, which wasn't supposed to progress like the disease.

"It's God's will," he said to the doctors, family, friends and the world. *"I'm being punished for my sins now, so I can spend eternity in heaven."*

Dad always believed his Parkinson's was a punishment and at the same time a blessing. He thought God gave it to him to show him and the world that it wasn't Muhammad Ali but God who was the greatest. He spent hours in his office reading the Quran and the Bible, looking for contradictions and making comparisons, wondering how with so much fame and admiration he'd make it into heaven.

"The Quran says you have to be humble to enter the gates of heaven," he said to Diane as they sat in his office one night. "I have the most recognized face in the world. People are always catering to me. I can drop a pen on the floor and everyone in the room rushes to pick it up for me. This is why I have to work at staying humble."

The next evening Diane walked into my father's office after work, eating a fruit salad. Like the night before, the fire was crackling and Dad was sitting behind his desk sipping coffee and reading his Quran.

"Watcha eating?" he asked.

"Fruit salad."

"Got any more?"

"Yeah, I'll get you a bowl," she said, heading back to the kitchen.

When Dad was finished, he slid his plate across his desk, as if to inform her she could take it to the kitchen.

Diane gave him a look.

"Oh!" he said, jumping up from behind his desk. He carried the plate over to her, where she was sitting on the sofa, and handed it to her. Diane smiled and put her plate on top of the one in his hand.

"Why, thank you, Muhammad," she said. "How humble of you to take my plate to the kitchen for me." He looked at her, confused for a moment, then his eyes lit up and he walked out the room to the kitchen and did the dishes, probably for the first time in his life.

My aunt Michelle was another story. She was sweet, but easily flustered. She was rather sensitive, complained a lot, and could be selfish at times. She also seemed to have a crush on my father and always behaved inappropriately around him: hovering, batting her eyes, telling him she needed to talk to him and begging him to meet her at my grandmother's, where she lived at the time.

"What do you want to talk about?" he asked on one of his recordings.

"I'll tell you when you get here," she said.

"Are you in trouble?"

"No, I just want to talk to you."

"Why do I have to come there ... why can't we talk on the phone?"

"Because I want to talk in person."

"Okay, let me tell Veronica ..."

"What do you have to tell her for? You need her permission?" she snapped.

"Michelle, what's the matter with you? She's my wife ... you sound crazy—you're talking like you like me ..."

Michelle was highly intelligent, overly sensitive—a perfectionist even. But she always seemed to be in her own world. Always lying in the bed in the guest room when she spent the night, talking on the telephone, or in the bathroom blowing cigarette smoke out of a cracked window.

"Go to your room, Hana," she said, noticing me staring up at her.

"I'm hungry ..."

"I'll take you down in five minutes," she said, waving away the remnants of another smoke ring. My parents didn't want her smoking in the house or around us. But she always did as she pleased. I guess it was her own pleasure, rather than our health, that she was most concerned with. Luckily, Michelle was only a temporary babysitter, watching us only when we were in between governesses or during the governess's time off.

When we were older, Michelle would drive us to school sometimes. I remember her fastening us into the back seat of her little Toyota and rolling down all four windows. She'd light a cigarette and pop her favorite tape into the player. We sang in unison to Prince's "When Doves Cry" as she drove us up Larchmont Blvd to Page School. She was the one who introduced me to my favorite album, *Purple Rain*. Naturally, when my parents got us VIP seats to Prince's concert at The Forum in 1985, Michelle volunteered to take us. Laila and I, together with our friends Kim and Karen, jumped for joy as we sang along to "Little Red Corvette" and "Raspberry Beret". And when, in the middle of his act, Prince tossed purple lace underwear with peppermint candy tied on the sides into the crowd, I jumped up and caught them. For a split second the underwear was mine, then Michelle yanked them out my hands.

What I remember most about my aunt Michelle living at Fremont is her frantic reactions to my misbehavior when I was four years old. She used to pace her room anxiously, threatening to walk out and leave us in the house alone, calling Grandma for help in the middle of the night.

"Mom, can you please come over here!" she once moaned. "Hana won't take a bath."

"What happened?"

"She jumped out the tub and is running naked all over the house. She's getting soap and water all over the floor ...!"

"Where is she now?" asked Granny.

"I don't know ... she's driving me nuts!"

"Calm down, Michelle ... I'm on my way."

Luckily, Grandma's house was only a ten-minute drive from Fremont Place.

On one occasion, after Granny had given me a bath and put me to bed, she drove back home. It was late, just after midnight, when she pulled in her driveway. She didn't see the man approaching her car as she reached over to the passenger seat for her purse, and before she knew it my grandmother was on the ground, clutching her purse as the man dragged her all the way down her driveway on Bonnie Brae Street. The flesh was scraped from her knees before the robber finally let go of her handbag.

"What were you thinking, Mom?" asked my mother. "Why didn't you let go of the purse? He could have killed you!"

"Are you kidding me?" said Grandma. "All my credit cards and ID cards were in there."

"Allah was looking after you," said my father.

"It was our lord and savior, Jesus Christ," said Grandma.

"I guess they were working together," he smiled.

My father loved to get into debates about religion with his family and friends. He'd pull out his tape recorder and get the conversation stirring with his opening statement: *"How can God have a son ..."* he'd ask, then let the comments roll.

He never got upset or took things personally, the way most people do when talking about religion. He simply enjoyed the discussion—the pulse and energy of the room. The fun and laughter. The back and forth of debate. The heated exchange of concepts and ideas. But he never took himself or the topic too seriously.

Then one day Grandma Ethel went too far.

One Sunday morning in the summer of 1980, my grandmother called Michelle and told her to get us dressed. "Put ribbons in their hair," she said.

"Ribbons ... why?"

"It's a special occasion. I'll pick them up in an hour."

Dad was supposed to be out all afternoon. He would be leaving to train for the Larry Holmes fight soon. He walked through the front door as Michelle, Laila and I came down the steps wearing our pretty ruffled dresses.

"Where are you guys going looking so pretty?" he asked.

"To church to get baptized!" I said.

My father stormed into his office and called my grandmother.

"I'm sorry, Muhammad," she said. "I just want them to get into heaven."

He didn't know it at the time, but I had been to church before. Grandma took me when he and Mom were in Hong Kong. She smiled at me sitting beside her in the huge row of benches, trying to sing along to the songs, making up my own words. But she couldn't understand why I lay on the floor during prayer.

"What are you doing, Hana?" Grandma asked as I got on my knees and bowed several times. "Get up," she whispered, as people stared out the corner of their eyes. "You're going to get your dress dirty."

It wasn't until later that she realized what I was doing.

"That's how Muslims pray at the mosque," my mother explained.

My grandmother meant no harm. She believed she was saving our souls. My parents understood that. Although my father was upset, he apologized for yelling at her that day on the telephone and quickly forgave her.

Grandma never did get us baptized, but after my parents' divorce she was always saying the Lord's Prayer over me when I spent the night, making me repeat the words as she said them: *"Our father, who art in heaven, hallowed be thy name, thy kingdom come; thy will be done on earth, as it is in heaven ..."*

In the morning, she'd have me recite the prayer from memory as she cleaned my soiled sheets. I had slip-ups from time to time at Fremont Place. One governess used to make me warm milk and honey, thinking it would help me hold it through the night. It worked occasionally, but when my mother remarried I started wetting the bed excessively.

"You have to learn to hold it, Hana," said Grandma. "What are you going to do when you get married? Pee-pee on your husband?"

I was about five years old when we met the new governess, Meg. Laila was four. I fell in love with Meg the moment I laid eyes on her. According to my father, Laila was still attached to Janet, so it took time for her to warm up to Meg.

"Laila," he said on one of his tape recordings, *"you're four years old now and you're always asking for Janet ..."*

Ironically, it was Laila's fascination with Meg that ultimately ended her employment. But the two and a half years she worked at Fremont Place were heavenly. Meg was a sweet, stocky Englishwoman, with bright blue eyes and long reddish-blonde hair. She spoke with a perfect English accent, which reminded us of our favorite television nanny, Mary Poppins. We met her over lunch one Saturday afternoon, and Laila and I giggled whenever she spoke.

"Would you kindly pass the sugar, please?" said Meg.

Afterwards, we ran around the house trying to imitate her accent: *"Pass the sugar, please ..."*

"No," said Laila. "It's *kindly* pass the sugar, please."

Meg was gentle, kind, patient, and fun. We sang songs on the way to school in the morning and played "Red light, Green light" after dinner.

"Green light!" she'd say as we ran towards her down the hall.

"*Red light!*" she called, as we froze in our tracks.

She let us comb her long straight hair and put make-up on her cheeks. She taught us how to say hello with an English accent and how to give butterfly kisses with our eyelashes. She played "Ring around the roses" with us before bed and let us play dress-up and run down to show Daddy.

"Are we disturbing you, Muhammad?" she'd ask as we ran into his office.

"No, come in."

"Look at me, Daddy!" I'd shout, wearing my favorite white dress with pink ribbons and ruffled lace sleeves. "Do I look pretty?"

"You look as pretty as your mother," he'd say.

After an hour or so, we'd head up to bed, and he'd tuck me in and tell me stories until I fell asleep, then he'd head to Laila's room and do the same. *The Three Little Pigs* was my favorite. Sometimes he'd make up a spin-off about the big bad wolf, howling and growling as I listened. It wasn't the typical story a parent would tell a child at night, but he made it fun and exciting, which meant that instead of falling asleep I was wide awake, requesting more stories and late-night snacks from the kitchen. He always obliged.

Best of all, like my father, Meg saw no harm in letting me eat popsicles in the morning—after breakfast, of course.

It was a fun-filled time with Meg—two years of laughter and play, building playhouses, picnics on the lawn, swimming in the sun. We spent so much time with her and enjoyed her so much that we wanted to be just like her—we even wanted to look like her and her friends. Meg had a friend in her twenties who used to visit her at the house. She was a pretty lady, with long blonde hair, who'd had a nose job and went jogging in Beverly Hills in the hope of meeting a rich man. Meg's brother was also handsome. She used to joke with Mom that he could make a living off his looks—like Richard Gere in the film *American Gigolo*. Then one day after school my father discovered a problem that would inevitably end Meg's employment at Fremont Place.

"When I grow up," said Laila, "I want blonde hair and blue eyes just like Meg."

"Me too," I added, coloring on the floor in my father's den. Dad pulled out his tape recorder, documenting the conversation.

"This is what I was afraid of . . ." he said into the recorder, as Laila started to cry because her skin wasn't as white as Meg's. *"This is how it starts,"* he explained. *"It's important for you all to love yourself—to have pride in yourself. To have people around you that you can identify with."*

He didn't fire her right away. When she was let go, it wasn't him—my mother handled that sort of thing. Dad would hire people all the time, finding odd jobs to get them off the streets or help someone out of a financial strain. But he never fired or reprimanded them—not a single disapproving word. He thought it would be too much coming from him—and if anyone begged for a second chance, claiming they needed the money to survive or pay bills, with my father in charge not only did they stay on as an employee but they were often given a raise.

"It would be too hard on them, coming from me," he said to my mother. "It might destroy them, having Muhammad Ali fire them."

"Please stop crying, Laila," said Meg. "You have a beautiful skin color."

"But I want to be white, like you," she pouted.

"I'm sorry, Muhammad," said Meg.

"You did nothing wrong," he said. "This is just an example of what happens when children of color have all white dolls and no toys that represent their culture to identify with . . ."

A few months later, Mom had her talk with Meg.

"I understand," she said. She knew it was coming. My father's Muslim advisers had long since commented on and warned him about a white Christian woman helping raise his little black girls and the identity issues it might cause. He also had his concerns, but he liked Meg, and most important we liked Meg, so he kept her. But as the years passed, his fears materialized.

"We'll miss you, Meg, please visit as much as you can," said Mom.

"Of course," she said. Mom told us Meg had to go home to take care of her mother and didn't know when, if ever, she might return. But she visited regularly for a while.

"Be the good little girls I know you are," she told us the last time we saw her. "Keep your rooms tidy, and always brush your teeth before bed."

It was the last time we heard her accent. Meg said her goodbyes, packed her bags, and probably moved back to England for good.

Mom started interviewing for the governess position immediately. A handful of women of varying ages and skills met with her over tea in the dining room adjacent to the front entrance of Fremont Place. This was where we would have large holiday dinners every year. My father sat at the head of the table drinking Pepsi out of a champagne glass.

One woman stands out in my mother's memory. "I'll never forget her," said Mom one day over breakfast. "She looked like a black Mary Poppins."

She was tall, thin, and elegant, and was dressed like a quintessential English nanny. She had on a long coat with a long black dress and old-fashioned boots. And she was wearing a black hat with her hair pinned in a bun.

John Young Brown, the governor of Kentucky (who purchased KFC from Colonel Sanders and turned it into a national company), was a friend of my father. His wife, Phyllis George, a former Miss America and commentator for NFL football, had told my mother about a New York governess agency. The following week my parents flew the woman to town for an interview.

"My job is to manage the household in all ways," she said, sipping her tea. "Not just affairs concerning the children, but the household budget and employees." According to the governess, Mom would no longer need Marge, our household administrator.

"I do it all," she said. "You can leave the rearing and raising of your children up to me. I'm stern but caring, and will raise them as I see fit."

She seemed to be the perfect example of an eighteenth-century governess.

"Thank you for your time," said Mom. "We'll be in touch."

For days, we begged Mom to hire her. *Mary Poppins* was one of my favorite films when I was a little girl. Mom admitted it would have been interesting having her around the house, but she wasn't what my parents were looking for.

My mother continued with the interviews for another couple of weeks. Grandma, Diane and Michelle took turns babysitting Laila and me.

One weekend stands out in my memory. My parents had gone out to dinner, so Mom's brother, Uncle Tony, was watching us and had brought my uncle Steven with him. Uncle Tony was fun, but I hated when Uncle Steven visited. He was sweet and playful, but he ate all the popsicles and hogged the large-screen television in the third-floor media room, watching his favorite show, *Star Trek*, for hours.

"I want to watch my cartoons!" I demanded, wrapped in a wet towel, fresh out the tub.

"I was here first," he said. "Watch TV downstairs."

When he got up to use the bathroom, I quickly scanned the channels looking for cartoons.

"Stop messing with the remote control, Hana," said Steven, as he walked back into the room and saw *Bugs Bunny* on screen. "I told you to watch your cartoons downstairs!"

"It's my house!" I shouted, then ran downstairs, dripping wet, straight out the front door and around the corner, where I complained to the guard on duty: "Uncle Steven won't let me watch my cartoons! Come arrest him!"

The guard stared at me in stunned disbelief, probably wondering why Muhammad Ali's six-year-old little girl was standing outside in the middle of the night, buck naked. I had dropped my towel somewhere along the way.

Just before my seventh birthday, we met our new governess—the lady I would come to refer to as Cruella de Vil.

Cruella had come via an agency in LA. She was a strict, rigid woman with a thick Jamaican accent. Her clothes were always ironed and her straight black hair, which she kept in a bun at all times, had a thick gray streak on the left side. She had a son in the army whom we never met and she was always listening to Jamaican music; she would switch her hips, holding a wine bottle in her hand, when she thought we were asleep.

"What are you drinking? Can I have some?"

"No, child! Go back to bed. This drink is for adults."

"What is it?"

"Lemonade," she chuckled.

"Kids can drink lemonade," I said.

"This is my special lemonade. It's hot and spicy—it'll burn your tongue, child."

"I want some," I insisted.

"I said no, child!" she barked back.

One thing my mother remembers about Cruella is that she once cut my and Laila's hair without her permission. "That took a lot of nerve!" said Mom. But she had gotten the impression that Cruella's son had joined the military to escape his mother's controlling ways, so maybe it wasn't that much of a surprise. I don't know how Cruella hid her drinking from my parents for so long, or when it started, but after three years her luck ran out.   .

One night when Mom and Dad were out, Cruella was sprawled out on the bed in a drunken slumber. Mom called her bedroom the Southern Room, because it was adorned with antebellum furniture she'd purchased in the south while Dad was filming *Freedom Road*.

Laila and I were obsessed with the female anatomy, particularly boobies. Cruella, even when lying flat on her back, had a large chest. We were lifting the edge of her shirt as she snored, hoping to get a peek at her boobs, when my mother walked into the room—to check up on us—home sooner than expected.

"What are you two doing?" she asked. "You should be in bed by now."

Mom realized something was off.

"Cruella," Mom said.

She lay there snoring.

"Cruella!" she said louder.

Cruella jumped up and quickly straightened her shirt but had no time to hide the empty wine bottle on her nightstand. She slipped out of bed and stumbled across the room to my mother. Laila and I giggled watching her.

"Have you been drinking?"

"Of course not," she said, pushing loose strands of hair out her face as she tried to regain composure.

"Pack your bags first thing in the morning," said Mom, then she grabbed our hands and walked out the room.

"No!" she said, stumbling down the hall behind us. "I love these bastards!"

"What did you say?" asked Mom.

Rushing towards her, she shouted, "I love these bastards!"

Laila and I watched wide-eyed as Mom pushed Cruella back and held her by the shirt against the wall. "Don't ever call my children bastards!"

Our jaws dropped. Laila and I looked at each other in disbelief. Aggression in any form was out of character for both my parents.

Dad had immense patience with me, but when his temper erupted it was out of nowhere. We called it the Papa Cash temper, after his father, Cassius Clay Sr. The temper would vanish as suddenly as it surfaced. It was the small things that would set it off, like me jumping on the sofa after he'd asked me to stop. Or playing with scissors after he'd told me they were dangerous. But he never lost it over the big stuff, like the time I pushed my fist through my bedroom window (I had been sent to my room for submerging my brother Muhammad Jr's head under the water too long), or playing in his Rolls and putting the car in reverse. Or, most notorious of all, putting Laila in the dryer and turning it on. He reprimanded me, of course. But when people complained, all he ever said was, "She'll grow out of it."

But I had never seen my mother lose her temper—*not ever!*

"I'm sorry!" said Cruella.

Mom let go of her shirt, and motioned for Laila and me to go into her room. Cruella followed, sniffling and groveling. She fell onto Mom's bed crying, wrapping her arms around both of us as if we were lifesavers keeping her afloat.

"Please, Veronica, give me another chance ... I love them."

I remember thinking her breath smelled like nail-polish remover and her clothes were damp and sticky. She had been a terrible governess. She never let me have popsicles when Daddy was away. She never let me keep my night light on and told me the bogie man would come get me if I was a bad girl. And she never let me play in my Wonder Woman costume.

"Take that off, child," she'd say. "It's not Halloween!"

Still, as she sat there that night in my mother's bedroom, begging and professing her love for us, I felt sorry for her.

But it was too late. Her fate was sealed the moment my mother discovered her drunk.

To say I was happy Cruella was gone would be an understatement. For weeks, I came straight home from school and put on my Wonder Woman outfit.

13

AFTER FREMONT PLACE I don't know what became of Cruella, but years later, when I was in my twenties, I spotted her walking through the Culver City Mall in Los Angeles. She looked the same, dressed in black, shirt buttoned to the top, and her hair was pulled back into a slick bun with the same gray streak—just like she wore it when I was a little girl.

I watched her walk past and said nothing.

Looking back, what I remember most about the day Mom fired Cruella was a feeling. As Laila and I stood there watching our mother defend us, I remember thinking, *Mom really does love us.* For a long time, we didn't believe she did. As I mentioned, she often ate alone, was off riding horses, practicing opera in her room, or running errands. She rarely came into Daddy's office. When she was there, she didn't play on the floor with us very long, or sit on the sofa and watch television with us. If she did, I have no memories of it. She often seemed preoccupied and busy. And when I was around her, sometimes she appeared understandably frustrated by my presence.

I remember her taking me to Griffith Park to ride ponies and shopping at Bullock's department store on Wilshire Blvd. She used to rush out the store embarrassed as I hollered and screamed at the top of my lungs when I couldn't have what I wanted. Dad had a different reaction to my tantrums. He'd holler and scream right back at me, mimicking my behavior. Sometimes it worked. I'd stop in the middle of my fits and stare at him as though he was the crazy one.

He'd just smile at the people staring at us, sign autographs and say, "She'll grow out of it."

But I must admit, my mother was kind and gentle, and she has many wonderful qualities. She took the time to do special things for us, but I never really felt her love as strongly as I felt my father's. I guess Dad's constant displays of affection, in contrast to my mother's quiet, shy nature may have had something to do with it.

"Marge told me she overheard your father say something in front of you and Laila once—that I act like I love my horses more than him and my children."

I guess Mom never considered that maybe, her absence—not being around or spending quality time with us daily—was what nourished the seed of this deeply rooted feeling I had about her. I guess it was easier for her to believe it was the comment Dad made.

I remember Marge, the executive secretary, with her scratchy voice and thick glasses, always reporting the happenings around Fremont Place to my mother.

"Veronica, I wanted to talk to you about the help. Doris [the house-keeper] has been acting up again ..."

"What now?" asked Mom.

"She's refusing to wear her uniform. Abdel caught her throwing it into the trash."

I referred to Abdel as my father's butler, but I'm not sure what he was really. I guess he was an assistant. He answered the door and hung out in my father's office, fetching him coffee, escorting guests, and catering to Dad's every need; driving around town with him, even traveling with him on occasion. He was a strange, thin, quiet man with stiff gray hair. I remember his pockets were full of Jolly Ranchers, which I accosted him for every morning.

"After breakfast, Hana," he'd say. "Sugar in the morning will give you worms."

But I knew better. And I knew how to get what I wanted. He quickly offered me two pieces of candy if I stopped trying to pull off his toupee.

"Daddy would never have said you loved your horses more than us, knowing we were listening," I told her. "You know Daddy has never and would never speak badly of you, especially in front of us. If he said it, it was out of pain—not intentional."

She could have told me the same of my father a hundred times and I wouldn't have believed it because his actions and my memories proved otherwise. I used to measure how much he loved me by the length of time he spent lying with me in the morning, telling me stories and showering me with kisses.

Daddy must really love me! I remember thinking as he lay beside me even after I told him I wet the bed. It's the quality of time they spend with us—the feelings their little acts of love create—that form our overall opinions of our parents.

Though Mom seemed to live a separate life at times, there are moments that stand out in my memory—occasions when she made time for us, when I felt important to her.

I remember her sitting Laila and me down on the blue silk bench at the foot of her bed and reading us a book about the birds and the bees. It was the beginning of a tradition. She had bought a series of twenty-four books called Value Tales. The stories taught moral and ethical life lessons through the experiences of significant people in history: *The Value of Believing in Yourself, The Value of Sharing, The Value of Honesty, The Value of Kindness, The Value of Humor* ... She read one to us every Sunday afternoon.

But the most memorable lesson, about the birds and the bees, didn't come from the Value Tales book set. Mom sat us down on the bed that morning and opened a little pink book. She began by describing the proper terms for the male and female anatomy. I remember the tight feeling in my stomach as I held in my laughter. When she read the various names for a woman's chest, "Breasts, boobies, bosoms ..." I fell onto the floor kicking and screaming, repeating the word that had sent me into my uncontrollable fit of laughter. "Bosoms!" I wailed. "Bosoms!"

Laila followed. Before long, Mom burst into laughter too.

That's when I became obsessed with boobs. "What is that?" I asked one morning as Mom got dressed.

"It's a bra," she said.

Laila (right) and me (left) in our parents' bedroom.

"What is it for?"

"It helps keep a woman's breasts up."

"When will I get some?"

"When you're older," said Mom.

"How old? When I'm eight?"

"No, when you're a woman," she said.

"When will I be a woman?"

"When you can wear a bra," she said.

And with that, an idea formed. I figured out a way to become a woman when I was just seven years old. I knew boobs were soft and round, like the dough that Edith, the cook, made our dinner rolls from. I used to sit on the kitchen island at Fremont holding my Cabbage Patch Kid doll in one hand and a pickle in my other, watching Edith prepare our meals. She'd get a large bowl and stir water, white powder and eggs into a mixture.

"What's that?" I asked.

"Flour ..."

The next day after school I came home, went into the kitchen, and poured water, flour, and eggs into a large bowl and started stirring.

"What are you making?" asked Edith, placing a bag of groceries on the counter.

"BOOBIES!" I said.

She watched amused as I molded the large dough balls into lopsided circles, powder and yoke smeared on my clothes and face. When the dough was firm, I put them into my shirt and then I frowned as my home-made boobs fell straight to the ground. I hadn't learned about gravity.

"You need a bra," said Edith, firing up the stove. "To keep them up."

"Oh yeah," I said, remembering what Mom told me.

I ran upstairs and hid my boobs in my dresser drawer. I'd have to figure out a way to get into Mom's closet unnoticed, which was the catalyst for my getting caught buck naked under the coffee table.

***

I WAITED PATIENTLY under the coffee table, unaware of the drama that would unfold around me. I'd been missing for nearly an hour before it was over. Everyone was frantic with worry. My father called the police, an ambulance, and the fire department. He was always overreacting to such things. When Laila slipped and slashed her chin on the swimming-pool steps, the house was filled with medical personnel, and when I cut my hand after falling on a piece of glass—playing hide and seek with Dad in the second-floor hall—he rushed me to the hospital.

Sneaking out of my bedroom at dawn for one of my morning adventures might have gone smoothly had I not gone back for my mother's fluffy French slippers. Laila and I were obsessed with Mom's wardrobe, particularly her shoes. We'd slip our little feet into her oversized one-inch heels and parade around our father as he worked.

On weekends, Dad let us stay up late watching television and playing dress-up. He watched warmly as we frolicked cheerfully around the room—our faces painted, hair flowing wild, looking like Diana Ross and Tina Turner, as usual draped in our mother's clothes, pretending to be grown-ups. With one hand on my hip, I circled around his desk.

"Do I look pretty, Daddy?" I asked.

"As pretty as your mother!" he always said.

"Do you think my hair is long like Mommy's too?" I asked, twirling my curls around my little fingers the way I noticed grown ladies doing on daytime television.

"It's longer than Mommy's!" he fibbed, filling my heart with pride.

Cruella, the governess, used to watch soap operas. *Days of Our Lives*, *One Life to Live*, and *General Hospital* were usually playing when Mom and Dad were away. Cruella was so busy hollering at Erica Kane, or Luke and Laura for making such a—as she put it—"fiasco" of their lives that she rarely noticed me sitting beside her, my wide eyes, mesmerized by the drama and glamor.

"Out child!" she'd holler when she eventually spotted me. "Your eyes are too young for this nonsense!" After scurrying me out, she'd immediately return her attention to the show, unaware that I was still watching from around the corner.

Looking back, it's no wonder I had such a flare for drama. When Laila and I put on our Wonder Woman outfits we'd spin cartwheels around the room like Lynda Carter, the beautiful heroine fighting for justice, love, peace, and gender equality. She possessed an arsenal of magic weapons, including the Lasso of Truth, a pair of indestructible bracelets, and my favorite, a tiara which served as a projectile and in some stories an invisible airplane. *Wonder Woman* was our favorite show. Day after day, we'd come home from school and slip into our sparkling red and blue suits, and act out our favorite scenes using our father as a target. We must have driven him crazy, but he never showed it.

Getting back to my nudity incident: as familiar voices called out my name, the longer I took to utter the words, "Here I am", the more calcified the words became. Like a deer caught in the headlights, I was frozen in silence. With good reason—after all, I was buck naked!

You're probably wondering how I got myself into that predicament. Looking back, it's rather funny: It was 5 a.m. that morning and Mom, Laila, and Cruella were still asleep. As usual, Dad was downstairs working in his office. I know this because my bedroom was directly above it. I used to press my ear against the floor, listening for any trace of him: his footsteps, his cough, the television, or the squawking of my mother's parrots, repeating their habitual "Bock, bock—I'm the Greatest! Bock, bock" whenever Dad entered the room. When I heard the faint sound of his voice talking on the phone, my adventure began.

I wanted to put on something pretty to see Daddy. Naturally, I snuck down the hall to the place where all the beautiful things—including bras (which my little hands were not allowed to touch)—were housed. My mother's closet.

Quiet as a mouse, I tiptoed around her bed as she slept. It was on my way out that it happened. I was treading towards the staircase, fully adorned in Mom's fine clothes and drenched in her Chanel perfume, when I heard the Big Bad Wolf—Cruella.

"Haaaana ... where are you, child?"

"Shit!" I yelped, freezing like a squirrel about to become roadkill. Cruella was up and she was hunting—for me. *Shit! Shit! Shit!* It was my new favorite word; I'd learned it a few days earlier, when my mother accidently blurted it out after stubbing her toe on the bathroom door. "Shit!" she'd cried out, catching herself as quickly as she said it. But it was too late. Like most little people, I retained information like a sponge, particularly the bits I was not supposed to hear. Cruella had washed my mouth out with soap a dozen times because of it. I might have forgotten about it had Mom not made the common grown-up mistake of tipping me off to the fact that my little ears had chanced upon a forbidden word.

"Haaaaana?" Cruella called again, her voice growing agitated.

"Shit!" I quickly slipped out of my mother's clothes: the stockings she told me I couldn't wear, the silk blouse she asked me not to put my sticky fingers on, and the one pair of shoes she never let me play in.

"Haaaaaana!"

"Shit! Shit! Shit!" I whispered, running *buck naked* down the hall and into the second-floor sitting room, where I made a kamikaze dive under the coffee table, finding refuge there until all the worried voices had faded into the background.

Ironically, it was Cruella's call that I finally answered. "Here I am," I uttered meekly. The Wolf had never looked happier to find me.

The next morning a latch was put on the top of my bedroom door. "To keep you from wandering into the streets," Cruella explained. But I knew better. She was trying to avoid the headache of having to search a thirty-room mansion for a determined little girl cleverly plotting to spend the day with her father.

Long before the coffee-table incident, Cruella had tried every trick in the book to keep me from reaching Dad on school-day mornings: first there was the stocking she tied from my bedroom doorknob to the staircase. It was a tight squeeze, but I slipped through. Next, there was the doorstopper she wedged beneath the outside entrance to my room. I used a hanger to dislodge it. Then came the lock at the top of my door. I climbed the bookshelf and pulled down the latch. Finally, she attached a string of bells, hoping the ringing would at least alert her to my impending escape. But, like a little Houdini, I managed to break free, unnoticed. Nothing could keep me from my father.

One incident shines vividly in my memory. One morning Cruella searched high and low for me, but I was nowhere to be found. I was already hiding in the back seat of my father's Rolls-Royce. It wasn't until after Dad drove past the guard, out of the Fremont gates, and onto the Miracle Mile that I finally peeked. Houses, trees, and road signs were rushing past. I was free! My uncombed hair flowed wildly in the breeze, as I cruised down Wilshire Blvd with my father. Hearing my giggles in the back seat, he pulled into the Carnation restaurant parking lot. When the car was parked, I jumped up from behind, "Surprise!"

"Aaaaahh!" he hollered, pretending to be frightened. Kissing my little face, he carried me into the diner for turkey bacon and scrambled eggs. During and after our meal he took pictures with adoring fans, shook hands, and signed autographs. Then he picked me up and headed back to the car as people gathered around him like moths to a flame. I understand how they felt; my father was like a light that constantly drew me too. Even when he was tired he turned no one away. Every autograph was signed, every smile returned.

We drove home, my mission accomplished. Another adventure with my father. Wonder Woman would have been proud of my perseverance.

Laila (left) and me in our Wonder Woman outfits in Dad's office.

14

I HEAR KEVIN turn on the shower as I leaf through the pile of newspapers and magazine articles on my lap: *Los Angeles Times, South China Morning Post, The Star, The Journal, U.S. Caribbean Voice*, and *Jet*, whose headline reads, "Muhammad Ali Takes a Beautiful Bride". I set this one aside. The photos on the front page of the *Los Angeles Sentinel* catch my eye. Bo Derek, the beautiful blonde actress who played in the movies *10* and *Tarzan*, is pictured strategically beneath my mother. Curious, I read the caption:

The Main Event—Muhammad Ali, the former boxing champion of the world, is the honored guest during "The Main Event" dinner, which was given for him May 22 in the Beverly Wilshire Hotel by Jose Sulaiman, president of the World Boxing Council ... In photo top left, Mayor Tom Bradley presents a citation from the City of Los Angeles while Sugar Ray Robinson, another former world champion, looks on ... At top center is Mrs Veronica Ali, the former champ's wife ... In the photo bottom left, Mayor Bradley, Robinson, Sugar Ray Leonard, Ken Norton, Ali, and flamboyant fight promoter Don King talk over old boxing times ... In center photo, bottom, is actress Bo Derek who, per *USA Today*, had been invited by Ali as his special guest but who was "stood up" when Ali brought his wife ...

I shake my head. The press can be so misleading, even mischievous at times. Bo Derek visited the house when I was a little girl. She was a nice lady. She let me run my fingers through her long, blonde hair and played "Patty cakes" with me. John Derek, her husband, asked my father if Bo could accompany him to the event for publicity. Dad agreed, but apparently the Dereks didn't realize that my parents were on good terms throughout their divorce proceedings and that the three of them would be arriving together in the limousine.

I checked the date beneath the caption: *Thursday, May 30, 1985*. The same evening that Dad received Mayor Bradley's Muhammad Ali Day Proclamation and one year before the divorce was final. I was nine years old and they were already sleeping in separate bedrooms. My mind traveled back to my first clue something was wrong—when the fairy tale began to crumble.

One morning I had woken up to find my father in the guest bedroom. Dad was normally up by 5 a.m. and working in his den. It was unusual to find him in bed in the morning, though he sometimes took a nap in the middle of the day.

It was the room my step-sisters Jamillah and Rasheda slept in when they flew in for the summer. A room full of memories of slumber parties and dance competitions, of singing "Billie Jean", "When Doves Cry", and "Purple Rain" as we jumped on the bed.

"Daddy," I said, my heart thumping in my chest at the sight of him sleeping alone, "why aren't you in bed with Mommy?"

"I snore too loud," he said, his smile belying the sadness in his eyes. "I don't want to disturb her."

He wasn't lying; it just wasn't the whole story. My parents started sleeping in separate bedrooms before their marriage was officially over—possibly before he wrote the first letter.

One night, after Dad was up late working in his office, he walked through the house. I imagine he was turning off lights and checking the windows and doors, which was something he always did before he went to bed. He'd roam the halls of Fremont Place making sure we were safe, then head to the kitchen for a midnight snack, standing at the counter eating cake and vanilla ice cream in the dim light, unaware that on this night when he got upstairs he would find the bedroom door locked.

There had been a few burglaries in the neighborhood and I guess Mom wanted to feel safe.

All those months leading up to their official separation, my mother assumed my father wasn't coming to bed. She had grown accustomed to him working late in his den. And he thought she intentionally locked him out. If only he had knocked on the door, or called her name, she would have opened it—and he would have known. But neither of them said a word. Knowing my father, he didn't want to wake her. Dad had a thing about letting people sleep peacefully— free of disturbance. And he didn't seem to face personal issues in the same way that he confronted the issues of the world. I think maybe it was because, with the world, he was fighting for something greater than himself. And there was a part of him that had never felt worthy of my mother—as if he had deserved to lose her. Or maybe he never knocked on the bedroom door because he knew what was coming—that it was the beginning of the end, and he wasn't ready to face the inevitable.

Those final two years of my parents' marriage, they traveled the world together, making appearances, always friendly and cordial with each other, "*like brother and sister*". Everything appeared normal to the press. All the while, my father clung to hope as he wrote his letters: "*I'm so sorry for the way I treated you. It hurts me that I cannot sleep with you ... I'm having a difficult time, and for me the meaning of this is not clear ... if you give me one more chance ... I love you so much ...*"

Twenty years after the divorce, Mom's sister, my aunt Diane, who lived with us at Fremont Place while she was going through her own separation, casually mentioned the day she found my father sleeping on the sofa in the third-floor media room. "He was just lying there," she told my mother over Thanksgiving dinner. "Beside the aquarium, with your exotic fish, without a pillow or blanket to comfort him."

Lying there uneasily, I imagined, in the company of his trophies and boxing memorabilia.

139

"Muhammad, why are you sleeping up here?" Diane had asked him.
"Veronica locked me out."

Maybe he thought, *Tomorrow will be different, tomorrow she might forgive me ... I'll give her the letters tomorrow.* But as time passed, my mother kept locking her bedroom door, distancing herself from my father. And he kept sleeping on the sofa, eventually moving into the guest bedroom across the hall from my room, where he would read me bedtime stories and we would fall asleep together, and I learned what my father learned: *hope hurts.*

I picked up another article: *Detroit News*, 1975. The more I read, the more I understood. "The Great Man looked out at us at a press conference and said that we [reporters] always miss the big point about him. He said everybody always asks him what's the toughest part of fighting and nobody has ever figured out what it really is. What it is, he said, are *women*: millions and millions of *women*—one more striking than the next. All so alluring and so beautiful."

"*Women* are the destruction of men," said Dad. "They have destroyed all the great men in history." This would have been base coming from anyone else, noted the reporter, but as he stood up there and smiled that angelic smile and told them of the great temptations of his life, the room shook with uncontrollable laughter.

He said, "Do you know what it's like to be desired by the most desirable women in the world?" And, of course, none of us really knew what he was talking about because it had never happened to any of us. But as he spoke you knew that it was something he must live with and it can't be easy—especially being married and portraying himself as a family man and devout religious figure.

He called a few ladies up to the podium and teased them about their beauty. To one he said: "Look at the skin ... so tan, so smooth ... and the pretty black hair, those eyes, those lips. Do you know what I say to women like this? I say, 'It's nice meeting you. Goodbye.' And that's so difficult to do!"

Everyone howled. It didn't come out dirty, lewd, or in bad taste. It was just plain funny. Dad leered at the girls: "That's my *big* problem. That's what you reporters never write about—never ask me about.

It's not getting hit. It's all these beautiful women in every city in the world. That's the big problem in my life ..."

"When your father was a teenager," my mother will tell me the day after the storage-room discoveries, "he only thought about boxing. There were only a few girls he had crushes on, but he was always shy and innocent. He fainted and fell down the stairs the first time he kissed a girl. It was the people around him who tried to corrupt him. If he had been left to be his natural self, he might have remained innocent."

I think I know why my mother had fallen so deeply in love with my father. He was charismatic and handsome. He made her laugh and feel beautiful. He said he adored her for all her grace, class, intelligence, and beauty. He gave her declarations of storybook love. He spoke of heartfelt emotions, feelings he claimed he had never felt for another woman. It was a promising beginning to a beautiful love story, with one major flaw: he was already married.

It's no secret my father fooled around. After all, he met my mother when he was still married to his second wife, Belinda Boyd aka Khalilah. What the world, *back then*, didn't know is my father's marriage to Belinda was already on the verge of divorce before meeting my mother in 1974. Contrary to the suspicions of my father's entourage, and rumors circulating at the time, my mother was neither a model nor a beauty queen, and she wasn't a spy sent over by the George Foreman camp, as some of Dad's entourage suspected and even tried to convince him.

She was an eighteen-year-old pre-medical student on a full scholarship at USC who entered a poster-girl contest which won her an unexpected trip to Salt Lake City and Africa. It's odd to think that if George Foreman hadn't cut his eye during a training session the fight my father dubbed "The Rumble in the Jungle" would not have been postponed thirty days and my parents may have never found the time to get to know each other.

"I remember the moment I knew I had fallen in love with him," Mom continued. "It was several weeks before the Foreman fight. We were in the living room of your father's private villa in the presidential compound in N'Sele, outside Kinshasa, Zaire. He was reciting several of his speeches and reflections about love and friendship. My favorite was *The Heart*: 'People look for miracles; people look for wonders—people expect surprises of all kinds. Yet, the greatest miracle, the greatest wonder, the greatest surprise is to be found in one's heart ...' As he spoke, the look on his face was so ethereal, my breath caught in my chest, and I knew."

They took long walks along the Congo river. He drew sketches of her and brought her dinner at night before going to bed. They hugged, cuddled, and did all the things people do when they're in love. My mother's beauty was overwhelming, but my father has repeatedly said how he admired her inner beauty more than her looks. "She was so sweet, classy, and intelligent—a real lady. I just couldn't let her go. I had to find a way to keep her with me."

He feared she would go back to college and forget about him, and fall in love with someone else—someone more intelligent and less complicated than him.

"Marry me," he said, a week before the fight. "Do you believe in one God?" he asked.

"Yes."

"Do you submit to his will?"

"Yes."

"Then you're a Muslim."

The following evening they were married in a spiritual ceremony under the African moon, the only witnesses the African Muslim minister who performed the service and my father's bodyguard.

"This is for you, and for me," he told her on the walk back to his villa. "So that I know you're mine, and you know I love you and intend to marry you officially when I'm free."

That was the beginning of their love story. But his freedom was to be three years out. Before he could make good on his promise, he'd need to get his wife to agree to a divorce and, not wanting to embarrass her or their four children, Maryam, Rasheda, Jamillah, and Muhammad Jr, he asked Belinda to file for it. But it was a path with more twists and turns than he or my mother imagined.

Mom and Dad, 1975.

15

AFTER WINNING THE Foreman fight, and regaining his championship title, my father talked my mother into taking a semester off from school. When she agreed, he called her parents and convinced them to let Mom stay with him. "I want her to be in my movie ... She can travel with me for a while—see the world. I'll take good care of her." And he did. The Porche family had no idea what they were in for. In the coming years, after my parents were officially together, he sometimes sent my grandmother money to help with bills, and years later he paid off the mortgage on their house. He flew my mother's parents, sisters and brothers first class on several trips around the world.

He gave them front-row seats to his fights, and spent money on them, giving them gifts and introducing them to heads of state and celebrities. My aunt Diane even dated a couple, comedian Richard Pryor and the actor Jimmie Walker, best known for his role as JJ Evans in the hit show *Good Times*. While my father and mother mostly kept the company of everyday people, and only occasionally hung out with celebrities, the Porche family's life had changed overnight and would be a constant adventure for the twelve years that my parents were together.

My father's generosity didn't begin and end with my mother's family. After every fight, Dad sent people money: his mother, Belinda's mother, all my siblings' mothers, his father, his brother, etc. And he gave bonuses to everyone who worked for him. The year after he met my mother he just included my grandmother to the already very long list.

"Steven," he said to my mother's youngest brother, "the baby of the family. You're so tall, you might be the next Larry Bird!" Everyone laughed. "Tony," he said to my favorite uncle, "I bet you're the ladies' man of the family, with those bright blue eyes.

"And, Leonard, your Afro is so neat and shiny." He clowned with the third brother, patting his own hair. "It almost looks as good as mine!"

"Michelle and Diane ..." His eyes enlarged as he greeted my mother's sisters. "You're both so beautiful, if I'd seen you first I might have married you instead of Veronica." He looked over his shoulder at my mother as he hugged them, teasing and hoping to rouse a reaction, but she was always good at ignoring his flirtatious behavior. She had heard that line many times before, and would hear it many times after.

"Look, Veronica," he'd say, hugging random women who asked for his autograph in airports, restaurants, or wherever. "I bet this will make you jealous." If it did, she never showed it. Mysterious and indifferent, she'd turn her head, seemingly unaffected. She'd grown used to his demonstrative behavior and fun-loving, flirtatious personality. It was part of the package. You couldn't separate one from the other, and she never tried. She let him be *himself*.

While my mother's family enjoyed the perks of being associated with the most famous man in the world, she would have a much different, and more difficult, experience. Portrayed as the beautiful temptress that seduced a legend and broke up his family, the press and Belinda loyalists were relentless in their condemnation of my mother. She was insulted and ridiculed by my father's staff and members of his entourage, and Dad's constant praise of her didn't help the situation. "I've been all over the world and I've never seen a woman as beautiful as Veronica," he said. "Pictures don't capture it."

Every day members of Daddy's crew brought countless women before him, hoping to change his mind and lure him from my mother. "Look at this one, Ali. She's a real beauty."

"Not more beautiful than Veronica," he'd always say.

This went on for years. I don't know how she handled it so gracefully. I never could have.

On the way home from Zaire, my mother boarded a separate flight, accompanied by my father's head bodyguard, Pat Patterson, who was also a Chicago policeman. "I'll meet you in Chicago," my father told her. "There are too many reporters on my plane."

Mom and Pat stopped in Spain and Italy, and spent the day sightseeing before catching their connecting flight to Chicago, where she reconnected with my father and was put up in the Continental Hotel, downtown, while he shopped for a more comfortable and suitable place for her. From there, she and my father spent a few nights at his business manager C.B. Atkins' sky-rise before settling into the two-bedroom condominium he bought for her on Hyde Park Boulevard.

My father, always wanting my mother with him, traveled everywhere with her. He based his fights out of Chicago for a while and they drove Blue Bird, his Winnebago motorhome, up to Fighters' Heaven in Pennsylvania—until Dad bought a forty-foot customized Greyhound bus, which was his pride and joy. "This is the BIG BOPPER," he'd shout over the radio. "I'm heading up the highway. Over and out!"

My parents spent a lot of time on that bus, as would I, driving to Florida, New York, Louisville, Pennsylvania—all over the place. Mom use to sit up late at night watching Dad drive, worried, after he'd almost driven into a house.

"The road was pitch black," said Mom. "The house was at the end of the street. Your father made a sharp left turn just in time."

Sometimes they drove to his eighty-eight-acre farm in Berrien Springs, Michigan. I was born there, at Berrien General Hospital at 2:01 p.m. on August 6, 1976. Daddy flew Mom's family in to visit and built her a large pond for her ducks. They rode his Clydesdale horse and went fishing on the lake.

In the city, Mom spent her free time shopping for furniture with Evelyn Potter—the decorator Dad hired to fix up her new condominium in Chicago—who would later become her matron of honor.

"Drive her around," he told Evelyn. "Let her pick out what she likes."

Mom chose a zebra rug and a light-blue tufted sofa, which was eventually refurbished in tan suede and placed against the wood-paneled wall of my father's home office at Fremont Place. She painted the living room her favorite color, baby blue, and chose peach for the walls of the bedroom. The second bedroom, an office, was the original home of the large wooden shelf that housed my father's trophies in our third-floor media room. It now stands on the main wall of my grandmother's family room.

Before Dad flew to Africa, he had purchased a beautiful brick house on Woodlawn Avenue, and arranged for it to be gutted and renovated. The plan was for him to move in with Belinda and the children, of course. But this was before something—having nothing to do with Mom—changed between them. But change it did, and this change, not surprisingly, was met with resistance by Belinda. Especially when the press started writing that my father had publicly introduced my mother as his wife in Manila before his separation was officially announced. It was already reported that Belinda's anger had manifested as a large scratch across my father's forehead. But the truth is the fight they had in Zaire had nothing to do with my mother—or my father's indiscretions (which Belinda recently admitted publicly). Mom left it out of her letters home and never spoke of it—but the infamous scratch can be seen in old photographs.

July 4, 1975
Dear Mom and Dad, and everyone,
Muhammad has decided to stay here in Kuala Lumpur for two more months. His next fight is in the Philippines (Manila) with Joe Frazier, and since we're already over here he doesn't want to go all the way home. (He said he's sending you a check by Howard Bingham. If he forgets, I'll mail it or something. I'm going to call in a few days after I'm sure Howard is there.) I'm sending some things I bought here in Malaysia. (The fight in Manila isn't until October 1st. We're going there a week before the fight.) The watch is for Dad. Also, the navy-blue lounge shirt. The black shirt is for Tony. The royal blue shirt is for Leonard and the red

one is for Steven. The silver chains are for Leonard and Steven also. The jewelry boxes are for Mom, Diane and Michelle. You have to fight over which color you want. There's a chance I may be able to come home before the fight, but I haven't asked him yet. He might not let me go.
Love, Veronica

I reached for another article. This one from the *Daily News,* Saturday, September 27, 1975. My mother and Belinda were featured in a split photo. The headline grabbed my attention: "Manila Thrilla: Ali Shuffle Leads to Domestic Scuffle". This should be interesting, I thought. I read the small print below the photo: "Veronica Porche and Belinda Ali—two sides of a triangle?"

Dick Young, sports editor of *The News,* wrote:

Muhammad Ali's wife, Belinda, showed the heavyweight king her own version of the Ali shuffle today, just five days before he defends his title against Smokin' Joe Frazier. The statuesque Belinda flew into Manila at dawn, and out again at sunset, after a shouting match with Ali over whether she is still champion or just another contender in his household. The source of the butterflies-and-bees conflict between the Alis is Veronica Porche, *nineteen* ... who has been his constant companion for more than a year, and who has been introduced as his wife in recent days.

"Belinda was supposed to fly to Manila with us," my mother told me. "But she decided to come later and didn't tell your father what time she'd be arriving that day." These were details Mom felt Belinda strategically left out of her comments to the press. "I think what upset her was the fact that nobody believed she was his wife when she arrived because I was there with your father."

When Dad met Filipino President Ferdinand Marcos, who was known for having an attractive wife, my father shook his hand and said, "You have a beautiful wife." Mom was standing behind Dad with some of the members of his entourage. After looking at my mother, President Marcos smiled at Daddy and said, "From the looks of your wife, you're not too far behind." Joe Frazier, who was also there, chuckled. My father said nothing.

"I'm going home to my family," is all Belinda said to reporters as she boarded a 6 p.m. flight back to Chicago, but during a stopover in Honolulu she had more to say: "He can see who he wants to see, but he's still married to me ... I'm not the jealous type—not one woman, not two, not six are going to come between me and Ali." She denied any rift between them and added that she'd be waiting to welcome him home after the fight.

Belinda had arrived in the Philippines capital twelve hours earlier and, after my father failed to meet her at the airport, went directly to the twenty-first-floor suite of his downtown hotel.

"We have something to talk about," she told him. And from there a shouting match ensued, ending with Belinda storming out of the hotel, headed for the airport.

Later, after knocking around a sparring partner in a heavy pre-fight workout, my father attempted to downplay the trouble, telling reporters it was "just publicity".

"My wife [Belinda] drives two Rolls-Royces and two Cadillac Eldorados," he said. "She is fixing up a sixteen-room mansion in Chicago. She has a couple of million dollars in the bank. She has four beautiful children. She has a couple of farms ... She knows she's my wife." Then, very softly, almost inaudibly, he said, "She knows I love her."

I believe he loved her. My father was bluntly honest, which could be confusing at times, but he did care about Belinda; she was the mother of his children. I think my mother understood that.

Reporters from around the world buzzed with conversation about whether the spat would affect his chances against Frazier on the Wednesday.

"It was the closest to death I've ever felt," my father said after winning the fight. "In the tenth round it's worse, and I have this feeling I've never had before in the ring—I'm close to death and every punch is taking me to the grave. Joe Frazier brings out the best in me. God bless him."

I skipped ahead and read the last two paragraphs of the article:

Today's prelude to Ali's promised "Thrilla in Manila" with Frazier has apparently been a long-time brewing. Ali, Belinda, and Veronica have appeared together often in the past year, with Ali insisting that the two women were close friends. But it was learned last June that Ali had asked for Muslim consent to take a second wife under Islamic code, only to be turned down because of a possible conflict with American bigamy laws.

Before that, in Zaire a year ago, while training for the George Foreman fight, Ali showed up one day with a scratched face and accompanying rumors that Belinda, a "karate expert," had clouted him. Whatever was going on, it apparently reached the boiling point in the last 10 days as Ali seemed to flaunt Veronica before the public.

It was not my father's intention to keep two wives. Dad was just trying to figure out a way to move forward with his life, without losing my mother, or hurting and embarrassing Belinda and their children by revealing the reason he wanted to divorce her in the first place.

Perhaps the most unusual and shocking detail to me about my parents' courtship was discovering that, in the beginning, Belinda traveled with them. On one occasion she was pictured wearing a matching dress with not only my mother but also Dad's fourth wife and widow, Lonnie, who was eighteen at the time, a year younger than Mom. When I first saw the photos, my mouth dropped. What in the world were they all doing together? And wearing identical clothes, no less. They looked like triplets. I laughed out loud. If I'm being completely honest, my first thought was, *Daddy was a smooth operator, like Casanova!* Who else in history has been photographed with their past, present, and future wives, all smiling agreeably, like old friends—when the past wife was in the process of, reluctantly, becoming the former. Unbelievable, right? For a moment, I considered going to tell Kevin about it, to see his reaction, but I was pulled back to the clippings.

The next page was torn. I couldn't make out the date or headline: "*My intention was always to marry her ...*" Obviously, I know that my dad is referring to his affair with my mother. Remember how he had already

150

made headlines in Manila, Philippines, after journalists started reporting that he had publicly introduced Mom as his wife? Well, before then, in photos and press releases, she was said to be his wife's cousin—a tale Belinda told, out of embarrassment, I imagine. Mom told me about how Belinda would sometimes introduce her to people that way when they were together. My father was traveling the world with another woman—my mother—whom he intended to leave her for. But Belinda wasn't ready to let go. She would fight to remain "Mrs Muhammad Ali".

One month after the Manila fight, Belinda gave an interview for the October 30 issue of *Jet* magazine entitled "Muhammad Ali's Wife Talks About Marriage Strains", in which she stated, among other things, she would rather share my father than lose him. But she only gave a fragmented piece of the puzzle, a fraction of a complicated and multilayered truth. She said nothing about the phone call, or her proposal regarding my mother.

"We were in your dad's hotel room in Las Vegas when the phone rang," my mother explained. "Your father was lying in bed and I was in the living room. He answered the phone, sat down in a chair and motioned for me to pick up the other line near the sofa.

"'It's Belinda,' he whispered, with one hand over the receiver. 'Pick up the phone. You have to hear this.'

"I remember him sitting there, in a chair with his back against the wall. His mouth wide open, as Belinda made her confessions. She asked for forgiveness, then offered to let him have another wife if he didn't divorce her."

My father convinced my mother Belinda's proposal would be good for him. "Just for a while," he promised. "So I don't have to give her all my money." A few days later he said, "I'll fly Lonnie in to town, to take some of the attention off you." Lonnie's mother, Margarite Williams, and my paternal grandmother were good friends and lived next door to each other. So, naturally, Lonnie saw a lot of my father over the years; somewhere along the way the two of them had formed their own relationship. Hence the photograph with the matching dresses.

Dad, Mom, and Belinda made a few public appearances together, but for the most part they lived separately and only traveled together a couple times. My father unintentionally fueled the gossip and confused the public further after he posed for a 1975 cover of *People* magazine, pictured at home with Belinda and the kids. With limited and biased information, the press continued to portray Belinda as a victim, Dad as a womanizer, and my mother as the villain, often reporting she was twenty-five when she was only nineteen.

The following year, at a White House dinner hosted by President Ford for Jordan's King Hussein, my father dropped another bombshell. As *Jet* magazine remembers, "He kicked the Capital's gossip into high gear when, perhaps in jest, he said within earshot of a reporter, 'I have to leave ... My wife is about to give birth.'" As the reporter stated, those who knew my father and his wife Belinda, knew they'd been living apart for months and she wasn't pregnant.

Belinda, still refusing to file for the divorce, seemed to be content with letting the public think my father was having a meaningless affair, even though she had privately agreed to the arrangement.

My mother was photographed holding hands and eating ice cream with Belinda's daughters Maryum and twins Jamillah and Rasheda, and her son, Muhammad Jr. I can only imagine what the public thought, not knowing the whole story.

You might have read about it when it happened. It was big news, so much so that Barbara Walters even mustered the nerve to ask my father about it in an old interview, questioning why he had a baby (me) with my mother, Veronica Porche, while still legally married to Belinda Boyd.

"My intention was always to marry her and be a gentleman," he explained. "To make it respectable and dignified." When Barbara pressed, he shifted in his seat. "Why are you pickin' on me? A lot of men fool around. A lot of men have other women on the side. I'm no different."

As I mentioned, my father was always bluntly honest. I'm told Barbara turned red with shock. No wonder she never added this to the list of her greatest interviews. Years later, the movie *Ali* would touch on the subject. Judging by my father's reaction, and what he said as we watched the film together one afternoon at his Michigan home, it wasn't an accurate portrayal of the events leading up to his divorce from Belinda, nor how he approached my mother in Zaire. The scenes are broken pieces of a large complicated puzzle and only a few people know the truth—or how to fit it together.

It was a humid day in August 2003 when Daddy and I watched the film. We had just returned from visiting Barnes & Noble, one of our favorite weekend pastimes. I set our bags, full of quote books and leather-bound journals, down on the kitchen floor, turned the television on and made my father a turkey sandwich with Swiss cheese, mustard and onions. Dad was sitting in his armchair eating his second piece of sweet-potato pie and I was beside him enjoying a bowl of my favorite ice cream, Häagen-Dazs Butter Pecan, when he told me.

"That's not what happened," he said, as Will Smith and Nona Gaye acted out the scene where Belinda confronts my father about my mother in the hotel room in Africa. "This movie makes it look like your mother broke us up, but I wanted a divorce before I ever met your mother." Then he gave his reasons. Details I have kept to myself.

Every family has its secrets. Ours is no different. But they aren't my secrets to tell.

Over the years, the media coverage of my parents' courtship and personal life was overwhelming. Book publishers and reporters constantly pursued my mother. She always graciously declined to share her side. I asked her once why she kept quiet, why she never defended herself.

"There was no way to clear my name or your father's without hurting people or revealing things about Belinda he didn't want the world to know," she said. "So we both remained silent."

But the questions kept coming.

"What do you think people misunderstand about you?" Marilyn Funt asked my mother in a 1978 interview, which I'll share in greater detail later. "The public thinks you broke up his marriage."

"The press has so distorted his divorce," said Mom, "and since we don't talk about things like that, no one will ever know the truth ..."

Belinda finally filed for divorce after I was born in 1976, freeing my father to marry my mother after nearly two years of waiting. I think maybe she was hoping he would eventually tire of Mom. I guess she never considered how much he *really* loved her.

In my mother's storage, I found a collection of professional photographs that she'd had taken of my father and his children by Belinda. The five of them are smiling in the living room of Fremont Place. Mom even posed with them in a couple of images. She bought the girls beautiful ruffled dresses, and Muhammad Jr was given a black suit. When I look at the pictures, I'm reminded of the porcelain dolls displayed on our bedroom shelves—the ones my mother never let us play with. It was their first summer visiting us at Fremont Place.

Because Belinda had moved to Los Angeles to pursue her film career, the children had been living with their grandparents, even before their parents' divorce was final. But despite that, after my father left Chicago, Belinda never let them come to visit him in Los Angeles. I guess, in the beginning, she didn't want them around my mother, especially after Dad had married her. Her wounds were too fresh.

In time, she relented, and my siblings spent their first summer at Fremont Place, swimming in the pool and watching movies in our third-floor media room. Including, of course, Dad's favorite, *Dracula*, starring Christopher Lee. We ate breakfast at Carnation's on Wilshire Boulevard. And drove around Los Angeles in his Rolls with the top down.

Regardless of the circumstances that caused the demise of my father's tumultuous relationship with his second wife, my mother often said that if she could go back, she would have done things differently. "I would have flown straight home from Africa," she once told me, "gone back to school, and waited until his divorce was final." But she didn't. Simply stated, my father liked beautiful women, and he liked to be married, and I'm glad, because my siblings and I are *all* here.

***

I SKIMMED THROUGH the *Los Angeles Sentinel* from Thursday, June 2, 1977: "The future Mrs Ali—Veronica Porche—is set to become the third Mrs Ali at the Beverly Wilshire Hotel on June 19th. Mrs Porche and the champion have been one of the most-talked-about couples in the world since their first meeting prior to Ali's title fight with George Foreman ..."

I read another article, published in *The Star* a year later: "Muhammad Ali has surprised friends—and two former wives—by saying the greatest moment of his life was finding Veronica Porche, the woman who became his third wife."

I scanned the stack of newspapers on the table beside me, looking for related headlines, and came across another old issue of *Jet*, from May 6, 1976—three months before my birth. I opened the magazine and saw a beautiful photo of Belinda. The headline read: "Khalilah Ali (aka Belinda) Breaks Out on Her Own". This should be interesting, I decided. Belinda gave a series of interviews over the years, promoting her acting career and accusing my mother of ruining her life. I wondered if this was one of them. I flipped through the pages, searching for the article, but its place was already marked. Mom must have read it long ago.

As I started to read about Belinda's plans for her future, living without my father, to my surprise she finally admitted the truth that she had long denied—that Mom had *nothing* to do with the impending divorce.

"The marriage was already in trouble ..." Belinda finally admitted. "And not because of any Veronica Porche."

My eyes were growing weary—flapping and fluttering, two butterflies struggling to stay afloat in turbulent skies. I'd been up since 7 a.m. and it was now just before midnight. A yawn escaped me as I reached for the glass of water on my nightstand. *Just a few more,* I told myself. *I'll read a few more, then I'll go to sleep.*

I picked up the July 7, 1977 issue of *Jet* magazine. I had set it aside earlier because it featured my parents' wedding: "Muhammad Ali Takes a Beautiful Bride". I leafed through it, reading random clips aloud, as if my spoken words were a divine ritual that would somehow transport me back in time.

The Wedding

Ali was smitten with Veronica. I remember once, on a television show, he said she was the best thing that ever happened to him ... But then (after twelve years together) things soured between Ali and Veronica. He got sick, and some people say she treated him bad. But I don't fault Veronica as much as others do. Ali was hard to live with at this point in his life. He's different now, but back then he wanted to have his cake and eat it too. Things fell apart, but don't blame it all on her. In my view, if Ali had treated Veronica right, she'd probably still be his wife today.

– Lloyd Wells in *Muhammad Ali: His Life and Times*, Thomas Hauser, 1991

16

MY MOTHER WAS the picture of composure in her suite at the Beverly Wilshire Hotel in Beverly Hills. She draped her veil over a chair and checked over the bridesmaids' bouquets.

"You know, I've been planning this day for three years," she said to the reporter with *Jet* magazine. Except for Dad's personal photographer Howard Bingham, who doubled as an usher, and his friend Gene Kilroy, Isaac Sutton, the chief photographer of *Jet*, West Coast, covered the wedding exclusively. Because of his special relationship with my father over the years, he was granted access to my parents' suites and to my grandmother's house later that evening.

Jet magazine had supported Dad's efforts to get a license to return to the boxing ring ten years earlier, after he was unjustly stripped of his heavyweight title for refusing induction into the US Army during the Vietnam War. Isaac Sutton kept my father in the public eye during his three-and-a-half-year legal battle.

Like justice, my father had a long memory.

"No, seriously," Mom quickly added, "it took about six months to plan our wedding."

The ringing telephone constantly interrupted her as she dressed.

"I don't have time to be nervous," she said, pulling rollers out of her hair and spraying her wrists with perfume. Several bridesmaids walked casually into the room carrying their tunics over their arms.

"You aren't ready yet?" said my mother, momentarily jolted. "It's almost time."

Well-wishers had crowded around the door and were trying to peek in as they entered the room. "Keep the door closed," said Mom. "Those people can see in here through the cracks."

My grandmother assisted the security guard posted outside, as bridesmaids paced the room. "Does anyone have any perfume I can use?" asked my nineteen-year-old aunt, Michelle.

"Are we going to wear the orchids on the left or right side of our hair?" asked the matron of honor, Evelyn Potter.

"Get dressed first; you can pin the orchids in your hair later," said my mother.

Her telephone never stopped ringing, and a messenger kept entering the room with details about the wedding crowd downstairs and how my father was fairing in his suite. Knowing Dad, he was probably already ready and checking his watch.

Dad spent most of his wedding morning meeting with his accountant, Eugene Dibble, and had watched a western later that afternoon, *The Return of Jesse James.* According to the *Jet* article, he seemed calm, but he told the reporter he was nervous, and joked with Dibble, "I changed my mind, get the luggage!"

The night before, Dad and Howard had gone to the speedway disco for his bachelor party, where he spent most of the night signing autographs and posing for pictures. Occasionally chanting, as he had at the wedding rehearsals, *"Muhammad Ali will be no longer free."*

Back in Mom's suite with just an hour to go a dozen people moved around the room shouting out questions, which my mother calmly answered. Then she walked into the next room, where someone helped her into her wedding dress designed by Christos of Bridal Couture of New York. "I'm saving this for Hana," she told the reporter. "If she wants to, she can wear it on her wedding day."

When the last covered button was fastened down the back of her beaded gown, my mother turned to face herself in the mirror. "It's lovely," she said, softly.

She walked back into the next room, where the bridesmaids were combing their hair and checking their lipstick.

"Oh, girl," said her maid of honor, "you look so good."

"Make sure they remember to put the runner down," Mom said to my grandmother as they walked out of the suite. The bridesmaids' dresses were designed by my mother: rainbow-colored chiffon tunics slit up to the waistline with matching silk pants beneath, set off with a pearl necklace and silver sandals.

Meanwhile, my father, political activist Dick Gregory, and some of the ushers in the wedding party lounged around in the living room area of Dad's suite cracking jokes and listening to Gregory discuss more serious matters.

As the star-studded audience awaited my parents' appearance, celebrities chatted amongst themselves. Warren Beatty was probably telling Mayor Tom Bradley about the movie he pitched to my father. Joe Louis was relaxing with his wife a few seats over from Christopher Lee. Japanese martial-arts champion Antonio Inoki—who gave my father a blood clot after kicking him in the leg in the ring the year before—was showing off the beautiful, multicolored Japanese doll he'd brought for my parents. A few rows away, actor Leon Isaac Kennedy was sitting with his wife, actress and NBC sportscaster Jayne Kennedy, who was the first black Miss Ohio and the first black woman to grace the cover of *Playboy*. She showed up wearing a long, white chiffon dress. (Several years later, when she was a commentator on *NFL Today*, an X-rated recording of her and her husband Leon was leaked—making her the first victim of a sex-tape gone public.) But that day in the Le Grand Trianon room of the Beverly Wilshire Hotel they were laughing and smiling as everyone listened to the ceremony's motif, Stevie Wonder's "You Are the Sunshine of My Life". Moments later the processional began, as the music eased into Mendelssohn's "Wedding March". My father and his best man, his brother Rahman, walked down the runway wearing white tuxedos, tails and gloves, and stood beside a seven-foot trellis entwined by white flowers. The foot of the altar was adorned with ferns, chrysanthemums, African gladiolus, carnations and snap dragons.

Then, one by one, the wedding party entered the room.

When my mother walked down the aisle, the 250 guests stood and admired her. The ivory gown featuring English net with Alençon lace was embroidered with pearls. It had a high neck and long sleeves with an empire bodice and an A-line skirt, which was covered with pearl buttons down the back that ended at her waistline. It was all set off with a matching ivory veil, and a long chapel train that followed her down the aisle. My mother was the picture of perfection—but people always said that photographs could not capture her beauty.

She gazed into my father's eyes and took his arm. "At first, I wasn't even paying attention to what the judge was saying," Mom confessed to the reporter. "Muhammad kept asking me if I was happy and saying things like, 'Well, here we are. We're finally getting married.' But when I heard the judge ask if I would take Muhammad to be my husband, I started paying attention."

Judge Billy Mills pronounced my parents man and wife as I, at eleven months old, cried loudly in the background. Although my mother wore a blue garter on each leg, Dad didn't remove and toss them for the single males to catch. That wasn't his style.

On the dance floor, my grandfather, Cassius Clay Sr, guided my grandmother around in a high-stylish waltz.

After the wedding, at about 11 p.m., my parents sat at a table in a Beverly Wilshire restaurant. As the reporter noted, "In between autograph requests, a starry-eyed champion lovingly praised his bride. With easily discernable, undeniable love in his eyes, he reflected a moment and declared, 'She's beautiful. This is a very sacred moment for me.'"

Later that evening two limousines carrying the bridal party were escorted to my grandmother's house. Dad was resting upstairs as Mom and her sisters sat on the sofa in the living room with their shoes off and feet propped up on chairs.

"I'm pleased with the way the wedding turned out," Mom said. "I'm just sorry so many uninvited people turned up. Even with all the security, there were so many faces inside I've never seen before." She walked over to the refrigerator. "Now that I think about it, I didn't even taste one hors d'oeuvre. And I know Muhammad was starving ..." She smiled. "When we were having the pictures taken of the bride feeding cake to the groom. I had to cut him two big slices instead of one." She poured a glass of milk, said goodnight and took it up to my father.

A few days later, they were off to Honolulu, Hawaii, for their honeymoon.

163

17

AS I READ through all the old newspapers, links were being made, I could feel them, but to put the pieces of the puzzle together and get to the bottom of the *lost love letters*, I'd have to face the ghosts head on. I would have to talk to my parents about them. The dozens of articles and magazine clippings I had read told only a fraction of the story. It was funny to think that some of them had once caused such a fuss, with their half-truths and silly gossip.

I marked my place in the magazine featuring my parents' wedding and set it down. I reached into my purse and pulled out the audio-tape I found in Mom's storage: *"For my Veronica, 1976"*, ten months before they were married. I took a deep breath, exhaled, and played the recording. To my surprise, my father was singing to my mother, spontaneously recapping the events surrounding their first meeting, as she lay beside him holding me, at one month old, in her arms.

August 21, 1976

"OH, OH, OH YES, I'm the great pretender—ooowooo—I pretend that you're doing well. I'm supposed to be, but I'm not you see, I'm lonely but no one can tell … Pretending, Veronica, you're doing well …

"Do you remember that day I first met you—ooowooo—I step off the plane. You were so beautiful you look so sweet, I knew one day you'd be mine.

"Then I went to the hotel—ooowooo—they got me a nice pretty room. I hoped you liked me but I really wasn't sure, then the other girls took you back to your room, you went to your hotel. I went to bed with you on my mind because you were so fine and soon, you would be mine. Then a few weeks and months went by. I continually tried to forget about you, but daily things would come to my mind because that girl I met in Salt Lake City was fine.

"Then I met you the night of the exhibition—ooowooo—George Foreman was there with Frazier. We all boxed our exhibitions and you, you were there. Oh, Veronica, you had on a two-piece bikini. I took you all aside, gave you a lecture, I saw that your heart was good. You went back to put on your (long) dress. I was proud because you listened to me. You were so sweet.

"That next morning after the exhibition, I got back on the private jet, not knowing that you would soon be in Zaire to see your daddy again. While in Zaire, Daddy heard you were coming. It was too good, too good to be true. I was at the airport waiting for you.

"Then Belinda, my wife, had to go. It made Daddy so mad. I didn't want her to come to the airport, but she did, but it couldn't keep me from you. James Brown and his band got off the jet, a crowd of black people. In the African moonlight, they came to see the fight. They all poured in to the airport. Now my heart was getting so shaky, waiting for that pretty tall girl. That pretty girl from the exhibition. I couldn't believe she was coming.

"Then I saw your beautiful face, she lit up like a doll. Her pretty, long hair, her pretty, cherry lips, she got off the big brown plane. She walked and she smiled and took pictures. My heart was beating so. Then Veronica, you looked and smiled at me. You walked over and said hello to people. Belinda following me close, she knew that the fine girls had got in, but she didn't know what I was thinking.

"And then I got to my car. As I walked away I saw you looking down at me, my heart beamed. Then Belinda drove back to N'Sele, she stayed with me that night, she left the next morning.

"You and your girlfriends came to my place. My heart was beating so fast. You sat on the couch. You looked so sweet. I went into the *kitchen for something sweet. I ate a piece of cake and drank some juice. I was so nervous this girl had come to see me.*

"You thought I liked your friend Trina, but I really didn't. You were so fine when I first met you at the exhibition, I couldn't say anything to you. In N'Sele, I knew you were true. You came away to see me.

"Well, to make a long story short, after all we did had been done, I knew you had to be mine. Then daily we talked on the phone. We walked on the Zaire river. I brought you your dinner. You comforted me. It helped me to destroy George Foreman.

"And now you have my little baby. My sweet, my sweet, little Ronca—her name is Hana—which means happiness and peace of mind, just like you. You're a Hana—for short they called you Ronca, but Ronca really means Hana. And now we see it in our little girl. You're with your daddy in your room, I'm making you this tape. After you hear my song I want you to kiss me. When I count three, Ronca, kiss meeeeee. ONE—TWO—THREEEEEEE."

They kissed and, as I listened from years in the future, my father speaks into the recorder. *"This hit song was cut in Show Low, Arizona, August 21, 1976. The time is now 5:25 a.m. I'm here with Veronica. Ronca, did you like that song?"*

"Yep."

"Did you love it, Ronca?"

"Yep,"

"Say, I love that song, Daddy."

"I loved that song, Daddy."

"Okay, Ronca ... it's 5:25 a.m. just after twenty minutes of road work [training for the second Ken Norton fight]. Signing off."

The recording was bittersweet. As one romance blossomed, another faded. As one family grew, another was torn apart. I thought about my siblings from my father's marriage to Belinda—Maryum, Muhammad Jr, and the twins, Jamillah and Rasheda.

I care about them deeply and wondered what it must have been like for them when he moved away. Did they also cry themselves to sleep, night after night, when they realized Daddy was never coming home? Did they have nightmares, waking their grandparents with screams and cries, like I had, begging her to give him another chance, promising to be a good little girl, thinking it was my fault? Helplessly trying to reason with her when she sat me down to explain, "We love each other and always will, but we're different people now ..."

"But you both like movies, you both like pickles ..." Tears streaming down my cheeks.

I thought, too, about the tape recordings between my father and his first family, perhaps the most heartbreaking and haunting of all.

"I'm calling Maryum, Rasheda, Jamillah, and little Muhammad at their grandmother's house in Chicago. Today is Friday, November the 30th 1979."

This was the year after we moved to Los Angeles and four years before Belinda finally agreed to let them come visit for the summer. Until then, they'd have to settle for short visits on his random trips to Chicago and fleeting telephone conversations.

"I'm still your daddy," he said to eleven-year-old Maryum. *"Parents get divorced all the time, but they don't stop loving their children. I'll always be your daddy, wont I?"*

"Of course! You will always be—ALWAYS!"

"Your daddy is Muhammad Ali. I can still run and play and get around. These are valuable years we're missing ... wouldn't it be nice if you were with your daddy more?"

"Yeah."

"One day soon I'm going to start coming out there to see you more and fly you all out here ..."

"Okay ..."

I'll have a similar conversation with him when I'm twelve, two years after my parents' divorce. I'll be sitting on the sofa in the living room of our new house, just like my sister Maryum, talking to my father on the phone.

I'm not sure when my happy childhood began to unravel. Did it happen all at once? Or bit by bit? Did I beg my father to take me with him—put up a fight when he left? How many nights did I cry myself to sleep? How long did I blame my mother? More importantly, have

I stopped blaming her? I don't have the answers because I locked them away long ago with my broken dreams, shattered hopes and painful memories.

"Maryum, your daddy is history conscious," he says on the same recording. *"I'm always thinking about history. Do you remember the day your sisters Khaliah and Miya were all at my Woodlawn house with you, and Hana and Laila, and I took those pictures of you all sitting on my big red steps?"*

"Yeah, I remember!"

"Well, I kept those pictures. So when you all get to be grown ladies and get married and when you look back to when you were coming up, you can say: I didn't live with all my sisters, but Daddy let me see them and we knew them, because Daddy let us play together. And, to prove it, we've got pictures ..."

I have the photos of which he spoke—framed images of my father sitting on the bottom of the red steps at the Woodlawn house, all of us gathered around him. We were all there: me, Laila, Maryum, the twins, little Muhammad, even Miya and Khaliah, his kids from women he was never married to. All his children, playing happily together, under one grand roof. A divided but blessed family.

"Maryum, I wanted to talk to you for a while. I love you so much and I never hear your voice ... I'm making tapes of Hana and Laila trying to sing and talk and playing. When I see you, I'm going to let you hear them. Then when they grow up I'm going to let them hear the tapes. I've got tapes of you and me talking on the phone from five years ago."

"You do?"

"Yeah ... you're going to hear them one day ..."

My memories of the house on Woodlawn are few. All I know is it was a large brick mansion where I first lived as a child. I was only three when we moved to Fremont Place in Los Angeles, but I remember the large winding staircase and its red steps. I remember my father playing fragmented melodies on the grand piano—playing only scales because it was all he knew. My parents' friends, Tim and

Helga, Mom, Laila and I lay on the white carpet, listening in front of the fireplace.

I can vaguely remember my siblings spending the night and eating breakfast together—Cheerios and Frosted Flakes. Dad took photos of us all gathered around the table like one big happy family. Those are my only memories of Woodlawn, which was never supposed to be ours to begin with. The memories I do recall feel stolen. They should belong to my siblings, Dad's first family.

"I love you, Muhammad," he said to his seven-year-old son on the recording. "I just love you so much. I think about you every day. I miss you. I'm not with Mommy any more so I don't see you much. Do you ever think about Daddy?"

"Yep."

"Do you want to see Daddy more?"

"Nope!"

"You don't? Tell me why."

"Because you have work to do—you have to go take care of business."

"No, I said do you ever WANT to see Daddy more?"

"No," he said again.

"Why don't you want to see me more? I want to see you more."

He paused as if considering. "It might be because you can't spend the night ..."

Dad had purchased the Woodlawn house for them, but as fate would have it they'd never move in. Instead they moved into their grandparents' house when their mother, Belinda, moved to Los Angeles.

"Rasheda and Jamillah, I just had to talk to you because I got real sad today and I didn't know why," he said on another tape, in 1979. "I said my prayers and something told me, 'Talk to your children more because they love you and you love them. You should talk to your children because one day they're going to be grown and you won't see them as much.' I want you all to know that Daddy always thinks about you. I'm trying to help you guys find your purpose in life. I have a lecture called 'The Purpose of Life' where everything

God made has a purpose. Horses have a purpose, chickens, cows, trees, grass, everything has a purpose ... You are a human being; if everything else has a purpose, humans have a purpose too. You don't have to really know yet, but you should know by age twelve, so you've got three more years to think about it because one day you're going to have to take care of yourself. You know that, right?"

"Yes, sir."

"I gave Mommy a lot of money when we got divorced so you all can go to college. Your money is already put up for you. So, find out what you want to go to school for—try to be something in life where you can make a good living. Don't depend on men and don't be living in the ghettoes. You know what a ghetto is, don't you?"

"Yes, sir."

"You see how nice Mommy's house is and Grandmommy's house is?"

"Yes, sir."

"Daddy helped them get all of that. I'm saving money for you, too, so that when you get big you can have nice clothes and your own car. You're going to be a woman with a good education, a nice house, and one day a nice family, right?"

"Yes, sir."

"So Daddy is going to help you do that—that's what I'm thinking about every day. I'm always working hard to save money to make a future for you all, so you can have nice things when you get big. I'm sorry I can't be around you more because I'm so busy. I've got Hana and Laila to take care of, and I got Miya and Khaliah. I've got you guys. I'm always working to take care of all of you. I give Mommy money to take care of you and I pray to God that I'll be able to keep doing it. One day soon I'm going to come back to Chicago and start seeing you more, so be good."

"Yes, sir ..."

Picking the phone back up, "Daddy," May May asked, "when are you going to come visit?"

"As soon as I get free—I promise you! I'm working on it ..."

"Daddy ... where are you?" Jamillah asked.

The photo my mother had taken. Los Angeles, summer of 1984.

"I'm at my house in California. I want you to come see it. This is your house too! You hear me?"

"Yes, sir!"

"Daddy, do we have your phone number?"

"Yeah, Maryum has it—call me sometime, you hear? I think about you all the time, but you never call me."

"Yes, sir!"

"Do you love Daddy?"

"Yes."

"Okay, I love you guys. Let me hear you say it together—say, 'We love our daddy.'"

"We love our daddy!"

"Okay, God bless you. I'll be thinking about you. Daddy loves you. Give Mommy the greetings for me ..."

***

I THOUGHT ABOUT Belinda and her relationship with my father. Listening to their conversations, you'd never know there was ever any discord between them.

"Salam Alaikum [Peace be with you], *how are you doing?"* she asked on December 9, 1979.

"I'm fine, what's happening?"

"Oh, nothing much," she said.

They sound like friends—joking and catching up about old times. Which is how two people who were once married should sound together.

"The kids are grown!" said Dad. *"They look extra big to me because I don't see them any more and when I see them it just shocks me. It seems like not too long ago, when you think back, that we were bringing them home from the hospital."*

"Yep, that was a long time ago ... a long time," she agreed. *"I took them to see your mother."*

"Yeah, I talk to her. It was so good that you did that, I'm so glad. I want them to see her more. Before you know it Maryum's going to be grown and she will be coming home with her own children and her man."

Belinda laughed. *"She better not bring nobody home."*

"If she's like you, she will be bringing her man home at seventeen. Think about that. That's only six more years. What is today's date?"

"I think it's the 9th," said Belinda.

"No, it's the 8th," said Dad.

"It's December the 9th, yesterday was the 8th," she said.

"No, it's December the 9th—check it out."

More laughter. *"No! You check it out,"* she said. *"Today is the 8th!"*

"I'll bet ya—I'll bet ya a hundred dollars—are you sure?" said Dad.

"I'm positive! Have you been asleep for two days?"

He checks the newspaper. *"You're right! You're right! You're right! I would have bet you were wrong,"* he said. *"The white man's paper doesn't lie!"*

They both laughed.

"Belinda, I never told you this but—right now—I'm really thirty-nine."

"Thirty-nine! You aren't thirty-nine; you'll be thirty-seven in January."

"I put my age back so I could marry you."

"You put your age back to marry who? You were twenty-five, fool!"

"I was twenty-seven—you thought I was twenty-five."

"What! You were twenty-seven? Why did you lie to me like that?"

"To trick your momma and daddy!"

"What!"

"Just kidding ..."

Another moment of laughter.

"So what are you doing today?" she asked.

"Harold Smith [Dad's business associate and friend] *is coming by, Herbert* [Dad's manager] *is in town and we're trying to start an organization where we sign and manage fighters ... Maaan, we got a camp here, it's ten times better than Deer Lake! It's for sale—the current owner wants 900,000 cash—so I'm trying to figure out how I can get it. I don't want to fight no more but the damn thing is terrible ... So I'm taking Harold and Herbert to see it ... that's all I'm doing today . . ."*

Dad describes the property with a passion that turns to melancholy, then he pauses for a moment. *"There's always something changing,"* he said. "At one time, I was back in Chicago and you were here. Now I'm here and you're back in Chicago. We're always rotating."

"Yeah, it's cold here, but according to the weatherman we're not supposed to have a bad winter."

His voice grew somber. "I wish the children were out here. Before I know it, Maryum is going to be grown, and I haven't even seen her much. I try not to let it bother me—it used to upset me, not being able to see them. But, hell, they're going to grow up and go their own ways. As long as they are healthy and have money, I'm happy. They'll get of age one day and I might see them more. I don't forget them, I just forget about having to see them all the time because I live too far away ... So what are you coming out here for this time?"

"I'm going to some meeting for my union to see about a film."

"You're going to do a film?"

"Yeah, but I don't know what it's about because we are still negotiating."

"Hold on, Belinda, Hana's cuttin' up."

"What's she doing?"

"I'm drinking coffee. Hana's got her spoon trying to get it. She's sucking on a popsicle begging me for coffee ..."

In the background: "I want some toffee, Daddy ..."

"Hana, please leave me alone, I'm talking on the phone."

"I want some ..."

"Belinda, Hana's crying. We'll talk later."

"Okay. Salam Alaikum ..."

***

I REMEMBER BELINDA walking around the grounds at Fremont Place once. It was the summer of 1985, after my parents' divorce was announced. My siblings were visiting and apparently Dad had a small gathering of businessmen at the house. My mother wasn't home at the time, but Belinda told the press a different story. According to the September 12, 1985 issue of the *Los Angeles Sentinel*, Belinda was walking around playing the gracious host, which fueled rumors of a possible reconnection between she and my father. After the gathering, she met up with the newspaper's staff writer at a Beverly Hills restaurant for an interview.

"It's taken a long time for me to feel completely confident with myself," she said between sips of ginger ale. "First, I was living in the shadow of Muhammad, then the divorce, then the marriage of he and Veronica."

The interviewer wanted to know if there was any truth to the rumors about her getting back together with my father.

"I don't need him any more," she said. "If anything, he needs me; he always did ... Ali is like a big brother to me now. We still talk on the phone and keep in touch ... There was a lot that happened between us. A lot the public didn't know about ..."

The magazine reported that Belinda waltzed around our estate, greeting guests and making small talk, while, according to her, my mother was in her bedroom hiding.

"Both of us knew where we were supposed to be," said Belinda. "I was down at the party and she was upstairs. Why would she want to come down and face me after taking my husband?"

My mother wasn't home, and she had no idea Belinda was ever even there. When the reporter asked why she was at our house in the first place, she said she was invited by her daughters, who were visiting from Chicago. They were young teens at the time. Belinda was living in Los Angeles, trying to pursue a film career. According to the article, she was then negotiating a contract with CBS to star in a series called *Jessy Clark* about a black female attorney in which she would play the main character.

Towards the end of the article, Belinda talks about her new love interest. The reporter writes about her two marriages after my father. How the first one lasted one month and the second ended after only two weeks.

"As a Muslim, I couldn't make love until I was married," she said. "It was probably for physical rather than spiritual reasons that I married. I admit I wasn't doing this whole thing properly, but we all make mistakes."

I bumped into Belinda that day when she was coming out the bathroom, around the corner from Dad's office. She smiled and started talking to me, imitating the voice of Daffy Duck. I remember laughing out loud, listening to her. She sounded just like him. But what stands out most in my memory about that day is her telling me about the book she was writing—about how my mother ruined her life.

I was nine years old at the time.

Belinda made many false statements to the press about my mother over the years, dragging her name through the mud. To this day my mother has never revealed Belinda's deepest, darkest secrets.

Muhammad Ali aka Daddy

At 10 o'clock in the morning my father edges his Rolls out of the driveway and drives through the gates onto Wilshire Blvd. Naturally, he leaves the top down, and within seconds a royal procession forms. Cars heading in his direction fall into line behind him, hooting their horns to catch his eye. On the sidewalk, passers-by suddenly freeze in their tracks as if paralyzed by one of those sci-fi laser guns. People scream and shout: "Aaaahhh!!! Aliiiiii!!!"

One young man does a kamikaze turn, screeches to a halt at the red light, leans out the window and yells, "Ali, you were right—you are 'The Greatest'!" Dad raises his fist in acknowledgement. At Crescent Heights Blvd, two garbage collectors almost smash a VW as they spot the champ. "How ya doin', baby?" screams a man pushing a cart out of a supermarket. "You're number one," yell a couple of black teenagers. "Thank you, brothers!" Dad shouts back. He doesn't miss one of the salutes along the way. By the time he turns onto Melrose he's left a trail of awed citizens—all ages, all sexes, all colors. It was a magic-carpet ride.

– *A Place in the Sun*, November 1979

18

WE ALL THINK we know our parents. The more we presume to know, the more shocking the discoveries when they are revealed.

For instance, I never knew that my father had two half-brothers, who he never knew existed until they turned up at his father's funeral in Louisville, Kentucky, on February 12, 1990. I was fourteen years old when my grandfather passed. Laila and I weren't at his service, but my siblings were there, and my stepmother Lonnie told me about it in later years. Dad was aware of his father's indiscretions, but he had no idea that Papa Cash had other children. My father never spoke much about things that upset him, so I've formed my own opinions based on what I know of him.

All his life my father treated strangers like family, inviting them into our homes, riding them around town in his Rolls, talking to them on the telephone. But when he saw his estranged brothers that day he didn't know what to say to them. He probably felt an emotional void when he looked in their eyes and saw his father's reflection. So he remained silent.

I don't know their names or who their mother was or what sort of relationship, if any, they had with my grandfather. And I don't know why he never told Dad or his brother about them. Maybe Papa Cash just didn't know how to handle the situation or how to bring all four of his sons together. Perhaps he didn't want my grandmother to know. Maybe the main reason my father worked so hard to unite

Me on the left, with my hand on Dad's knee. Laila is on the far right.

his own children was so none of us would one day bump into the other in the distant future and view him or her as a stranger. I only wish that my father and his estranged brothers had had the same opportunity. Papa Cash was a good man but he didn't give his sons the gift that Dad would later give to his own children: the chance to grow up with their siblings.

Every summer my father brought all his children together. Belinda's kids—May May, Muhammad Jr and the twins—flew in from Chicago. Pat's daughter, Miya, flew in from New Jersey, and Aaisha's daughter, Khaliah, flew in from Pennsylvania.

Once there, he'd pile us all into his Rolls-Royce and drive around Los Angeles with the top down. Dad loved putting himself and his family on full display. I remember the sting of the wind blowing my hair in my face as we drove up Wilshire Blvd to Dad's favorite diner, Carnation's, or Bob's Big Boy for lunch. His order was always the same: a cheeseburger with mustard and onions, clam chowder, coffee with cream and three packets of Sweet 'n' Low.

I looked forward to the summers, knowing that my sisters and brother were coming to stay with us.

I might have been able to show my sisters Carnation's, Bob's Big Boy and Wilshire Blvd, but when it came to pop music, and dancing, I was very much the little sister and, being a year older than Laila, it was a summer role reversal I enjoyed. May May used to put Prince, New Edition, Salt-N-Pepa and Doug E. Fresh on her Walkman cassette player, and dance in Dad's office as we sat on his sofa watching her. Sometimes she'd teach us her dance moves, then we'd go to the kitchen for ice cream and popsicles—I didn't mind sharing with them.

May May was the oldest and somewhat of a mother figure to us all, especially the twins and Muhammad Jr, who, like me, always seemed to be in some sort of trouble. Once when we were all sitting around the kitchen table eating lunch after our morning swim, little Muhammad was twirling his silverware between his fingers and poked Laila, then aged six, in the eye with his fork. Unfortunately, he didn't always listen to May May, as she had warned only moments before, "Muhammad! Put down your fork before you hurt somebody."

May May and I resembled each other the most, so naturally I felt close to her. In fact, Dad was always trying to keep us all connected.

"Maryum," said Dad on one of his recordings, a few years before Belinda let them come visit, "does Hana look like you?"

"A lot like me."

"That right!"

"How old is Hana, now?"

"Hana is three and Laila is two."

"Where are they now?"

"Hana is at preschool and Laila's upstairs with the babysitter, Janet … Do you love your sisters, Hana and Laila?"

"Yeah."

"Let me hear you say it."

"I love my sisters Hana and Laila."

"No, you don't."

"I do!"

"You don't love them—you don't know them yet. But I'm going to start flying you all out here, so when you grow up you can say, 'I didn't live with all my sisters, but I knew them because Daddy let us play together ...'"

I had the time of my life following my older siblings around the house, driving them crazy with kisses and endless questions: *"Who do you like best—Michael Jackson or Prince?"* or, *"Who do you think dances better, Madonna or Cyndi Lauper?"*

Everywhere they went, I wanted to go with them. Their only refuge was sleep and a hideaway outside the kitchen door at the bottom of the steps that led to an outdoor entrance to the basement. It was a narrow, dark stairwell—they knew I wouldn't follow. Sometimes I'd give up and go swimming or run to my father's office to see what he was up to. But usually it was a waiting game to see who tired first. I knew they couldn't hide forever. I'd sit at the top of the stairs sucking on a popsicle, waiting patiently for them to reappear.

At night, before bed, I'd scoop a handful of Vaseline and spread it over my hair, trying to straighten my long curls. I wanted it to look as silky as Jamillah's and Rasheda's hair. The twins were six years older than me and I thought everything about them was cool. The way they laughed wholeheartedly with their mouths wide open, or the way they rolled their eyes in unison when something annoyed them. And how they each called out the other's name, even when they weren't in the same room together, putting emphasis on the vowels—*"Rasheeeeeedaaaa!"*—after a funny scene in a movie or when I did something silly, or unbelievable, like the time they found out what I said to Michael Jackson when he came over to visit. I'll tell you that story later.

"Jamiiiiiiillaaaah!"

One morning I got the scissors out the kitchen drawer and snuck up to the third-floor media room. They had fallen asleep there the night before while watching Daddy's film, *The Greatest*. We had all watched it together, enjoying Daddy's reactions to his life on screen.

182

"Wasn't I somethin'?" he'd say, as we rewound our favorite scenes again and again. We especially loved the part when Dad called a reporter from a telephone booth in the middle of the night and disguised his voice to sound like an old lady.

"Cassius Clay is outside Sonny Liston's house right now with a bus full of people . . ." he squeaked into the receiver. *"Well, I don't like to say that word, but yes, they're Niggers!"*

Dad was trying to agitate Sonny Liston into a fight. At that time, Sonny was the heavyweight champion of the world and he wouldn't give my father a shot at the title. Or he didn't, at least, until Dad rode his bus to his house in the middle of the night, shouting over a microphone, *"Sonny Liston! Come out here, you big, ugly bear!"*

My father named all his opponents and Sonny Liston was "the bear".

By the time Sonny came outside, the press had arrived and all his neighbors were either peeking out their windows or standing on the sidewalks in their pajamas. Sonny ran across his lawn in his robe shouting and throwing rocks at Dad's bus: "Get out of here, you crazy fool, before I call the police!"

As Dad pulled away Sonny tripped on something in his front lawn.

"What the hell is that?" he asked a reporter, poking at the thick black metal with his foot.

"That's a bear trap!" said the reporter.

I tiptoed over to the sofa, careful not to wake up Laila, Miya, Little Muhammad or Khaliah, and grabbed a handful of either Rasheda's or Jamillah's hair. Like my father, I could never tell them apart. They were identical when they were younger. Dad often called them twin 1 and twin 2.

As I slid my sister's hair into the open scissors, May May walked into the room.

"Hana!" she shouted, startling me and waking the twins. "Put down those scissors!"

"Daddy!" she said to my father, "guess what I caught Hana doin' now?"

"She'll grow out of it," he said.

The twins always stuck together. They were social and playful but, like most identical twins, they had their own special relationship. They always seemed to be sneaking off to the corner of a room, whispering amongst themselves and telling secrets. Like two best friends in their own little world. They were fun, high-spirited and feisty, but they were sometimes rude to my mother.

"This is our father's house," they told her. "We don't have to listen to you."

As far as they knew, Mom was the reason Dad had left their mother. They had no idea what was really going on. How could they? They were just little girls at the time.

My sister Khaliah was two years older than me. She was shy and quiet, and often asked to go home before the summer ended. I'm not sure why, really. I never asked her. Maybe she missed her mother and grandmother. Or maybe she felt like Laila—that the house was too crowded.

But when she was at Fremont, she was always playing in my room. We looked a lot alike and had so much in common. The moment my father brought us together, at the house on Woodlawn Avenue in Chicago, we were drawn to each other. We are still close today. And her son, my nephew Jacob, an exceptional athlete, was recently accepted into Harvard University. My father would be incredibly proud.

Miya was the fun sister. She got along with everyone and was particularly close to my mother. After the divorce, Mom flew her into town to visit us at our new house. We had the time of our life when she visited. She used to eat Cap'n Crunch cereal at night and teach us how to say bad words in Jamaican.

"*Bumbaclot* ..."

"*Bumbabot* ..."

"No," she laughed. "*Bum-ba-clot!*"

I had no idea what it meant. But I liked how it sounded. When the boys at school were teasing me—pulling on my ponytails—I shouted, "Leave me alone, you *bumbaclot!*"

It was a good thing my teacher didn't know what it meant either.

May May was also polite, but she had her suspicions about my mother and she was a detective by nature—always watching, trying to size people up, and figure things out. That first summer when my siblings visited, Mom was with a man in the dining room. It was her friend Terry Scott, an interior designer who was helping her decorate Fremont Place. They were going over ideas for the living-room draperies. Mom met Terry, who was gay, when Dad was filming *Freedom Road*. He lived with Buzz Harper, a well-known antique dealer in Natchez, Mississippi. Harper had invited my parents over to dinner one night after filming. What Mom remembers most about that evening was when my father sat on one of the antique settees and broke it.

"It didn't actually collapse, he probably only cracked it," said Mom. "But it made a loud creak and every head turned in the room."

I pictured my father sitting there, wide-eyed, like a kid caught with his hand in the cookie jar. I laughed out loud at the image. This was probably why white ropes were tied across the arms of certain antique chairs in our living room.

Mom and Terry were looking at a decorating book when May May suddenly jumped in the doorway.

"Aha!" she shouted, then quickly snapped a Polaroid picture and ran off.

Mom and Terry looked at each other and laughed.

"She looked like a little detective," Mom told Dad later that night.

"What did Terry do?" he asked.

"He just laughed ..."

My mother was very patient with my siblings. She never complained or gave my father any trouble or stress about them—no matter how rude they were to her. She welcomed all of his children into her home. I think she understood why they sometimes treated her the way they did and silently forgave them. Years after my parents' divorce, Muhammad Jr called me and asked for my mother's number.

"I want to thank her," he said, "for never coming between me and my father."

Little Muhammad was obedient mostly, but, as I said, he was a magnet for mischief. Playing too rough with our dog, or hitting me in the swimming pool. It was May May who reprimanded him mostly: "Stop it, Muhammad!"

"Hana tried to drown me!" he said after she yelled at him for bopping me in the head.

"In that case," said May May, "if she does it again, slap her again!"

Muhammad Jr was the only one who actually called and apologized to my mother for the way he treated her. Perhaps May May and the twins, like the world at the time, thought Mom married Dad for his money. They didn't know about the prenuptial agreement she willingly signed at the request of Dad's lawyers. Nor did they know that the man she married after my father was far from wealthy. If anything, she had more money than he did. Mom could have had anyone in the world; celebrities, wealthy businessmen, even politicians were sending messages to her through their assistants and mutual friends. She turned them all down. Regardless of how or why their fairy tale ended, once upon a time my mother and father were deeply and genuinely in love with each other. They made wonderful memories together.

It's strange the things we can remember. The single images that stay with us through the years. Like the first time I waited barefoot on the patio for my father to come home. And how in that moment I realized that there was no one in the world I loved more. Somehow, in my mind, images of my childhood grow fainter with each passing day, but I can still recall every detail about that day on the patio. And the first time I drove up Wilshire Blvd with my siblings in our father's Rolls.

***

I WAVED TO the crowds and smiled as they chanted my father's name. We swept along the street, the wind whipping my hair in my face as cars, trees, and street signs flew by. It was Muhammad Jr's and Miya's turn in the front seat of our father's Rolls. Normally I would have minded, but that day I didn't care. It was my siblings' first summer visiting us at Fremont Place.

186

"You guys, tell your mother that you want to come to California one day," Dad had said to Little Muhammad, May May and the twins. *"She's not going to do it unless you ask her—let her know you want to come."*

"Okay."

"Don't tell her that I said it, just say, 'Mommy, we want to go out and see Daddy. He said we can come one weekend when we're not in school and meet the stars.' Say, 'Daddy said that you'll have to okay it.' Give her respect, you hear?"

"Okay ..."

Squashed in the back between my big sisters May May, Khaliah, Jamillah and Rasheda, I couldn't wait to show them the fun that Daddy and I had when we went out driving. I was in heaven and so was my father. He wanted the whole world to see us all together. It was something he'd tried to arrange every summer for years. Now he was finally able to do it.

"Daddy!" I yelled over the crowds.

"Yeah?"

"Daddy, are we taking them to Carnation's for cheeseburgers?"

"We're going to Bob's Big Boy today," he said.

"Okay!"

I turned to my siblings and filled them in on Bob's Big Boy, where I loved to order strawberry shakes and french fries. The staff there were always happy to see my father—he over-tipped the waitresses, signed autographs for customers, and performed magic tricks. There was even a framed photo of Dad and me on the wall. We are sitting in a booth eating cheeseburgers.

On our way home from lunch, Dad would thrill us with his theatrics.

"I kill! Aaaaaaaaaaaahh!" he'd shout, slamming his foot on the gas.

"Aaaaaaaaaaaahh!" we all screamed, with butterflies in our tummies. He was only going about 35mph but his dramatic expressions made us feel like we were riding the wind like a roller-coaster. My father was a big-hearted kid and he was always fun to be with. He turned the simple things in life, like driving down the street, into an unforgettable adventure.

A few blocks later, Dad spotted a crowd of people waiting at the bus stop. He pulled over, walked into the middle of the stunned crowd, and put on a show. We all watched from the car as Dad pulled a false thumb from his pocket and performed one of his signature tricks, the disappearing scarf. Then a black case was produced from the trunk of his car: cards were laid out, minds were read, copper coins were turned into silver, unequal lengths of rope were made even again, and large dice were turned into small ones. Then he took a scarf from his briefcase, laid it flat on the hood of his Rolls, and ordered everyone to be silent as his voice grew louder: "Rise, Ghost! Rise, Ghost!"

We all screamed, then he slammed his hand on top of the scarf, to flatten it.

"Wasn't that somethin'?" he asked, bright-eyed.

But he saved his best trick for last—his levitation act. We watched as he turned his back to us, told everyone to watch his feet, then raised both heels slowly off the ground, shifting his weight onto the tip of his front right toe, just enough to make it appear, to everyone watching from behind, that he had levitated a few inches from the ground.

"He can fly!" one man called out as "Oooooos" and "Ahhhhhhs" buzzed around the crowd. Before leaving, he showed everyone how the tricks were accomplished.

"This is all deception," he said. "I'm doing this to teach you a lesson and it is this: do not believe your eyes. There are people who will tell you lies and try to trick you, but you must always be on your guard."

My father didn't like deceiving people—not even with a little magic. It's no wonder the magicians' society kicked him out their union, depriving him of the honor they'd once bestowed on him. *"The secrets he's giving away are bread and butter to magicians . . ."*

We pulled back onto Wilshire Blvd, as people called out, *"We love you, Ali! You're the People's Champ! You will always be 'The Greatest'!"* I rested my elbows on the back seat, smiling and waving at them, then Daddy blew them a kiss, held up his victory fist and drove home—their echoes following us in the wind.

The summer was full of lively adventure. Whatever stunts I pulled—putting Laila in the clothes dryer, trying to cut the twins' hair, running into the street without underwear, holding my brother's head under the water too long, or breaking into the house of the famous singer Lou Rawls, who lived around the corner, and accidently setting off the alarm—Daddy always replied the same: *"She'll grow out of it ..."*

He was right. Eventually I did.

19

MY FATHER ONCE said, "It is an expensive price I have to pay to be the most famous man on earth."

The price he was referring to was *lost time* with his children. Like most kids, when I was a little girl I only thought about my own sorrow—my own pain. But now, as an adult, knowing all that I do, I can finally see his. For all that he had, my father did not have everything he wanted. He suffered, too.

Although my father had more time to spend with Laila and me than he did with Miya and Khaliah or with his first family, he still missed out on some of our special moments. Dad made a comment to this effect in the middle of an interview he was giving in his hotel room in May of 1977. He was in Maryland to fight Alfredo Evangelista in his ninth defense of both his WBC and WBA heavyweight titles. My mother was with him but I, at nine months old, was at the Woodlawn house in Chicago with Gertrude. My father was speaking to the interviewer when my mother walked into the room and whispered into his ear. "Hana's walking!"

He proudly relayed this information to the journalist. "My daughter is walking!" he said. "We left Chicago two days ago and she couldn't walk. Now Veronica called home and the babysitter said that she walks." He looked at my mother. "Give me a kiss," he said tenderly.

A moment before Mom walked into the room, the reporter had asked my father if he had enough time to see all his children. There were eight of us in total, including Laila, who was still in Mom's belly at the time.

"No," he said. "I don't. I suffer for that."

I was usually with my parents when they traveled, but sometimes they left me at home with the babysitter. But from then on my parents brought me—and in the months to come, Laila—nearly everywhere with them. I think this was one of the main reasons why my father made so many audio recordings over the years. He wanted to capture all the incredible events and moments that people weren't witnessing in his everyday personal life and preserve them for his children and posterity. Perhaps so many of the recordings are of Laila and me laughing, singing, crying, playing, and getting ready for school because he lost valuable time with his first family and he wanted all of his children to have proof that he was doing his duty as a loving father whenever he could.

But, like all fathers, he thought his children were growing up way too fast and wanted to preserve some of the intimate moments we shared. Laila never seemed to mind him leaving; it was my heart he had to ease, my tears he had to wipe.

"I wanna go bye-bye with you—I wanna go bye-bye ..."

"This tape is being made on December 16th, Sunday, 1979. Hana Ali, three years old, is crying because she cannot go with us to Hong Kong and Peking. With me on this trip is my wife Veronica, her sister Diane, and my father, who came in from Louisville, Kentucky ... Hana Ali is in the background crying because she can't go ..."

He walked into the room. *"Laila, pick that up and put it back ..."* He spoke into the recorder. *"Laila's got the toothpaste all over the floor. Put it back, Laila."*

"Hana, please stop crying," my mother was pleading in the background.

"Why are you crying?" my father asked me.

"I wanna go bye-bye with you—I wanna go bye-bye with you!"

"Me and Mommy are going on the airplane to China and Hong Kong. We can't take you, but we're going to buy you some dolls and toys—we'll bring them back."

"You'll be back?"

"Yeah—I'll be back."

"I want to go with you, Daddy. I wanna go bye-bye with you."

"Hana, please stop crying. Please stop crying, Hana. I'll be back—I'll be right back ..."

My father's career kept him away from home, but after marrying my mother and eventually retiring from boxing, although he still traveled, Dad had more time to spend with us.

"Hana, I'm going to go eat. Do you want to come with me?"

"Come on, Laila, hurry up," my mother calls in the background. "Go eat with Daddy."

"Now I'm going downstairs to eat breakfast," he said into the recorder. "Hana wants me to pick her up. Okay, Daddy's got you ... why are you crying, Hana?" he asked again, carrying me into the kitchen with him.

"I wanna go bye-bye—I wanna go bye-bye!"

At the kitchen table, he spoke into the recorder. "I'm trying to eat and Hana wants to sit on my lap."

"I want some bacon," I said.

"Okay, you want some turkey bacon?"

"Yeah, I want to cut it."

"Here's the best way." He picks up the bacon. "Don't cut it. Bite it." I did as he did.

"There you go!" He smiled. "Okay, that concludes this segment of Hana Ali and her daddy, Muhammad Ali, just before leaving for Hong Kong, Peking, and a few more countries on a little tour of China ..."

My father made two trips to China. The first was in December of 1979. Chairman Deng Xiaoping extended the invitation, with the hope that Dad would help bring boxing back to his country. My father's visit was also of diplomatic importance. He was the first foreign athlete to be invited by the Chinese Olympic Committee and the All-China Sports Federation. He was also acting as an emissary of President Jimmy Carter, who hoped my father could persuade China to participate in the 1984 Olympics.

Boxing had been banned in China a couple of decades previous, when, in 1959, a fighter died in the ring. Many Chinese believed boxing was too brutal, savage, and ruthless. My father, always grateful for the opportunities boxing offered him, defended the sport that introduced him to the world. Long after he won the gold medal at the 1960 Rome Olympics, he stated: "If we stopped all the things that caused accidents, cars would be first. Airplanes would be second. Boxing should be improved, not abolished. It's a route to wealth and fame for the underprivileged. A sport where all sizes of men can truly play. There's no other sport where a 110-pound guy can become a millionaire overnight ..."

In 1966, during the Cultural Revolution in China, competitive sports were banned by the Communist Party. When the revolution collapsed in 1969, China used table-tennis matches to reconnect with the world. Deng believed that to win friends and respect his country had to win medals. Thus, in December 1979 he invited my father to meet with China's political leaders, hoping Muhammad Ali could help their cause.

And for those who wondered what he was doing in his hotel room, or in between flights, as he traveled the world, he recorded the moments.

The recording on December 22nd opens with an elegant English voice on Hong Kong Radio News: "Yesterday, London had its first snowfall of the winter after weeks of unseasonal mild weather which brought out spring flowers. The snow lasted ten minutes but melted as soon as it fell. In Kent, there was heavy overnight snow and the traffic was stalled on roads leading to Dover. And now to end this news, here are the main points again:

"The Ayatollah Khomeini has ordered that Christian Priests should be allowed to visit the hostages in Tehran over Christmas. President Carter says he will ask the United Nations to impose economic sanctions on Iran. The two sides in the 'Guerrilla war' have signed a peace treaty. A letter bomb addressed to a British cabinet minister has been discovered by London postal workers.

"And that ends this news from Radio Television, Hong Kong."

My father spoke into the recorder: *"That was a little example of what radio sounds like in Hong Kong, as far as the news is concerned. This is December 22nd, 1979, in my Hong Kong hotel room ... Now we'll hear some more radio programs ..."*

He whispered into the recorder as symphony music played: *"It's a few days before Christmas and they're playing Christmas carols ..."* He flipped through the radio stations for a while, listening to random channels. *"Well, so much for that ... I'll be back when we have something else. Signing off—hotel, Hong Kong."*

My father remembered Deng as a kind, honorable man. "We hugged, ate, and talked, and he treated me like family ..."

Dad's second trip to China was in 1985. By then, his personal life and health had both taken unexpected turns. He'd lost his championship title to Larry Holmes in 1980, he was on the verge of a divorce he didn't want, he'd been diagnosed with Parkinson's syndrome the year before, and Fremont Place was officially on the market.

When the call came to return to China, my father remembered his warm welcome several years earlier, and he and my mother accepted the invitation. The Communist government hoped he'd follow through with their plans for him to train their boxers for the Olympics. While his health would eventually make this difficult, Dad flew across the ocean again and showed the people of China the Muhammad Ali of old.

Accompanied by my mother, Howard Bingham, and a few others, Dad was mobbed by fans wherever his limousine went. As always, he signed autographs, kissed children, shook hands, and waved at roaring crowds. As reported in a local Peking newspaper, twenty-year-old lightweights got the chance of a lifetime when they sparred with "the Greatest of All Times" in a makeshift ring at the Peking Sports Institute.

Dad took off his suit jacket and tie, and stepped into the ring for the one-minute bouts, swinging his right uppercuts that weren't meant to land, dancing and floating and faking a TKO at the hands of his much smaller foes, making it the most memorable day of their lives.

195

"They've got great potential," he said of boxers in Peking and Shanghai. "They're not big, but they can take a punch, and they are determined and courageous. I hope to come back with a program to train Chinese boxers." When questioned about his ill health's correlation with boxing, he declared, "If I had to do it all over again, I'd do it exactly the same way."

After my father's 1985 trip to China, the sport of boxing steadily recovered. By 1986, boxing regained its validity, with Chinese boxers appearing on the international stage.

Before leaving the country, he delivered a few words of advice. "Now that you are open to the world," he said, "never lose your culture, because others will try to give you theirs. It will be a great fight." Then he waved goodbye and promised to return.

My father reportedly said the most moving experience of his ten-day tour, on his second trip in 1985, was praying with 1,000 fellow Muslims in the great mosque of Xian, which dates back to AD 742, the period of the Tang dynasty.

"I was surprised that so many people still knew me," he said humbly. "To be there with my brothers, people so different and from so far away, was unforgettable."

My father was always a lover of people, nations, and cultures. While he adored his religion, he saw the truth and beauty in all faiths, and treated everyone with respect and kindness. His initial visit to China, in 1979, was a step towards understanding and friendship between our two countries. It wasn't the first or last time my father's name would improve foreign relations or open the lines of communication between nations. When he returned home, President Carter invited Dad to the White House to be briefed on the trip.

"This is the only place I get nervous," said Dad, as he looked around the Oval Office. They talked about some of his past fights—Carter's mother was a fan. They joked, exchanged pleasantries, and discussed his trip, among other things. On his way out, Dad turned to look back over his shoulder at the White House. "I like this place," he said. "Couple of carpets I'd change ..."

That same month, January of 1980, a reporter for the *Los Angeles Times* asked my father about the Ayatollah Khomeini and the hostage crisis in Iran. As always, Dad answered uninhibitedly: "Khomeini has been a spiritual, religious man. This is the worst thing he could let happen. At his age now, which is near death, the worst thing a Muslim can do is mislead his followers ..."

In December of 1979, the Russians invaded Afghanistan. President Carter asked my father to visit five African nations to represent the United States' position on boycotting the 1980 Olympics in Moscow (due to the extreme abuse inflicted upon the citizens of Afghanistan). Ambassador Andrew Young was a confidant to Martin Luther King and was in close personal contact with my father. Young felt Dad was the ideal representative to defend the civil rights and liberties of not only Americans but all people around the world whose basic human rights were being violated.

My father made the trip, unaware that the United States had refused to join twenty-five African countries in boycotting the Montreal Olympics four years earlier over South Africa's place in the sporting world. He later stated that had he known the history he might not have made the trip at all. After learning the truth, my father felt used and embarrassed, reportedly stating, "President Carter put me on the spot. He sent me around the world to take a whoopin' for American politics."

Dad had become something of an emissary for President Carter. He made decisions based on how information was presented to him. Not all of his diplomatic choices were wise, but his intentions were always pure. He did whatever he could to help people in need.

My father was always aware of the responsibilities that came with fame, but after that experience I think he was more cautious and mindful about the invitations he accepted. Where he had once readily agreed to travel to Africa and Israel without a second thought, he found himself having to stop and think about how his presence in certain countries was being viewed and used. On one of my father's recordings, an Israeli reporter calls from overseas, inviting him to visit. Dad took the time to explain why he couldn't freely accept the invitation.

"*Two groups from South Africa invited me over,*" he said. "*When I accepted their invitation, or talked about it publicly, I got calls from all the African nations asking me not to go. They said that the United Nations or the African countries voted for me to stay home. A group of white people wanted to improve the education among blacks and build better schools in black neighborhoods in South Africa. I thought that was a nice gesture for peace and equality.*

"*So I wanted to accept their invitation. But people asked me not to go because they said it would make it look like I was ordaining South Africa's works, and that South Africa wasn't doing what they pretended to. With so many people protesting about South Africa, and me going to South Africa, they could use my presence there to say, 'Muhammad Ali came, so why do you say we are not just to blacks?'*

"*It was a political thing. So many native South Africans wanted to see me—so many of them like me, so I was going mainly to see them—to inspire them and uplift them and make them feel good. Regardless of who invited me, that was in my heart. I'm just sorry that all of these things have to get involved because, to me, humans are humans and people are people.*

"*So what I'm saying to you, my friend, is that I want your invitation, and I will gladly consider coming, but I don't want to come if it's going to stir up all my people against me or cause controversy, or if they make it a political issue. I have many Israeli friends in this country. On Miami Beach, so many of the Jewish people support me—the old ladies—they come to see me train. They like me, and I like them.*

"*Send me your proposal, and I'll have it looked at to be sure the world isn't going to condemn me if I come. Just like Anwar Sadat. He made peace and now all of the Arabs and the Muslims are condemning him because he is tired of seeing his boys killed, he's tired of always being attacked or fighting for whatever the reason is that causes death. So, I can sympathize with Sadat, but the whole Arab world is cut off from him and looks at him as though he is an extension of Israel. I don't want them to look at me like that just because I made a trip, you understand?*"

"*Yes, I do,*" said the reporter.

"So, send me your proposal, and I will have it looked at ..."

After three wars and decades of tension between Israel and the Arab states, on March 27, 1979, the government of Egypt and the government of the state of Israel signed a peace treaty. Egyptian President Anwar Sadat was under extreme pressure from Arab countries not to sign a separate accord. However, after intense negotiations, the agreement was sealed in hopes of assuring peace and security for all surrounding countries, making Sadat the first Arab leader to broker peace with Israel. Dubbed "The Man of the Year" by *Time* magazine in 1977, Sadat was one of the most important and influential Egyptian and Arab figures in modern history. He served as Egypt's third president from October 15, 1970, until his assassination on October 6, 1981, when he was gunned down on the platform of a military parade by Islamic infiltrators in the Egyptian Army. The Peace Treaty of 1979 notably made Egypt the first Arab country to officially recognize Israel.

At the beginning of the call, the same reporter had asked my father, *"Muhammad, what do you think about the peace treaty between Israel and Egypt—do you find it a good one?"*

"I know nothing about the politics of Israel and Egypt," Dad said. *"Although I am a Muslim, I don't understand the problems the two countries have been dealing with over the years. But I know all people are God's people, regardless of race or religion, and I know that God, Allah, is not for war. I know God, Allah, is not for violence, and I know he is for peace. So I think whatever people are involved—whether they are Israelis or Arabs or Puerto Ricans or Chinese ... I think it's nice to see the countries who don't agree religiously on many things— countries who don't agree politically—it's nice to see they can make a bond to stop killing, regardless of what other countries may say.*

"I think that would be nice because I'm sure the Israeli people are saddened when their boys are killed in a war. I'm sure the Egyptian people are hurt when their boys are killed. If they can do anything, they can stop fighting. I can understand why they don't want to keep suffering so much. So I can sympathize with Israel, and I can sympathize with Egypt. I can sympathize with any country, regardless

of their beliefs—whether I agree with them or not. I understand why they are tired of suffering so many casualties. Whatever they can do to help lessen them, I think that is good."

"Very nice . . . Very nice, Champ. I wish you all the best, Muhammad . . ."

"Thank you. May Allah bless you."

During 1979, Dad was involved with the Tehran hostage crisis and other political and humanitarian endeavors, which would occupy most of his time and eventually propel him into a much bigger role as a mediator for world peace. But on December 24, 1979, he was just a father coming home to his children.

20

December 25, 1979

IT WAS CHRISTMAS morning; my parents had just come home from Hong Kong with dozens of colorfully wrapped packages full of toys from around the world. Every morning the sun shone through my window, illuminating all my beautiful dolls, especially the porcelain faces of the ones that my mother never let us play with and my father wouldn't let me take to school for show-and-tell, thinking it would make less fortunate children feel bad.

"Hana ..." he'd say, removing the doll from my arms, "You will find in life that most people get pleasure out of showing off, and knowing they have things that others don't. When we follow the rules of Islam, compassion, and kindness, it teaches we should want for others what we want for ourselves ..."

And with that, the doll was put back on the shelf. I was a little disappointed that day, but it wasn't so terrible; the following week I ended up bringing something much better to school than my exotic porcelain doll.

I know, I thought to myself, I'll bring something fun and exciting that everyone in my class has—but not like mine! So I brought my father to school for show-and-tell.

He hugged and kissed my classmates and performed magic tricks. Then he turned on his tape recorder and interviewed my teacher and classmates, trying to find out what boy I had a crush on.

"Who does Hana like?" he asked.

"Nobody in here," I said. We were in Laila's classroom. Thank God!

"Little girl," he said to one student, *"What's your name?"*

"Cheyenne." She blushed.

"Are you friends with my daughters, Hana and Laila?"

"Yes."

"Tell me, are Hana and Laila good little girls?"

She paused before replying, *"NO."*

"What do they do?"

"Laila hit me." She pouted.

"That's not true!" said Laila in the background. *"She hit me first, then I hit her."*

"Cheyenne, are you bad?" he asked.

She pouted and lowered her head.

"It's okay," he said. *"I'm bad sometimes too, you just can't be bad ALL the time ..."*

***

OUR CHRISTMAS TREE was upstairs in the governess's bedroom. It had originally been downstairs in the foyer just outside of my father's office, but my mother asked my aunt Diane to help her move it. Dad was a devout Muslim, and he respected my mother's wishes, but she knew how often he changed his mind. He could be rather mercurial at times. She knew that if one of my father's Muslim friends said something to him about the Christmas tree in the entrance hall, there was a good chance he'd forget why he had agreed to let us have one in the first place.

"Then he'll just get mad at me," said Mom, as she and Auntie Diane carried the tree upstairs.

My mother was raised Catholic and wanted her children to experience the holiday as she had. My aunt Diane loves telling the story about how a conversation with my father was instrumental in him deciding to let us have a tree.

"Oh Muhammad," she said one day in his den after dinner, "don't you remember how happy you were when you were a little boy opening your presents on Christmas morning? And what it felt like seeing the colorfully wrapped gifts under the Christmas tree?"

"Yeah," he said, wide-eyed.

"That's too bad," she sighed.

"What?" he asked.

"I was just thinking how sad it is that Hana and Laila won't have those wonderful memories that you and Veronica have."

Diane had many talents, but her knack for manipulation was, and still is, exceptionally effective. She knew my father occasionally wrestled

204

with his desire and ideology. He would perform magic tricks for a while, then store them away for months at a time, explaining how it was against Islam to practice trickery. Then, after a time, he'd bring them out again, resolving it would be okay if he showed people how the trick was done. As I said, he was sometimes mercurial.

I think he found a similar reasoning when letting us have a Christmas tree. After all, we were only celebrating the spirit of giving and gratitude.

Then one day I came home from school, walked into my father's office and said: *"Jesus is the son of God."* The next morning Dad checked me out of Page School in Hancock Park and enrolled me in a Muslim academy at the mosque on Vermont, near downtown Los Angeles. Where every day he would bring me my lunch of Pioneer Chicken and a strawberry soda, standing in the doorway with the paper bag in his hand, as I learned about the Prophet Muhammad, the five pillars of the Islamic faith, and why it was important to give to charity and to treat people with love, respect, and kindness.

But on that Christmas morning in 1979 my father was wrapped in his terry bathrobe with both of my grandfathers, Papa Cash and Horace Porche, sitting beside our beautifully decorated tree, watching and recording us opening our gifts.

"There was no way to keep it from you," he explained into the tape recorder. *"We are not Christian, we're Muslim. But you hear about Christmas everywhere so we let you have a tree and open gifts ..."*

Even after he enrolled me in the Muslim academy, every Christmas Dad let Mom buy us a tree. As we jumped with joy watching our mother decorate it and hang stockings from the fireplace in the governess's room, Dad was always careful to explain that we were celebrating the spirit of giving and receiving, which is what Christmas is really about.

Our three bedrooms were adjoining, like a hotel suite, each room flowing into the next. My bedroom had pink walls, two large picture windows overlooking the swimming pool in our backyard and, most importantly, the door opened out onto the hall and a second flight of stairs that led to the third floor. Thank God for that door. Without it, my most treasured childhood memories might not exist.

It provided an escape route for me on the countless mornings I snuck out of bed before school, looking for my father. I usually found him sitting behind his desk, shuffling through papers, or on the sofa watching the news, or sitting in a chair sipping coffee and soaking up the heat from the crackling fire.

A door on the other side of my bedroom led to an adjoining bathroom, which opened into the middle room, where the governess slept. It was a bright room with a fireplace and blueish-green walls, and had a large picture window with a view of the front lawn and the sidewalk of Fremont Place itself. That bedroom had three doors—one led to the bathroom and my room, another led to the hall, and the third to Laila's room, a small cozy space with butter-yellow walls and a large circle balcony overlooking the swimming pool, garden and driveway. Unless she walked through either my bedroom or the governess's room, the balcony was the only way out of Laila's bedroom. This may be why she fantasized about jumping off it.

Just outside, on the opposite end of the hall, was my parents' bedroom. A large, beautiful master suite with its own large circular balcony—the one with the vines—which overlooked the manicured lawn and the two-story carriage house, which my mother's father, Horace Porche, moved into.

Dad made a recording, talking to him about life, women, and why he split up with my grandmother. "*The way Ethel tells it, it was all your fault,*" said Dad, "*but there's another side to the story, isn't there?*"

My favorite part of my mother's room was the huge walk-in closet where she hid all our Christmas presents and birthday gifts. It reminded me of Grace's dressing room in the movie *Annie*. I would often find my mother sitting on the blue brocade loveseat in the middle of the dressing room, her beautiful brown hair flowing backwards as she extended her long graceful legs to pull off her pantyhose.

Every day after school I'd run upstairs and into her room, begging her to let me try on her clothes and wear her fluffy French slippers. She let me play dress-up and wear those nightgowns and dresses, which, looking back now, I imagine she didn't mind us damaging. This must have been the case because anything I put on resulted in stains, rips, and tears. After I slipped into her one-inch heels I flopped around the room, slipping on the tail of the skirt or dress I was wearing.

"Careful, Hana," she'd say as I sashayed across the room, staring at my reflection in the mirror, wondering if I looked as beautiful as my mother. Then I'd throw off the clothes and beg to try on something from the section of the closet I was never allowed to play in. Her silk shirts and pantyhose were also off limits.

"No!" she said, grabbing the pantyhose from my hands. "These are my good pair."

"Please!" I begged.

"No, you might poke a hole in them."

"Then give me your bad pair."

"I don't have a bad pair," she said.

"Can you get a bad pair so I can wear them?"

Naturally, not being allowed to put them on made them more alluring, and I fantasized about how and when I could get my little hands on Mom's stockings without her knowing. I knew I would have to be clever about it. The last time I'd gotten caught in her closet I broke her crystal perfume bottles, and got honey and dough all over her dressing table and lace bra.

Remember how I was obsessed with having boobs and had made a pair from dough that I'd stashed in a drawer in my bedroom? Well, the next morning I'd snuck into my mother's closet and borrowed a bra and pantyhose from the forbidden drawer. Had I known it would end up as it did, with the police and fire department at our house, I would have stayed in bed that morning or at least put on some clothes before sneaking into Mom's closet.

***

THE DAY AFTER Christmas my father received a phone call from Stevie Wonder.

"Stevie! Hello, my brother. It's nice hearing your voice."

"How are you?"

"Oh, I'm just here recuperating from all this holiday action," said Dad. *"Where are you now?"*

"I'm visiting with my children," said Stevie.

"Oh, you have children, how many you got?"

"I've got two. They're four and two."

"Isn't that cute?" said Dad.

"How are you feeling?" asked Stevie.

"I'm glad you called, I'm always glad to hear from you," said Dad. *"You're one of the great black men of our times."*

"You're the ONE," said Stevie.

"I'm just trying to do all I can," said Dad. *"I just left Peking, China ..."*

"Listen," said Stevie, *"I want you to do me a favor. You know I bought radio station KJLH ... We celebrate Christmas and Kwanzaa, so I wanted you to call, if you don't mind, and wish everybody a Happy Kwanzaa."*

"Okay ... I'll call right now. Are they on the air?" Dad asked.

"Yeah, hold on one second, let me call them ..."

"Okay ..."

Dad speaks into the recorder while he waits: *"I'm talking to Stevie Wonder, this is December 26, 1979, in my Los Angeles home. It's about 6:49 p.m., Tim Shanahan is here with me, Hana and Laila are hollering in the kitchen, Veronica's here and my father is in town, Cassius Clay Sr. He got here three days before Christmas and he'll leave three days from now ..."*

"Muhammad," said Stevie, clicking back on the line, *"can I hang up and call you right back? What I want is to set up a conference call."*

"Okay, I'll wait here," said Dad.

The phone rings a few minutes later, and my father and Stevie hold on the line as they wait for the operator to connect them to go on air. *"Stevie,"* said Dad, *"when you get back to LA, I want to hang out with you."*

"I would love to hang out with you too ... I'd love to talk to you. I wanted to tell you something while we're on the phone. I have a special surprise I'd like to give you, as a friend and for what you've

done for black people, and just for all people period. The thing is, what I want to give to you, as an artist, I don't want any kind of commercialism or anything getting in the way because it's very special to me and you are very special to me."

"Thank you, I appreciate that, Stevie. I understand what you're saying."

"Okay, because I don't want you to ever think for any moment that I have been any less than someone that is very fond of you ..."

"I know. I'll never forget some advice you gave me once. You said, 'Champ, please don't fight any more—please retire, Champ.'"

The operator interrupts them: "Hold, please, I'm trying to connect you."

"Stevie, isn't Kwanzaa celebrated in Africa?"

"Yes, I'm going to get you a card or something with all the days of Kwanzaa ... All people could celebrate it if they wanted to."

They chat some more on the recording, but Dad ends up having to call the radio station, as the line is bad, and Stevie wants the people to hear the message from him. When Ted Terry answers and puts him on air, Dad says, "This is Muhammad Ali ... I wanted to wish the people a Happy Kwanzaa and I want everybody to get out and promote it, because Kwanzaa will be the greatest holiday of ALL TIME ..."

21

MY FATHER NEVER did find out who I had a crush on, thank goodness. I'd probably still be recovering from the embarrassment if he had. Joshua was in the third grade and he had a girlfriend named Jennifer. But that didn't stop me from inviting him to my birthday party. I had Kim and Karen Richardson, my oldest childhood friends, help me plan how I'd give Joshua the invitation. Kim was a couple years older than me—in the same grade as Joshua—and she knew Jennifer.

"You should do it at recess," Kim said. "Joshua and Jennifer don't eat together."

Karen and I walked over to the table he was sitting at with his friends. "Hi Joshua," I said, my knees shaking. "I just wanted to give you this—it's an invitation to my birthday party next weekend."

"Cool, thanks." He smiled and put the invitation into his jacket pocket.

"I hope you can come," I said. "There will be ponies and clowns and a magic show and a DJ ..."

"Wow! Can I bring my little brother?"

"Yeah, that's okay."

"Cool!" he said.

Just don't bring Jennifer, I wanted to say, but didn't.

The bell rang. "Okay, hope to see you there," I said and waved goodbye.

Karen and I hurried across the playground to Mrs Brown's class, a huge grin on both our faces. I was so excited about Joshua coming to my birthday party that I decided I wanted a new hair-do—to look pretty for him, the way Mommy got pretty for Daddy.

It was the '80s, the time of Wham!, George Michael, Prince, The Jackson 5, Cyndi Lauper and Madonna. My theme song was "Girls Just Want to Have Fun".

Kim and Karen had just gotten new bangs. Naturally, I had to have them too.

"Mommy, I want bangs! Can you cut them for me? In time for my party on Saturday?"

"I'll take you to Supercuts on Friday after school."

"But I want them now," I said.

"Hana, be patient," she replied, flipping through a stack of mail on the dining-room table. "Friday's only three days from now."

To me, three days felt like three months. I was desperate to see what bangs looked like on me. And as my mother would soon discover, a curious, impatient, and naughty little girl was a recipe for disaster.

The next day after school Connye Richardson, Kim and Karen's mother, picked us up from Page School, on Larchmont, and brought Laila and I back to her house for a play date. Mom was busy shopping for my birthday party. Connye and our governess, Cruella De Vil, were friends of a sort and they'd often sit in the living room talking and laughing about grown-up stuff while Laila, Kim, Karen and I swam in the pool or rode our bikes around the neighborhood. But that day my mother was picking us up from Connye's.

After swimming in the afternoon, I was the first to run up and take a shower. As I stared in the mirror at my curly wet hair, which hung past my shoulders, I had a bright idea—or so I thought. *I'll just see what they look like*, I said to myself. *Then I'll cut the bangs off after and Mom will never know.*

I opened the drawer, pulled out the scissors, and chopped away.

Bangs look good on me, I thought. I played with them for a while, flipping them to either side of my face, and practiced saying "Hi" to Joshua in the mirror: *"Hi Joshua, like my bangs? Hey, Joshua, glad you could make it ..."*

"Haaaaana?" I heard Connye call from downstairs. "Get your things, honey, your mother's here."

"SHIT! Okay, coming ..."

I gathered the bangs in my hand, picked up the scissors, chopped them off and threw them in the trash beside the toilet under a pile of crumpled-up tissue.

"Open up, Hana!" said Laila, banging on the bathroom door. "Mom's here, I have to get dressed."

"One minute!" I shouted.

I put the scissors back in the drawer, unlocked the door, then snuck out the side door that led into the bedroom of Kelly, Kim and Karen's older sister. I peeked out the door, then headed down the hall.

Then I heard talking and footsteps. Kim and Karen were coming up the stairs.

"Oh my god!" said Kim at the sight of me. Karen just burst into laughter.

"Shut up," I said.

"Why do you have a bald spot on the front of your head?" asked Kim.

"Oooh, you're going to be in big trouble," teased Karen, walking off to her room.

I put my hand over the bald spot just above my forehead. "Let me borrow a hat," I said.

Kim went into her room and returned with a white sun-visor cap. It covered the bald spot perfectly.

"Don't tell my mom," I said.

"Tell her ..." Kim laughed. "She's going to see it! You can't sleep in the hat."

"They'll grow back by Saturday," I said, walking downstairs.

"Sure they will." Kim laughed.

When I walked into the kitchen, Mom and Connye were talking. *So far so good*, I thought.

A few minutes later Laila, Kim and Karen came flying down the stairs.

"Hana, why don't you take off the hat?" said Karen.

The way she said it got my mother's attention. "Hana, what did you do?" she asked.

"She cut bangs," blurted Karen.

"Shut up, big mouth!" I said.

"Take it off," Karen said, "show them what you did."

All eyes were on me.

Karen ran back upstairs. Laila and Kim were just staring at me.

I slowly removed the sun-visor.

"Hana!" Mom shouted, half-shocked and half-amused. "Why is there a bald spot on your head?"

"Here they are!" said Karen, running back down the stairs, waving my severed bangs in her hand.

"What in the world were you thinking?" asked Mom.

"I wanted to see what they looked like—I thought I'd cut them off after, so you wouldn't know … I didn't think about the bald spot until afterwards."

Everyone burst into laughter, including me. And the following Saturday at my birthday I wore a floral headband my mother made to help cover the bald spot.

Joshua never noticed.

The following day my parents were off to the Los Angeles Equestrian Center's Riding and Polo Club, for the "Polo for Pandas" benefit. Other than at Dad's training camp in Deer Lake, the Equestrian Center is the only other place I can remember spending quality time together as a family on a regular basis.

Mom and Dad exchanged pleasantries with His Royal Highness Prince Philip. As usual Daddy had a few tricks up his sleeve. During the reception, he entertained everyone with his disappearing scarf magic trick, posed for pictures with the Duke of Edinburgh, and signed autographs on cocktail napkins. The day was all laughter and cheers.

Only one reporter noticed his slow, deliberate hand.

22

AT THREE O'CLOCK in the afternoon, a little girl arrives home from school. She runs upstairs to her room and, from the hand-carved trunk that her parents brought her from Asia, she grabs her white glove and black fedora hat. She rushes back down the steps to her father's office, where she performs Michael Jackson's famous song "Billie Jean" for him and his guests. Her father watches wide-eyed, on the edge of the sofa, as his young daughter bounces around the room, dancing and singing. She hears the sound of his laughter and cheers as she attempts to moonwalk, throws off her black hat, flashes her sparkling white glove, and slides across the floor.

***

ONE OF THE various side effects of my father's fame was that he knew a lot of celebrities, many of whom came to our house on Fremont Place. The status of some of them was unknown to me at the time—John Travolta, Clint Eastwood, Johnny Carson, Sylvester Stallone and Diana Ross—but I'll never forget the man who visited my father in 1984.

Laila and I had arrived home from Kim and Karen's house, where we'd been swimming, and noticed a black Mercedes with tinted windows in front of the house. I knew it belonged to someone important. Mysterious cars with tinted windows were a usual occurrence at Fremont Place. Not that any of my father's cars had tinted windows; Dad liked to drive convertibles and kept the top down most of the time. He didn't like concealing himself from the world. He wanted people to see him up close—to be able to reach out and touch him. He would pull his Rolls out the driveway, past the guard gate and onto Wilshire Blvd, wave, smile, and sign autographs at red lights and stop signs, feeling at home with the crowds of people gathering around him. When driving down Crenshaw Blvd, on his way to the 10 Freeway, if he saw a group of boys shooting dice on the corner he'd pull over and surprise them.

"Awww man," he'd say, jumping out the car. "I'll run all you brothas off this corner with these dice. Give me a quarter, man!"

"MUHAMMAD ALI!" they'd gasp, wide-eyed. "What are you doing over here?" They just couldn't believe the world champion, who they had just seen on television, was out on the street corner shooting dice with them. No press, no announcement, no campaigning. Just him and the people, talking to them about living a clean life and staying off drugs.

"Little things like this don't cost nothing," he'd say. "So, when you become rich and great, remember when you were scuffling out here on the street, remember the people who didn't make it like you, and every so often go and walk down the same block where you used to live, and talk to the people you used to see, and let them know you're still with them. It will make you greater ..."

My father used to say that most of his knowledge came from talking to people on the street, old men, wine-heads and drunks—people who were once scientists and doctors but who lost their way or went crazy and ended up on the corner.

"People don't realize how much gold and wisdom is out in the streets," he once said. "In ghettos or in places where you don't think it is."

He sometimes quoted scripture, telling all who'd listen, "When God comes, He will come as a thief in the night." Meaning we wouldn't recognize him. Then he'd tell the story about the old man he met when he was a teenager: "He had all white hair and a long beard," he'd say. "He was sitting on a street corner holding a wine bottle. I walked past him one day after training. 'Please give me a dollar,' said the man.

"I stopped and I looked at him, and he looked at me. When I handed him the dollar, he looked at me long and hard, then he shook my hand and said, 'I will bless you.'"

He wasn't saying the man was God, but he wondered, "How do you know that isn't God out here walking around to test you, just to see what you will do?"

It wasn't until I was an adult that I could appreciate why my father was always talking to us about drugs and alcohol. Neither of my parents drank. Mom would sometimes have a few sips of wine on Thanksgiving but that was the extent of her drinking. The closest my father ever came to experimenting with drugs was sniffing gas once when he was a teenager.

I think maybe seeing his father coming home drunk and arguing with his mother was enough to turn him off drugs and alcohol entirely. My mother's parents weren't drinkers either, so, aside from my aunts Diane and Michelle sneaking an occasional cigarette, for the most part we were surrounded by clean-living adults.

Laila tried smoking weed and used to sneak the miniature liquor bottles out of Dad's hotel fridge when we were young teens, but I never so much as took a sip of alcohol until I was in my early twenties. It was a glass of wine and I remember thinking it tasted like nail-polish remover; I didn't like the warm, fuzzy feeling in my chest. I've always stayed away from drugs in all forms. I'm not sure if it's in my genes or had something to do with my father's constant lecturing, but I never had any interest in drugs or alcohol. Not even an occasional glass of wine. Even now, when my friends order fruity intoxicating drinks, my order is always the same: "Diet Coke with lemon, please."

Dad always had a way of keeping us spiritually conscious—aware of the little things most people didn't notice. And he taught me early in life to treat all people with equal respect.

"The heart accommodates the heavens and the earth, all the seas and all the land," he said on one of his recordings. "The greatness or smallness of a man does not depend on his outer things. Regardless of a man's title, wealth, rank or position, if his heart is not great then he cannot be great ... But if his heart is great," he continued, "then he remains great under all circumstances. Rich or poor. Great or small."

These were the lessons he taught, the simple wisdom that nature told and etched into his soul. "Always remember, it is only the heart that makes us large or small ..."

I looked at the Mercedes parked in the front of the house and wondered who was visiting Daddy this time, then I waved goodbye to Kim and Karen and walked up the driveway. The week before I'd come home to find Mr T, best known for his role on The A-Team, sitting on the sofa in my father's den. He was wearing his signature gold chains around his neck, with his infamous Mohawk. I recognized him immediately. "What's up, Mr T!" I said, walking into my father's office. "Where's the rest of the A-Team?" I must have driven him crazy asking him to repeat his signature line from the show: "I pity the fool!" Again, and again. He always did.

"I pity the fool!"

As we walked through the front door that afternoon, Laila ran off to find my mother. As usual, I only had one thing on my mind—my father. I raced off to where I knew he'd be waiting to sweep me into his arms. He wasn't in his office, so I ran into the kitchen, where Edith, the cook, was preparing lunch. Turkey sandwiches and lemonade.

"Are you hungry, Hana?"

"No," I said, grabbing a pickle and a popsicle from the refrigerator. "Where is Daddy?"

"Upstairs, resting. Go comb your hair. He has—" Before Edith could finish her sentence, I ran out of the kitchen, straight upstairs into the guest bedroom where Dad usually took his daytime naps—a habit he'd acquired from years of training and fighting.

I pushed open the bedroom door. "Daddy ..." I began, wanting to tell him that I'd swum a width of the pool all by myself. "Daddy, I ..." I stopped dead in my tracks. My father was lying in bed, under a white sheet with one hand behind his head, and sitting in a chair beside him was the unmistakable figure of Michael Jackson. Politicians, actors, even most singers might have been unrecognizable to my young eyes, but the King of Pop? He was one of my favorites, pure and simple. I was never the type to be a fan of anyone, even as a child, but this was two years after *Thriller* and Michael was a megastar. I didn't have any posters of MJ pinned on my wall or a pile of magazines with him on the cover, but I'd been performing his "Billie Jean" act for my father for months and the fact that he was now at my house, sitting in the bedroom with us ... It was enough to send me into a hysterical fit.

Michael was lifting his black fedora hat, showing my father his white bandages. He'd been injured filming a Pepsi commercial when pyrotechnics had set his hair on fire. It was a massive news story. And some believe that the painkillers he was given at that time eventually contributed to his addiction to anesthetics, which ultimately led to his death in 2009.

I stepped out the room for a minute and closed the door. "Michael Jackson!" I screamed. "Michael Jackson!"

Laila came running out of my mother's room. "Where is he?" she asked.

"In there," I pointed. "With Daddy!"

My mother had already told her. She had changed into her pink dress with the white ruffles. I was still in my swimsuit and shorts, my curly hair reaching in all directions, as if I'd just stuck a fork in an electric socket! Michael probably thought I looked like the beast that swallowed Tokyo. And if he didn't already, he would before he left—especially after the question I asked him. But that was still an hour or so away. In this moment, I hadn't marked him with any lasting impression of me. To him, I was still just Muhammad Ali's eight-year-old daughter. A wild little girl excited to find Michael Jackson in her house.

Dad used to visit the Jacksons at their house in Encino. He'd bring his black briefcase and perform magic for them. Sometimes Michael came to the house when we were at school and sat on the sofa in Dad's office, where so many celebrities and politicians who the world admired came to admire him. I think he was their guiding light, the man the celebrities looked up to.

"Hana, do you know who this is?" asked Dad as Laila and I walked back into the room. "This is the most famous singer in the world." I stood there for a second, with my mouth wide open. I knew exactly who I was looking at.

As Michael sat smiling at me, with his hat in his hand, I couldn't stop staring at the white bandages wrapped around the top of his head.

"Hi, Michael Jackson," said Laila.

"Hello."

"What happened to your head?" I asked.

"I had an accident," he said.

"Does it hurt?"

"Not any more," he smiled.

I smiled back, then quickly shut the door and ran around the house, screaming to anyone that would listen that Michael Jackson just smiled at me and was in my daddy's bedroom. Jose, our neighbor's housekeeper's son, didn't believe me. Sara, the teenager who lived up the street that Mom let babysit us sometimes, didn't believe me. Lora and Felisha, the two girls I sometimes played with, didn't believe me. And the man sitting in his red sports car across the street couldn't be convinced either.

I went back in and out of the room again at some point before Michael left. I wanted to call Kim and Karen to tell them who'd been at my house when they'd dropped me off.

"Karen!" I shouted. "Guess who's here?"

"Who?"

"Michael Jackson!"

"Liar!" she said.

"It's true!" I said.

"Hana said Michael Jackson is at her house," Karen said in the background.

"Sure he is," shouted Kim, probably rolling her eyes.

"He's here!" I said again. "Upstairs with Daddy, eating a sandwich ..."

Their loss, I thought to myself.

After the excitement settled I went back upstairs and jumped on my father's bed. I don't remember what they were talking about, but for the next hour or so I lay next to Dad, staring at Michael, wondering what really happened between him and Billie Jean.

The first time Michael came to the house I was too young to remember. My mom had invited him back to Fremont Place as a surprise for my father. Mom casually mentioned years afterwards that while we were still living at Fremont she used to eat at a vegetarian restaurant called the Golden Temple, a quaint little place on 3rd Street, a ten-minute drive from the house. After leaving Jane Fonda's workout studio on Robertson Blvd she would stop there for lunch. Michael Jackson was usually the only other person eating there. Eventually he and Mom sat together—until Michael hired the chef to work for him privately and the restaurant closed. One day my grandmother was there with Mom, trying to sell Michael Avon cosmetics over lunch. I can only imagine the look on my mother's face! Michael was sweet and nice about it, but Mom was embarrassed.

On other visits to Fremont Place, he brought a friend, Emmanuel Lewis, with him. Emmanuel was an actor from the sitcom *Webster* that I watched. Another time Michael brought his pet monkey Bubbles with him. I wish I could go back and relive the moment—tell you exactly what was seen, felt and said. But I was just a little girl. And at the time I had no idea who Michael Jackson was. That all changed, of course, after I saw his ground-breaking video *Thriller*. I closed my eyes on the scary parts—especially when he turns into a werewolf—but I must have watched it a thousand times. I started playing his music every day after school, and came home and practiced my moonwalk for Daddy and his friends.

As I got used to the idea of having Michael Jackson in my house, I started drilling him about his *Thriller* video.

"Michael Jackson," I said, scooting to the edge of the bed, "how did you turn into a werewolf?"

"They used a lot of make-up and masks."

"Did it hurt?"

"No, it didn't hurt."

What I remember most about Michael was his kindness. He was very patient, soft-spoken and moved with a gentle, graceful pace.

When it came time for Michael to leave, I followed him out the back patio door. He and my father paused as they chatted. They were standing in the middle of the driveway where Sheba and Sampson usually lay, sprawled out in front of the steps that led to the swimming pool.

"Michael Jackson, wait!" I shouted after he said his final goodbyes to my father. "I want to ask you something." I had a question that couldn't wait any longer.

He turned to me and smiled softly. "Yes, Hana?" he said.

"Michael," I said, "why do you talk like a girl?"

Laila, gasped. Half-shocked, half-embarrassed.

There was a pause. "Well," he said, looking up at the blue sky, "I guess God made me that way."

Then he turned and walked away.

The next weekend James Anderson, my father's bodyguard, brought his boys over to play with us. When I told them what I had said to Michael, Jamal looked at me wide-eyed.

"You fool," he said. "Now he's never coming back!"

"I just wanted to know why he talks that way," I said, shrugging my shoulders. "I don't care if he doesn't come back," I fibbed. "I like Prince better anyway."

In the 1970s James Anderson went almost everywhere with Dad. He was a very kind man with beautiful eyes and he stayed married to the same woman, Zenobia, his entire life. James had five sons, the oldest of whom was JJ. The twins, Jamillah and Rasheda, had a crush on JJ Anderson and I was no different. And I didn't mind he was seven years older than me. One Christmas he chased me around the tree when we were all having a sleepover at his house and his towel fell off. We had just come from the swimming pool and I had done something to agitate him. I saw everything down south, but no one would believe me. I especially enjoyed telling Rasheda, as she was one of JJ's biggest admirers. Unlike Jamillah, Rasheda was aloof, which I think he liked.

Like Daddy use to say, "What you resist, persists and what you persist, resists." He always loved giving us advice, especially about boys. "It's nature to chase what's running from you and to run from what's chasing you," he clarified.

221

I started going to my father for advice when I was twelve, after he'd given me his version of the birds and bees lecture. It was different from the one my mother had given me when I was seven. Dad was married to Lonnie by then, and they were in Los Angeles on business.

For nearly two decades, starting in 1987, Harlan J. Werner handled marketing and licensing for my father. Dad was in town for one of his sports collector's conventions at the Disneyland Hotel in Anaheim when he first gave me the lecture about respecting my body and keeping it covered.

"Everything that God made valuable is covered and protected ... you should be covered too."

As usual, I stayed behind in the hotel room with my father as Laila and Lonnie went shopping for shoes. I didn't like the idea of him being alone. He didn't mind it—he was at peace with himself and enjoyed reading, writing and signing Islamic pamphlets, hoping to spread the message and clarify misunderstandings about his faith. I sat beside him putting all the signed ones in a neat pile and handing him the blank ones.

"People will save this and read it," he said. "Because my signature is on it."

We ordered room service, apple pie and two scoops of vanilla ice cream, and watched TV. Dad asked me if there were any boys I liked at school. I told him yes. We talked and joked about it for a while, then he looked at me seriously.

"Hana, I can tell you this now because you're getting older," he said. "You're pretty and shaped nice, so a lot of boys are going to like you. And they'll brag about it because you're my daughter." He shifted in his seat. "The worst thing you can ever do is get on your knees like a dog and suck some boy's dick. That's the worst thing you can do."

My eyes popped out of their sockets. Dad was always blunt and talked about things most parents avoided, especially fathers. But he caught me off guard that day. We both burst into laughter.

"But seriously ..." he said. "Always respect yourself and your body."

It was some of the best advice he ever gave me. And I took it.

My friends were always whispering around me. I would walk into the homeroom and hear them exchanging stories about what they did in the closet with boys while playing spin the bottle over the weekend. Or how they snuck into their parents' liquor cabinet or smoked weed at the party they'd been to. I guess they thought I was a goodie-two-shoes—or worse, that I'd judge them.

My first kiss came at eighteen and I lost my virginity to the same boy—my boyfriend—two years later, one week before my twentieth birthday. And I told my parents all about it. Laila was shy and kept her personal business to herself. But I was an open book. I went straight home and told my mother, then I called Dad the next morning. Mom ran through the house covering her ears. But Dad was always eager to listen and bestow his valuable advice, and I cherished every conversation.

"Daddy, I did something last night."

"What did you do?" he asked.

"I touched his private parts, but I didn't put my mouth on it," I assured him.

"That's not so bad," he said.

Okay, so I chickened out. I didn't tell him I'd had sex. He figured it out before I could. A few months later I walked into his hotel room and Dad looked at Lonnie and said, "She's screwing!"

"How did you know?" I asked, stopping in my tracks.

Daddy always had a sixth sense. I think he was a little psychic. Sometimes he'd say that a plane was going to crash, and the next day a plane crashed. Once we were at the stop light on the corner of Wilshire and Fairfax in Los Angeles where the rapper Biggie Smalls was gunned down. My father knows nothing about rap or the tragic incident. At the time, it had been almost a decade since it had happened. Even if he had known, he wouldn't have remembered the details or where it had happened. As we sat waiting for the light to change Dad asked, "Have you ever heard of someone called Biggie Smalls?"

"Daddy, he was a rapper—he was killed on this corner ten years ago."

Eyes wide, he said nothing.

"Did you know who he was?" I asked him.

"No."

"How did you know his name?"

"I don't know," he said. "It just came to me."

Things like that happened all the time. Then there was the matter of his fights. He used to predict the round his opponent would fall in. Mainly to sell tickets and entertain people, but twenty-six of his predictions—the rounds he said he'd KO his opponent in—came true. He only stopped because people were approaching him in the streets telling him how they bet their houses and cars on what he'd said, how they'd lose everything if he was wrong.

My father never believed he was psychic. He just didn't put much faith or energy into such things. But I always believed he had a gift.

***

SWIMMING WAS SOMETHING we did a lot of in the summers. It was especially fun when my siblings were visiting. When we got together with Howard Bingham's sons, Dustin and Damon, and the Anderson boys, it was heaven on earth. JJ would put me on his shoulders and jump to the bottom of the pool in the deep end and stay down there for five seconds.

After JJ came Jamal, Jaleel, Jabriel, and then Jazen, the youngest. Jamal went on to play for the Atlanta Falcons, among other teams, and is known for creating the Dirty Bird celebratory touchdown dance, which he did for the first time during the 1998 Super Bowl.

The Anderson boys had three sisters, Kenia, Keisha, and Little Zenobia. When I visited, I would make Kenia nervous by going outside to the ice-cream truck, chatting to people sitting in their cars. "Hi," I'd said, licking my dripping popsicle. "My name is Hana ... My father is Muhammad Ali."

"Hana, don't do that!" shouted Kenia. "You might get kidnapped or something!"

Everyone was afraid I'd get kidnapped—including my father. I'm not sure where the fear came from, but it was a constant concern throughout my childhood.

"Don't worry, Muhammad," Cruella reminded him time and again. "If anyone took this child, they'd bring her right back!"

I never did see Michael Jackson at the house again after that visit. I often wondered if Jamal was right—if it was because of the question I had asked him. But it may have been because the divorce was imminent and we were leaving Fremont the following year.

My father often spoke to Michael and his brothers over the telephone, but at that time I was too young to know who they were. I was three years old and sitting in his lap dripping my popsicle all over him as Dad's ever-rolling tape recorder captured one of their conversations, on December 8, 1979:

"Hey Marlon," said my father. "Do your kids like popsicles?"

"Yeah, they love them."

"Mine too!" he said. "I don't know what it is about them. My little girl, Hana, is only three years old and she's always asking for a popsicle ..."

"So does my little girl," he said.

Marlon had called my father to see if Dad would introduce them on stage. They were performing at The Forum in Los Angeles.

"I wish I could," he said, "but I'll be in Hong Kong ..."

A few days later Marlon called back to see if anyone in the family wanted tickets to the show.

"Marlon Jackson of the Jackson 5!"

"Did I wake you?"

"No ... you all aren't the Jackson 5 any more, are you?"

"No, we had to change our name when we left Motown because they claimed they owned it. Now we're just the Jacksons."

"Who are you with now?"

"We're with CBS—Epic Records."

"I thought y'all were with Kenny Gamble."

"We used to be with Kenny Gamble, we were with CBS and they wanted us to record with him, but we're doing our own stuff, we're writing and producing our own songs. The Temptations just rejoined and signed with Kenny Gamble."

"They're not doing anything much now, are they?" Dad asked.

"Yeah, they're getting ready to come back out—the original Temptations ..."

"Hold on ... Put those back, Laila," he said in the background. "My two daughters are in here cuttin' up, tearing up and drawing. Talkin' about 'Daddy, I want to write,' then they take my pen and scribble on paper."

"That's sweet," said Marlon.

"I take all that stuff and mark the date on it. When they get older, I'm going to show it to them. It's valuable."

"Yeah, we save our little girl's drawings too. She goes to nursery school ..."

"Yeah, keep all that stuff ... So, what's up, Boss?"

"We just wanted to know if anyone in your family needed tickets to the show."

"Yeah, when is the show?"

"December 18th, which is next Tuesday, at The Forum."

"Hold on—let me see where I'll be ..." He reached for his date book.

"No," said Marlon, "you'll be in Hong Kong, I wanted to know if your in-laws wanted tickets."

"Yeah, man, I'd like to get five of them—my sisters and brothers-in-law would love to go to the show. Can you mail them to me?"

"Yeah, no problem, I'll mail them. I have your address ... You live on 55 Fremont?"

"Yeah man, the zip code is 90005."

"Okay, I'll get you five tickets. My wife Carol wants to know if Veronica is going to Hong Kong with you?"

"Yeah, she's going ... Well, I sure am thankful you're calling me and are going to give me those tickets. I'm so honored I'm going to give them to my sisters and brothers-in-law, they'll want to go see you."

"Okay, I'll get this right out to you."

"We've got to hang out one day, you hear?"

"Okay, we will."

"Okay, take care," said Marlon. "I love you."

"I got your phone number, I'll call you as soon as I get free," said Dad. "Thank you, brother."

Dad hung up the phone and spoke into the recorder: *"That was Marlon Jackson of the Jackson 5; they left Motown, so they're now called the Jacksons. This is December 8, 1979. I'm downstairs with Hana and Laila ... What's Laila doing, Hana?"*

"She's messing with your papers ..."

***

LIKE I SAID, there were always celebrities visiting Fremont Place. Actors, athletes, rock stars, politicians—even royalty. And they all wanted my father's time and attention. They enjoyed being at home with Muhammad Ali. One afternoon Dad's friend Tim Shanahan carried me into his office after taking me out for ice cream. "Tim Shanahan! My Main Man!" Dad greeted exuberantly as always. He did that often, shouted Tim's first and last name whenever he walked into the room or called on the telephone, especially when he was with people Tim didn't know. I guess it was to make him feel good and to announce he was a friend. Tim loved to tell the story about what happened that afternoon.

"To my surprise your father was sitting behind his desk talking with Don Henley and Glen Frey, the lead members of the Eagles singing group," said Tim.

Of course, at the time I had no idea who they were. I ran right past them and jumped into my father's arms to kiss him. Then I jumped back down and ran out the room to find Laila.

"Tim Shanahan!" Dad repeated. "Do you know who these guys are?" He knew that he did because Tim played the Eagles in Dad's Rolls all the time. Ron Levin, a friend of my parents, had brought them over to the house.

"Wow! Don Henley and Glen Frey!" said Tim. "My all-time favorite singers. It's great to meet you guys. Has Muhammad talked you out of taking drugs yet?"

Dad cracked up laughing. He thought Tim was joking. When he realized he was serious, he turned to Don and Glen, who looked as though they had just seen a ghost.

"Are you two really into drugs?" asked Dad.

At a loss for words, they remained silent.

"That's bad stuff, man ..." he said. Then he talked to them for a while about why drugs were bad for them and ended with saying, "Why do you need drugs? You should be high on life. You're singing to thousands of fans all over the world [they were getting ready to tour South America], all the girls are screaming and fainting for you ... Maaaaan, you don't need no drugs."

When he was finished, Glen Frey looked at Don Henley and said, "I don't know about you, but I want to quit usin' right now!"

Trying to lighten the conversation with a joke, Dad pointed at Tim. "He looks white, doesn't he?"

"Yeah, he does," said Don, looking Tim over.

"He's my cousin," said Dad. "He's been passin' for years—look at him closer ..."

Tim Shanahan met my father in the spring of 1976, before the third Ken Norton fight. One warm April night in Chicago, Tim peered through the window at 4944 Woodlawn Avenue and saw Dad standing on top of the red stairs that greeted you as you entered the front door.

"He was wearing his gray and maroon Egyptian cotton bathrobe," said Tim one night over dinner. He and his wife, Helga, became friends of my parents and spent a lot of time with us at the Woodlawn house in Chicago, sprawled out on the white carpet in the living room in front of the fireplace, and eventually at the house on Fremont Place. After my parents' divorce we saw less of Tim and Helga, but they always kept in touch, with regular phone calls, emails, and occasional dinners when Tim was passing through town on business. Tim is old enough to be my dad but we always had one thing in common, our love for my father, and he always had stories to share. But until that night in 2010, over dinner, I hadn't heard the story of their first meeting.

Tim had gotten my father's address somehow and, like so many fans before him, had heard stories about people from around the world who had bumped into my father on the street and were invited home with him. Tales of admirers who walked right up to

Muhammad Ali's doorstep and he invited them in, signed autographs and performed magic tricks. So, on that fateful evening in April of 1976, four months before I was born, Tim decided to walk up and knock on my father's door.

"As I stood there waiting for him to open the door, I thought, 'Oh, Lord, what do I call him?'" said Tim, "Mr Ali? Muhammad? Champ?"

When the door opened, he froze, but eventually got the words out. "Hello, Mr Ali, my name is Tim Shanahan ..."

"Come on in ..."

"I sat next to him on the stairs," said Tim. "*Wow*, I thought. *Muhammad Ali asked me to sit next to him in his home.* He made me feel like the luckiest person in the world."

As they talked about upcoming fights and his movie, *The Greatest*, Dad reached over on the telephone table and picked up his black book filled with celebrity names and phone numbers. He opened it and said, "Do you know him?" *Leonard Bernstein.* "Do you know him?" *Johnny Carson.* "Him?" *Bill Cosby.* "How about him?" *Paul Newman.* "Let's call her ..." *Diana Ross.* He dialed the number, the maid answered, so he left a message. "Let's try this one." *Tony Orlando.*

He answers.

"Tony, I have a friend here that I want you to talk to, he is a big fan of yours."

"Hi Tony, I just met Muhammad a few minutes ago and here I am on the phone with you."

"So, Tim," said Tony. "You, too, are now one of those special people who are one of Muhammad's 10,999 closest friends, as am I!"

"It was unbelievable, Hana," said Tim. "One of the most memorable moments in my life."

I knew exactly how Tim felt. My life is full of unforgettable moments and stories. My father made his mark on so many people's lives. I often wonder about all the stories I have never heard.

"You should write a book one day," I said.

"Maybe I will." Tim smiled.

A few years later he wrote *Running with the Champ: My Forty-Year Friendship with Muhammad Ali.*

Dad loved pulling out his phone book and calling his famous friends to amuse people. But there were times when he and my mother were hanging out at home when he'd pick up the phone just to call and say hello.

"Hello, may I speak to Mr Newman?"

"He isn't home right now. May I ask who's calling?"

"Tell him, MUHAMMAD ALI called!"

"Hello Muhammad, this is his wife, Joanne ..."

Paul Newman's wife, Joanne Woodward, was also a famous actress but had chosen to keep her maiden name. Not realizing this, Dad replied, *"Joanne Newman—nice to meet you."*

One of my favorite celebrity stories involving my father was one he liked to tell about the night he spent with Elvis Presley. On February 14, 1973, Elvis Presley presented my father with a white jeweled robe. On the back, rhinestones and jewels spelled out "The People's Choice". It was meant to say "The People's Champion", but Dad didn't mind. He loved the robe and was grateful Elvis had taken the time, that he cared enough to have it made. On March 31, 1974, when he fought Ken Norton, my father entered the ring proudly wearing the robe.

"A few years ago, Elvis came to my training camp in Pennsylvania," Dad told reporters. *"Nobody knew about it. I said, 'Elvis, please do me a favor. I got a guitar. Come with me down to Pottsville, a little town nearby, to this redneck place called Spoonies.' I called the owner, told him to let us come in the back door. It was Saturday night, dancing inside. Elvis went up to the mike with a towel over his face, then I snatched off the towel and he started singing 'Hound Dog'. Then we jumped off the stage and flew out the back door again.*

"Can you imagine being in that little one-horse town and Elvis Presley runs on stage?" he asked the reporters. *"Man, people ran all outta the place, looking, getting in cars, trying to find us. Elvis said, 'Champ, I've never done that before in my life.'"*

I think my father was joking. But you could never tell with Dad. People were always doing things for him that they wouldn't normally do.

When he was filming *Freedom Road,* he asked Kris Kristofferson to play the part of Abner Lait, which he did as a favor to my father. And Dad once had John Travolta dancing in the streets of Mississippi with random people, in hotel lobbies and taverns around town. I don't know about Elvis, but Dad did that sort of thing all the time—and his friends readily indulged his whims. He liked to shock and amaze, turn up in places and on street corners where they'd never expect to see Muhammad Ali. If he had told the reporter that he and Elvis walked off the stage and signed autographs, I would not have questioned it. But there's no way Dad would have run out the back door without talking to the people.

My father loved his fans so much that when there weren't any people around he went looking for them. *"Let's go outside and stand on the corner, see how long it takes for people to recognize me."* He said this one day when we were sitting in his hotel room in New York City.

"Okay." I grabbed a handful of his pre-signed autographs, then we walked out his hotel through the revolving doors onto 5th Avenue.

"What up, Ali!" said one man.

"Look! It's 'The Greatest'!" said another.

In less than a minute, people had gathered around him, like moths to a flame. As always, Dad stood patiently handing out his autographs, performing magic tricks, and taking photographs for as long as his health would permit. He could still walk on his own back then and seemed to have bursts of stored energy he probably conserved for moments like those.

"I'm the King of New York!" he had said as our private jet landed at JFK International Airport. It was my first trip to New York City. I was seventeen at the time. "They love me here."

"They love you everywhere, Daddy," I said. "But I thought you were the king of the world," I teased.

"I had to start somewhere," he shot back, with a wink.

A couple of hours later, a police officer on horseback was escorting us out of the crowd. They were all chanting my father's name as we made our way back to the hotel. Daddy's eyes lit up, and he raised his fist, giving them the old victory sign. He was always most alive in moments like those. When we were back in the hotel room, a look of serenity washed over his face as he sat back in his chair. "We did a good deed today, Hana," he said. "You helped me make all of those people happy. God will bless you."

While most celebrities spent their time finding ways to escape their fans, Dad went searching for his.

"When your father and I were guests of the ruler of Bangladesh, President Rahman," my mother once told me, "he hosted an elaborate dinner in our honor. Halfway through the banquet, your father disappeared. Do you know where we found him? In the kitchen, performing magic tricks for the staff. People tell stories about legends and superheroes all the time," she said. "But your father was real."

I often wondered about the stories Dad told about Elvis. I asked three of his friends about it once. Tim, who was acquainted with Elvis Presley's best friend, Jerry Schilling, Howard Bingham, and Gene Kilroy. All of them had spent a considerable amount of time with my father at his training camp in Deer Lake, especially Howard and Gene. If Dad took Elvis out for a night on the town, surely one of them would have known of it, I thought.

"No, that wasn't true," said Howard. "He probably made that up."

"No, that never happened," said Gene.

"I don't think so," said Tim. "But who knows."

Elvis called my father at the farm in Michigan a couple months before he died, to congratulate him on his recent marriage to my mother. Dad missed the call. He and Mom were on their honeymoon in Hawaii.

"Tell him he married a real beauty this time," said Elvis.

"I'll give him the message," said Lana Shabazz, Dad's fight cook. "He'll be home in a couple of days."

Howard Bingham and his camera went almost everywhere with my father. He captured unforgettable images over the years. He even took the only pictures of my father and Elvis together. But no one I asked seemed to think there was any truth to Dad's story, so I wrote it off as an amusing tale and forgot about it.

Years later, I was up late surfing the internet for old photos of my father when I came across a statement he once made to the press.

"Elvis was my friend," he said, after hearing of his passing on August 16, 1977. "He came to my camp in Deer Lake about two years before he died. He said he didn't want anybody to bother us. He wanted peace and quiet, so I gave him one of the cabins in my camp. When the cameras started rolling, watching me train, he was up on the hill sleeping in the cabin, and nobody even knew it. I don't admire anyone, but Elvis Presley was the sweetest, most humble and nicest man you would ever want to know."

I guess some things will always be a mystery.

***

BUNDINI BROWN, WHO was portrayed by Jamie Foxx in the movie *Ali*, was my father's friend and corner man. He coined the phrase that would become permanent in Dad's repertoire, *Float like a butterfly, sting like a bee*. Bundini once said my father had seven people inside of him, but only three were around all the time: the fighter, the prophet, and the little boy.

My dad was a constant performer. The ever-present child within him loved to entertain and make people smile. Of all the titles he has acquired over the course of his life, the People's Champion was his favorite. And it suited him.

As long as I can remember, people have told me stories about how my father changed their lives—they found the courage to face their fears, stand by their convictions, follow their dreams, or simply love themselves; he made them feel like they could do anything, and convinced them that they were the greatest too.

234

23

IN JULY OF 1979, the renowned film critic Roger Ebert spent a day interviewing my father. By the end of their time together, he would have a unique story to tell. And, because my father let the outside world in, Mr Ebert's article would transport me back in time, allowing me to relive the moments I was once too young to remember.

On a Tuesday afternoon, Roger Ebert was standing in the entrance of Fremont Place admiring the mahogany paneling, the stained-glass window in the stairway, and the Turkish rug on which he was standing, when an insect started buzzing near his ear. He slapped it away but missed. Then it started buzzing at his other ear. He struck at the air, but nothing seemed to be there. My father was smiling to himself, pretending to be looking down the hall. When Roger turned his back, the insect attacked again. Dad grinned mischievously as Mr Ebert turned in circles, slapping at his hair.

Killer Bees was Dad's signature prank. Kings and presidents all over the world had experienced the buzzing. After Dad had his fun, he always explained.

"Make sure your hand is dry. Then rub your thumb hard across the side of your index finger, like this, see ..." Dad showed Roger, making a vibrating noise. "Then hold it behind somebody's ear, sneak up on 'em, and they'll think it's killer bees. I catch people all the time ..." He smiled. "It never fails."

A black limousine pulled up in the driveway. Dad was on his way to the NBC studios to film *The Tonight Show* with Diana Ross. It was her first night as guest host. After the taping, he was taking Mom and me to the movies—a private screening of *Rocky II*. Throughout the film, my father would play movie critic with Roger Ebert.

"*Rocky Part II*," he said, "starring Apollo Creed as Muhammad Ali."

The taping with Diana Ross went smoothly. Dad joked with her about her age, leaned over to read her notes, talked about his official retirement benefit, and asked her to sing at the party. Then he was back in another limousine, a blue and beige Rolls-Royce, heading home. My father sat in the front seat, next to the driver, with his window down. His face positioned in the frame, waiting. The entire seven-mile drive, not a single person failed to recognize him. People shouted his name as the Rolls passed, his fist clenched in a victory sign.

As Roger witnessed that day, riding down the road with my father was no ordinary venture—it was a hero's parade.

When we were setting off for the private screening, five cars pulled out of the driveway like a presidential procession. Dad, Mom, and I were second in line. We were en route to the United Artists headquarters on the old MGM lot. As Mr Ebert noted, all five cars' emergency flashers were blinking the entire way: it was the day's second parade.

When we arrived, a crowd of young kids was waiting for Dad in the parking lot. He shook their hands, spoke to them briefly, then we were inside a private screening room about to watch the most popular movie of the summer—the sequel to *Rocky*, which had won the Academy Award for Best Picture two years earlier, making Sylvester Stallone a household name.

Dad liked the original movie and was eager to see *Rocky II*, I'm sure. He settled down in the back row, with Mom and me on his right, and Roger Ebert on his left. If my father was reflecting on his career as the film began, he didn't say so. And he made no mention to Roger that he was thinking of coming out of retirement to fight Larry Holmes. Dad knew how to keep a secret. Especially his own.

My father watched the opening scenes in silence. He didn't speak until the moment when Apollo Creed, the heavyweight champion, delivers a televised challenge designed to lure Rocky back into the ring. And with that, his commentary began.

"That's me, all right," Dad said softly. "Apollo sounds just like me—insulting his opponent in the press to psych him out. That's me exactly."

Back at Rocky's new house, the doorbell rang.

"You know who that's gotta be," said Dad. "That's gotta be his trainer."

Rocky opened the door to find his old trainer, Mickey, standing on the doorstep.

"That's how Angelo Dundee used to get me," Dad remembered. "A good trainer knows a good fighter can't stand to have people talk about him badly on TV."

Now Mickey was giving Rocky advice: "We've got to get you fighting with your other hand. Use your right, save your left, protect that bad eye ..."

"Maybe it could be possible," said Dad. "If you started on a kid early ... he might be able to change the hand he leads with, but it doesn't happen overnight."

Now Mickey was making Rocky chase chickens to improve his footwork. "That one goes back to the days of Jack Johnson and Joe Louis—chasing chickens," said my father. "You don't see chickens at training camps any more—except on the table."

Mickey was shouting fiercely at Rocky, "JAB! JAB! JAB!" as he pounded the heavy bag.

"You don't have to tell a great fighter to jab," said Dad. "He goes at the bag like a robot. I never had anybody telling me to jab. If you don't want to jab, what are you doing being a fighter?"

There was a wider shot of the gym, with Rocky in the foreground. A dozen fighters were working out, jumping rope, and sparring in the background. "What you see here, if you know how to look for it," he explained, "is the difference between real fighters and actors. A real boxer can see Stallone isn't a professional; he doesn't have the moves. It's good acting, but it's not boxing. Look in the background—at that guy in the red trunks. He's a real fighter."

Now Rocky was in the ring with a sparring partner. "The other guy's a real fighter," he said, again. "Stallone doesn't have the moves, but it's perfect acting. The average layman couldn't see what I see.

And the way they're painting the trainer is all wrong. Look at him, screaming 'do this' and 'do that'! No one told me what to do—I just did it. Shouting at the fighter that way makes him look like an animal—like a horse to be trained."

"Is the character of Rocky inspired by you?" asked Mr Ebert.

"No way," said Dad. "Rocky acts nothing like me. Apollo Creed, the way he dances and jabs, the way he talks—that's me."

And he was right. Stallone would later reveal that he wrote Apollo Creed's character based on my father.

On the screen, a moment of crisis unfolded in Rocky Balboa's personal life. After giving birth to their son, his wife had slipped into a coma. Rocky had just left her bedside and was praying in the hospital chapel.

"Now he doesn't feel like fighting because his wife is sick," said Dad. "The same thing happened to me when I was in training camp—during one of my divorces. It's hard to keep your mind on fighting when you're thinking about a woman. You can't keep your concentration."

He must have been referring to his divorce from Belinda. Mom was pregnant with me before it was final. Towards the end of her pregnancy, she had a complication. At the hospital, the doctors had to deliver me by C-section. After I was born, Dad flew to Show Low, Arizona, and Mom stayed in Michigan at the farm to recover. My grandmother, being a registered nurse and mother of six, taught my mother how to care for me. The following week, Mom and I flew to Show Low. And a few days later he made the tape of him singing to my mother.

"You feel like sleeping all the time," he continued. "I'm going to make a prediction. Rocky's wife is going to get better, then he's gonna beat the hell out of Apollo Creed."

Back in the hospital room, Rocky's wife opens her eyes. Dad nodded. "My first prediction is proven right," he said.

Then Rocky's wife turned to Stallone and said, "There's one thing I want you to do for me. Win."

"Yeah!" said Dad. "Beat that Nigga's ass!"

The nurse walks into the room with Little Rocky Jr. The baby had a head full of thick black hair. "They got a baby in line to win the Academy Award," Dad laughed. "Look at that Italian hair!" he said. "Rocky couldn't deny the baby in court—in real life!"

In an inspirational montage, Rocky threw himself into his training regime with renewed fury. "That's right," said Dad. "He's happy now that he's got his woman back. Now, I'm gonna further predict that, in the big fight, they'll make it look like Rocky's losing. His eye will get cut, and he'll look the worst before he wins. And after the movie the men will be crying louder than the women."

Now Rocky was weightlifting: "That's the worst thing a boxer can do," said Dad. "It tightens the muscles. A fighter doesn't lift weights, but it looks good in the movie."

In an inspirational scene, Rocky was running through the streets of Philadelphia, as a crowd of cheering children followed him up the steps of the Philadelphia Museum of Art.

"Now that's something people will think is artificial—all the crowds running after him—but that's real," said Dad. "I had the same kind of crowds follow me in the streets of New York."

It was now time for the climactic fight scene—more grueling and violent than in the original *Rocky*. In his dressing room, Apollo Creed is jabbing at his image in a mirror.

"The way he's fighting in the mirror, those aren't real fighting moves," said Dad, "but for the movie, they look good. And the motivation here is right. Apollo won the first fight, but some people thought Rocky should have won it. If you lose a big fight, it will worry you all of your life, plague you until you get your revenge. As the champion, almost beaten by a club fighter, Apollo has to have his revenge."

I was asleep in my father's arms as Rocky Balboa was on his knees praying in the locker room. Dad was absorbed in the scene. When Rocky stood up, Dad told Roger, "The scariest time in a fighter's life is the moment before the fight—in your dressing room. All the training is behind you. All the advice in the world doesn't mean a thing. In a moment, you'll be in the ring. Everything is on the line, and you're scared."

Now Apollo Creed and Rocky Balboa came dancing down the aisles of the Philadelphia Spectrum, Apollo taunting Rocky: "You're going down! I'll destroy you! I am the Master of Disaster."

"Those first two lines should have been my lines," Dad mused. "That 'Master of Disaster' ... I like that. I wish I'd thought of that."

On the screen, the big fight was in progress. Between rounds, in the fighters' corners, their trainers are pumping out instructions.

"Angelo doesn't tell me nothing between rounds," said Dad. "I don't allow him to. I fight the fight. All I want to know is if I won the round. It's too late for advice."

"How long do you predict the fight will last?" asked Roger.

"Hard to say. Foreman, they stopped in eight. Liston, they finished in eight ... The movie might take something from that. I can't predict. But look at that ..." Dad pointed at the screen. "Apollo is using my rope-a-dope defense."

In the tenth round, Dad leaned in: "Here's where the great fighters get their second wind," he said. "Where determination steps in." On the screen, Rocky was taking a beating, and his eyes, as Dad had predicted, were severely swollen. "In a real fight," he said, "they would never allow the eyes to close like that and let the fighter continue. They would stop it."

But in *Rocky II* they didn't stop it. The fight would go the distance. And my father continued his commentary, explaining how in real life no fighter could absorb as much punishment as Apollo and Rocky had. A minute later the theater filled with the *Rocky* theme. When the lights came on, my father's entourage was applauding the movie. Dad stood carefully, so as not to wake me, and handed me to my mother.

"That was a great movie," he said. "It will be a hit. It has all the ingredients: love, violence, emotion—the excitement never dulled ..."

***

THREE YEARS LATER, in 1982, our house and its furnishings were used in multiple scenes in *Rocky III*. Sylvester Stallone was sitting on the bench in the Southern Room in one of the scenes. Mom and

Dad's bedroom and the back patio that I used to wait for my father on was also featured in the film. They even captured our courtyard furniture and my parents' lace bedspread and blue moire headboard.

They say life imitates art. But sometimes it's the other way around. While there may not have been an intentional connection between Stallone's character, Rocky Balboa, and my father, ironically in *Rocky III* he loses his championship title, just like my dad did in 1980. And Rocky and his family had to move out of the beautiful mansion, just as we would four years later.

But at that moment, while everyone sat there applauding the film, the house on Fremont Place was still home. The phone in Dad's office was ringing off the hook with endorsement offers and greetings from friends. And Sylvester Stallone's next movie, *Rocky III*, along with my father's last two fights, had yet to be seen.

242

24

WHENEVER I ASKED my father which fight meant the most to him, he always said the Rumble in the Jungle. "Nobody believed I could do it. They thought Foreman was too strong—too big. 'He's got youth on his side,' they said." George Foreman had beaten two of my father's toughest opponents, Joe Frazier and Ken Norton, fighters to whom my father had lost one out of three bouts each.

"I didn't know how," said Dad, "but somehow I just knew in my heart that, with God's help, I could do it. I had to."

I think the secret to my father's success was how he always believed it was never him but God working through him—and the fight was always for something bigger than himself.

"If I had walked into that ring only for myself, yeah, then he would have seemed scary, he might have got me. But when I thought of all the good winning the title could do, when I thought of all the people I could help ... George seemed small by comparison."

As Foreman fell to the ground in an eighth-round knockout, the crowd burst into a thunderous roar—as did the heavens. Rain poured from the sky, drenching the people of Kinshasa as they danced in the street. He had done it; Dad had achieved the impossible. That night he'd regained his world championship ten years after he'd first won it in 1964—showing himself and the world how great he really was.

"My God, he has done it!" the commentator shouted over the radio, as Foreman fell to the canvas. "The great man has done it!

Muhammad Ali has regained his heavyweight title at the age of thirty-three! He must be The Greatest!"

The moment my father stepped onto African soil, he felt a kinship with the people there. After the fight, he saw a group of kids playing barefoot near the Congo river. He told them they had a dignity in their poverty that American blacks had lost. He told them he would use his title for good, that he would use it to bring awareness of their country, and that he would never do anything to disgrace them.

And he didn't.

Five years later, on December 3, 1979, Dad picked up the phone and called George Foreman at home in Houston, Texas.

"George Foreman!"

"Praise God, man! It's a miracle," said George.

"How you doin', George?"

"I'm doin' just fine, man. I'm just thinking about you every day ... just sitting down here, working for the Lord ..."

The fated encounter that inspired this phone call and friendship is a story in itself. Dad, Howard Bingham and my mother were driving down a road in Houston when they suddenly spotted George Foreman. Following his devastating defeat by my father, George fell into a deep depression, eventually leaving boxing and emerging with a new-found purpose. Foreman was a changed man. Realizing the true meaning of his life, George sold everything he owned and embarked on a spiritual path.

"It was unbelievable," said my mother. "Like something out of a movie. He was just standing there on top of a wooden crate in the middle of a vacant dirt lot, preaching to a small crowd of people."

My father had heard rumors about George after losing the title to him in Africa. Shortly after that fight, George retired from boxing. My father was shocked to hear that George sold all of his material possessions, his houses and his cars, and devoted himself entirely to preaching the word of God. His sacrifices were so extreme that it caught my father's attention. The details were different but, until then, Dad thought he himself was the only person to take such a noble stand—walking away from worldly riches in the name of his principles and faith. Now he heard George had done the same. The fact that he belonged to a different faith intrigued Dad further. He wanted to know what had happened to him.

That night in Texas my father couldn't believe his eyes; he was mesmerized at the sight of George Foreman, former heavyweight champion of the world, a man who was once invincible, now standing humble in the street, in the middle of nowhere, with an open Bible in his hand. Naturally, Dad wanted to know more about what motivated George to such an extreme. He parked the car and eagerly walked across the street. After a brief discussion, photographs were taken. Telephone numbers were exchanged. Then Dad got back into his car and promised George he'd call.

"Hey, George," said Dad. "Have you ever thought about getting some type of building—somewhere you can get a lot of people in one place and not on the street—where they can hear you good?"

"Well, see, this Gospel here is, 'Preach to the poor people.' And the way you find them is where you and I used to be when we were little kids, just hanging around the streets."

"Right."

"Jesus said, 'Go to the highways and to the hedges.' But right now I've been in a place ... It's just a small, common place which can hold a thousand people."

"A thousand people, that's a big place."

"And then, in a few more months, I'm going to move to an even bigger place ... And that's when you're going to come," said George.

"Okay ..."

But George didn't tell Dad just yet about the dream he had. His warning would come later in the conversation, when two men, once adversaries in the ring, came together in the spirit of peace and brotherhood, each trying to understand the other's religion.

"God spoke to me, man," said George, "and told me you were going to call today—and it worked out just like that. Man, God loves you. Do you hear what I'm saying? You're loved by God, the man who makes this whole planet go around. He's right there, keeping his eye on you ..."

"Right," said Dad. "One thing I want to ask you. I never understood this, maybe you could help me. Was Jesus the Son of God?"

"He is the Son of God, and he's alive."

"Well, I've had people tell me God don't have children."

"Yeah, God has got this Son, man. What happens is that you become one of his sons by adoption, by taking on Jesus yourself, you see."

"I always wonder why the preachers talk about Jesus so much," said Dad. "Why can't you just pray to God and serve God and follow just God?"

"You see," said George, "he's the Son of God. He's the mediator between man and God. It's the name of Jesus that's great, not the man. It's the name that's great. You see?"

"I'm not trying to say that you're wrong," said Dad, "I'm trying to learn ..."

"Yeah, I know. I understand that," said George.

"What do they mean when they say, 'God the Father, God the Son, and God the Holy Ghost'?"

"What happened was there was a scripture when Jesus spoke to his disciples. He said, 'You go, ye, and teach all nations. Baptize them in the name of the Father and of the Son and of the Holy Ghost.' So, he told them to do it in the name of the Father and of the Son and of the Holy Ghost, right?"

"Mmm-hmm," said Dad.

"But they got it wrong. See, like the name of your child and of you and of your wife is one. It's one name for all of you. That's Ali, you see?"

"I see."

"But that doesn't mean that you are the mother or that you are the daughter. You are just the father, but you all have the same name."

"That makes sense," said Dad. "I'm glad you straightened that out for me."

"Jesus can't do nothing alone," said George. "It's God that's in him."

"Here's another question," said Dad. "Are the Father, the Son, and the Holy Ghost all equal?"

"No!"

"I'm glad to hear that, too," said Dad.

"See, the Holy Ghost itself is like the spirit of the living God. The Son, he is subject to God himself, and there's one power of them all. That's God. You see?"

"So, what you're preaching is the real, the true Christianity?"

"Yes," said George.

They spoke a little about Billy Graham and other religious figures, then Dad said, *"George, there are one billion Muslims on Earth, which is a thousand million, enough to fill America ten times. Saudi Arabia is Muslim, Morocco, Egypt, Syria, Pakistan, and all the Muslim countries. Prophet Muhammad was sent to Arabia 1,400 years ago—to the Arabs who had gone astray. And they say Buddha was sent to the Chinese, and Krishna sent to the Indians, and Jesus sent to the Jews and Gentiles. All the Muslims pray to Allah, they say that the divine name of the supreme being is Allah, which they revere ... Jesus didn't speak English 2,000 years ago ..."*

George shared his opinion, then Dad asked, *"George, do you run into the Muslim Brothers in Texas?"*

"Oh, yeah, man."

"You're friendly?"

"I start talking and they get violent-acting," said George. *"But they know what I've got. They don't bother me ..."*

"Muslims are supposed to be peaceful—we're not violent. Muslims are peaceful people. They're misrepresenting us. George, what are you preaching—what's the title?"

"I teach the death, burial, and resurrection of Jesus Christ ... I'm a Jesus's name preacher."

"You're a Christian?"

"Yes, I'm a Christian, but I'm a Jesus's name preacher."

"Where are you living now, George?"

"I live here in Houston now, man. I gave up my ranch, because I had to come down here and preach to these people. Man, I tried to preach just to big-time people, but they're not going to have it. We're preaching at a little common church now for anybody who wants to come here—white or black."

"The big-timers won't listen?"

"No," said George. "The Bible says, 'Not many men are noble, or mighty men are chosen.'"

"You gave up all of your earthly stuff, like land and houses and cars and all of that?" asked Dad.

"What happened is I sold all of that stuff, man, because it just spread me out thin, you know? I can't be taking care of all of that stuff. I sold it."

"You're right," said Dad. "All of the stuff I've got—I feel it, too."

"Yeah, it just spreads you out too thin ... So I got rid of it, you know."

"What do you do for income, George?"

"I've been living off the stuff I sold, so far."

"How old are you now? I'm thirty-seven," said Dad.

"I'm thirty," said George.

"Damn—you're young!"

"Yeah, but you are, too, man," said George. "In the past, you did some great things, but the greatest thing you're going to ever do is save your own soul."

"I'm going to tell you something, George. I think God has control over all people, all minds. I think he knows what's in your heart. A man judges a man's actions, but God judges a man's heart. I think if your heart is right and you really mean right ... and you help people, you give to charity, you hold no hate in your heart. I think you'll go to heaven, no matter what you call your religion ...

"Catholic, Baptist, or Jew," Dad continued. "See, Man named it Catholic. God didn't name them Baptist, Jehovah's Witness, or Muslim. God never gave them those titles. Man gave the titles. And that's what separates and divides people. There is only one religion, and that's the religion of the heart. And if you've got the right heart and you mean right ... George Foreman don't know what's in my heart."

"I know what's in your heart, man."

"No. You ain't God, George."

"No, see, you love me the same way you love yourself. You have the spirit of God ..."

248

"Have you ever heard God's voice?" asked Dad. "You said God showed you this and God showed you that. You don't hear no sound, do you?"

"Yeah," said George.

"What do you hear?"

"Well, first I was shown a dream ... God showed me how I was going to talk to you ... Then God told me once that he didn't want my money. He wanted me. I heard it, right within—and it shook my whole soul, man. He said, 'I don't want your money. I want you.' That scared me, man."

"It happened after the Jimmy Young fight, didn't it?" said Dad.

"Yeah, that scared me worse than I've ever been scared in my life. I don't want to hear that no more. You know ... God will speak to you in dreams and visions, because you wouldn't be able to stand to hear the voice of God right in your mortal body. You couldn't take it."

"Right," said Dad.

"You know, what I want you to do," said George. "Come and go to church with me one day. I'll come and pick you up from the airport and take you to church, then take you right back to the airport."

"The worst thing a Muslim can do," said Dad, "is to leave the Holy Quran and Allah and then go back to the white man's Christianity. All my draft, all my Vietnam stuff, all of my success, my praying before fights, all of my power comes from Allah, and I can't leave Allah now for something else. I can't leave all the Muslims. I have a big following in the world. I can't leave them."

"I'm not trying to change you," said George. "But, see, if you could just come down one day ... I'll pick you up from the airport. Just come to church with me, and I'll take you back to the airport."

"Well, we have to make a deal," said Dad. "You'll have to go with me one day, and I'll go with you one day. Then it won't look bad. If the press or somebody said, 'What are you doing? Are you leaving the Muslims?'"

"Ain't no press going to know you're coming down here—unless you call them."

249

"They'll know. When I get off the plane or I'm at your church, it'll be out, because it's in all the magazines now. I read somewhere, Time or some magazine, where you were saying you talked to me about Christ and about being born again … it's in some magazine … So you've got to come to the mosque with me one day, and then I'll go with you. That would make it better. Then, when I go with you, I'll say, 'I came here because he came with me, too.' I want to take you to Chicago one day when Wallace Muhammad is ministering—you don't have to say nothing. You don't have to join nothing. All you've got to do is go in and listen, and when it's over we leave. Then I'll go with you. That'll make it better. If I just go with you, that'll look bad. It will look like I'm leaving my religion."

"Man, I'll make sure you don't look bad," said George.

"If my mind is open enough to go to listen to something that's never done nothing for me, I'm a world power because I'm Muhammad Ali. The name Muhammad is the most common name in the world. There are more Muslims than anybody. I'm recognized in Asia and Africa, and it's done so much for me. I'd look crazy to my people. But if I can say, 'I came with him because he came with me,' then it justifies my going. You did me a favor; I'll do you a favor. But if I just go myself, then word would get all out. 'George Foreman is converting Muhammad Ali.' Then some crazy person might come and shoot me."

"Man, nobody is going to shoot you."

"You don't know that, George."

"I'd lay my life down for you," said George.

"I know that," said Dad.

"I'll come stay with you," said George. "You can come stay at my house with me."

"You don't have to do that, George. You've just got to come one day with me, then I'll go one day with you. Why should I just go with you when you won't come with me? I want you to see 5,000 clean men and women praying and listening to Wallace Muhammad, the most powerful black preacher in America."

"Man, I know what that is. A lot of those people have murdering spirits, man."

"*Throughout history, Christians have done more killing than anybody.*"

"*Them ain't no Christians,*" said George.

"*Well, them ain't no Muslims if they murder,*" said Dad. "*Those ain't true Muslims if they can murder. Muslims don't murder. We don't kill nobody. We give charity, and we ain't breeding no hate. Christianity and Islam is almost alike, the closest two religions in the world. I heard you preaching, and I liked what you were saying. You said, 'I was the champion of the world. I had this, and I had that.' Man, that's powerful, because people knew it was true, because if you want to you can still have women and big houses. You can still be trying to fight, and you ain't that old. You can fight if you want to, so they know that you're really giving all of that up. That makes people believe you, because you did it ... Are you still married, George?*"

"*No, I'm not married.*"

"*You don't have a girlfriend?*"

"*No, I don't do that, man.*"

"*Look, George, nature is nature.*"

"*I used to breed animals. I used to get dogs and put them together, and they'd smell each other and start breeding. God didn't make man in the image of a dog. He made us in his image. If a man wants to marry, that's good, but if he doesn't, you know, that's all right, too.*"

"*You aren't getting married any more?*" asked Dad.

"*I'm not worried about that. You know, if I find a woman to help me, but I don't need nobody just to lay in the bed with me. I'm not a teenage boy. I'm a thirty-year-old man. I don't have the hots for every woman walking down the street no more. I don't need that. Do you know what I mean?*"

"*Yeah,*" said Dad. "*You know, if you want to, you're young enough to fight again.*"

"*Oh, yeah, but, man, I am fighting. I'm fighting right now. If you can hear what I'm saying, then that means I've lived a good life.*"

"*God knows what's in your heart, George. If you mean right, God wants you to get famous to help the cause. Didn't you say God said, 'I don't want your money; I want you'? Well, if he wants you, he wouldn't mind making you extra great. When I was boxing, my*" purpose wasn't to hurt anybody. You can go in the ring and box without wanting to hurt people. You pray to God you don't hurt them or get hurt and, if the man is going down, you pull off of him—don't hit him. I did that with Jimmy Ellis, I did it with Jerry Quarry. I pulled off them and told the referee to stop it because I didn't want to hurt them. God knows my intentions. All I'm saying is ... with the modern-day technology, we ..."

"Right there—that's why God loves you," said George. "You're one of the most decent people I've ever known in my life."

"Yeah, I want you to come back and take the heavyweight title, George."

"Oh, no," said George. "I could never do that any more ... God don't want you back in that stuff no more either."

"I'm not fighting," said Dad. "I'm through with fighting. I'm thirty-seven, man. I'm way older than you."

"Yeah, but he doesn't want you in the ring any more—he doesn't want you in any more boxing exhibitions either."

"No boxing exhibitions?"

"No," said George. "I had a dream that you were having an exhibition, but it would lead to another fight."

"Yeah, that was gonna be in Chicago. That didn't happen."

"No, but evidently there's one coming up again. Don't do that stuff. Stay out of the ring."

"My purpose was this," said Dad. "If I do the exhibition for $100,000, there's a school in Chicago that needs $50,000 to build a gymnasium, and the school is to help the children in the ghetto—poor children. It's a kind of a spiritual, Islamic school. My purpose is to help build the school."

"Can you please call me a little bit more?" said George. "You and I are closer than you think ... We're going to be old men and old friends together. You should call me up at least once every month, man."

"I'll call you once a week," said Dad.

"Could you?"

"Yeah ... Okay, George. We had a good talk."

"I didn't offend you, did I?" asked George.

"No, man. We're brothers—I'm learning."

"I just don't want you to be mad at me."

"Mad at you? What are you talking about? Why do you think I am on the phone for an hour?" said Dad.

"Yeah, you're all right," said George. *"I'm with you all the way."*

"Okay, I'll get back to you," said Dad.

"All right," said George. *"God bless you ..."*

***

HELPING OTHERS WAS always Daddy's driving force. People's love for him gave him extra strength, energy, and purpose. It also gave him a bit of extra magic. A spark that he could store away, deep within his spirit, and summon at will. When the world was trying him unjustly, when his bouts in the ring were exhausting, and later, when his reflexes slowed and his speech grew softer, he'd reach down in the bottom of the well and find the strength to defy seemingly impossible odds. Showing the world, and himself, what we are *all* capable of.

Like my father, George Foreman shook up the boxing world. Twenty years after he lost his title to Dad in Zaire, and fifteen years after this conversation, George came out of his long retirement and won back his heavyweight championship at the age of forty-five. He went out a winner, like my father hoped he would.

Over the years, Dad and George remained friends. It was an improbable friendship, but a friendship it was. On an old video recording, someone asked my dad if there was any animosity between him and the men he fought.

"No," he said. "We're all friends. We only fought for the money."

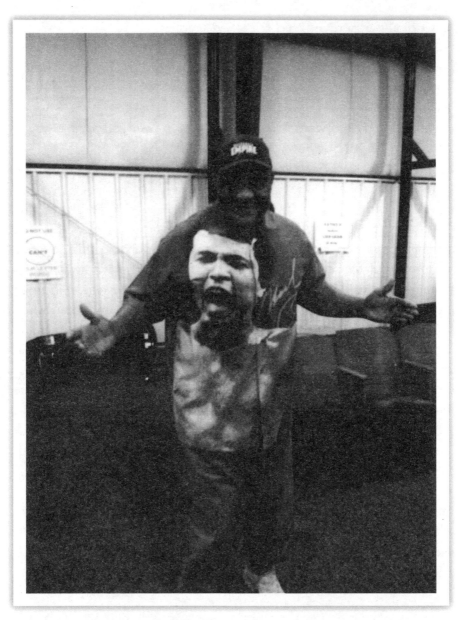

A photo George sent me of him wearing a Muhammad Ali shirt.

25

December 27, 1979

A SERIES OF clunking sounds echo from my father's office. Upstairs, my mother picks up the telephone intercom.

"Hello?"

"You heard the pop?" Dad asks.

"Yeah, what is it? I was in the bathroom."

"Mike Douglas is on the other line; can we go to his house in an hour to watch a movie and have dinner?"

"I can't."

"Can I go?"

"Can't you tell him we'll go tomorrow?"

"He's screening a movie tonight." (*Going in Style*, starring George Burns.)

"I would go, but I promised my brother I would take him somewhere and I have an appointment at five o'clock."

"Oh, I can just go," says Dad.

"Okay."

He says goodbye and picks up the flashing line. "Yeah, Mike, I just spoke to my wife. There's no way she can make it, but it looks like I might ... I've got my daddy here with me. Can I bring my daddy?"

"Sure..."

Later, as my father is rushing out the door, the phone rings. Dad answers the call.

"Hello?"

"Mr Ali, I hate to bug you about this, but there's so much money involved I just couldn't pass it up ..." It's Mr Lomax, calling from the Chicago office. "Gloria Vanderbilt wanted you to do a commercial with her about women's sports apparel. They didn't want to put your name on it, they just wanted you to do a commercial. First, they offered us $200,000. Today, they went up to $600,000 and that's just for one year. They want a three-year deal!"

"Women's clothes?"

"No, women's jogging trousers like your jump suit, and tennis apparel for women."

"Well, I don't ..."

"I talked to Jabber [Dad's manager] about it," said Mr Lomax. "And first, when they offered $200,000 he turned it down flat. Jabber said, 'Muslim men don't mind women wearing pants, so long as they wear them within the house for their man.' And he said, 'If Ali has any reservation about it, I'm not going to encourage him to do it.' When they came back to me today with $400,000 and then again with $600,000 per year, Mr Jabber said, 'Well, maybe if at the end of the commercial you could say, "Muslim men don't like women to wear trousers in public and I'm not endorsing this for Muslim women ..."' How do you feel about that?"

"I don't think they'll let us say something like that on a commercial," said Dad.

"I think they want it so bad they'll work with us, and all I need is for you to tell me to go ahead and work on it."

The other line clicks. "Damn it—shit—hold on ..."

"Hello ..." No one is there. Dad returns to Lomax.

"Yeah, I'm back ..."

"There's so much money!" said Lomax. "For example, they said to me today—"

Dad interrupts, "So much money is good, but—" His other line clicks in the middle of his sentence. "Damn it! Shit! Wait—hold on ..." He could never resist a ringing telephone. Laila and I used to laugh watching him run back and forth from different rooms in the house to answer the phone. The only time he ever tried not to let it disturb him was during prayer. But even then it sometimes got the better of him.

He clicks over hastily. Without asking who is calling, he says, *"I'm on the phone, call back in twenty minutes ..."*

He returns to the other line, picking up where he left off. *"When you're talking about so much money and you're talking about compromising on the beliefs of Islam, or something with Allah and the Muslim laws, I don't care if they call back and say, 'Here's ten or fourteen million.' That is just a test from God, to see if I'm going to like the money more. I hope Jabber isn't getting weak over money ..."*

"No," said Lomax. *"He's not. This is my point of view, not his. My point of view is that they want you to do it so badly ..."*

Dad interrupts. *"Why? Why do they want me to do it so badly, if you don't think they have nothing bad in mind ... by getting me in trouble?"*

"Because they said the best TV commercial you ever did was D-Con. They said it was the best thing in the business and that if you could do that for D-Con, you might be able to do it for Vanderbilt."

After a brief pause, *"I'm not turning down something good ... Tell Herbert I'll be in Chicago on the 8th and let me, uh ..."*

"You want to think about it?"

"Yeah, let me meet with Wallace, and if Wallace Muhammad tells me that, Islamically, it's all right, I'll do it. That's all! I've got to go."

"Okay. Thank you, bye."

My father was very careful with how his image was used. He didn't want to contradict the teachings of Islam. He knew he was the most famous Muslim in the world and had a huge Islamic following. He took his unique position very seriously and was always on guard so as not to do anything to embarrass his fellow Muslims.

A month before Christmas, in November of 1979, he was on the phone with the State Department and the White House, trying to negotiate with a group of tyrannical Islamic students who had taken

Americans hostage in the US Embassy in Tehran. The mere mention of my father's name had opened the lines of communication.

One morning stands out in my memory. Laila and I laughed as usual, watching Dad run back and forth from the living room to his office to answer the telephone—never knowing the importance of the phone call he was waiting on.

26

November 1979

AT FIVE O'CLOCK in the morning, a man rises. Careful not to wake his beautiful wife, he eases out of bed, slips on his house shoes, and wraps himself in a brown terry bathrobe. In the bathroom, he stares at his reflection in the mirror. He examines the smooth mocha skin that belies his age, thinking of how quickly time passes. After a moment, he brushes his teeth, washes his hands and face, and then heads down the hall to his daughter's room. He sits on the edge of her bed and wakes her with soft kisses. "Wake up, Hana," he whispers. "It's time for morning prayer." Yawning and rubbing her weary eyes, Hana reaches for her father. Muhammad Ali picks up his young daughter and carries her into the next room to wake her sister Laila. Still in their pajamas, the two little girls walk downstairs holding their father's hands ...

Unlike our older siblings Maryum, Jamillah, Rasheda, and Muhammad Jr, who had Muslim grandparents and grew up accustomed to the religion's traditions, Laila and I were two wild little rascals. I never called my daddy "Sir" like they did. When I was three, my father tried to teach me to do that, but all I would say was, "Yes, Poopoo Head!"

"Poopoo Head!" he said. Then he laughed and gave up.

259

One Sunday in November of 1979 stands out in my memory. The morning began as usual with my father waking us and walking us downstairs to the living room, where he had placed three prayer rugs on the floor facing east. Laila and I didn't spend much time in the living room. It was where my mother displayed her Louis XVI antique furnishings, with the white ropes tied across like in an art gallery in front of priceless masterpieces to let you know that they weren't meant for touching.

My father probably chose this room because of the large picture window centered on the east wall. When the sun rose, the room took on a beautiful, spiritual ambience as the first glimmers of daylight shimmered across the horizon.

This morning the sound of my father reciting the traditional prayer, "All praise be to Allah, the magnificent the graceful. He alone we worship, he alone we seek for help ...", was interrupted by the sound of the telephone ringing from his den. The sound was relentless, but this was not unusual. The phone rang often and when it happened during prayer Daddy tried his best to ignore it. But this morning he could not resist and several times he rushed down the hall as if his life depended on it. I didn't know at the time that my father was waiting on a call from the American Embassy and, if it went his way, that call would change hundreds of lives and jeopardize his own. The week before, he offered to fly to Tehran to negotiate for the release of the American hostages being held by militant Islamic students.

But the callers at that early hour were not the people my father was waiting for; instead, they were more of the same calls he'd been receiving all winter. Like the news reporters from overseas wanting to know his future plans; heads of state inviting him to their country; the President requesting his presence at the White House to be briefed on my father's recent trip to China; politicians, such as Ted Kennedy, calling for my father's support; The Jacksons, asking him to introduce them in their final concert. The list went on.

Laila and I couldn't sit still or be silent for ten seconds, let alone a ten-minute prayer, and watching our father bustle back and forth muttering "shit" and "damn it" under his breath every time he stopped to answer the phone appeared hilarious. He would speak quickly to whoever was on the line, then return to us, picking up where he left off.

We were both "cuttin' up", as Dad put it, before he reentered the room. I'd taken my chance to get up and bounce on the forbidden furniture. I knew when my father was coming back down the hall because my mother's parrots would screech in unison, "Bye Chap! Bock Bock!" But my guilty pleasure—thinking I'd gotten away with something naughty—was short-lived. My father had an inner knowing, and perhaps my flawless memory of that morning and all the mornings that followed over the years has more to do with the lessons he taught me than the pleasure I experienced watching him run back and forth to answer the relentless telephone.

On one occasion when we were a little older, after a few minutes of enduring our giggles and whispers, Dad turned to face us both and said something I'll always remember.

"Hana! Please stop cuttin' up," he said. "There's an angel on each of your shoulders. The angel on the left is writing down all of your good deeds and the angel on your right is writing down all of your bad deeds." Now he had my attention. I listened wide-eyed. "When you die and go to heaven," he explained, "God is going to present you with both lists. Make sure that the good list is the longest." My eyes grew wider. "Always remember," he advised, "even when your mother and me aren't watching you, God sees everything that you do."

My father always had a way of getting his message across in a profound way. As many reporters experienced over the years, verbal sparring with The Greatest was no contest. He was way ahead on points before they even warmed up and he was impossible to corner.

The idea that we all die was not new to me. My father had told me this many times over the years. He would sit Laila and me down on the sofa in his den and explain how everything God made has a purpose. "Birds have a purpose, trees have a purpose, ants and cows have a purpose and you have a purpose too ... When you're about twelve years old," he said, just as he had told my siblings, "you should know what your purpose is. I discovered my purpose when I was twelve, after my bike was stolen ..." I was only six years old the first time he told me this, and Laila was five. "So you still have a few years to figure it out," he explained.

"Nothing lasts forever," he'd say. "We're all going to die one day. I will die, your mother will die, and you and your sister will die. But there is another life after this one—the eternal life. This life is short—it goes by so fast. Thirty years ago I was a little boy running around with my brother. You're just little girls now, but before you know it you'll be all grown up with your own children. Remember, this life is the preparation for the eternal life. What we do for God is all that matters. It's all that will last."

After our many talks, I had become anxious about life and death. As I grew, my father's words stayed with me. When walking barefoot in the grass I was careful not to step on ants. I never killed a spider or a fly, and when riding my bike with childhood friends Kim and Karen I warned them not to roll over the snails in our driveway. "All life is sacred!" I shouted, flying down the driveway on my red bicycle past the swimming pool and my father's parked Rolls.

"That snail has a purpose!"

But I was mostly obsessed with the idea that my father would die—that I would one day lose him. The thought was too much to face. I remember sitting in my first-grade class and thinking about how much I loved him, how I wanted everyone to know how much I loved him, and that when he went to heaven I would be so sad I'd want to go with him. I know it sounds melodramatic, but children's minds are imaginative and at times unreasonable.

I could never imagine ever loving anyone as much as I loved my father, and I asumed he felt the same about me. But when I was five years old I discovered I wasn't the greatest love of my father's life and it broke my heart. Dad had taken Laila and me to the mosque with him for Friday prayer and since we were so young he took us into the men's prayer section with him. It's customary for men to sit in the front of women, so as not to distract the men from prayer. Dad found a quiet place in the corner and did his best to keep us quiet. But as usual I was messing about, giggling and laughing.

262

"Hana, Laila, please stop cuttin' up," he said. "You have to love God more than anyone, even me. I love God *more* than I love you."

My heart sank. I didn't completely understand the concept of God yet, but I could not believe that there was something my daddy loved more than me. I remember wanting to understand why my daddy loved God so much. My father prayed all the time—five times a day. I didn't know that anyone else prayed, so I assumed God and my father were telling each other things. When you're little you try to make sense of stuff and, to me, it seemed that Daddy was extra special in God's eyes. I thought this was why there were crowds everywhere he went. He was like my own personal superhero, with love and attention coming at him from all directions. I remember thinking, *God must really love my father,* so I clung to his every word and for that reason, along with the fact that he told me the same stories year after year, I never forgot my father's words about the angels on my shoulders.

When I was nine years old, one year before my parents' divorce was final, I was playing with Jose. He was a couple of years older than me and I had a small crush on him. This afternoon we were playing hide-and-seek, and as Laila counted to ten Jose and I hid in the bushes together.

"Ready or not, here I come ..." Laila shouted.

"Hana," Jose whispered.

"Be quiet." I said. "She's done counting." I tried not to make too much noise pushing aside the branches that were scratching my arms and tearing small holes in the pretty pink shirt that I had snuck out of Mom's closet. *I'll have to throw this one away,* I thought. It was torn in too many places, and there was no way soap and water would get those stains out. I always wanted to look pretty, like my mother. For me, that meant wearing her clothes. As you can imagine, a lot of Mom's belongings went missing over the years.

"Hana ... can I have a kiss?" Jose asked.

Without a second thought, I offered my cheek. But he wasn't satisfied. He looked at me with puppy-dog eyes.

"I want to kiss you on the lips," he said.

"I can't kiss you on the lips, Daddy wouldn't like it."

"Your dad isn't here. He can't see us. He'll never know."

I looked at Jose as though he were clueless. "But God will see," I said, "and God tells my daddy EVERYTHING!"

27

Monday morning, November 12, 1979

THE CALL MY father was waiting for finally came on the morning of November 12, 1979. Eight days earlier, on November 4th, a group of Iranian college students and militants had stormed the American Embassy in Tehran and had taken hostages. Some escaped, others were freed but fifty-two people remained in captivity for 444 days before it was over. The students refused to communicate with our government, demanding only that President Carter return the Shah of Iran to Iranian authorities for trial and execution for the alleged mistreatment of the citizens.

The Shah was King of Iran and the descendant of a great dynasty that stretched back generations. Known for having his lunch flown in by Concorde and his wife rumored to have bathed in milk, the Shah was overthrown by the Islamic revolution in January of 1979. Having lost his country, the Shah fled to New York in exile, where he was given diplomatic immunity by President Carter and received treatment for cancer.

In the Shah's wake, one of his political opponents, the Ayatollah Khomeini, seized power, allowing the students to take over the embassy.

On November 7th, after my father heard the news, he went on national television and offered to go over and speak to the students personally. The mention of his name alone opened the lines of communication between the United States and Iran. As you can imagine, the telephone was ringing relentlessly at home. The State Department, the Cultural Counselor to the Iranian Embassy, news reporters, concerned family and friends, and—in the days to come— even the White House would call.

Eager to resolve the country's troubles and help bring the hostages home safely, as he waited for the call confirming his visa for Iran, my father made a few calls of his own.

***

DAD SPOKE INTO his recorder as he dialed: *"This is November 10th, 1979, the time is around twelve-noon. I'm calling Washington DC, for Mr Farhay, concerning the problem in Iran and doing whatever I can to help ..."*

"Hello Mr Farhay, this is Muhammad Ali calling."

"Hello Muhammad, how are you?"

"I'm good. I'm very happy to hear your voice. How are you?"

"Good, thank you. I talked to your assistant in Chicago, Mr Lomax, and he gave me your message. This afternoon we are going to send the message home, and as soon as we hear from them we will inform your office."

"Thank you, who are you representing, sir?"

"The Embassy."

"You're the Ambassador?"

"No, I am the Cultural Counselor to Iran."

"Thank you. What message did you send?"

"It said that you, Muhammad Ali, were interested in going to Iran and seeing Iranian authorities, including Khomeini, if possible, and you're interested in taking part in, if possible, resolving the present crisis."

"Yes. What I suggested, sir, was that if Brother Khomeini or the students didn't want to negotiate with no Americans or nobody, I figured that maybe I could go in and if there is any message to be brought back to President Carter, or I could take something from

President Carter to them. I figured that they would know my sincerity, being a Muslim. I would not do anything to betray them or nothing that was considered wrong. According to Islam, probably, they could trust me better than they could a Christian American."

"Well, they know you, so it is not necessary to write the details. You are very well known in Iran. As soon as they get the message, they will respond to us and we will inform your office."

"Okay, thank you, sir."

"Thank you, Muhammad."

"Salam Alaikum [Peace be with you]."

My father made another call, and spoke into the recorder as he dialed. "I'm calling Mr Wayne Grover of Miami, Florida—a newsman—concerning helping me to get to Iran, and he's doing a good job."

"Hello ..."

"Wayne Grover! It's Ali."

"Yes, Muhammad ... what's the news?"

"I just called Mr Farhay of the Embassy. He told me they got my message and they're trying to get through to the students. As soon as they find out something, they'll call me."

"Okay. In the meantime, the Saudi Arabian Ambassador's wife just called me. The Ambassador has still not returned, so I am now drafting a telegram direct to the King of Arabia."

"King Khalid?"

"Yes, King Khalid," said Wayne. "We'll sign both of our names to it and tell him what we're proposing to do."

"If your dreams could be fulfilled," asked my father, "with what we're trying to accomplish, what would happen?"

"If my dreams are fulfilled," said Wayne, "first we will open communication and the Ayatollah will finally talk to someone. He will realize he has refused everything; and our president has refused everything, as far as letting go of the Shah. Before we can start making anything happen, we must communicate. We've got to talk to each other first. Once we talk, then we will work something out. The Ayatollah will become a hero in the eyes of Islam because he has stepped in and eliminated the situation that's bringing the world to a crisis standpoint. At that point, Muhammad, you will have done something that nobody else in the world was able to do—period. If King Khalid comes along, then it will be the trio of you, King Khalid and the Ayatollah. So right now we are trying to get to King Khalid, and if he replies faithfully we'll fly to London. From London, we'll fly to Riyadh, the capital of Saudi Arabia, and meet the King. And then, along with the King and his staff, on the royal airplane, we will plan to go into Tehran and be met by whoever oversees the government now and be led to the Ayatollah."

"So we're going on the King's private plane?"

"Hopefully, yes. If he goes, he'll go on that private airplane."

"If we can go with him, that's a big honor," said Dad. "What do we have to do when we get to the Ayatollah? What do you think our appeal should be?"

"Well, in your case, Muhammad, you will be appealing to the Ayatollah to make him realize he alone can now eliminate this situation and bring the world off this stage of crisis, and that Islam stands for peace and for love, as you know, and nonviolence ..."

"That's right!" said Dad.

"He can eliminate the possibility of worldwide violence and confrontation by doing something now and understanding the position of the American people and the position of the president—that we have the Shah here in a hospital and we can't be blackmailed. It just can't be done. But if our president and the Ayatollah say 'Absolutely not!' then nothing can be done. So, we have to start with King Khalid. The Ayatollah will listen to the King and he will listen to you, Muhammad. King Khalid also commands the city of Mecca, which you know, of course, is the Holy of all Holies ... I spoke to the State Department again. They are working on their own level, but they are not getting anything accomplished."

"So our main goal right now," said Dad, "is to reach the King, who will help us promote peace. We know he's a religious man and we know he doesn't want these people dead. We know he doesn't want trouble and disunity, so if he makes his move and just releases these people, that will be a great thing."

"He will listen to you, Muhammad. He may be a crazy man, but he will listen to you. And if he won't, so many other people there will, because they know and love you ... the State Department called and got through this morning to the students that are holding the people hostage in the Embassy in Iran. They called several times before but got no response. This morning they mentioned that you, Muhammad Ali, would be willing to come over there, and for the first time the students got excited and showed a definite reception to the idea that perhaps you were going to come over and help do something about this crisis."

"Who made that call?" asked Dad.

"That was the State Department's crisis group this morning. A man called Sheldon Kris, I believe ... I'm going to call the Western Union and send our telegram directly to the King."

"Okay, God bless you."

"Same to you, Muhammad."

***

LATER THAT EVENING, my father and Tim Shanahan were alone in his office waiting to hear back from the State Department. The house was unusually quiet. The phone had finally stopped ringing, everyone had gone home, and Mom, Laila, and I were fast asleep.

My father was sitting in his armchair in front of a crackling fire, staring pensively at the flames. Tim was sitting on the couch across from him. Dad had asked the State Department for clearance for two friends: Howard Bingham and Wayne Grover, whom he'd never actually met in person. If everything went according to plan, the three of them would soon fly to Iran.

Suddenly, Dad broke the silence. "You know, there's a chance we might not come back."

"Yes," said Tim.

"How do you think they would kill us?"

"It would probably be a gunshot to the head," Tim said.

"How would it feel?" Dad asked, wide-eyed. "Do you think it would hurt?"

Dad at home in his office.

Tim walked over to my father's chair and stood behind him. He took his index finger and poked Dad in the temple, quick. "That's it, Champ," he said. "You wouldn't feel much more than that."

"Good!" said Dad. "Let's go!"

They watched the news for a while, then Tim asked, "Are you sure you want to go?"

Without hesitation, Dad turned to face him and said, "They're holding fifty-two people hostage, and each one of them has worried family members and friends who love and miss them. So, for every single person I help, I'm really helping hundreds. If you add them all up—all the mothers, all the fathers, all the sisters and brothers, all the aunts and uncles and all the friends and co-workers—you see, I'm not just going for fifty-two people, I'm going for thousands!"

In the end, the State Department couldn't guarantee his safety and canceled the trip. But my father had been willing to risk his life to help bring strangers home safely.

Two days later, on November 12, 1979, my father had a little fun playing a prank on one of his friends (whose name I have changed for anonymity). Mr Jack Elliot called, worried out of his mind after watching Dad on television a few days earlier offering himself in exchange for the release of the Americans being held captive in Tehran. Jack was best known for his lavish parties, thrown on his seaside estates all over the country, and his lively, eccentric personality.

My father didn't tell Jack that the trip to Iran had been canceled. He let him believe he was still going and that he wanted to bring him along. Jack had been calling and pleading with him all morning. Dad found his hysteria, and nervous, quirky voice, so amusing, he had to get it on tape.

"This is Muhammad Ali making a tape for future reference. We're now in a crisis where the Iranian college students are holding over fifty Americans hostage. People have been calling me and pleading for me not to go. They're very frightened when it comes to taking a stand for what is right and for God ... This call is coming from Mr Jack Elliot, a big businessman, a multimillionaire. He has been calling me all day, pleading and telling me why I should not go and why it is not worth going. This is the typical frightened man that you're going to hear, who believes just in money and that's all. He says he is my friend. He has always told me there is nothing he won't do for me, but listen to how he talks on this tape coming up. Thank you."

"Yeah, Jack, I just got a call from Iran's embassy in Washington. It looks like I might go, but I'm not sure."

In a shaky voice, *"MUHAMMAD! DON'T GO OVER! THOSE PEOPLE OVER THERE ARE CRAZY! All those students are neurotic. They're all crazy! I read in the paper and I saw it on TV, and I said to myself, I am going to call you and tell you not to go! Don't go over, Muhammad—it's foolish!"*

"Jack, you're a friend of mine, right?"

"Right!"

Dad, joking, *"Why don't you go with me?"*

271

"Oh, no-no-no! I'm going to go to, uh ... Tonight, I'm leaving to go to, uh ... uh ... I'm going to go to, uh ... I'm leaving right now for the airport to go to Australia."

"I had some people coming there to meet you—"

Jack cut him off. "No-no-no! NOT ME! No-no! I'm going to Australia tonight. Then tomorrow I've got to go to, uh ... Georgia, and ... uh ... Alabama!"

"Why do you have to? When I spoke to you earlier you didn't have to go anywhere."

"Yeah, I did. I have to go to all these places. I'm going to be gone for about six months or a year!"

"You're not running, are you? I want you to go with me to Iran."

"No, Muhammad, I can't go! I've got to go to ... uh ... uh ... to Alabama tonight. I've got to leave early, right now, as a matter of fact."

"Doggone it, I was hoping you would go with me."

"Muhammad, I've got to leave. As a matter of fact, I'm going to leave in just ... well, I'm late now. I'm all packed. I'm going to go to the airport tonight. So please do me a favor—don't go!"

"In about ten more minutes, there might be somebody out there to meet you."

Jack was frantic. "No-no-no!"

"Because I got some people close by—the mob ..."

"Muhammad, I'm going to take the train. I'm going to go by train to New York and then I'm going to go ... Muhammad, I'm telling you something, do me a favor. Please don't go!"

"Well, if fifty Americans were going to be shot, wouldn't you risk your life for them?"

"Muhammad, please don't go. Please don't go! Those people are all kids! They're all crazy! Everyone has a gun! You don't know what the hell they're going to do, Muhammad! You have no idea what they're going to do!"

"Well, I was almost sure I could count on you to go with me."

Stumbling on his words, Jack blurted, "I've got business—I've got business! Then I've got to go to England—yeah, that's where I'm going to go, I'm going to go to England. England!"

"Okay, well, I'll have somebody watch your house until you get back."

"Oh, no! No-no-no-no-no, because, uh ... I don't know when I'm going to come back. But please don't go, Muhammad! DO NOT GO!"

"Well, I put my word on the line now. I told the world I would go."

"Muhammad, that was foolish! I saw you on television and it said that you want to go and they'd release the fifty hostages in exchange for you. You've got to be crazy! Those people are all nuts over there!"

"I want to ask you something, Jack. Do you believe America is a great country?"

"Yes."

"And if fifty Americans can be set free in exchange for holding you, wouldn't you go for fifty?"

"Muhammad, I got to go to, uh ... I'm going to go to, uh ... Nebraska tonight."

My father bursts into laughter.

"Yeah, I've got to go to, uh ... Idaho—Idaho and Nebraska!"

Dad was still joking when he said, "All right. Well, I'll call the airports and have them watch for you—they'll wait for you there."

"No! I'm going to go by train! I can't fly! I wanna go by train tonight and then I'm gonna leave."

"Are you serious?"

"Honest to God—yeah!"

"Jack, a businessman like you—"

Jack interrupted. "So, don't check on me because I just won't be here."

"Well, I'll consider what you were saying. Those people are acting crazy, they got guns. And like you said, they ain't got no reasoning. I'm glad I called you. Maybe I'll just forget all about it."

"Take my advice and forget all about it! I've gotta go to Idaho tonight."

"If you had to do one, would you contribute twenty thousand dollars or would you go?"

Jack was relieved. "Yeah, money I'll give, yeah!"

"What did you say?"

"I swear to God, I'll send a check for twenty thousand!"

"No, I don't need it. I don't need any money. I was just saying ..."

"I'll give you a hundred thousand dollars for that WORLD thing that you were going to do. I'll give you a hundred thousand dollars!"

"You would rather give one hundred thousand before you would go to Iran?"

"I swear to God, for the WORLD—what was that WORLD thing?"

"You would give one hundred thousand dollars before you'd go to Iran, Jack?"

"Yes, before I'd go to Iran. As a matter of fact—wait—Iran! I'm not going to Iran! Wait a minute, I'm not—I've got to go to, uh ... Missouri! I'm not going to Iran! What was that WORLD thing you were going to do?"

Dad gets more detailed with his prank. "I called the man at the embassy and he said, 'Do you know any people worth money that are influential? Because we can't hold just anybody. If we let fifty people go.' He said I'm good, but he wanted to know if I knew any people who have money who have something to give up. I told him I know Jack Elliot."

"I swear I'll give a hundred thousand dollars if you don't go. I swear to God I'll send you a check for one hundred thousand dollars! I'm telling you, you've got to be stupid—you got to be stupid to go! Think of your wife, the kids, those Rolls-Royces of yours, that briefcase and that picture in People magazine! You cannot go. I'm telling you!"

"All right, I won't go."

"Honest to God! You can't go!"

"Are you really worried about it?"

"Yeah, honest to God. I saw you the other night on the television. They said you were going to go in place of fifty hostages. And I said, 'You've gotta be crazy! You have got to be absolutely crazy!' Who knows what's going to happen! They may just want to shoot you to get attention!"

"Those guys from the Iranian embassy ... look outside your front door and see if there is a red car there. They might be waiting. Look out your front door."

"Hold on a second ..."

Once Jack was off the line going to his door, my father whispered into his recorder: "*I'm just joking with him, but this man is really scared. I'm talking while he goes to check the door.*"

A moment later, Jack picked the phone back up. "*No, there's no car! Doggone it, I can't even see—*"

"*Well, the guys were supposed to come and bring you to me ...*"

Jack was frantic once more. "*Me? No—no! I'm gone! I've left for Australia! I've got to go! I'm late now for the, uh ... I've got to go, Muhammad! I've got to go now!*"

"*Okay, look ...*"

He cut Dad off with, "*No—no! Honest to God, I've got to leave. I'm late for the plane!*"

"*Wait, Jack, don't hang up, I want to tell you something.*"

"*What?*"

My father laughed hard.

"*No, I've got to go!*"

More laughter. "*Can I say one thing to you?*"

"*No, I've got to go to Alabama!*"

"*Jack! I have to say something to you.*"

"*What?*"

"*All this time I was joking. Since you've been on the phone, I've been joking.*"

Relief flooded over him. "*Oh ... Okay.*"

"*Listen, you sound so funny. First, you said you were going to Alabama, and then you said Australia. I want you to know I was only joking. Nobody is coming to your house, and I'm not going anywhere. They told me they didn't want me. I was going to go, but they said no, and I couldn't get clearance ... I'm not going any more.*"

Jack was relaxed now. "*Thank God. Those people are crazy, Muhammad. So when are you going to come over to the house to eat?*"

"*Sometime soon ...*" said Dad.

They made casual conversation for a while. As Jack calmed down, my father saw another opportunity to rekindle the joke.

275

"Okay, well, I'll tell you what," said Dad. "I'll cancel that Iran trip and I'll call the people to tell them not to come by your house because they were going to pick you up."

"Oh, no-no, not me because I won't be around. I sold the house! Tell them I sold the house!"

"Okay, I'll cancel the call because I asked the Iranian students to come by your house to take you."

"Oh, Jesus Christ! No! Not me because I sold the house! They painted it—and I'm going to leave tonight! Let me tell you something. I swear to God, for that WORLD thing—you said something about some WORLD thing ... I'll give a hundred thousand dollars to the WORLD ... what was that WORLD program?"

"The World Organization for Rights and Liberty and Dignity," said Dad.

"Right! I will give a hundred thousand dollars for whatever that is!"

"Well, just hold it; you don't have to worry about it now."

The line clicked. "Hold on, Jack ..."

"Muhammad," my mother said, calling from the telephone intercom upstairs. "Are we still going out to dinner?"

"Yeah, in about twenty minutes."

"What are you doing?"

"I'm talking to Jack Elliot—I want you to hear the tape."

"Okay."

Dad clicked back over to the other line, picking up where he left off. "Yeah, Jack, so let me hurry up and call the Iranian students there, so I can tell them you aren't going to go with me and I might not go either."

"Just tell them that I'm not around and that you got the wrong name because some of those people might just come out here by mistake."

"Okay, let me go call them now."

"Just tell them I left two months ago!"

"Okay, I'll tell them you left two months ago."

"Say hello to Veronica, and give her my love and the kids."

"Okay, bye-bye."

"Don't go over!"

276

"Okay ..."

Dad hung up the phone and spoke into the recorder. *"This is November 12th, 1979. Jack Elliot, scared to death!"*

Although the Iran trip was canceled my father didn't give up trying to find a way to secure the release of the hostages. Twelve days later he picked up the telephone and called Jeremiah Shabazz, his friend and Muslim minister from Philadelphia.

"I hate to wake you," Dad said, *"but something important has come up. Wake up—wake up—are you woke?"*

"Yeah, I'm up." Jeremiah yawned.

"I got a call from Arafat's people a couple nights ago. One of them came by when I was at my brother's house in Chicago and said that Arafat had invited me to Lebanon. He wants me to go with him to try and talk to the Ayatollah—to release the hostages. He left three plane tickets. One for me, one for Howard Bingham and one for whoever else I want to bring. I was wondering if you would go too?"

"Yeah, I'll go with you."

"Will it get us in trouble, meeting with Arafat?" Dad asked.

"No, not really ... I'd meet with the devil himself to help somebody."

"That's a good one," said Dad, *"I'll meet with the devil himself to help somebody. I like that ... So the plane tickets are here. If Khomeini gives us an invitation, that's some kind of small progress, isn't it?"*

"Yeah, that's progress," said Jeremiah. *"I think that Arafat can probably get in to see Khomeini. He knows his way around, and everybody knows him, and everybody knows you. The combination is pretty good, really."*

"What would you say standing in front of Khomeini—about releasing the hostages?"

"First I would tell him to keep the lines of communication open and to be open to reason. Mainly to keep negotiating—as long as they're talking there is a chance. Listen, Ali, don't think you're going to go over there and get them people out. Just keep in

mind that wherever you go and whatever you do, the world sees that you tried to do something. That's the best you can do. You can say, 'I tried.' I agree that they should let them go but you are not the powers that make up the United States and you are not against the United States. The only position that you stand for is justice ..."

While my father wasn't able to secure the release of the hostages in Iran, in 1985 he flew to Lebanon in an attempt to secure the release of four hostages. Then, in 1990, he flew to Iraq and successfully negotiated the release of fifteen American hostages. I remember watching him bringing them home on the news when I was a teenager and thinking that he was like a golden key that could unlock any door around the world.

Like Dr Martin Luther King Jr once said after my father refused to be inducted into the United States Army, "You might not agree with Mr Ali's religious beliefs, but you certainly have to admire his courage ..."

My father was called to rise many times in his life, and every time he rose to the occasion. He proved over and over, in and out of the ring, that he wasn't afraid of a challenge. In my eyes, he was—and always will be—the measure of greatness.

After Dad got off the phone with Jack Elliot, my parents made plans to go out to dinner. As usual, I was determined to go with them. For as long as I can remember, I knew my tears were like kryptonite to my father; he was defenseless against them. All I had to do was turn on the theatrics or poke out my lip and he would melt. Dad had a weak spot for children and the elderly. While he was a fierce opponent in the ring, he never stood a chance against his three-year-old daughter. And he knew it.

"Hana, this is 1979 November the 12th and it's about 8 p.m. Me and your mother, Veronica, are going out to have dinner ..."

I interrupt. *"Now?"*

"Yeah ... I'm going to take Mommy to have some dinner."

"I want soooome! I want to eat with yoooou."

Dad talked into the recorder, speaking to the future-me. "*Hana, this was you typically when you were a little girl, this is how you always talked ...*"

I could be heard pleading in the background. "*I want to—I want to, Daddy—I want to go bye-bye with you ... I want to go bye-bye with you, Daddy ...*"

"*Why don't you stay here, Hana? It's dark outside. It's time for you to go to bed.*"

"*No! You'll be back?*"

"*I'll be back. Every night I go out, you say this—every night—and you cry.*" He returned to the recorder as I pulled out the kryptonite. "*See, Hana,*" he said to my future self as I sat listening beside him, "*this tape is to show how little girls are persistent. They keep crying, using their feelings to get what they want from men. You're three years old—one day you'll be thirty years old, conning men ...*"

I continued to beg him.

"*Okay, you can go. Give me a kiss. Daddy will take you. I just can't help it.*"

We walked down the hall together to my mother's room. "*I'm going to go out to eat with you, Mommy. I'm going to go bye-bye with you and Daddy.*"

"*You went bye-bye with Auntie Diane already,*" she said.

I looked at my father. "*Daddy ...*"

He looks at my mother. "*Mama, I'm taking Hana to eat with us, you hear?*"

I looked at my mother. "*He said yes, Mommy!*"

"*Okay,*" she said. "*I'll let you go this time.*"

Dad finished the recording as I talked to my mother in the background.

"*The time is about 8:27 p.m. and I'm here upstairs with Hana and Veronica in the house at 55 Fremont Place in Los Angeles. The date is November 12, 1979, and Hana is in the background talking. What did you say, Hana?*"

"*She said she'll go this time and tomorrow night she will stay home.*"

"Oh good," he said. *"Come give me a kiss."*

"You'll come back later and I'll go this time—I'll go now?"

"Yes. I'll come back later and you'll go now, but tomorrow you'll stay home. Let me hear you say it."

"I go now, but tomorrow I stay home."

"Good girl ... Signing off, until tomorrow."

I was always worrying my father wouldn't come home. It was as if I'd always known that, one day, he wouldn't.

28

"CAN YOU GRAB me a pencil and notepad?" I called out.

It was nearly 2 a.m. and Kevin was still watching his favorite movie, *The Godfather*. Any other film and he would have fallen asleep by now. He came to the bedroom door and gave me a look. "You have a drawer full in your nightstand," he said.

"I can't move!" I said, sitting in the middle of the bed. "I have these papers in order and I need to write down the stuff I want to ask my mother about. And the notepad is in my office desk drawer."

He grabbed an ice tea from the refrigerator and returned with a notepad and a handful of pens and pencils. "Any chance of us going to bed soon?" he asked.

"Can you give me thirty minutes?"

"Okay," he said, then kissed me and left the room.

As I flicked through one of Mom's old decorating books, an envelope fell into my lap. I stared at the beautiful penmanship; it was my mother's handwriting and it was addressed to Laila and me. *This letter looks ancient*, I thought. But for a moment I ignored it. I told myself I was no longer in the mood to be reminded of things and places past. But who was I kidding? I'd been consumed with thoughts about the past since the moment my father revealed his tape recordings to me. I just wasn't ready to face my own ghosts yet. I'd spent years trying to forgive my mother for leaving my father.

Curiosity and frustration battled within me. Why hadn't Mom given this to us? And what in the world was it doing in a book about decorating? I started to call her but stopped myself. Knowing my mother, she would still be distraught over the discovery of my father's letters, and if she'd managed to sleep it was best she stay that way.

This is crazy, I thought. First Dad, now Mom. Mercury must have been in a perpetual retrograde when these two were born. I peeled the letter from its envelope, my mind racing. Would this also break my heart the way my father's letters had?

Dear Hana and Laila,
There was a lot you were too young to remember.
Love Mom

I noted the date: December 22, 1986. She must have written this at the time of the divorce. I examined the pages. It wasn't a letter, but a copy of a long interview titled, "Are You Anybody?" I read the opening lines:

Veronica is 5 feet 10 inches tall. She is very striking, with a wonderful face and regal bearing. She has light mocha skin and huge, dark brown eyes framed with thick eyelashes (not false). She wears little makeup—lip-gloss, mascara, and cheek color. Her rich, long, wavy, henna brown hair is pulled to one side with a barrette. Hers is the kind of face you don't get tired of looking at! Veronica is the perfect mate for Muhammad Ali. They certainly make a beautiful couple ...

I was quite impressed with Veronica's sensitivity and intelligence. She understood her husband's problem and found a way to handle the situation with great dignity. I could never have done as well ... Her beauty, which is overwhelming, is far among her lessor assets ...

I wondered if I should keep reading. Although I'd confronted similar memories before, this was different. My mother's message made me feel guilty somehow. I knew where it was heading. It had something to do with the reason she left my father. This wasn't the first time I'd been abruptly confronted by the past. When the memory becomes too painful, I block it from my consciousness. There isn't much I remember about our final days at Fremont.

My father was my world. In my eyes, he was responsible for making the sun rise and I had unfairly cast my mother in the role of the villain, just as she had been cast by the world over the break-up of my father's marriage to Belinda. Beautiful women often get blamed in these situations, but really, if anyone is to blame, it is the partner who is being unfaithful. Usually.

Now, for the first time in my life, I was forced to consider her feelings—what she went through. I knew it was time to face it, to finally admit to myself and the world—after all these years—that it was not entirely her fault.

***

IN 1979, MARILYN Funt, then wife of Allen Funt, best known for his hit television show *Candid Camera,* conducted a series of interviews with the wives of famous men. She hoped to give a voice to the women—a chance to let *their* light shine. Getting Dad to agree to the interview was a story in itself.

Mrs Funt arrived at my grandmother's house at 1 p.m. for a two-hour scheduled interview. As she rang the bell, the pleasant empty street behind her suddenly filled with cars. Up front was my father's convertible Rolls-Royce. My mother got out and invited Marilyn into the house: a five-bedroom home built by my grandfather with rich red brick, an ornately carved mahogany front door and individually shingled roofing. The yard was landscaped with shrubbery and small trees. All the women in Mom's family loved gardening.

Before they went inside, Dad called my mother back to the car to ask her a question. Mom then went to ask Marilyn if she'd mind going to the screening of Dad's new movie, *Freedom Road.* Marilyn agreed and got into the back seat of my father's Rolls. They drove through Los Angeles with the top down as Dad smiled and waved at fans all the way to the Film Institute. Mrs Funt later wrote that she had the feeling she was in a presidential cavalcade. They watched the film. She was impressed with Dad's acting. "He's good," she said.

By five o'clock they were back at my grandmother's house. She and my mother sat down on the living-room sofa. Before they could begin Dad said, "I can't think of any reason why I should let her talk to you." And walked into the kitchen, where he began eating rice and beans. Marilyn followed him in and sat down at the table to face him.

"What did you say?" she asked.

"I can't think of any reason why I should let her talk to you about our personal life."

"I can't think of any for you either. The interview is not for you, it is for Veronica. It will make her feel good about herself."

"She feels good enough! She's my wife!"

"The world sees her as some kind of doll you keep locked away. She needs to express herself."

"That's the last thing she needs!"

"You seem to be a man who is afraid to let her speak."

Dad was having fun with her now. "Why does she have to speak?"

"Because she is a human being. Do you want everyone to think you are controlling her this much?"

"Yeah, hell yeah! As soon as she would be in your book, everyone will be coming around after her. What do I want that for?"

"This book is a very special collection of women. Obviously, I think she should be a part of it. I do understand your feelings, but because of the way you have her hidden people assume she can't even think. She happens to be very intelligent and nobody knows it."

"How do you know they think she can't think?"

"The image of her is not flattering because of how you keep her locked away."

"Good! That's what I want. I have the whole Muslim world to think about."

"So, what should we do? Do you want me to interview you? I came all the way from New York."

"I'll talk to you. I'll give you all you want."

285

"How about if the three of us talk together? You will be there the whole time."

"Well, let's see how it goes." He called Mom to come back in. Then he left. "What do you think happened to change his mind?" asked Marilyn.

"I don't know; it is hard to say. He changes his mind quite often. I don't think he remembers you are the same person he talked to on the phone."

Dad entered the room again and my mother left to check on me.

"Why don't you pay her?" he said. "Your bosses are going to make a lot of money, why should she talk for nothing?"

"It's a good question. I don't know, no one asked it before."

"She's a lady, she wouldn't ask. She would do it for free."

"I haven't paid anyone, but I will consider it. These women, who are in this book, are not interested in the money; they want to express their values, their thoughts and their identities. If I offered Veronica a lot of money now, would you care or are you just looking for another reason for her not to do it?"

"This just doesn't make sense," he said. "This is a stupid idea—for someone to talk about their marriage. That's nobody's business."

"I respect your feelings. Even though you said okay to me when we spoke before. You have every right to change your mind."

"You caught me when I wasn't thinking," he said.

"You had reservations then, so I understand how you feel."

"I'm sorry about it; I think she would have enjoyed it. Do you think she would have enjoyed it?"

"Why don't you ask her?"

"All right ... go on ... just let me hear the kind of questions you will ask, all right?"

"Here are a few: What are some of the things you do well? What are some of your favorite pleasures in life? How do you spend time with your children? What do you and your husband like to do together? How do you handle jealousy? What do you hope for as you grow older? I'm not going to trick her. You will be right there anyway."

"Okay," he conceded.

***

"WELL, ALONE AT last," said Marilyn. "I suppose you can begin by telling me about your background."

"I am twenty-three, Muhammad is thirty-seven. My parents are both from Louisiana, and they both moved here before I was born. My father started as a baker, but then he got into the construction business. He is retired now. As long as I can remember, I always wanted to be a nurse. My mother was a nurse. It was sometime in elementary school that I began to have that desire, but by the time I was twelve my sister and I went to a boarding school. It was there that I decided I wanted to be a doctor, not just a nurse. I think it's because I wanted to do something more ... but I always wanted to be the best at whatever I did."

"You mean when you were growing up, you actually thought about being the best?"

"Yes, I wanted to be the best nurse—until I realized it would be even better to be a doctor."

"'The Best' and 'The Greatest'—quite a combination. Were you very influenced in these feelings by your mother?"

"Not really. My parents were always interested in me, but I was very independent. I motivated myself. I never needed pushing to get me to get out and do something. I was always good in school. I've been lucky because I didn't really have to try hard."

"What kind of a man was your father?"

"He is pretty quiet now, but I can remember that when my father said something he meant it, and when my mother said something you could wonder and try to figure out ways to work on her emotions and get around her. I am the same way with my children. I have to practice being firmer. I feel sorry for my daughters when they do something wrong—they look so pitiful when they are crying that I can't help myself."

"What type of financial environment were you raised in?"

"We were always comfortable. I have three brothers and two sisters, and I never remember being hungry. We were a happy family. My whole family is artistic, especially my older sister Diane; my brothers are, too. My father, who is in construction, is also artistic. He rebuilt this whole house with the help of his friends."

My mom as a girl, and her parents on their wedding day.

"Why did you leave your family to go to boarding school?"

"I spent two years in boarding school in Louisiana. My sister was going, and I just went with her. We went because a good friend of my mother's told her about this particular school and she thought it was a good idea. It was there that I became more disciplined as far as studying and keeping a schedule was concerned. I was there until I was fourteen, and then I returned to Los Angeles to finish high school, where I was a very active student at Belmont High."

"What were some of your teenage activities?"

"I was a cheerleader for a while. I was on the pep squad. In boarding school, I was on the softball team, volleyball and basketball team. I'm a pretty good athlete. I was in the band. I played the clarinet. In high school, I was Prom Queen. I did not date very much. I had one boyfriend all through high school. He lived down the block, but when I got into my senior year we sort of outgrew each other."

It's a good thing they did. A few years after Mom met Dad, she found out her high-school boyfriend and his new girlfriend were the victims of a random shooting.

"Were your parents strict with you?"

"They really didn't have to be. They were, but not overly. People always felt I was older because of the way I carried myself. I always seemed more mature. I don't remember being pushed to study, or to do what I had to. This sounds like bragging, but ever since I was in boarding school I never made anything but straight As. That was bad for my brothers and sisters. I was always the example to them. I was the role model. Something that was very important to me happened when I was sixteen. I won a scholarship to work in a hospital over the summer. I was serious about being a doctor. My favorite part was working in the emergency room. We were supposed to work there a week. I stayed a month. I really got into it."

"Before Ali, was there any important boy or man in your life?"

"No, I just had the boyfriend I mentioned, but I began to lose interest in him before I met Muhammad."

"You are very, very beautiful. You say that when you were young your head was filled with academic thoughts. Were you treated in any special way because of your looks?"

"I never even thought about the way I looked until I went to boarding school. My family never made me aware of being special. It was at school that the kids started to compliment me, but you know how it is when you are growing up—you think you are ugly. I thought I was too tall. I was also shy, and I think the attention made me even more shy, because I had the feeling people were staring at me."

"Throughout high school, here in Los Angeles, what kind of a life did you lead?"

"I remember taking science courses in preparation for college, I was active in afterschool clubs and events, and I was generally home studying. I didn't go out very much, and when I graduated I was accepted at several eastern colleges, too. I didn't go because of the weather, and I ended up at USC. I am a very precise person. I probably got it from my science courses, but my brothers and sisters are like that too, so it must have also been my upbringing. I should mention the colleges, because my parents were so proud of them. I had four-year scholarships wherever I applied. I was accepted at USC, UCLA, Princeton and Yale. What is ironic is that I ended up in the bad weather with Muhammad anyway."

"What about your religious background?"

"We were practicing Catholics. I went to Catholic schools. Elementary and boarding."

"How did you change from being a Catholic to a Muslim?"

"When I met Muhammad, he said I was already a Muslim. It is just the way you live. I think he said to you that I'm a better one than he is. [Like him] I don't smoke, or drink, or eat pork—I live very decently, as I did before. There was no ceremony. My family is still Catholic. All religions are really the same; if you are a good person, you are a good person in any religion."

"How old were you when you began college, and what was your major?"

"I was seventeen and was studying pre-med. Even though the first couple of years are general study, I was taking all science courses. I was doing very well, I was on the dean's list. I went there for one year, and was about to begin the second year and I met him."

"How did you meet him?"

"I had a summer job at a department store. I heard they were looking for two representatives. One for Ali and one for George Foreman, whom he was going to fight at that time. It was a contest, and I had done some modeling work before. I had won several titles, and did some department-store modeling. The titles were school titles, like Prom Queen, Girl of the Month."

"Did you think about going into modeling and giving up your education?"

"No, never. It was just a diversion. I was never serious about it."

"Didn't you feel very special, winning titles for your looks and receiving such high grades?"

"I guess that is why I am the way that I am. I don't try to compete with Muhammad. If I didn't really feel like something before I married him, I could see really feeling like a nothing. I think that is what he experienced before—a constant sense of competition. He does not have that with me. I'll never try to prove I'm someone with him. I don't have to. I could go out and try to be famous but I don't need to. Fame isn't important to me. I might want to do some commercials just for fun, as I did modeling in school as a diversion."

"Let's go back to when you met Ali ..."

"I was interviewed by a group [Booker Griffin, who ran the fight promotions' West Coast office] who wanted several girls who would represent [Foreman and Ali] for a poster to advertise the fight. We were going around showing people slides and trying to get people interested in going to Zaire, Africa, for the fight. We went to a boxing exhibition [in Salt Lake City] and that's where I met him. We picked him up at the airport, drove him to his hotel ..."

"How did he react to you?"

"He ignored me when he first met me. If you are ever around, you will notice when he meets people he likes to clown, it depends on his mood, but he likes to grab and hug people—that was a lot different from the way he treated me. He was doing that to everyone else but me. Later I asked him why, and he said he was afraid of me. He said he was afraid he might say the wrong thing. Actually, I didn't realize it then."

"What was your first impression of him?"

"I was impressed with him—he seemed to have high morals. I admired him."

"How did you really get to know him?"

"I went to Africa with a separate group; he was already there. We just got to know each other by talking and being around. [George Foreman cut his eye, so the fight was postponed a month. Dad invited my mother to the presidential compound, where he was training, in N'Sele.] By the end of the month, we had begun to care for each other ... He told me that his marriage was really over. Before I would let myself get involved, I checked with those close to him to see if it was true. You know men lie! I was convinced that his marriage was over emotionally, and they were going to get a divorce."

"I know he doesn't want us to talk about that whole period before your marriage, so we won't. You were married after Hana was born. Your life must have changed radically as soon as you started seeing him, even before you actually married him?"

"We have known each other for five years. Our youngest child, Laila, is thirteen months old. Hana is two and a half. In the past five years things have been so frantic that I don't feel as if we have begun to settle down. Perhaps we can't for quite a while."

"What did it feel like, being a mother at such an early age? You were just twenty."

"Well, when I realized that my plans about my future had changed, and that my future was Muhammad, I was very anxious to have a child. I was very happy when I knew I was going to have Hana. I wanted children, and I just had them and they fit in. I did not think about it that much. We travel with them, and when we can't I have family and responsible people who stay with them when we are away."

"Did you have any problems about their being so close in age?"

"Hana seems to have been troubled by Laila's presence. She was drinking out of a cup, and now she has gone back to the bottle, and in general reverted to some baby ways that she had outgrown. They are very attached to each other—it will work out. I want the children to be proud, but I don't want them to be arrogant and think they are better than anyone else because their father is Muhammad Ali. I know that is a very hard job. When we come here to my mother's, the kids just seem to come alive. They are pretty good at home [the Woodlawn house in Chicago]. We travel so much with them, but this house is so small, they do much better here."

My father enters the room.

"Hello," said Marilyn, "are you going to join us?"

"I'll just sit around," said Dad.

"How many homes do you have?"

Dad looked at my mother. "Tell her how since you've been with me," he said, "you haven't been able to settle down and fix up a home. How you never know where you are ..."

"Yeah," said Marilyn, "it must be crazy being married to him."

"It is!" said Mom. "We have several places—"

Dad interjects. "Our summer home is here in California [they had just purchased Fremont Place, but we had not moved in], our main home is in Chicago."

"In the past five years," said Mom, "he's been fighting ever since I met him. So he's training most of the time. We live in one training camp for three months, then move to the city where he is fighting, and then go home for a couple of weeks, then in between he has appearances to make."

"What do you do when he is so busy with his life?"

"I just take care of the kids. I play tennis; I love birds and I collect them. When I was pregnant with Hana, I raised farm animals just to keep busy. I like to paint. I do oils, and watercolors. I have several at the farm. I did a lot of painting there while I was carrying Hana ... My painting is literal; I don't do abstracts. I like the old Master type of paintings."

Dad gets up. "Your questions are all right. I'm going upstairs."

"He's so tired that he doesn't care," said Mom, laughing.

"I won't take advantage ..." replied Marilyn.

"I have very little free time," said Mom. "We are always traveling. I love antiques and I go window shopping a lot. I love to admire beautiful old things and paintings. Every once in a while I see something I really love and I will buy it. I am anxious to be able to decorate our new home here, in California."

"What are some of the problems with all the fame, which is different from that of most celebrities? His fame is worldwide."

"I'm sort of shy, so I am a little self-conscious in crowds, people staring at us. Sometimes when we are tired and trying to spend some quiet time I wish people wouldn't come around, but there are always people around. I don't mind very much, he doesn't mind at all ..."

"You are very striking and very intelligent, and you would have pursued a career in medicine had you not married him. Does it bother you that all the attention is going to him?"

"Not at all. I prefer it that way. I'm getting out of my shyness—I guess I have to—but I am more comfortable with his being the center of attraction."

"I am interviewing you here in your mother's house, a simple place by comparison to where you could be staying. I know your family is very important to you. Do you ever worry that all the glamor might take you away from your roots?"

"No, I have never felt that way, or even thought about it. When we are in town we enjoy being here ..."

"Hello again," Marilyn said to my father as he walked back into the room.

"We feel the family—grandmother and father and brothers and sisters—should not be deprived from seeing the children," said Dad. "The family feeling is very important. Hana knows all the names. We have to be together as much as we can ..."

"Veronica, how do you handle jealousy?" Marilyn looked at my father. "Is that okay to ask?"

"Yes, that is okay. She can talk about that," said Dad.

"When I first met him, I had to get used to him hugging everyone. Now I'm used to it. I can't say I like it, but I try not to pay attention to it. It doesn't make me angry, but if I had a choice I would rather he didn't do it. But it is his personality. Sometimes I just get disgusted with the boldness of the women today. Even in front of me, they sort of push you aside, and don't acknowledge you. They are really bad, sometimes."

"Veronica, what are some of the things you feel you do well?"

"I feel that I have a lot of artistic ability, but I don't have enough time to express myself that way. I am good in just about any sport. We play tennis together, and on the farm we ride horses and ride bikes together."

"What makes you angry?"

"I get angry when I can't understand why people can't live in peace together. People should be able to live the way they want—without so much interference."

Marilyn looks at my father. "Can I ask her what makes her angry about you?"

"Yeah," he said.

"I would have to think about that for a while," said Mom.

"You want to know what makes her angry about me?" said Dad. "Wearing the same clothes too often. She says they are dirty—I don't think so. If I wear a black shirt and pants, I say it's not dirty."

"It may not be dirty, but it is strong," said Mom, laughing. "I would not have told that, but since you did, it is okay." Both Mom and Dad laugh.

"It makes her angry when I am up early and won't let her sleep ..."

"So you wake her up because you are up?"

"Well, I kiss her on the cheek and she gets mad and pushes me away."

"Did you ever hit him?"

"She hit me once. Nothing serious. I can't remember when, but she knocked me down one day." He laughs.

"I did not!"

"She did. She took a poke and then she stomped me."

295

They all laugh.

"I'm only joking," he said.

"Seriously, does it ever bother you to know how strong he is?"

"No, I never think about it," said Mom.

"Oh yeah?" said Dad. "One morning she said, 'Ali, you are strong—put on some Ban Roll-On.'"

"Veronica, do you think there is anything about you he doesn't like?"

"I don't know. I don't think he would tell me."

"She takes too long to get dressed. She has a hard time deciding what to order in a restaurant," said Dad.

"That's because I'm particular about food. You don't even need a menu," said Mom.

Marilyn changes the subject. "Muhammad, you have said that when you have ten thousand tax-free bonds you are going to give it all up and preach. Do you seriously think the two of you can devote yourself to the religion?"

"That's my goal in life," said Dad.

"Veronica, do you think you can share this dream with him?"

"I will be a part of it. I'm not sure in what way."

"In the Muslim religion, the woman's job is not the same," said Dad. "She is beside me to comfort me, help me, raise the family, travel with me, help me make decisions."

"What decisions does she help you with?"

"A lot of them ... Where we should live. She has even helped me make decisions on certain fights, by helping me to decide where to train, and planning our schedules."

"Do you feel he is dependent on you?"

"Not at all. I don't feel that. I really don't know how I have helped him make any decisions about the fights," she said.

"Muhammad, are you very dependent on her?"

"I am, but she doesn't know it, she doesn't feel it."

"Why doesn't she feel it, if it is true?"

"Because she isn't an arrogant, sassy kind of woman. She is 100 percent my woman—even in thought. She never uses words of profanity, she never wants to party or disco. She never talks bad about people."

"It's interesting, people think how lucky she is. I think you are a lot luckier to have her."

"She is a saint," said Dad. "She is sweet and nice. I am the lucky one."

At this point my father stood and walked out the room. "Goodbye, girls," he said.

Marilyn then focused her attention back on Mom. "Veronica, we really didn't get into what makes you angry when he was here. Let's go back to it."

"It is hard to get me mad. I never really get mad at anyone. My family will tell you that."

"Is it that you feel it mostly inside, but do not show it?"

"Yes, I guess you can put it that way. I don't know if I can tell you what makes me mad, but some things can. Like things in the newspaper that are untrue get me angry. I don't stay upset very long. I get over things quickly. I do get mad when he rushes me. He tells me to get ready at a certain time, and he keeps coming in and bothering me long before it's time. He'll actually time me with his watch, and if it's thirty seconds past he will say, 'I told you, you wouldn't be ready.' He's been brought up that way—he thinks if you are supposed to there at 10:00, get there at 9:30. I try to get him to go to certain places later—he's not supposed to arrive before everyone else. He ends up waiting for the people when they are coming to see him."

"I was very surprised today," said Marilyn. "All the people around him seemed so comfortable. For a celebrity of his level, that is surprising. Usually they have to let a few people down, he didn't."

"Once you get to know him, you will see he treats everyone the same. He likes to be around common people more than celebrities."

"You told me about how he spoils people around him. Does he spoil you?"

"I don't think he spoils me. I'm the one he doesn't spoil. The people he spoils are the ones that are not close. The ones that are close he treats normally. He is generous with me, but I don't spend a lot of money."

"If you wanted a fur coat, would you go out and buy it, or ask him for it?"

"I would be afraid to ask him. I just don't like asking. I always wanted a Mercedes and I never told him, so one day he got his cook a Mercedes and I still didn't say anything."

"You say you don't get mad, but you must have been really mad this time."

Laughing, "Yeah, I was. I didn't say anything for a while, but finally when I let it out he said I should have told him. He did get me one. He is so generous. He gives people houses and cars. I am trying to get him to act more normal. It is working—he's changing."

"Do you think he does it because he wants to be loved by everyone?"

"No, not at all. He really loves helping people. He enjoys making people happy ..."

Dad walked back into the room. "You two still at it?"

"Veronica, do you ever think about going back to school, to study medicine?"

"I'm thinking about it."

"I have been talking to her about it," said Dad.

"Wait a minute," said Marilyn. "Are you saying you would be supportive of her going to school?"

"Yeah. I don't want her sitting around waiting for me, with her life going by. I want her to be busy and not be dependent on me. I would be the happiest man in the world if she went back to college."

"Wait a minute," said Marilyn, "you were afraid of this interview—how can you imagine you could handle her being involved with her own life?"

"I'm not worried about men, I want her to go back to school to be a doctor."

"I'm very shocked—I asked that question assuming I'd get the opposite answer."

"I'm thinking about it," said Mom. "But the children are still very young, and our lives are not settled. I know how much time school takes, and how serious you have to be with your studies."

"I would be so happy if I could see her in the morning and say, 'Give me a kiss,' and she would say, 'Ali, I'm busy. I have to jump in the car and go to school.'"

"I can't believe this," said Marilyn. "Knowing you, I would think you would only want her on standby."

"When I first met her, I was like that. I didn't want her to go to school or anywhere. But now that I know her and know that she really loves me, she can go anywhere in the world. I wouldn't even worry about it ... She is much smarter than me. She was top in her school."

"Veronica, do you think he really means any of this?"

"He means it about my studying to become a doctor. Going anywhere in the world without him is something else."

"If I die, I want her to be self-supporting. A good doctor can make two- to three-hundred thousand a year," said Dad.

"I think he is really looking forward to picking me up at school," said Mom. "He would really be proud."

"Can you imagine him at your graduation? When do you think you might make a decision about a return to college?"

"It would have to be after he decides how much longer he is going to fight. We travel so much that last year we were only home one month."

"Why do you think he is so anxious for you to do something?"

"He has just become like that in the last few months ... He wants me to be happy. He knows I want to do something, I think that's why. Because before, he didn't want me to do anything. He also knows that if I had stayed in school, by the time I reached twenty-five I would have been a doctor. That is just two years away."

"Ali, do you feel guilty that she didn't go to medical school?"

"No, I just want her to go now."

Dad leaves for a while again, and Mom and Marilyn continue to talk.

"About the movie that I saw today. Whose idea was it for you to have a cameo role?"

"It was the producer's idea. He actually offered me the part of Muhammad's wife, but I knew I wasn't right for it, and I also knew I didn't have any training to be a good actress."

"Do you think he would have let you take the role of the wife? It was such a prominent one in the movie."

"I don't know. He said he didn't mind, but he also knew I didn't want it. If I did, he might have felt very differently. I was not right for the part, even physically. I knew it."

"Do you feel you know your husband?"

"I feel I do, but sometimes he can even puzzle me. Occasionally he throws me. I certainly did not expect him to encourage me to go back to school. It's funny, in the beginning I wanted to go back, and he didn't; now he is encouraging and I am not so sure because of the children. I know I'm going to do something ... I just have to find something I am interested in, and know I have the time for it."

"What do you think people misunderstand about you?"

"Well, you said it today, when you were talking to Muhammad. People must think, 'I wonder why he won't let her do interviews ... he must be hiding something.' That is one reason I would want to do an interview, to dispel that impression. Also the press so distorted his divorce, and since we don't talk about things like that, no one will ever know the real truth."

"You feel the public thinks you broke up his marriage, and you feel you didn't. Does that trouble you much?"

"I have a sense of what is really important. Even big things that don't actually affect our daily lives are not important. For instance, the stories in the papers don't really have any bearing on how we live. The main thing is that God knows the truth and that is what counts. I am a substantial person."

"How is Ali as a father?"

"You wouldn't believe it, he is so good. He is wonderful with the children."

"What do you think is your greatest strength of character?"

"Sometimes I think something is wrong with me because things don't worry me or get me down like I think they should. Even with all this publicity from his divorce, it didn't affect me as I think it could have someone else. I think about why I am like that, and I think it's because I have an inner self-worth ... Being married to him has strengthened that feeling."

My father re-entered the room.

"We are almost finished," said Marilyn. "Veronica," she continued, "what do you consider a weakness?"

"Oh—I have to think ..."

"The fact that you need all this time is the answer," said Marilyn.

"Well, I think I am weak with the children. I don't discipline well enough. They often see me smiling when I'm trying to be firm."

"You want some sensational answer to that question. You are not going to get that," said Dad. "She doesn't have any weaknesses. A poem to my wife, Veronica Ali, by Muhammad Ali: *I told her to go to college and get some knowledge. Stay there until you are through. If they can make penicillin out of moldy BREAD, they sure can make something out of you.*"

"Is that supposed to be a compliment?" asked Marilyn.

"I'm only kidding," said my father. "She is a beautiful woman. Not just her looks. You can't find anyone like her."

29

THERE WAS A letter wedged between the last two pages of Mom's copy of the interview, addressed to my father from Marilyn Funt. The letter wasn't dated but judging by her comment about President Reagan, and what she wrote, it had to have been written sometime between 1981 and 1984. After my father lost his last fight in December 1981 and his first Parkinson's diagnosis was made public, there were stories in the press about him not feeling well and how abnormally exhausted he had been before the fight. She could have written it then. But if it was the latter, five years after she had interviewed my mother, things had changed by then between my parents.

> Dear Muhammad Ali,
> It so really hurt me to learn that you are sick. As I continue to tell friends and associates, I have never met a star who treats the people around him as decently as you do. If you remember I spent a whole day with you when I was interviewing Veronica. I know you will beat this. You are "The Greatest," and always will be ...! Please don't back Reagan ... Even if you do, I still love you and I'm rooting for you to get well!
> Marilyn Funt

By 1983, Mom and Dad were probably sleeping in separate bedrooms. And Dad had written his first letter to my mother. In 1984, she told him she wanted the divorce. Then on June 26, 1985, my mother's lawyer released a statement to the press:

USA TODAY LOS ANGELES: Three-time heavyweight boxing champion Muhammad Ali is down for the count for the third time in marriage—he and wife Veronica filed Tuesday for divorce. Ali, 43, and the 29-year-old were married for eight years. They have two children, Hana Yasmeen, 9, and Laila, 8. Ali retired in 1981.

"An amicable agreement on the major issues has already been worked out," said Frederick J. Glassman, the lawyer representing my mother. She had prepared a statement that read: "The decision to dissolve the marriage was mutually agreed upon ... Both parties maintain the utmost admiration, love and respect for each other and their deep friendship remains intact."

Mom told me she was trying to save my father any embarrassment. She made no mention of his infidelities and let the world believe that they had both decided to file for divorce.

But his love letters to her told a different story.

***

A FEW MONTHS after Marilyn Funt's interview in 1979, we officially moved into the house on Fremont Place. One of my favorite things was calling my father over the telephone intercom. I was only three years old, but it's the first thing I actually remember learning how to do. Probably from watching the adults around me. The house was so large, everyone called each other rather than running up and down one or two flights of stairs just to ask a question or deliver a message.

Every morning I picked up the telephone in my bedroom, which my mother had installed for emergencies, pushed a button, and my father would answer from his office downstairs.

"Daddy! What are you doing, Daddy?"

I'm sure Marilyn Funt would have been intrigued by all of the tape recordings my father made, eavesdropping on conversations, or talking to me and countless acquaintances, friends and celebrities.

Especially the one of him talking to my mother on December 29, 1979.

My father spoke into the recorder: *"This is December 29, 1979, in the Los Angeles home, at 10:30 p.m. I'm talking to Veronica on the telephone intercom ..."*

He clicked over to connect the line, picking up the recording in the middle of my mother's sentence: *"Frankie* [the housekeeper] *borrowed $500, then she borrowed $200. Now her television went out, so I let her borrow a TV. Now she just asked to borrow some more money and she said, 'Whenever I want to borrow money, I come to you. I don't believe in going behind somebody's back, asking their husband.'"*

"Who said that—Frankie?" Dad asked.

"Yes ..."

"Is she saying that somebody else does it?"

"No, that's all she said, but the other day she told me that when she used to work for another lady, the woman's husband kept bothering her. She said, 'If anybody's husband bothers me, I'll come tell or I just won't work any more.'"

"Why did she say that?"

"She was just talking about the people she used to work for. The husband was flirting with her, and she told the wife that she wasn't going to work for her any more unless the husband wasn't there."

"Do you think that all people who have houses and helpers have problems with them?"

"I don't know. I bet you that no one in their right mind tells the help that they don't have to listen to the wife, and that they're the big authority."

"No, I never said that."

"You said that to Doris, in the Chicago house."

"No. Something happened one day, I can't remember what it was, but she had a problem and I told her she should come to me about it. It wasn't anything to do with housework."

"Well, she shouldn't go to you about anything," Mom scolded him. "Even if it has nothing to do with her housework."

"Do you think you're going to keep Janet [the babysitter]?" He was changing the subject.

"Eventually I'm going to find somebody else," Mom said. "Because, when the kids get a little older, they're going to need somebody who has good sense and can teach them something. Janet's nice and I like her, but sometimes she's sloppy and her English is bad ... Do you have that tape on?"

"No," Dad fibs. "Do you want me to get the tape?"

"No, I was just wondering if you had the tape on because one day she might pick it up and listen to us talking about her. Especially if she sees her name written on it. 'Talking about Janet.'"

"She doesn't meddle in our business," he said.

"That's what I'm saying. She's nice."

"If an emergency came up, does she know how to call 911?" he asked.

"Well, she would, but, you know, you wonder. I've told her I've got all the emergency numbers on the phone and I had my father put locks on Hana's and Laila's doors, so if someone got into the house they wouldn't be able to get into their rooms. And I have her keep my gun in her room when we are gone."

"I'll take her out one day and teach her how to shoot it," he said.

"You aren't ever going to take Janet anywhere." Her voice was slightly raised. "Don't ever take Janet any place—not you!"

"What?" he stutters. "Take her where?"

"You were about to say that you're going to take her to the shooting range and let her practice shooting."

"No, not me," he recanted. "You should go somewhere and take her."

"I'm going to do that, just for myself. I'm going to go learn how to shoot again."

Laughing, he asked, "Why can't I take her?"

"Because you don't do things like that! Doris [the Chicago house-keeper] didn't start acting up until you drove her to the hospital with her daughter when she got shot in the head with the BB gun. You just shouldn't be out with a woman, that's all. You should just keep away from them, and don't give me any excuse because too many times before I trusted you with people like that and something happened. So now, if I get suspicious, I'll just say forget it and get rid of them."

"You think I might be hittin' on Janet?"

"I don't know what you might do—you're always talking and flirting ..."

"That's terrible," he said.

"Listen, do you think I'd have her in the house if I thought you would? I just know there's a chance."

"The girl that takes care of my children?" He sighed, innocently.

"Muhammad, I would have never thought you would have messed with Tammy [a previous babysitter]. I would have never thought that."

"Allah is my witness, I never—"

"Muhammad," she interrupted, "don't you say Allah because you already told me you did!"

"But I didn't, though ..." he fibbed.

"You did too, at the farm. You got mad and finally admitted it to me."

"I just said that because you made me mad—"

"You did not."

"You just said I got mad, didn't you?"

"Yeah, because Tammy was blaming the baby on you and she was going everywhere with us and telling people that she was pregnant. Crazy girl. And she used to talk like a crazy person, too, going around telling people you were her master."

"She was crazy, wasn't she?"

"And another time I came home and you had a lady sitting on your lap."

"Where?"

"In Chicago, and then another time you were in the bus with that woman in the bathroom. Anyway, I'm just telling you ... If I thought you would bother Janet, I would have never hired her and, just to make sure, just don't take her anywhere."

Joking, he said, "I'll tell you the truth, I talked to Janet last week. She likes me. She's my woman now ..."

My mother was annoyed. "Ooooh, I'm just telling you ..."

He laughs.

"And don't tell them to come to you or anything like that because if I get suspicious I'll just get rid of them, and Janet's all right, I don't want to fire her, but she does have faults."

"How's everyone else acting, how's Edith [the cook]?"

"She's fine, and Carol is okay too. She just doesn't wear her [maid's] uniform. She said it makes her feel like a slave, so I told her I'd find her some pants."

"What's the uniform look like?"

"It's the standard uniform. It's pretty. It's black and it has lace on the collar and on the sleeves, and a white apron."

"Okay, well, I won't say anything to that girl any more. If she comes in here talking about money, I'm going to tell her to go see you."

"Okay. Well, you can speak to them, just don't say things like, 'If you don't like something, come see me,' like you're over me. You're supposed to discuss it with me."

"You're right. It doesn't make any sense. You won't get any respect out of them."

"I know—that's what was wrong with all the Chicago crew. You know what they'd tell me? 'I was here before you.' That's what all their attitudes were."

"Don't let it upset you," he said. "It's all over now."

"I'm just saying, don't start that around here."

"Okay, I won't. I'll talk to you later."

30

I WAS BEGINNING to see my father through my mother's eyes. She had devoted so much of her life to him that in some ways she had lost herself in him. It's no wonder she eventually felt the need to break away.

Mom had a lot to deal with in the years she was married to my father. As I've mentioned, women were always chasing after him, and some even tried to pin their children on him. One lady claimed Dad had fathered her newborn child, which he would have eagerly accepted as his own for no other reason than he loved being a father. But judging from the birthdate of the child in question, Mom figured out that, while not improbable, it was impossible. It would've had to have been conceived during the period they were on a month-long tour of Europe.

"I knew there was no way it was his," said Mom.

The blood test also proved it. But its results didn't stop the offsprings of women who had allegedly spent the night with my father from copying our baby photos offline and passing them off as their own. I can't say that I blame them. I can understand how a person without a father would want to believe that they were the long-lost love child of Muhammad Ali.

I never actually witnessed my father seriously flirting with another woman. I know he was a lady's man till the end. His eyes lit up like the sun whenever a pretty girl walked by, but I've never seen him *really* look at anyone the way he looked at my mother.

I remember the way he sat up in his chair and straightened his shirt the first time he saw Mom after he'd moved to Michigan with Lonnie in 1987. Dad visited us regularly at our new house after the divorce. He'd sit in the living room with her, drinking coffee, and telling her how much he still did and always would love her. Sometimes he'd tell jokes, and he once said to her before leaving, "I had your best years." He always found the humor in life—even in painful situations.

But after a couple years had passed without seeing her, it must have brought back all his pain and love when Mom came up to his hotel room to pick us up. "Ronca," he said, walking across the room to hug her, "you're still beautiful."

"So are you," she whispered. Tears welled in both of their eyes.

My parents shared a great romance. Laila and I were born out of their love, and a lot of beautiful memories, adventures, and sometimes pain and sorrow were experienced in the twelve years they were together. They were just two remarkable people trying to find their way in the world. My father would be the first to admit he made mistakes. It saddens me to think they cost him the love of his life.

***

I LAY ON my bed for a while, staring at the ceiling, pondering about everything: their fairy tale courtship, the letters, the tape recording and the divorce. I thought, too, about my father and his pain. How he had blamed himself when Mom left him, his conviction that he deserved to lose her. When I first asked him about it, years ago, he denied it of course. It was the same afternoon that we were watching the movie *Ali* at the house in Michigan. After discussing the circumstances surrounding the demise of his relationship with Belinda, I asked Dad why he cheated on my mother, if he loved her so deeply.

"No," he said. His brows squinted, as if I had just accused him of murder. "I never cheated on your mother."

"Yes, you did, Daddy."

"No." His eyes were wide with denial.

310

"Daddy, you have kids by different women who are the same age," I gently reminded him, with a chuckle. "You brought us all together, every summer, and made sure we knew about each other so we could grow up and be friends. And we did."

He said nothing.

"Daddy, the whole world knows. Admitting it to me won't make me love you any less. Nothing you could *ever* do or say will make me love you less. I'm not going to judge you. I just want to know why you cheated."

"She didn't satisfy me!" he blurts, abruptly.

"Daddy! That's not fair. I know that's not true."

He shifted in his seat, staring in his lap, as if considering—searching. "I don't know ..." he finally answered. "I was wrong. I'm sorry."

"It's okay, Daddy," I assured him. "No one is perfect. We all make mistakes." I hugged him and reminded him once more, "All of your children grew up to be friends because you brought us together. You did good, Daddy."

He nodded and neither of us spoke further about it. We shifted our attention back to the movie and our dessert.

He had asked for forgiveness and I gave it. But the truth is, I had forgiven him for everything he had ever done, or ever could do, long before that day. Something about the way he looked when he answered me—the sadness in his eyes, perhaps, reminded me about the time I tried to take him to visit the house on Fremont Place.

We were driving down Wilshire Blvd in January of 2002 on our way to his hotel, the Beverly Hilton. Dad was in town for the unveiling of his star on the Hollywood Walk of Fame. An honor that is generally reserved for filmmakers, actors, and musicians was awarded to him for, among other reasons, "living his life as live theater". And since he first gained world recognition with his Olympic gold medal in 1960 he had been a constant showman and entertainer—"walking theater".

But of the 2,500-plus stars that line the sidewalks on the fifteen-block stretch in Hollywood, my father's is the only one that has never been walked on. At his request, it was placed on a wall—at

6801 Hollywood Blvd, in the entrance of the Dolby Theater, home of the Academy Awards.

Dad had originally declined the invitation to receive a star from the Hollywood Chamber of Commerce because he didn't want his name and what it represented disrespected.

"It will have to be on a wall," he said. "I bare the name of the beloved prophet of Islam. I can't allow it to be trampled on by people and urinated on by dogs ..."

Respecting my father's wishes, Johnny Grant, then chairman of the Walk of Fame Committee, broke tradition to honor Dad's request and decided that the 2,189th star would be the first and, so far, only one mounted on the wall. No other honoree has ever been granted a similar request, and probably never will.

I stopped at a red light on the corner of Rossmore Avenue, adjacent to Fremont Place. I saw my youthful self soaring down the street on my bicycle en route to 7-Eleven. I remembered Laila and I riding over bumps on the sidewalk as our friends Kim and Karen trailed close behind. Wendy was my name and my bike was a red Corvette. Laila was Heidi and she drove a white Porsche. These were the games we played; the adventures we etched into the heart of the street. Eating Jolly Ranchers and red licorice, bought with the fifty-dollar bills my father pulled from the small round safe he kept under his desk.

"Look, Daddy," I said, as we waited for the light to turn green. "Want to drive by and see the old house?"

He looked up but said nothing.

"A lawyer and his wife live there now," I said. "They have two children."

He closed his eyes and shook his head.

"Maybe another time." Tears swelled in my eyes and I leaned over to kiss him. When the light turned green, I glanced at the huge stone pillars that frame the guarded entrance to Fremont Place and drove away.

Remembering that day made me think of one of my father's last letters to my mother. I felt his pain as if it were my own, especially now, knowing what he suffered: living under the same roof with Mom, unable to sleep in the same bedroom with her. Hoping and praying, day after day, while traveling the world together, knowing the end was near. Those final years of their marriage he endured the uncertainty looming above like a dreary cloud waiting to unleash its storm.

"Veronica, our love has now come to its end, simply because we are only friends ... For it is never easy to understand how heartache and despair can take command ..."

I was in my twenties when I learned my father's strategy for over-coming a broken heart. I had just broken up with a boyfriend and asked Dad for advice. He was always happy when we came to him for help. I think hearing about our problems made him feel closer to us, made him feel needed, like a father.

I explained my dilemma. "What should I do, Daddy?" I asked.

"If he's sorry, and he's worth it, give him another chance," he said. "If you decide not to, first you should get rid of everything that reminds you of him, moving away helps. Then it will take twice as long as you were together for it to happen."

"For what to happen?"

There was an enduring pause. "For the pain to end." There was a sadness in his voice that haunts me to this day. I knew he was probably thinking of my mother. He had loved and lost before, but in those situations he was the one who'd walked away. I think it's a much deeper agony when you're the one being left.

I did the math: two years, for me. Twenty-four, for him. According to his philosophy, at the time he still had eleven years to go. But there are some things in life—some people—we never really get over. We just learn to live through the pain. Dad was always good at that—living through pain.

Several years ago, Mom asked me to tell my father she will always love him and that she forgave him for all her pain. When I conveyed the message, Dad stared down in his lap, as if remembering his own sorrow. After a moment, he looked up and said, *"Tell her that I love and forgive her, too."* I nodded in agreement wondering *how* love ends up this way.

313

Most women think that men cheat on them because they're lacking in some way—not beautiful enough, thin enough, etc. Because my mother was so exceptionally beautiful and intelligent, and my father still cheated on her, I learned that it has absolutely nothing to do with a woman's looks. It's more to do with men having problems and issues of their own.

I thought about my mother and her decision to leave my father. Did she come home one day and realize she was no longer in love with him, or did it happen gradually, over time? I have so many unanswered questions, questions I never asked either of them, fearing I don't know what, really—the answer, maybe? Or worse, the painful memories that might resurface on hearing the details: the months following the divorce when I would smile watching my father walk up the brick driveway to visit us at the new house, then cry when it was time for him to leave and walk away, his suffering only outweighed by *my own*.

***

I SAT ON my bed thinking about all my father was dealing with. It seemed like torture for him—knowing, yet not knowing, what would become of his marriage, his health. It was such a melancholy and unsettled time. *"Faith comes easy when things are going smooth in life,"* he once said. *"The test is holding on to it when the winds of change and uncertainty blow."*

He got through it, of course; he's always had a remarkable tolerance for discomfort, both physical and emotional. So much so that we never knew when something was bothering him. A headache, cramped hands, a limp in his walk. You had to watch him closely, especially near the end. He never complained. And he always had an extraordinary ability to turn a negative situation into a positive one. He came to the earth that way.

Dad started boxing when he was twelve, after his bike was stolen. Every day after school he'd go to Nazareth College to help the nuns Sister Allen and Sister Christina dust the shelves, sweep the floors, and take care of the library. From there, he crossed the street to Columbia gym to train with Joe Martin, the

315

policeman who had introduced him to boxing, whom he met just after the bike was stolen. I imagined him in the gym—sparring, jumping rope, and hitting the speed bag; he could never pass a mirror without shadow-boxing.

Joe Martin introduced my father to the sport, but Dad always said that it was a black man named Fred Stoner who he had to train with in secret who taught him the science of boxing. After training six to eight at Martin's gym, he'd sneak over to Stoner's—"*To get my real training,*" said Dad. Joe Martin had one rule: no one could train with Stoner or his boy.

Day after day, Dad repeated the process.

My father was embarrassed to tell his friends that he didn't always have a nickel to ride the bus to school, so he found a creative way to deal with the situation. The walk from his house on Grand Avenue to Central High was long. *This is a good chance for exercise*, he thought, as the big city bus drove past one morning. And with that he ran out beside it, his classmates and friends waving and smiling at the sight of him. He never knew what they were saying. He just smiled and waved back, as he jogged beside the bus all the way to school, with his peers shaking their heads and saying, "That Cassius is as nutty as can be."

31

THEY SAY MEN learn how to be good husbands from their fathers, and women learn from their mothers. I think my mom had the advantage here. She grew up in a modest but comfortable house in Los Angeles, with two sisters, Michelle and Diane, and three brothers, Tony, Leonard, and Steven. My grandfather, Horace Porche, was a carpenter. He built the house they grew up in after my grandmother, Ethel, a registered nurse, received a $30,000 inheritance from one of her private-duty patients.

My mother's father was the opposite of Papa Cash, my dad's father. Grampa Porche was a quiet, reserved, loving but unaffectionate man who liked to spend his time fishing with his friends, watching baseball, and cooking gumbo.

"You act like you love fishing more than you love your family," my grandmother often complained.

"I'll be home at five," he'd say, and walk out the door. He was a man of few words.

My grandmother was a fashionable, hard-working homemaker. She cooked dinner every night after work, did everyone's laundry, and always found time to doll herself up. Her hair was always freshly rolled and she wore red lipstick to match her pretty dresses. She loved to sing my mother's praises, then and now. "Of all my children, your mother never gave me any trouble," she said one afternoon, not too long ago, while cleaning out one of her closets. She was making space for more of Mom's storage boxes. Almost every room in my grandmother's house was stuffed with boxes and bundles of clothes and furnishings from Fremont Place—things my mother wanted to sort through before throwing them out.

"She'd go straight to her room after school and do her homework," Grandma said proudly. "And when she was a little girl and got her clothes dirty playing outside, she went upstairs and put on a clean dress."

My mother was a goodie-two-shoes. She spent most of her time studying in her room, earning the perfect record of straight "A" grades that my grandma loved to show off. Mom was voted Prom Queen, Homecoming Princess, Senior Class President, and she received four full scholarships to Princeton, Yale, USC, and UCLA. Grandma had been Prom Queen and valedictorian herself.

"Why can't you be more like Veronica?" she'd say to my aunt Diane, the rebel of the family, who regularly snuck out of her bedroom window to meet her boyfriends, listing the names of the ones she kissed on a notepad in her nightstand. This had been the catalyst for my grandmother's decision to send both she and my mother off to Catholic boarding school, where she hoped the nuns would manage to teach Auntie Diane how not to sin.

"I'm sending you with her, Veronica, so she isn't alone," she explained on a Saturday afternoon, as my twelve-year-old mother reluctantly packed her bags. "The year will fly by. You'll be home before you know it."

Two years later, Mom returned with a perfect report card; Diana came back with a handful of names to add to her list.

From then on, my mother's young life was uneventful. While her sisters fought over the telephone and her brothers debated about sports, she spent most of her time, as she always had, studying in her room. Unaware that the poster hanging on her brother's wall of the handsome, outspoken boxer—whom she thought was conceited, and whom the world and the boys in chemistry class referred to as "The Greatest of All Times"—would one day be her husband.

My grandparents separated after my mother graduated high school. Grandma, still young, beautiful, and in need of attention, found herself a boyfriend, and my grandfather eventually moved into the guest-house at Fremont Place. For the most part, my mother's youth was ordinary. Dad, on the other hand, observed more than any little boy should, growing up in the segregated south of Louisville, Kentucky.

Louise Hay wrote in her bestselling book *You Can Heal Your Life*, "We're all victims, of victims ... when we learn about our parents' childhood we learn where their fears and rigid patterns come from."

Like so many parents around the world, my parents were doing the best they could with what they had been taught as children.

***

I FORGOT ABOUT the newspapers and magazine articles for a while and let my thoughts roam. I thought about my father's childhood, and how different it was from mine and my mother's. I wondered what it was like for him when his parents separated. He was an adult when his father moved out, but still I wondered if it had the same effect on him as it did me.

I thought, too, about my father's parents, Papa Cash and Mama Bird, and the little pink house Dad grew up in on 3302 Grand Avenue, with its leaky roof and walls, and lopsided front porch. The porch my father, as a seven-year-old little boy, used to go outside and sit on and look up at the stars waiting for God, or one of his angels, to tell him his divine mission in life. He always believed he'd been born for a special purpose.

I wished I could go back in time and tell that little boy—my dad—that he was right. He *was* born for a special purpose, and he would grow up and fulfill it a thousand-fold and come to be known all over the world as The Greatest.

My Father's Childhood

Everything Muhammad did seemed different as a child. He even had the measles and the chicken pox at the same time ... His mind was like the March wind, blowing every which way. And whenever I thought I could predict what he'd do, he turned around and proved me wrong.

One time he tied a string to our curtains in the bedroom and ran the string out the window around the house to his own room. Then when we went to sleep, he'd pull on the string to make the curtains move. He always had confidence in himself. And that gave me confidence in him. He started boxing when he was twelve and he'd sit up at night and tell me how someday he was going to be the champion of the world. I always felt like God made Muhammad special, but I don't know why God chose me to carry this child.
– Odessa Grady Clay aka Mama Bird, in *Muhammad Ali: His Life and Times*

32

EVERY GREAT PERSON has a story of how they came to be. A place, a reason, a moment when their purpose became clear and the journey began. And there comes a time in every person's life when they'll have to choose the course their life will take, inspiring a series of events which will ultimately shape their destiny. For my father Muhammad Ali, born Cassius Marcellus Clay Jr, *"the only man in history to become famous under two names"*, the story began when he was twelve. But his road to glory was paved with humble beginnings.

On October 9, 1984 a reporter from *Star* magazine asked my dad, if he could go back and relive his life, would he do everything the same way?

"No!" he said emphatically. *"I would never want to relive my life again. Before, I didn't know what I was going to live—what pains I would have to suffer. I didn't have any answer. Now that I know, I say never again! I've made sixty million dollars and still I wouldn't live the same life."*

My father was born in Louisville, Kentucky, on January 17, 1942. The first horror story he ever heard was the one his father told him about when he was born—how he almost killed his mother in the process.

"Your mother was so overdue the doctors couldn't figure it out. It was your big head," his father said. "It was too big to come out! They tried everything. Pushing it out, pulling it out, praying it out! But your mother stayed in labor ... Finally, when enough of your head

323

was showing, the doctors used forceps to yank you out, leaving two faint marks on your neck that are still visible today."

My father was almost named Rudolph Clay. My grandfather always loved the name Rudolph, but my grandmother convinced him his firstborn son should be named after him, and that's how Dad came to be Cassius Marcellus Clay Jr. His parents weren't happy when he changed his name to Muhammad Ali; the Clay name had a long and complicated history.

The original Cassius Marcellus Clay was a slave owner best known for being a Southern abolitionist and US Ambassador to Russia. He was also a lawyer, a politician who worked closely with Abraham Lincoln, a newspaper publisher, a farmer, and a soldier in the first Kentucky Cavalry, ranking as a Captain and Major-General in the Mexican-American War and the American Civil War. He was married and divorced twice, had eight children, and died in Madison County, Kentucky, on July 22, 1903, at the age of ninety-two.

My grandfather was proud to carry the Clay name, but my father saw it as a constant reminder that his ancestors were once in chains. All slaves were stripped of their names and became the property of the people who bought them. If you were sold to the Smith family, you became Smith's property. If you were bought by the Anderson family, you were Anderson's property. If you were sold or traded at auction, you took on the name of your new owner. And so on. Cassius Marcellus Clay emancipated his slaves, but they carried his name nonetheless, passing it down from one generation to the next. Until my father's great-grandfather John Herman Clay—who was a slave born in Virginia in 1861, owned by the family of Henry Clay, the US Senator from Kentucky—married Sarah Fray and had nine children together. One of their sons, Herman Heaton Clay, was my father's grandfather. Herman married Edith Greathouse and had four girls and eight boys with her. He named their second child, my grandfather, after the only man to whom he could trace his genealogy, Cassius Marcellus Clay.

My father loved the way his name sounded. But as he grew he learned more about its history, and his name became a symbol of slavery. He was free, and he wanted a name that represented freedom. So, in 1964, after he became a Muslim, he changed his name to Muhammad Ali. *"Muhammad means worthy of all praise, and Ali means most high,"* he told an enquiring reporter a few days before receiving a letter informing him he'd been drafted into the United States Army.

When my father's parents brought him home from Louisville General Hospital, the rest of the world was preparing to fight the Second World War. It was a hectic time in America. Only a month before, Japanese warplanes attacked Pearl Harbor. Little did my grandparents know world wars and political controversy would play a major role in their son's life story—but all that would come later.

Even getting my father home from the hospital was eventful. After he was born, they almost lost him. The nurse put the wrong baby in my grandmother's bed. She was satisfied for a while until she noticed the child in her arms wore a tag that said "Brown", not "Clay".

"We should have known something was wrong because that baby was far too quiet, and you came out kicking and screaming! Waking up all the other babies in the ward. But you sure were a beautiful baby," Grandpa told him.

My grandfather was always telling my father that he was "as pretty as a picture" and warning him not to mess up his beauty. When Dad was in grade school, he slipped and hit his forehead on his aunt Coretta's dining-room table.

"Cassius fell and tore the skin on his forehead," Coretta explained.

"My God!" my grandfather said. "I hope he didn't mess up that pretty face!"

The next thing my father knew, he was at the mirror saying to himself, *"I hope I didn't mess up this pretty face."*

As I read all the old newspaper articles and listened to my father's recordings, I thought of the stories my grandparents told about my father when he was young, how he used to run around the house in his diapers, misbehaving. My grandmother would throw her fox fur coat in the middle of the living-room floor and he'd crawl into the corner and wouldn't move. "That's how I used to tame him when he was running wild," she told my mother. "He wouldn't come out of that corner until I picked that fur up. He thought it would come to life and bite him."

And then there was the story of how my father always liked to be the leader. *"Today I'm going to be the daddy,"* he'd say when playing with his friends and his younger brother, Rudy. When Dad changed his name to Muhammad Ali, Rudy also changed his, to Rahman. My father was always protective of his brother. When he was five years old and my grandmother tried to spank him, Dad ran and grabbed her hand. *"Don't you hit my baby!"* Only eighteen months separated them. My father loved Rudy from the day he was born. And as they grew he and his brother remained close. They did everything together.

I imagined my father and his brother at seven and eight years old, making horses out of broomsticks, running out the front door of their little pink house (my grandfather painted it his favorite color), playing cowboys and Indians on the front lawn. *"I'm the cowboy, Rudy,"* Daddy would say. *"You can be the Indian."*

I thought, too, about the sound of my grandmother's voice, her sweet Southern accent calling after them: *"Don't get your clothes dirty; dinner will be ready soon."*

"Okay, Bird," they'd call back to her as they shaped their fingers into mock guns and began shooting.

"Bang! Bang!" my father would shout. *"I'm the meanest cowboy in town!"* he'd holler, chasing his brother down the block. Ronnie King and Laurence Montgomery, their childhood friends, would join in the fun too.

Sometimes they'd play tag football, and Dad would ask his brother to throw small rocks at him to see if he could hit him. But he never could. Dad was too fast.

Years later, my father ran into the actor Clint Eastwood. For those too young to know him, Clint was once best known for his role as Dirty Harry, but he also starred in cowboy films. When Dad met him for the first time in the waiting room of a popular television talk show, he looked at him wide-eyed and said, "Clint, walk across the room, turn around and tell me, 'You've got three days to get out of town.'" He did, and they became fast friends.

My father thought his mother was "pert and sweet", and she had a little bird nose, so he christened her "Mama Bird" and he called his father "Papa Cash". I imagine the four of them sitting around the television after dinner, watching westerns: *Bonanza* and *Gunsmoke* and *Wyatt Earp*, starring Hugh O'Brian. After my father began his professional boxing career, Hugh came to a few of his early fights, cheering for my father the way Dad had once cheered for him when he was a boy watching him on the television in the living room. There he would watch boxing greats like Joe Louis and, his favorite, Sugar Ray Robinson—the first boxer in history to win a divisional world championship five times. It stirred something deep within him—a vision and a dream.

"I wanted to be just like him," my father once said. "I used to listen to his fights over the radio. 'And still the welterweight champion of the world . . . Sugar Ray Robinson!' I'd jump around the living room, shadow-boxing—throwing punches in the air, pretending I was Sugar Ray." He did all this never knowing that, one day, he'd meet Sugar Ray, who'd break his heart, and they'd later become friends.

My father thought Sugar Ray was classy, well-dressed, and well-spoken. And he sure knew how to draw everyone's attention. He traveled with a huge entourage and drove around in a big pink Cadillac. My father used to dream about buying a pink Cadillac just like it, and one day he did. When he started his professional boxing career, Dad also traveled with a large entourage, and he chose black and white Everlast boxing trunks, just like his boyhood hero wore.

"That's the kind of fighter I want to be," he said to his family when he was a young boy. "Fast, classy, and PRETTY!"

Eleven years later, when my father was twenty-two, he stood on the podium at a press conference in Miami Beach, Florida, after winning his first world championship fight against Sonny Liston, aka the Bear. It was February of 1964, and Sugar Ray Robinson was standing beside him, smiling up at the new heavyweight champion. He playfully tried to cover my father's mouth as he shouted, "*I shook up the world!*" He'd won the fight no one believed he could. "*I'm so pretty! I don't have a mark on my face … I must be 'The Greatest'!*"

But there's another scene I heard about, which was set five years before, when my father was still an unknown, dreaming teenager—two years away from winning his gold medal at the Olympic Games. A sixteen-year-old aspiring athlete, passing through New York City on the way to winning his second Golden Gloves tournament, is patiently waiting outside Sugar Ray Robinson's Harlem nightclub, Sugar Ray's, to get his autograph.

"Sugar Ray!" my father called, after waiting six hours in the cold. "My name is Cassius Marcellus Clay Jr, I'm training for the 1960 Olympic Games in Rome, Italy. I'm going to be the heavyweight champion of the world one day. I've watched all your fights. Can I please have your autograph, sir?"

"Sorry, kid," Ray said. "I don't have time for autographs."

Then he climbed into his pink Cadillac and drove away, leaving my heartbroken father standing in the parking lot.

The pain of being rejected by his childhood idol hurt so deeply he vowed that when he became famous he would sign his autograph for every person who asked him. And he did. Sometimes he didn't wait for people to ask. Whether we were in restaurants or airports, Dad would sign his name on a pamphlet or card with one of his favorite sayings—*Serve God, he is the goal*—and he'd pass those cards or pamphlets out to everyone he came across, sometimes startling people in the process.

"Oh, thank you," they'd say, taken aback. "Wow! Muhammad Ali!"

***

I SAT ON my bed for a while, with all the newspaper articles spread out around me, thinking about the stories my grandparents told. I envisioned my grandfather, Papa Cash, sitting on a stool painting his signs on all kinds of delivery trucks: the cleaner's, the bakery's, the grocery's, and the milk trucks. His murals were displayed on tavern walls, churches, and above factories all over Louisville.

I thought of how he sometimes brought my father to work with him. Dad, then Cassius Marcellus Clay Jr, a ten-year-old boy, would be up at midnight watching his father paint pictures of Moses on Mount Sinai, John the Baptist, the Virgin Mary, the Lord's Supper, the Holy Angels, and his infamous portrait of the Crucifixion, which my father said was *"so beautiful it made people cry"*.

I pictured my father helping his father as a bucket boy, running up and down the ladder, bringing Papa Cash the paint, both of them shivering in the cold as they climbed back down to the truck every ten minutes to get warm again. My grandfather's pay for the job: $25 and a chicken dinner, the latter of which he shared with his son.

Cash taught him about the art of sign painting, and my father admired him for the great care and pride he put into his work, whether it was a sign on a door or a mural on a tavern wall. And Cash loved singing his favorite tunes while he worked, "Mona Lisa" and "The Little Boy That Santa Claus Forgot".

"Boy, did Cash love to sing," my father once told me. "And his voice was beautiful. He always said, if times had been different for blacks in America when he was growing up, things might have turned out differently for him. He might have been a great singer—like Frank Sinatra or Nat King Cole."

My father admired his father's talent, hard work, and determination, but he knew he wouldn't follow in his footsteps. And my grandfather didn't want him to. "You'll be a teacher or a lawyer," he'd say. But after he saw his son in the ring, that changed. He was the first to shout: "This is going to be the next world champion!" It startled Dad at first; he'd only had one fight. But Cash couldn't help himself. "I've got another Joe Louis!" he'd boast.

His loud and dramatic encouragement spurred my father on. Not long after, Dad won his first fight on a local television show called *Tomorrow's Champions*, against Ronnie O'Keefe, a name my father would always remember. Cash took him to see a telephone pole that Joe Louis had once leaned against when he was a champion. My grandfather just stood there with his hand pressed against it, staring at it.

"I remember watching my father and the way he looked at that pole," said Dad, "and thinking that, one day, I wanted to have that effect on people."

The telephone pole was the neighborhood shrine. He and Rudy used to stand around it and touch it for luck. Neither of them suspected then just where it would lead.

It was through watching his father's struggle for recognition and success that he concluded early in life that there was little future in Louisville for a talented black artist. Nowadays the South is different, but when my father was growing up Louisville was segregated, and all he wanted to do was change it. He, too, sometimes wondered what might have been had things been different for blacks when his father was growing up.

"He might have become a famous painter or singer."

My grandfather was a natural actor. He liked to imitate the movie stars, especially the lovers. When my father was a little boy, Cash used to sit in a corner and paint as he sang, "Mona Lisa ... many dreams have been brought to your doorstep ..."

My father had a close, loving family growing up, but they had their share of problems, too. My grandparents were an affectionate couple, but they were always arguing. Cash was arrested a few times for reckless driving, disorderly conduct, and assault and battery. He had even once spent the night in jail after hitting my grandmother. Papa Cash liked to chase women, and his indiscretions caused discord at home. My father often witnessed his parents arguing when he was growing up, but he never spoke about those memories. I learned most of what I know about my paternal grandparents from my father's recordings, family members, and old interviews.

Dad would run to his room and hide beneath his covers until the yelling stopped. Probably remembering the time he was accidently slashed by the knife his father was waving around in a drunken rage. Luckily, Cash had a quick temper that cooled as swiftly as it heated. But he was also known around town for being a drinker and had a reputation for bar fighting. His womanizing was no secret either. Cash was far from perfect, and made a handful of mistakes, but he was known for his softer side too. He wasn't afraid to show affection. He was always hugging and kissing Dad, his brother, and my grandmother.

My grandparents were so different I often wondered how they came together. Cash was high-spirited and outspoken, and Mama Bird was sweet and gentle. Cash liked to hang out in smoky jazz clubs and taverns, dancing and drinking. She was a homemaker, who cooked and cleaned. He was a Methodist who seldom went to church. She was a Baptist who worshipped regularly. He protested the wrongs of racial injustice. She held her head high and grieved silently. But for all their differences the one thing they shared was their love for family and laughter. Cash and Bird were opposite in many ways, but together they blended to make the perfect recipe of Muhammad Ali—fire and love, conviction and forgiveness.

My grandparents weren't wealthy. Sometimes Dad and his brother would get a new shirt for Christmas, but most of their clothes came from goodwill. Including their second-hand shoes. Having had to make his own shoes last as a child, Papa Cash was an expert at cutting out cardboard and fitting it inside the lining.

As I sat on my bed thinking about my father's childhood, I wondered how deeply he was affected by what his youthful eyes had seen, growing up in his little pink house on Grand Avenue, in the west end of Louisville, Kentucky.

"I remember one summer my mother didn't have bus fare," my father once said. "So we walked all the way from downtown Louisville. It was hot and I was thirsty, so Bird walked me into a five-and-dime store and asked the clerk if she could have a cup of water for her son."

"I'm sorry, but we don't serve Negros. I could lose my job."

Then the store manager asked my grandmother to leave and even escorted them to the door. Tired, hot, and thirsty, Daddy cried all the way home. But his most heartfelt pain still lay ahead of him. "Nothing would ever shake me up more," he said, "than the story of Emmett Till."

Emmett Till was a fourteen-year-old boy from Chicago who spent the summer of 1953 in Mississippi with his uncle. He was taken from his front porch by a group of young white men and beaten to death, beyond recognition, for whistling at a white woman. The four white men who kidnapped him from his uncle's front lawn were identified in court by eyewitnesses, but the all-white male jury let them go free.

"I cried for months just thinking about it," my father said. "We were almost the same age and we looked so much alike. It could've happened to me."

My father was born into a segregated, prejudiced world during the Second World War. A world that wouldn't give a pleading mother a cup of water for her thirsty three-year-old son on a scorching summer day. Yet somehow he managed to keep love and forgiveness in his heart, just as his mother did, and she taught him, as he taught us, that prejudice and hate were wrong, no matter who did the hating. "Cassius," she said to my young father, "the world can be cruel and unfair, but you must always treat people with respect, kindness, and love."

My grandmother was a Baptist. Every Sunday, she dressed my dad and his brother up and took them to church. She taught them everything that she believed was right about God. She taught them to love all people and treat everybody with kindness. She taught them that prejudice and hate were wrong.

"I may have changed my religion," my father once said, "but the God my mother taught me about is still God; I just call him by another name."

My father adored his mother. He was always hugging and kissing her, and pinching her fat cheeks. He said she never spoke bad about anyone and described her as "*a sweet, heavyset, wonderful woman who loved to cook, eat, make clothes, and spend time with family*". He said she never meddled in other people's business or caused anybody any trouble, and that in his entire life there was no one who had treated him better. From the moment he was born to the day she died, his mother called him "Tinkie Baby". I don't know where she got the nickname, but, as Dad's recordings show, she called him this his entire life. Sometimes she called him *GG*, because *GG* were my father's first words. He later told her he was trying to say: *Golden Gloves*.

My grandmother cleaned houses for a living. Every day she dropped my father off at his aunt Coretta's house and she'd take the bus downtown to cook and clean for a white family my father never met.

Mama Bird had a hard life growing up. Her parents were separated when she was a child, so she never knew her father. She had three sisters, but her mother couldn't afford to raise them all so she lived with her aunt. She worked hard and made her own clothes for school. One day when she was sixteen years old she and a friend were walking home from school when a boy, four years her senior, my grandfather, Cassius Clay Sr, aka Papa Cash, walked across the street and started talking to her.

"I loved her the moment I laid eyes on her," Papa Cash once said.

"He walked me all the way home and never stopped talking," my grandmother added.

My grandparents were both affectionate. They were always hugging and kissing each other, my father, and his brother. But, as in any family, things weren't always perfect between them. Cash had a temper. And a wandering eye. As I mentioned earlier, he loved women—especially big-leg ladies. One day, after dinner, beef stew with cornbread and cherry pie, my grandfather grabbed some money from his wallet, then slipped out the door. My grandmother followed him down the street and found another woman waiting in a car for him. When they saw her, both Cash and the lady jumped out of the car and took off running.

My father, four years old at the time, stood in the doorway watching his mother chase them both down the alley. They laughed about it later, but when Dad was a little boy it wasn't funny. He used to cuddle up with his brother in their room. He didn't like hearing his parents arguing.

Years later, on November 30, 1979, my father pulled out his tape recorder and called his mother.

"Mama Bird," he said. *"I want to ask you something. Make me laugh one more time ... Do you remember that day Daddy came home to get some money or something, and you followed him outside and chased him down the street?"*

With her sweet Southern accent, she replied, *"Yeah, I remember! And he was running down the alley! Sure, I remember."* She laughed.

"He had a woman in a car!" said Dad.

"You were a little boy, wasn't that funny?"

"Yeah ... he had a woman ... he ran so fast the dirt flew up!"

"And they were flying down the alley and everything! You remember that?"

"You started walking towards the car," Dad said, *"and Cash got in the car and told the woman you were coming, then they both got out and ran!"*

"They got out and ran down the alley! And I ran them down! Hee-hee-hee—you remember that? You were a little boy!"

"You remember that, too," he said. *"Were you mad?"*

"Yes, I was mad!"

"You took a lot of mess off him," said Dad.

"I sure did. For about fifty years!"

"Now that I'm married, I see it," he said.

"He was chasing women before you were born! So now you see what I've gone through all my life!"

"You're separated now," said Dad. *"You don't want him back?"*

"NO! NEVER! NEVER-NEVER-NEVER! I'm enjoying life, and I have peace of mind, and it's going to stay that way ... I am so glad! I don't care where he goes or what he does! Just leave me alone!"

"So, if you heard he was out with two or three big, fine ladies, it wouldn't bother you?"

"Wouldn't bother me at all!" she said.

"You hope he has a good time, huh?" He laughs.

"That's right!"

"I thought maybe, by now, you would be missing him and wanting him back."

"Oh, no! Not with his lifestyle. I can't! NO! NO! NO!"

Dad laughs harder.

"You think it's funny," said Mama Bird, *"but I don't think it's funny. You laugh—laugh—laugh. It's not funny."* She burst into laughter with him. *"Hee-hee–hee ... No, but really! That is the truth! I don't*

care where he goes or what he does! My peace of mind is the best thing in the world."

"Well, I'm going to tell you why I've been asking you all these questions ..."

"Why—why?"

"I'm taping you!"

"Oh, you're taping me! I don't care if you are taping me. I'm going to tell the truth! You little devil!" She laughs. "No, I don't miss him. Tape all you like. I'm going to tell the truth!"

"This will be fun for you to hear one day," he said. "Will you be scared if Cash hears this tape?"

"No! I won't be scared if he hears this. I always say it pays to tell the truth!"

"Let's imagine he's listening. Pretend I'm him."

They acted out the imaginary conversation.

"If he says, 'Odessa, Odessa, I want you back. Give me another chance.'"

"No—no, I couldn't!"

"I've just got to have another chance!"

"No! I can't!"

"I'll kill myself, Odessa!"

"Oh, just kill yourself then, shoot!"

More laughter.

As I listened to their conversation, I wondered if this was the reason Daddy never handed Mommy the letters. Maybe a part of him knew he had already lost her—that after all she had lived through she would never give him another chance. He'd caused too much pain.

"Oh, you little devil," Mama Bird said. "My little Tinkie Baby. Are you taping me, my little Tinkie Baby?"

"Yeah, I'm going to always have your voice ..."

He plays the recording back for her, then Laila gets on the phone. He asks her about her trip to Chicago. She tells him she saw Belinda and the kids. They laugh and reminisce together, then he promises to visit her soon.

"Everyone's going to be here for Christmas. I'm just going to have a ball!" she said.

"I might be in China and Indonesia some time in December—I'm not sure yet. But if I can, I'm going to be home with you—and eat your food ... I'll get Veronica, Hana, and Laila, and Rudy and we'll all be there."

"Oh, that's the best news in the world! That will make me so happy ..."

"I'm getting ready to go now. I love my Bird."

"I know you love your Bird, honey, and I love my Tinkie Baby."

"I'm always going to look out for you."

"Okay, honey. Bye-bye ..."

My grandfather wasn't perfect, but he always made sure there was food on the table, and that his wife and children were taken care of. He was a painter by trade, but he came home in the evenings and practiced his singing. He taught my father and his brother to always face their fears and to try to be the best at whatever they did. *"You don't learn these things by accident,"* Cash said. *"They have to be taught."*

Papa Cash was a funny, fast-talking man who loved to dance, sing, and give kisses. Whenever Cash visited us at Fremont Place, he'd grab Laila and me and say, *"Give me them jaws!"* His whiskers tickled our cheeks as we giggled and screamed.

I faintly remember the sound of my grandmother's soft Southern accent and how her words flowed like a song when she spoke. "Hi, Tinkie Baby!" she said whenever my father walked in a room or called her on the phone. "How are you doing, Tinkie Tinks?"

My father made several recordings talking to his parents over the telephone and while visiting them at home in Louisville. A few tapes were made in 1979. The other recordings were made in the early to mid-eighties, mostly November of 1982, two years after Dad had come out of retirement to attempt to regain his championship for an unprecedented fourth time.

Their recorded conversations gave me a better understanding of my father and his childhood. As I listened, I caught a glimpse of the boy inside the man—that theoretical child within us all, navigating our subconscious mind throughout our lives.

33

ON THE EVENING of November 20, 1982, Papa Cash, Mama Bird, my father's uncle William, and a few of their family and friends were gathered around the breakfast table in my grandmother's kitchen—laughing, singing, and reminiscing about old times. In the middle of it all, my father turned on his tape recorder.

"This is Muhammad Ali, The Greatest of All Times! Introducing a man that the world doesn't know, who's greater than Frank Sinatra and Nat King Cole and all the rest! Now, I want you to hear from the uncrowned greatest singer of all times, Mr. Cassius Marcellus Clay Sr, the father of me, Muhammad Ali."

Cash looked at Mama Bird and started to sing one of his favorite songs, "Mona Lisa". When he'd finished, my father spoke into the recorder again.

"Ladies and gentlemen, I'm very glad that you came to the Cassius Clay Show. I got a break in boxing, but I was never good at singing. This is why I'm making this tape, to show that my father is the uncrowned great! Cassius Clay Sr ..."

Papa Cash turned his attention to Mama Bird then, and started speaking. *"After all, everything hasn't been so bad. Think of the good times we had. You only speak of the bad times, but there were some good times, and better times to come."* Then he started singing to her, *"Don't look so sad ... I know it's over, but life goes on and this old world will keep on turning ... We had some time to spend together ... Make believe you'll love me one more time ..."*

Dad whispered into the recorder, describing the scene as his father sings to his mother in the background. *"Cash is singing to my mother, and my mother's laughing."*

"So lay your head upon my pillow ..." Cash sang.

"My mother is laughing," Dad whispered.

"Hold your warm body next to mine ..." Cash sang.

"My father's singing to my mother."

"Hear the whisper of the raindrops blowing soft against my window and make believe you will love me one more time ..." Cash finished the song and kissed my grandmother on her cheek. Everyone applauded and my father spoke back into the recorder. *"That was Cassius Marcellus Clay singing at my mother's house in Louisville, Kentucky. The time is 9:01 p.m. Cash, would you please sing another great number? One day, as you know, we're all going to die. I hope that I die before you, but you might go before me and we will always have this to listen to. Cash, will you now sing a song called 'My Way'?"*

He finished the song, *"I did it myyyyyyyy waaaaaaay"*, and everyone applauded some more, then my father spoke into the recorder.

"Ladies and gentlemen, thank you very much. Now, to wind up the show, that was Mr Cassius Clay, the father of Muhammad Ali. Again, the date is November 20th, 1982, at my mother's house in Louisville. The time 9:15 p.m. One day we will hear these songs when Cash is long gone! Signing off!"

That same day, three hours earlier, my father had spoken into the recorder: *"I'm in my mother's Louisville home, it's 6:35 p.m."* Cash was at his house, he hadn't come over to my grandmother's yet and was talking to her about my father on the telephone when Dad walked into the living room. After a few minutes, Mama Bird hung up the phone and walked over to my father, who was now sitting in a chair next to the sofa, his recorder hidden in his lap.

"Are you taping my voice, Tinkie Tink?"

"What's Cash doing?" Dad asked.

"He called me today saying he's coming over later. He said, 'GG's home! GG's home!' Like I didn't know it. 'GG's home!'" she said, laughing her way over to the sofa.

"He isn't fussing any more?" asked my father.

"No! He's gotten too old and tired to fuss too much. He comes over here and sits on that couch and throws his head back and just sleeps all the time."

"So he just lies down?"

"Yeah, but sometimes he gets to fussin' about you and Rock [Rudy] like you all are still little boys!"

"He still makes you mad?"

"Yes!"

"How many years has he been on you?"

"How old are you, forty?"

"Yeah."

She did the math. *"You're forty, so I guess about ... oh, I guess just about forty years!"*

They both laughed. *"Damn, that's too long,"* she said. *"That's where I got that ulcer from. His mouth over the years, worrying the hell out of my soul! That mouth will kill anybody, child! You know how that mouth is!"*

They both laughed loud and hard.

"Sometimes we'll try to tell Cash something for his own good, but you can't tell Cassius nothin'! Like that yard ..."

"What about the yard?" asked Dad.

"We keep trying to tell him to clean up that yard, and he keeps talking about, 'That's good stuff—good stuff! You just want me to throw away everything!' Oh, you should see that back yard ... How did it look when you went over last night?"

"Real nice! All cleaned up and everything."

Her eyes widened. "Really?"

"Naw! Just kidding." He laughed.

"Cash has more money than I do," she said. "If I can pay the garbage man, he can too."

"Where does he get all the money?"

"He still paints signs—great big signs sometimes."

"What is today's date?"

"November the 20th."

"1982," he adds.

"Awww, I bet you're taping me," she said.

Dad noticed someone impersonating him on television. "Turn the sound up!" he said.

On TV: "Ali is down! The referee is counting 6 ... 7 ... 8 ... on 9 Ali is up again! I told you I was The Greatest! I AM THE GREATEST OF ALLLLLL TIIIIIMES!"

Dad speaks into the recorder. "We just saw a commercial of a man on television imitating me ..."

His father's brother walked into the room at this point.

"Uncle William!" said Dad. "How ya doing, big boy? You still look good."

"Hey, Ali, how ya doin'?"

"I just came back home to see the family."

My father spoke into the recorder. "This is Muhammad Ali at my mother's house. For the record, what's your name?"

"My name is William Clay ... Where's Big Cash?"

"He's at home," said Dad. "He'll be over later. William, how old are you now?"

Papa Cash.

"I'm fifty-seven and Cash is seventy."

"Tell me something, when you were little boys, what was Cash like as a kid?"

"You know what he was like. The same as he is now. He likes a bowl of beans, a bowl of beef stew and some pie and ice cream ..."

"And cornbread," my father added, laughing.

"Yeah," said William.

"Did he argue much when he was young?"

"No, he didn't argue back then," said William.

"Did my grandaddy use to whoop you guys when you were bad?" Dad asked.

"No," said William. "Dad didn't whoop us, our mother whooped us."

"William, what school did you and Cash go to?"

"Central—same as you. We went to Old Central. You went to New Central."

"When Cash was a boy, did he fight?"

"Big Cash—yeah, he'd fight."

"Who would have thought the greatest boxer in all history would come out of the Clay family?" Dad said.

"You didn't come out of just the Clay family. You're Clay, you're Grady, you're Greyhouse, you're Morehead ..."

"I'm all mixed up." Dad laughed.

"You should have seen your grandaddy, boy," said William. "Your grandaddy was about six foot four, and he wore a size thirteen shoe."

"My father's daddy?"

"No, I'm talkin' about your mother Odessa's daddy. He's a Grady!"

"Somebody told me that your daddy, my grandaddy, wouldn't take no mess off white folks."

"No, he wouldn't take nothin' off white people."

"William, when you were small, did you hang out with Cash? In those days, did he turn around every time he'd see a big-leg woman walk by?"

"Yeah!" They both laughed. "He wasn't too bad then: he'd look at them—stop and talk to them—that's all."

"Big women?"

"Yeah, big fat ones."

Mama Bird chuckled. *"All you Clay boys like big women. Claude [my father's uncle] had a great big fat woman once when he came to Louisville, a great big fat girl—bigger than me! She's twice as big as I am, or she used to be."*

"Her name was Ophelia," said William.

"Is that her name?" said Mama Bird. *"Yeah, he had a big fat one!"*

"Mama, what elementary school did you go to?" Dad asked.

"The same one you and Rock went to, Virginia Avenue. And I had the same teacher you did, too. She taught me in the second grade, and Mrs Halley Wilson ... She's dead now. And Mrs Victor Perry taught you in high school, and she taught me—all those teachers who taught me, taught you all."

"What high school did you go to?"

"Central. I graduated high school when I was eighteen."

"Where did you live?"

"12th and Oak," she said.

"When did you first meet Cash?"

"On 12th and Oak—across the street at another girl's house, Loraine's house. He was sittin' out in the front yard one day."

"Tell me what happened,' my father said.

"Oh, I don't feel like talkin' about it ..."

"That's when you met a lot of trouble, wasn't it?" he said.

"Yep." She laughed.

"What did he do? Walk by?"

"Yeah, he just came over and started talking."

"What church did you go to in Louisville as a little girl?"

"Centennial. You went to the old one. I took you when you were a baby and you'd get to hollerin', and I'd stick that milk bottle in your mouth, and the Reverend would just laugh. Yeah, I took you to church every Sunday when you were a baby."

"You told me once the Reverend used to kiss me," he said.

"Yeah, he'd kiss you because you were a baby. I took you to church every Sunday, and you were so cute everybody just wanted to hold you. You were a pretty baby."

"The way you remember who kissed me, all the people who gave me, Muhammad Ali, that baby, a kiss, they'll always remember that, won't they?"

"Yeah."

"Tell me, William," Dad said, *"at your age ... can you still chase a pretty woman—are you too old?"*

"I can do anything that I used to do when I was seventeen, boy! I just don't do it as often."

My father laughed, then said into the recorder, *"Cash is seventy and William is fifty-seven—still a baby. This is Muhammad Ali at my mother's house. Mama, what's your address?"*

"4032 Lambert Avenue."

"All of us are here making tapes. I just got in the mood to make some tapes for history. Cash is not here right now, but we'll get him on tape later." Dad looked at his mother. *"Bird, what you got for me to eat?"*

"Steak and salad ... do you want to eat in here?"

"Yeah ..." He turned his attention back to his uncle. *"William, where are you going to take me tonight?"*

"Where do you want to go, son?"

They both laughed, and spoke a little more about old times, then my father said for posterity, *"Now I'd like to dedicate a little poem called 'Truth'":*

The face of truth is open; the eyes of truth are bright.
The lips of truth are never closed. The head of truth is upright.
The breast of truth stands forward. The gaze of truth is straight.
Truth has neither fear nor doubt. Truth has patience to wait.
The words of truth are touching. The voice of truth is deep.
The law of truth is simple; all that you sow you reap.
The soul of truth is flaming, the heart of truth is warm.
The mind of truth is clear, and firm through rain and storm.
Facts are only its shadow. Truth stands above all sin.
Great be the battle of life; Truth, in the end, shall win.
The life of Truth is eternal. The soul of Truth is God.
Truth has the power to endure. Truth shall always last.

"Signing off from Bird's house in Louisville, Kentucky. Today is November 20, 1982 ... I'm taping this for history."

I don't remember too much about my paternal grandparents. My only clear memory of Mama Bird is of her sitting in her hot, humid kitchen at the square table just off the back-patio door at her house at 4302 Lambert Avenue. I remember the white-and-blue checkered tablecloth and the freshly baked chocolate-chip cookies piled on a large plate next to a stack of white napkins with pink flowers on them. I remember watching her put on her apron as she prepared to cook dinner for my father.

"*Are you hungry, Tinkie Baby?*" she asked as he walked through the screen door and sat down at the small square table in the corner.

Dad picked up a cookie. "Yeah, whatcha got for me, Bird?"

"Steak and salad," she said, firing up the stove.

Although my grandparents were separated, they remained friends for the rest of their lives. Just as my father remained friendly with all his children's mothers.

On May 8, 2012, my father's childhood home on 3302 Grand Avenue received a historical marker. I wish his parents had lived to see it. Cash and Bird died four years apart, both at the age of seventy-seven. Thanks to my father's recordings, we'll always have the sound of their voices, song and laughter.

***

"*NO!*" MY FATHER had said. "*I would never want to relive my life again. Now that I know, I say never again!*"

While I look upon my childhood with fond memories, I can't say that I'd want to relive it entirely either. The year leading up to and following my parents' divorce was no fairy tale. There were times that I'd wake my mother in the middle of the night with my cries and screams, having to breathe in a paper bag until I calmed down and fell back to sleep. My night terrors didn't begin until after Mom, Laila and I moved into our new house in 1986, but the seeds were planted at Fremont Place a couple years after my father's last fight.

Being a parent and being married is hard. My father may not have done everything perfectly, but he learned from some of his parents' mistakes, and my mother learned from hers, just as Laila and I will learn from their missteps and do better with our children. I guess that's what we all hope will happen until someone, someday, many years from now, finally has a perfect childhood.

Farewells

Oh, yes, he knows the butterfly's secret. Knows it, and doesn't even know he knows it. To transform himself, a man must first be able to lose, able to keep letting his old self die. Part of such a man will never grow old.
— Gary Smith, *Sports Illustrated*, November 15, 1989

34

I SAT ON my bed separating all the newspaper articles into three piles: things I'd already read, things I hadn't, and things I wanted to ask my mother about. My notes and doodles were circled around the headlines that interested me most. Such as "Ali Is Grilled in Federal Court", *USA Today*. What in the world was my father doing in Federal Court? The articles were beginning to frustrate me. They left me with more questions than they gave answers. Unlike my father's tape recordings. As I listened to *them*, I learned so much about him that I never knew.

I learned about his fears, faults, dreams, and plans for his future—the reason behind his fight with Larry Holmes. Like most people at the time, I always thought my father came out of retirement in 1980 because he needed the money. It was true, to some degree—he had documented as much in his recorded conversations with his lawyer, Mike Phenner, expressing his anxieties about his finances. But the more tapes I listened to, the more I learned and discovered that there was *more* to the story.

On December 7, 1979, Harold Smith, a friend of my father's from back east, with an exuberant personality—who drove around Los Angeles in a black vintage car that resembled an old British taxicab—called my father with news about their business. Dad always engaged in lively banter with his friends, and this conversation was no different.

"Hello!"

"Maaaaan!" said Harold Smith.

351

"*MAAAAAAN!*" Dad shot back.

Harold laughed. "*MAAAN!*" he repeated.

"*AW, MAAAAAN!*" said my father. "*I'M GOING TO MESS YOU UP, MAN!*"

Chuckling, "*What happened, Ali?*"

"*Oh, you're messed up now!*" said Dad. "*I've got something that's going to mess you up, man! You're really going to be messed up! This messes up everything!*"

"*What's happening? What you got going on, Champ?*"

"*I've got a whole boxing training camp, already built on fifty-five acres! It's a four-hour drive from here, man! The guy sent us the pictures of the place—the land, the layout, and everything. Man, we've got to drive out tonight, man. Aw, maaan! We'll come back for this! If this place is like I want it, I'll come back and we'll take $100,000 and have some trees cut down, and we'll build a gym that's going to equal two Deer Lakes! We'll train there. I'll come back for that—only for that! They'll ask, 'Why are you fighting again, Ali?' and I'll say, 'Because I can't afford this camp. I want this camp ...'*"

"*Where is it?*"

"*Paso Robles [north-east of Santa Barbara].*"

"*Ali, that's the place I told you about earlier today!*" said Harold.

"*The place you told me I could put a camp? That's the same place?*"

"*Yeah! I brought that to you. They want $900,000 cash for it!*"

"*Yep, that's the same place! MAAAN! AW, MAAAN!*"

They both laughed and Harold said, "*You're crazy! I'm the one that told you about it, Ali!*"

One year earlier, in 1978, when we were still living in Chicago, my father called Tim Shanahan and asked him to pick up someone at O'Hare Airport and bring him to the house on Woodlawn. "His name is Harold Smith," said Dad. "He's coming in from Tennessee on an American flight."

Harold had met my father in 1969, when he was a track star at the University of Tennessee. Dad was giving one of his college lectures there, after he was forced into an early retirement by the Supreme Court between 1967 and 1970. Only Harold's name wasn't Harold

Smith back then. It was Ross Fields. Dad didn't discover this until two FBI agents showed up at Fremont Place in 1981.

Tim waited outside the terminal, looking for a man that matched the description my father had given him. "He's a tall, black guy—about six foot one, with a beard."

Harold Smith walked off the flight wearing a cowboy hat and carrying a briefcase. His plan was to get my father to sign an agreement for him to start a promotional organization called the Muhammad Ali Amateur Sports Program, which would seek out low-income-area black athletes who were good enough to make the Olympic team but didn't have the support, or the grades, to earn a college scholarship to compete in their sport. The focus was mainly track and field and boxing.

Sitting on the sofa in Dad's office, Harold said, "I'll seek out the best young black athletes in the country from low-income neighborhoods. Your name will be immortal with this organization."

"Ali's name is already immortal," said Tim. "He doesn't need your organization for that."

"I like that idea," Dad said. "Helping kids in low-income areas. I used to be one of them. This can be a route to wealth and fame for the underprivileged."

Harold opened up his briefcase, which contained $40,000 in cash and offered it to my father as seed money for the organization. He then asked Dad to sign a contract that gave Harold the right to use his name as CEO of the organization: Muhammad Ali Amateur Sports.

Dad didn't know it at the time, but Harold Smith's goal was to set up Muhammad Ali Professional Sports, where he was intending to be a promoter of professional heavyweight fights.

"Harold gained your father's confidence and support, acting as if he was doing it all to honor his name," said Tim. "By helping poor black kids in the ghetto get an education, which may have been genuine, but—in reality—his goal was to become the godfather of fight promoters."

A few months later, Harold showed up with another contract, naming himself the fight promoter for Muhammad Ali Professional Sports

[MAPS]. Dad would receive 25 percent of each fight or $10,000, whichever was higher. This led to my father's idea of building a Triple Crown World Headquarters where he could train the fighters that Harold signed.

"You know what I'll do," Dad said. "On my property that I have now, if I like the place, I'll borrow it and then I'll get it. We'll put in about $100,000 and build a gym. It will be worth it! Then we'll announce the fight and we'll stay there and train and we won't go nowhere! We'll tell the world to go to hell! Now look, man—we've got to go up and see it tonight!"

"We don't have to go tonight," said Harold. "Let's go up early in the morning. We can leave at 5 a.m.—I've got to pick up Tommy Hearns at the airport in an hour."

Dad thinks about it. "Okay, that sounds better ... So, you're going to get Tommy Hearns? Is he really good?"

"Champ, he'll knock Sugar Ray Leonard and all of them fighters out!"

"Well, then he's got to see it too! He isn't going to fight for us, is he?"

"They're having a championship title fight tomorrow. He wants to do the guy just like you did Sonny Liston. I got some tickets for you. They're fighting at the Los Angeles Sports Arena. I got ringside tickets for us."

"What's today's date?" Dad asked.

"December 7, 1979."

The line clicks. "Hold on, Harold ..."

***

"HELLO?"

"Salam Alaikum. Where's my girl, Veronica?"

"Wa-Alaikum Salam, Lana [his old fight cook]. Boy, these calls are coming in just right. Something might happen, I'm not going to say it is—but it might ... We've got another Deer Lake four hours from here, a man is up there lookin' to sell it now. It's got log cabins on it, it's already got a kitchen that will hold one hundred people, and it's got a big gym ..."

"Doesn't that sound good!" said Lana.

"Aw, man ... they're asking $900,000 cash for it."

"Listen, Ali ... think before you buy something else."

"Before I do, I'll fight again. I'll fight for it! And you'll come back and cook for us ..."

They reminisced about old times for a minute. Then Dad clicked back over to Harold, picking up where he left off.

"So, Tommy Hearns is coming in tonight. How old is he?"

"Twenty-three. Champ, he's undefeated. Tommy Hearns is the one that none of them will fight! He's the one Joe Louis came in to see—Joe loves him! He's got twenty-four fights and twenty-four knockouts ..."

"All this is good, Harold, but I'm thinking about this camp—this place is bothering me." Dad looks at Bundini, his corner man, who was sitting on the sofa in his office. *"How many log cabins does it have again?"*

Bundini tells him.

"Damn!" said Dad. *"It's got twenty-five cabins!"*

"Champ," said Harold, *"my man here has a two-engine plane. He can get us there in 30 minutes tomorrow. He said we could leave at 6:30 a.m."*

"Who?"

"The pilot I was telling you about. He's flown a lot of places. It's a nice safe plane. It's a million-dollar plane. I can have him ready to go at 6:30 in the morning."

Dad considers it again, *"I'm not messing with that small plane."*

"Champ, if you see it ..."

"Look—forget the airplane!"

Harold laughed. *"You want to drive. All right. What time do you want to leave tomorrow?"*

"We'll leave in one hour ..."

"No, Champ! Don't drive up tonight! You can't see the scenery. Let's leave at 5.30 ... six o'clock ... something like that. I'll meet you at your house, I'll pick Bundini up on my way over there."

"He's already here."

"Oh, he's already with you—okay."

"I don't know if it's possible to get this place," said Dad. *"I've got so much property that I can't sell. If I sold something, it would make it easy."*

"That's right. See, Champ, that's another reason you should fly up there to see it—because you may not like what you see, then we've got that long drive back."

"Well, I'd rather drive than go by private plane, I don't care for those private planes."

"It's a good plane, Champ—I've flown in it ten times ... Ask Bundini. He's been in it too."

Dad looks at Bundini, *"The plane looks good?"*

Bundini replies, *"Yep ..."*

"It's got two good motors?" Dad asked.

"Yeah!" said Harold, adding, *"The plane cost a million dollars."*

"Where would we land?"

"At the nearest airport. Do you want me to call the pilot and tell him to get it ready? Champ, this cat's good—he flew us all the way to Mexico!"

Dad took a moment to consider it. *"I'd still rather drive."*

Once more, Harold laughed. *"You'd still rather drive!"*

"Is that your conscience laughing?" said Dad.

"No! It's my wife," said Harold.

"I thought I heard your conscience ..."

"That's a good plane, Champ!"

"I know, but still, I'd rather drive ..."

My father developed a fear of flying when he was sixteen years old. He'd experienced an especially rough flight on his way to Chicago for the Golden Gloves tournament. When he landed, he vowed never to board another plane. A couple years later, after he secured his place in the 1960 Rome Olympics, he almost didn't go.

"That's a long flight. I'd rather take a train or boat," he said to his father, Papa Cash, after reading his acceptance letter.

"Son, if you're going to be the champion of the world one day, you'll have to face your fears. You'll have to fly to Italy."

I remember watching Dad in old interviews talking about what scared him, and being surprised that he even had fears—he was always so strong and confident.

"I'll tell you what I really fear," he said. "Airplanes! Whenever the plane starts shaking, I look out the window and think: *What if one of the wings breaks off!? Where would we land? What if we have to land in the water? What if my life raft doesn't inflate? And then, what if a shark comes and pokes a hole in it? Or worse—THINKS I'M DINNER!* During the entire flight all these scenarios run through my head and I say to myself, *Man, you could have taken a bus or a train!*"

Dad always had a vivid imagination. It's a good thing he learned to face his fears early in life. He boarded his flight to Rome wearing a backpack stuffed with a parachute. Several days later, he won his gold medal.

My father used to say, "Courage is acting in the face of your fears—not the absence of them." But he still traveled by ground whenever he could, driving back and forth from Michigan to Chicago, and Chicago to Pennsylvania on Blue Bird, his Winnebago bus. The land is also my preferred choice of travel. I'm more comfortable on a cross-county train ride than a three-hour flight.

"You got that from your father," my mother once said. "We were on a small four-seater plane once in the middle of a thunderstorm. It was shaking and bouncing so hard we both thought we were going to die." I think they were coming back from Show Low, Arizona. It was the day after my father made the tape on which he sang to my mother. I was just one month old.

"On another flight you were in your father's arms when he jumped out of his seat," said Mom. "He started shouting, '*Allahu Akbar, Allahu Akbar!* [God is Great!]'" I laughed out loud, picturing his animated expressions, his furrowed brows, and the wide-eyed look he wore when he was excited, surprised, or fearful.

Then I imagined the panic people would go into today if someone started shouting "*Allahu Akbar*" in the middle of a commercial flight. It saddens me to think that this spiritual phrase my father so often said, which brought peace to his heart, has come to invoke fear in the hearts of so many due to its misuse by those who claim to love the faith they so tragically misrepresent.

***

357

"When is the fighter coming in?" Dad asked.

"He's coming in tonight to go to this fight tomorrow and to meet you. You told me to bring him over at nine o'clock in the morning," said Harold. *"You know what he did, down in New Orleans? He fought the number four contender in the world, from the junior middleweights, which is heavier than he is. He knocked the guy down five times and broke his jaw in four places!"*

"Sounds like a bad brotha!" said Dad.

"Oh, he's bad! They call him 'Hit Man'!"

"Hit Man—that's gangsta!" said Dad.

"They call him Tommy 'the Hit Man' Hearns."

"Tommy 'the Hit Man' GANGSTA Hearns!" Dad shot back.

"Yeah, he'll knock Sugar Ray Leonard and all of them out!" said Harold.

"This land I want is bothering me," said Dad, *"and I've got to meet this fighter ..."*

Harold chuckled. *"Then we can go up and see the land Sunday morning—that's even better."*

The line clicks. *"Okay, Harold, my other line is ringing ..."*

"Okay, Champ. I'll see you in the morning."

By January of 1981, Harold Smith had promotional contracts with Ken Norton, Gerry Cooney, Thomas Hearns, Aaron Pryor, Michael Spinks, and Wilfred Benitez, among others. The future of his organization looked promising, and the whole thing might have worked out. What my father didn't know was that his friend had a dark secret. One that would ultimately end the organization and land him in prison.

"Harold was very outgoing and charismatic," said my mother. "Your father liked that about him."

According to reports, "From the late 1970s through early '81, more than $20 million was embezzled from the Wells Fargo Bank in California. Two Wells Fargo executives, who were high enough in the bank's hierarchy to do so without attracting attention, put the money in Harold's pockets ..." It was also reported that his "inside" man at the bank had given him more money in one day than Bonnie and Clyde stole in their lifetimes.

No one else was aware of the scam, and they might have gotten away with it had it not been for the minor slip-ups which led to their exposure.

Dad called Tim to let him know the FBI wanted to question them. Of course, my father wasn't involved in the embezzlement in any way, though he was paid $500,000 of Wells Fargo's money. My father couldn't understand how a con of this magnitude could succeed. A lot of others didn't understand, either, including the FBI agents, who spent a day at Wells Fargo for a briefing on how the con was pulled off.

Dad, who allowed Harold to set up a company using his name in return for payments by means of Wells Fargo cashier's checks, was asked by a reporter what he thought of Harold Smith's dealings. Harold had once ordered a rush-order check for $223,000 made out to my father, whose lawyer insisted on the payment before Dad would fly to Australia for one of Harold's promotions. He walked into the bank and came out ten minutes later with the money.

"I saw him with all those beautiful girls, planes, boats ..." Dad said. "I don't know where he got his money. I'm still wondering ..."

Harold Smith was convicted of passing hundreds of bad checks in twenty-one states under the name Ross Fields. According to Tim, Harold used his connections at the Wells Fargo branch near our house on Wilshire Blvd to set up the Muhammad Ali Pro Sports account. He convinced the bank manager to give him a line of credit, which he used up quickly. Allegedly, he started writing bad checks. The bank covered for him, allowing the scam to proliferate.

"One morning, I got a call from your father," said Tim, "asking me to come to the house the following day: *The FBI wants to talk to us about Harold ...*"

Tim walked into the house and saw two FBI agents seated in front of Dad's desk. They started to question Tim about his connection with Harold Smith and MAPS. He told them everything he knew. Which was nothing about the scam.

"What did Harold do?" Dad asked.

"He embezzled over $21 million from Wells Fargo," said one of the agents.

"Man, that's crazy! I don't believe it," said my father. "No brotha could embezzle $21 million from a bank. Ten brothas couldn't embezzle that much from Wells Fargo. All of those smart Harvard men guarding our money; Harold Smith is not smarter than those bank executives. No way. I can't believe it."

He was serious. He didn't believe it. Dad never believed anything extraordinary—good or bad—about anyone, until it was proven. He had to see it with his own eyes. And, in the months to come, he would.

"Harold had an office at his gym in Santa Monica," said Tim. "The FBI set up their field office there. They had a blackboard with a flow chart of all the people who were involved with Harold Smith and my name was near the top. I was scared for a while, but it all worked out."

My father attended the last day of Harold's trial. He tried to act as a character witness for him before his conviction was delivered. When most people had turned their backs on Harold Smith, my father remained a loyal friend.

Ross Fields, aka Harold Smith, received a ten-year sentence but only served six of those years. He's captured on some of my father's tape recordings, calling collect from prison. Dad always accepted the call.

After Harold was convicted, that was the end of Dad's idea of a Triple Crown World Headquarters for fighters. My father never bought the ranch in Paso Robles. His lawyer, Mike Phenner, advised him against it. It wasn't a wise investment.

But in 1979, Dad's dream hadn't been crushed yet. It was very much alive and would be the ultimate incentive for his *final* return to the ring.

***

THE MORNING AFTER his call with Harold Smith, my father was preparing to leave for Paso Robles when the phone rang. It was my eleven-year-old sister May May. Dad put her on hold for a moment to turn on his tape recorder, before returning to the line.

"Maryum! I'm so surprised you called me. Boy, you really surprised me—caught me off guard."

"What were you doing?" she asked.

"I was just getting dressed. I'm getting ready to go look at another place like Deer Lake."

"You are?"

"Yes. It's out here in California, near the mountains, with all the trees. It's got a lake. There's a river by it and there's a lot of log cabins already built where I can put another training camp and I can start training fighters ... Did you go to school today?"

"It's Saturday!"

"Oh, that's right ... Maryum, you were born 1968. Daddy won the title in 1964, so four years after I won my title you were born. I was in exile at that time. They took my title because I didn't go to Vietnam. You were too little to remember, but it's history now ..."

"Yeah, but I know about it ..."

"So, I'm going to ride up to look at this place and it might be possible that if I like it ... I might fight again."

"Nooo! Don't fight again, Daddy, please!"

"I might come back to challenge the new champion, Larry Holmes, and take the title back for the fourth time. Can you imagine that?"

"Don't fight again, Daddy, you're getting old!"

"I'm getting what?"

"Old!"

"How old is your daddy?"

"Are you thirty-seven?"

"That's right ..."

After hanging up the phone with my sister, Dad, Harold, Bundini, and Herbert Muhammad, my father's manager, flew up to see the land. When he returned home, he'd fallen even deeper in love with it. Later that evening my father was sitting behind his desk in his office when the phone rang. It was Jeremiah Shabazz, a former Muslim Imam from Pennsylvania, who was sometimes involved in my father's business dealings.

"Man, I went to see a training camp today," said Dad. "God is my witness—it's ten times better than Deer Lake! There are twenty-five cabins, a coffee shop—real big. All the cooking utensils and stoves are there, with old English furniture—all brand new. It has enough tables to seat a hundred people. There's a big rec room, a big office ... a place to build a gym. It has private roads on it with parking lots ... For the whole place, the man wants one million six, but he said he'd take $900,000 cash! Mountains all around—real pretty—a four-hour drive from my house in LA!"

"Where you could really run," said Jeremiah.

"Oh man, that would make me want to fight! If I bought that thing and got up and saw it. Jerry, it's so pretty—there are trees ..."

"It may be pretty, Ali, but you don't want to buy it. Why don't you just lease it? Why put out that kind of money for one or two more fights?"

"It wouldn't be for the fight—it would be to train fighters. They'd live there—to manage them."

"Oh, you mean like a camp."

"Yeah ... a business—a world headquarters for fighters ..."

"That's nice, it's almost as big as your farm," said Jerry.

"You wouldn't believe it!" Dad started dreaming again. "Hills and trees, and rocks ... Fifty-five acres of rolling hills with a big stable—with horses. It has a big heated swimming pool and a big tennis court on top of a hill. Each individual cabin has two rooms in it—a bedroom, a living room, and two bathrooms in each cabin. Twenty-five cabins encircled all over the place. It's pretty, man! I'm telling you, there's nothing in the world like it ... I'll fight just for that!

"Then we'll have a press conference there—call the world and tell them, 'Ali is making an announcement. Do you want to come see his camp?' Then, after I'm through, it will be a Triple Crown World Headquarters for all boxers. I took Herbert up to see it in a small plane and he said if I fought again I could get it easy. Oh yeah ..." he said distractedly, as if he were suddenly reminded of something. "If I fought again, I could get it easy! Then I could build a gym there out of real logs where at least 300 people could watch me train. Maaaaan, then I could run all of that as a business when I'm through fighting!"

"Well, look," said Jerry, "does Herbert have anything better than eight million for you to fight Larry Holmes?"

"No, he said realistically he was looking at about seven million, but an out-of-state fight would make it more, but eight million to fight Holmes, where?" asked Dad.

"Anywhere ..."

There was a pause ...

"Tell them to challenge me ..."

***

BOTH MOVIES ABOUT my father's life, *The Greatest*, in which he played himself, and *Ali*, which starred Will Smith, end the same way: in 1974, after he won the World Championship title for the second time in an eighth-round TKO over George Foreman. Perhaps this is because that is when the people who love and admire him wish he'd retired. If he had, Shakespeare himself could not have written a better ending. But he did not.

Two years later, in 1976, after winning a controversial decision over Ken Norton, during a *Sports Illustrated* interview my father was reflecting about a suitable ending to his unequaled career. He suddenly turned to his host and said, "Maybe I should reach up and pull down the mike in the middle of the ring and announce, 'Laaaaadies and gentlemen, you have seen the last of the eighth wonderrrrrr of the world. Muhammad retires!'"

"No," replied Harold Conrad, a journalist and fight promoter who helped get my father his title bout with Sonny Liston. "You did that in Manila, you did it in Malaysia. Who would believe you?"

Again, my father announced his retirement. In 1978, after losing—then regaining—his championship title for an unprecedented third time against Leon Spinks, Dad retired once more.

In less than two years, he was back ...

"I want Larry Holmes!"

Soon after, Dad left for Deer Lake.

"Hana ... I have to go soon. Give me a kiss goodbye."

"You're not my daddy," I had said. *"You're Muhammad Ali!"*

The following week he sent for Laila and me.

Dad trained hard and sculpted his body into remarkable condition for a man of his age. According to reporters who were there, "In terms of physical appearance, he looked like the Ali of old. He even dyed his hair to hide the gray."

While he had defied seemingly impossible odds his entire life, people could see my father no longer belonged in the ring.

"I wouldn't come back if I thought I'd go out a loser," he said in an interview given around that time. "I know I can whoop Holmes. We all live in a world of limitations, but some people can see further than others. When people judge what I'm doing with *their* logic, they say, 'It can't be done.' Their reasoning says it can't or shouldn't be done. Their knowledge of history says it can't be done."

He leaned forward in his seat, "So, their reasoning, their knowledge, and their logic clashes with my superior belief. And the result is they don't believe. But I'm on the mountain and they are looking up at me. Being so high, I can see further than them. But everyone is looking up at me saying, 'Ali, don't do it! Ali, please stop! You might get hurt . . .' I'm at such a high level that I don't think like them. I'm not like them, I can see further—*I believe.*"

As I watched the interview, I realized that if Dad hadn't contracted Parkinson's he may have never stopped fighting. When you've lived a life defying impossible odds and performing miracles, the only place to learn the odds have turned against you and that you've run out of miracles is in the arena where you once performed them. For my father, that was the boxing ring.

We all run out of wonders, sooner or later. But it was a lesson my father had to learn on his own. He knew this. He realized it on his mountain at Fighters' Heaven. His arms were tired and his legs were sluggish, but he kept climbing—towards the echo of victories long past.

When he stepped into the ring, his boxing skills were a shadow of what they once were.

"All that remained was the courage which had sustained him through three championship reigns," said one reporter. "And sixty fights against the best heavyweights that a three-decade career could offer."

My father once said, "I'm not superman. If the fans believed I could do everything I said I could do, then they're crazier than I was."

He also said, "Life is a fair trade where all adjusts itself in time. For all that you take from it, you must pay the price sooner or later. For some things, you must pay in advance. For some things, you must pay on delivery. And for others you pay later, when the bill is presented."

35

"ALI AGAINST LARRY Holmes ... Oh God, that was painful," said Sylvester Stallone in *The Lost Legacy of Muhammad Ali*. "Like seeing your child playing on the railroad tracks with a train coming, and you can't get him out of the way. I just sat there and watched. And I also felt for Larry Holmes because he had a terrible job to do, and he knew it. He had to go out and dismember a monument."

I've never seen my father's last two fights and I probably never will. I don't want the images imprinted in my mind. It was an emotional victory for Larry Holmes, who wept in the ring afterwards and told my father, "I love you, man." Larry was his sparring partner for four years.

After losing the bout, Dad sat solemnly in his dressing room, then came a knock on the door. It was Larry Holmes.

"I'm sorry, Champ," he said again, tears falling. "I love you."

Dad looked up at him, somehow mustering a smile. "Then why did you beat me up like that?" he said.

Larry also burst into tears at the press conference after the fight. And again when he talked to Howard Cosell. He adored my father—respected him and looked up to him.

"When you fight a friend and a brother, you can't get happiness," Larry said. "All I achieved was money. I fought the best heavyweight fighter in the world. Ali is a hell of a fighter and a hell of a man. He proved he could go for the title a fourth time, and that's a great achievement ... I was trying to knock him out, but I couldn't. If I could have got rid of him in the first round, I would have. He tried to psych

366

me, but I worked with the guy for four years and I knew everything he could do. Ali fooled some of the writers, but he couldn't fool me."

After the fight, there were reports in the paper about Dad not feeling well. How he had drained his body of energy by taking his prescribed thyroid pills while he was training. His doctor had prescribed them for him to help him lose weight. Which he did quickly—going from 246lbs to 218lbs. The rapid weight loss was no doubt the main factor in his loss of energy and endurance. If he had not taken the pills, the world would have seen a better performance.

"A month before the Holmes fight, I started to think something was wrong," said Dad. "Two weeks before, I started getting more tired. But I thought it was because I was reaching the peak of my conditioning. If it's age, I'm finished. I'm washed-up. I'll face it. But if it's because I wasn't healthy—because of the drugs ... *I shall return!*"

His doctors confirmed his thyroid prescription had drained his body of energy. So he came back once more. After the unexplained fatigue and exhaustion, he wasn't yet convinced that he was through—and he wanted to go out a winner. Or at least looking and feeling better than he had the night he fought Holmes.

"They always remember your last fight," he said softly after losing. "Joe Louis was on the floor—everybody remembers that. So was Sugar Ray. I don't want to end that way."

But as a reporter once wrote: "When you're Muhammad Ali, there's always one more mountain to climb."

When my father's bruises healed and his body stopped aching, he started to dream yet again. On December 11, 1981, in Nassau, Bahamas, my father laced up his gloves for the final time. He fought his last fight against twenty-eight-year-old Trevor Berbick. Dad was one month shy of his fortieth birthday.

"It was close," he told a reporter after the fight. "If Berbick had been thirty-nine, like me, I would have beaten him. I found I couldn't tie him up and move the way I wanted to. It was a good fight, but he was too young and too tough for me ..."

Dad had performed better than he did the year before against Larry Holmes, and he felt much better too. The sluggish, exhausted feeling that came over him before and during the Holmes fight was gone. But people could see something was still wrong. There were concerns before the fight about my father's slurred speech and physical deterioration. Not to mention the fierce heat in the open-air arena. He'd fought under trying conditions before, but he was much younger then, and Parkinson's wasn't knocking on his door.

When his last fight was over and the scorecards came in, my father lost by decision.

"Father Time has caught up with me. I'm finished," Dad said to a reporter after the fight. "I've got to face the facts. We all lose sometimes. We all grow old. This is the end."

When I was a little girl I saw an old issue of *Time* magazine on my father's desk. The image on the cover made me cry. Daddy was pictured sitting on his stool in the corner of the ring, slumped over with his head hanging down. The headline above him read, "The Greatest Is Gone!"

It was an image I had seen before; not on a magazine but in real life. I remember my father standing outside the boxing ring after his last fight. He was wearing a blue pinstriped suit, holding onto the ropes and staring into the ring. When Laila and I ran into the empty arena and jumped into his arms, his face lit up.

I don't know what he was doing in there, after everyone had gone, or if I'm remembering it correctly; we might have been at Fighters' Heaven. But in those seconds before we ran up to him I remember feeling something was wrong; something about the way he was standing felt forlorn. He had been in the ring before looking tired after his training sessions and boxing expositions. Slumped over, resting his elbows on his thighs and his fists on his cheeks. The twinkle in his eyes only coming back at the sight of Laila and me. It's probably why he always sent for us during training. Our presence brought him joy. But that day I was too young to understand that this was different. It wasn't a sparring session. It was his last fight after nearly thirty years in the ring. A fight he'd hoped and believed he would win.

Everyone wanted to know *why* he kept coming back. But there was no complicated answer. He had a vision and a dream. He believed in himself when no one else did, and he'd shown the world, and himself, so many times before what he was capable of. My father was born to do great things, and he found himself in many circumstances in his life where great things happened.

When he stepped into the ring for his last two bouts, he wasn't fighting Larry Holmes or Trevor Berbick—he was fighting Parkinson's.

"Ali knows he can't go on forever," said Sugar Ray Robinson in a 1979 issue of *Jet* magazine. "You can only go up so high, and then you've got to come down. He's gone as high as any one boxer can go. He would be wise to retire."

Everyone has something to say about how great men live their lives—their triumphs and losses, their choices and mistakes. How they should have made better decisions, in the end.

When it comes to reflecting upon a legacy like my father's—and the decisions he made—I think Theodore Roosevelt said it best:

There is no effort without error and shortcoming; but who does actually strive to do the deeds; who knows great enthusiasms, the great devotions; who spends himself in a worthy cause; who, at the best, knows in the end the triumph of high achievement, and who, at the worst, if he fails, at least fails while daring greatly, so that his place shall never be with those cold and timid souls who neither know victory nor defeat.

After the Berbick fight, it was time to say a final farewell to Deer Lake, Fighters' Heaven. Farewell to the whistling winds, clear skies, and fresh mountain air. Farewell to the sound of branches crackling beneath my father's boots as he jogged up Agony Hill: *"The fight is won or lost long before I dance under those pearly lights."*

Farewell to riding in the back seat of the Cadillac, following behind him in case he tired. If he did, he never stopped. He always kept going. There was always another mountain to climb.

Farewell to his cabin in the woods. Farewell to the large stone rocks—*Sonny Liston, Jack Johnson, Sugar Ray Robinson, Kid Gavilan* … Farewell to the evergreens that reached for the sky and the sparkling stars he so often dreamed on. Farewell to the look in my father's eyes as he admired the land. *"I'm close to God up here."* Farewell to the sound of the bell that awoke his crew. Farewell to the sound of his axe chopping trees, *"Teeeeeeeeeemberrrrrr!"*

Farewell to the smell of Lana's cooking—roasted chicken and beans. And the scent of her greens, luring us in from the meadows and woods. *"What you got cookin', Lana?"*

And farewell to the sound of hopes and dreams. *"Float like a butterfly! Sting like a bee! Rumble, young man, rumble ..."*

"Hana, what's your daddy's name?"

"Muhammad Ali!"

"What do I do?"

"Box!"

Farewell.

***

"WHAT NEXT?" ASKED Robert Lipsyte in an interview from 1978, when my father was at the height of his fame—the looming, inescapable question so many athletes and entertainers are confronted with, and often haunted by. "What next?" was asked of my father countless times over the course of his life; Dad had the most recognized face on the planet, and he wasn't going to hide it.

Sometimes he'd say, "Now I will become the world's greatest movie star!" To others, he said, "I will become the world's greatest businessman!" And sometimes he'd answer, "I don't worry about such things. God will tell me what to do when the time comes."

Once, when asked that question, he stared at the ground. "We're all like little ants," he said. "God sees all these little ants, millions of them, and he can't answer all of their prayers and bless every one of them. But he sees one ant with a little influence that the other ants will follow. Then he might give that one ant some extra special powers. I'm like that special ant. Lots of other ants know me—follow me. So God gives me some extra strength."

Back home, the routine events that usually dominated the calm of day in our household had settled with the sun. My father was resting

comfortably on the suede tufted sofa in his office. The television was playing softly in the background, and Laila and I were fast asleep. When the phone rang, Dad reached for his tape recorder and quickly answered the call, as though not quite ready for the adventures of his bustling day to end.

"Hello ..."

"Muhammad, what will become of boxing now that you have (truly) retired?"

"Boxing will always continue with or without me. Just like presidents die, get old, or get assassinated. There will always be someone who will next take the job. You just have to get adjusted. The Concorde airplane is not very economical, and I understand they're thinking about drowning it out. If they do, jet planes will still fly, you just won't have a Concorde. I was the Concorde of boxing, and the other fighters are jets. I flew at a higher altitude than the rest, moving faster than the rest, and [I was] more progressive. But you'll just have to get used to riding on jets again. You can't ride the Concorde any more ..."

36

I PICKED UP a copy of *Star* magazine and noted the date: October 9, 1984.

"Being famous, rich and respected, what else do you want from life?" a reporter asked my father after his Parkinson's syndrome diagnosis was made public.

"I want the strength to do good for those who aren't as fortunate," said Dad. "To make others a little happier. See a frowning face—turn it into a smiling one. I want no more starving children, begging for food or money, or crying in front of a dead parent or brother or sister killed by a bomb, by human madness ..."

A photograph of Dad sitting on the suede sofa in his office with me and all of my siblings around him graced the cover. I'm sitting on his lap. I read the headline: "Ali Comes Out Punching as He Embarks on World Peace Tour with Kids". I put an extra pillow behind me, got comfortable and settled in to read the article.

"His face has all the vibrancy and good looks of his youthful prime when he was *The Greatest*. But the voice, once so booming and clear, is an inaudible murmur. He talks in monosyllables. His right hand holds the left one to stop its trembling. Yet the mind is alert. The sense of humor remains. He's still a jokester and a prankster.

"In his shaky mid-life, which has been complicated by a debilitating illness, Muhammad Ali has mellowed. The world now sees a more human side. The Champ refuses to accept any suggestion his life is at stake. Yet if he were to learn differently, what would he say?"

"If they tell me I've got one, two, three, six months left, I'll be happy. I'll be happy because I would tell myself that it's Allah's will and that it'll be that much sooner that I'd get to meet Him."

"Since his ailment was diagnosed as Parkinson's syndrome, a progressive disorder marked by tremors and weakness of muscles, Ali is giving the future a fresh look with the same confidence he has exuded throughout his memorable boxing career."

"I feel fine," Dad said as he packed for a quick trip to an Islamic conference in Africa's Sudan, to be followed by a global journey with his favorite people—twenty-five children from different countries. He was planning to take them on visits to the Vatican, the White House, Buckingham Palace, the Kremlin, Peking, and India among other sites and nations around the world.

"These children will meet the Pope," said Dad, "President Reagan, Queen Elizabeth, Konstantin Chernenko, Deng Xiaoping, and Indira Gandhi, to ask them what they're doing and building for the children of the world."

When asked about his health, my father said, "Contrary to what others have been saying, I am not suffering. I am not crazy. And I am not dying of Parkinson's disease. My hands do tremble a bit and my speech has slowed down, but it's because of another problem, nothing as serious as Parkinson's."

"My life is definitely not at stake," said Dad. "The Champ is not dead yet."

His physician, Dr Martin Ecker, clarified that recent tests conducted in New York's Presbyterian Hospital indicated my father suffered Parkinson-like symptoms, which might have been brought on by punches to his head during his twenty-five years in the ring. His slurred speech and shakes, Dad conceded, could have been the cumulative result of the 1.5 million blows to the head he estimates to have taken in the 150,000 rounds he'd boxed.

"Or," he added thoughtfully, "it could be from a motorcycle accident eleven years ago. I fell and, although I had on a helmet, I could have suffered a head injury I wasn't aware of."

"Boxing means everything to me," he went on. "I wore the Golden Gloves at sixteen, won the Olympic gold at eighteen, and was heavyweight champion three times. I became famous. And I'm now using my fame and world credibility to promote wonderful causes. I'm loved. People are constantly visiting me. I'm not an idiot. I have my eyes opened and I know some people take advantage of me, or try to. But I can be smart and clever. Muhammad Ali is not ruined … He is still 'The Greatest', the Champ."

***

THE FINAL ARTICLE I read came from *Jet* magazine, dated May 13, 1985. My father gave the interview one year after he was diagnosed with Parkinson's syndrome. His symptoms continued to progress and the following year he would be diagnosed with the disease.

> Although the forty-three-year-old suffers no discomfort, it pains him when he is constantly asked about his health. One afternoon he sat down and told *Jet* magazine what to tell his fans: "Tell them I'm happy." He smiled as he spoke softly. There was a touch of sadness in his face as he mustered the smile to respond to those who say they feel sorry for him.
>
> "I don't know why they feel sorry," he said. "I have a beautiful wife. I have two beautiful daughters I'm living with. I have eight kids in all—seven girls and one boy. All are healthy. I have more fans and more loved ones than any one person in the world. I've been invited to countries of the world. I stay busy from day to day. I have so many people who love me—and I love them. I'm the last person they should feel sorry for." He paused, then said with deliberate emphasis: "Don't feel sorry for me. I'm happy and doing really good. I'm happier now than when I was boxing."

Three months earlier, in February of 1985, my father had sat behind his desk in his office dressed in a basic brown suit and a short-sleeve white shirt—his favorite attire at the time. A reporter from the *Los Angeles Times* was in the chair beside him. He was surrounded by hundreds of letters from people all around the globe. A few thousand posts from children from Australia, Lebanon, Africa, England, Japan sat in a neat stack in the corner of the room. They would be placed in the basement soon, with the twenty-two trunks full of answered mail.

"You must have answered every child in the world by now, Muhammad," said Marge, our household administrator, picking up a huge stack of envelopes. "I'll get these to the post office today."

My father always read his own fan mail. Letters from children touched him most. Especially after losing his championship title. Dad feared that people—the world as a whole—might forget him. As if that could ever happen.

Like many before him, the reporter sitting with my father that day wondered why a forty-two-year-old retired boxer was still among the most recognized superstars on the planet. He wondered why my father was approached with an attitude of awe. "When he travels to other countries, he is besieged: by Chinese in Hong Kong, by Japanese in Tokyo, by children too young to remember the Greatest's great moments in the ring," the reporter wrote.

Later that evening, my father sat down at his desk and prepared a personal message for the *National Enquirer*. He hoped to defuse the rumor of his failing health.

"The world is seeing the old Muhammad Ali again, and with God's help I'll be around for a long, long time! My doctors tell me I've knocked my medical problems out of the ring, and I can do anything I want with no holds barred.

"I'm busier now than when I was fighting. I just got back from the Middle East and Africa. For three weeks, I was the guest of King Fahd of Saudi Arabia at his palace.

"I also attended an Islamic conference. Then I was a guest of the Nigerian government for ten days.

"I feel absolutely great and I'm preparing for the greatest battle of my life—the battle for peace. I intend to devote the rest of my life to bringing the peoples of the world together. Boxing can never compare to something like that."

***

AFTER MY FATHER married Lonnie in 1986, his health slowly began to decline, but he continued to show the world that he was still the playful, fun-loving man they'd fallen in love with. He just moved a little slower and spoke less often. It wasn't easy for him; there were challenges, especially in the beginning stages, before he had come to terms with it, when he seemed to be in denial. In an old interview, he was holding out his hands showing the reporter how still they were. "People with Parkinson's shake," he said. "Look, I'm not shaking ..." He refused to be held prisoner by ghosts of the past and faced his new challenges as he always did, with the faith, grace, and dignity that marked his life.

My father never liked taking his medicine. He used to hide his pills in plants or flush them down the toilet. "If I keep taking them, eventually they'll stop working." Then there were the little experiments he used to do. "I want to see how I feel if I don't take them for a while." Sometimes he was fine—better, even. But he always asked Lonnie for his meds after a few days.

When he made appearances, he would smile graciously but wouldn't speak. He didn't like it when people had a hard time understanding what he was trying to say. One day, when I was a teenager, we were at the Los Angeles marathon. The founder and president Bill Burke was a friend of my father's and invited Dad and Lonnie every year. We were sitting at our table in a VIP tent. A long-time admirer of my father walked over and told him how happy he was to meet him. Dad shook the man's hand and smiled, as he always did, but said nothing. He was probably hoping the man would be satisfied and walk away, so he didn't have to speak. But the man stayed right where he was and tried to spark a conversation. Dad just nodded and smiled. The man turned to me and asked, "Can he talk?"

With the strength and clarity of the voice with which he had once spoken, my father looked up at him and said, "What makes you think I can't talk, man?"

No one goes through life without hardships. Sometimes they are out of our control. But we can decide how we will react to them. My father looked for the deeper meaning in things and, in the end, he

377

grew from life's lesson. As he always said, "*The man who views the world the same at fifty as he did at twenty has wasted thirty years of his life.*"

Over the years, a lot changed for my father. His speech and motor skills became a shadow of what they once were, but his indomitable spirit remained utterly intact.

Dad standing on Jack Johnson's rock at Fighters' Heaven.

37

I LAY IN bed for a while thinking about everything and staring at a photograph taken on the steps of Fremont Place—before the divorce. It's one of the few photos I have of myself sitting in my mother's lap, with Laila on my father's. It was usually the other way around. For years, the image made me sad—it served as a painful reminder of all that was lost. Now, it sits on my dresser beside another photograph, taken the year after my parents' divorce: the four of us—Mom, Dad, Laila and I—are snuggled together in the doorframe of our new house.

My mind traveled back to weekend afternoons, when Dad would say, "Let's go cruising, Hana."

Mom, not wanting to mess up her freshly rolled hair, stayed home with Laila as my father and I drove up Crenshaw Boulevard in the convertible like Bonnie and Clyde—the sun beaming down on my smiling face. He bought the bean pies packed in pink boxes from the Muslim men who stood on the corners dressed in bow ties and suits. He always overpaid.

"Thanks, Champ! You're lookin' good!"

"Thank you, brother!" he'd say, holding up his victory fist as the light turned green and we drove away. As we cruised the streets, people spotted him and tooted their horns and shouted in excitement: "Look, there goes Muhammad Ali!"

"You'll always be 'The Greatest', Champ!"

Another victory fist goes up.

Once, a tour bus was passing by and a passenger spotted Dad as we were waiting at the light. He motioned for the driver to pull over. He did, and my father signed countless autographs and performed his disappearing thumb trick.

Then, on our way home, he would let me sit on his lap and pretend I was driving.

The memories will always shine.

I looked at the picture again. Photographs are beautiful things. They provide another way to feel, touch, love, and remember. They take an instant out of time and alter life by holding it still. A fleeting moment is captured and preserved—frozen in a place where it will live *forever*. When I look at both photographs of us now, before and after the divorce, I realize that, somewhere in time, we will always be a family.

***

"HANA, LAILA," DAD said on an old tape recording. "*Come give Mommy a kiss goodbye ... Where are you going, Veronica?*"

"*To the dentist to get my two front teeth fixed.*"

"*I want to go with you, Mommy.*"

"*Laila, stay home with Daddy and Hana. I'll be back.*"

"*What's wrong with your teeth, Veronica?*"

"*They died.*"

"*How did they die?*"

"*I got hit in the mouth with a baseball in the second grade.*"

His voice softens, "*You did?*"

"*Uh-huh. I'm going to make you an appointment while I'm there,*" she said heading towards the door. "*To get your teeth cleaned.*"

"*Okay ...*"

Suddenly, a memory stirred and shifted.

I wondered if my father wrote those letters to my mother because of what *not* writing one had once cost him. Gene Kilroy, my father's old business manager and life-long friend, told me about a girl Dad had had a crush on when he was a teenager.

"It was when he flew to Rome, for the Olympics. He went over there and never wrote to her. By the time he got back, she had a new boyfriend."

He never wrote to the girl because he didn't know how to spell Louisville and was too embarrassed to ask anyone in the Olympic Village. When he got home, he went to her house and found her sitting on the front porch with another boy.

"I'm sorry, Cassius," she said. "I thought you lost interest because you never wrote me."

The relationship was too new to be love, but I'm sure my father remembered the feeling of losing what *might have been*.

Maybe he wrote so many letters to my mother because he didn't want to make the same mistake twice.

At last, after all the interviews, recordings and newspaper articles I finally opened the envelope containing my father's letters to my mother. I flipped through the pages, reading the various titles: *Let's Try Again, Our Melody of Love, Veronica, It's Never Too Late, Veronica, Princess of Enchantment, Dear Veronica, Love Always, For My Veronica, When It's Over* ... Some of the pages weren't dated or titled. They opened without an introduction:

I've been so many places and I've seen so many faces
until I felt lost in between places.
After all the love in my life,
after all the pains in my life,
I think you are going to remain my wife.
Where have you been, my love?
Where have you been, my dove ...?
I've been searching so long for happiness;
somehow, I've never found tenderness ...
Now you've become my sunshine ...
Yes, my love, we are one heart ...
we both knew from the start.

I read one of his poems next:

> You are admired for many reasons,
> for you are a pearl of wisdom that keeps its beauty in all seasons.
> Your smile is beautiful and priceless ...
> Even your eyes sparkle like a star ...
> Veronica, my Princess of Enchantment, you are rare.
> Today your golden glow shows you care ...
> So please, Veronica, let's laugh together without hesitation,
> this will bring about a beautiful sensation ...

As I read the next one, I laughed out loud; it was a nice feeling for a change. Most of his letters made me cry:

> I have found that you have the disposition of an angel.
> The way you get around every day, you have the endurance of
>   a camel.
> From the first day that I saw you, I saw the tenderness of a shepherd.
> You have always had the devotion of a true mother.
> The way you always see things, you have the vision of an eagle.
> You are a peaceful person and you have the gentleness of a sheep.
> Every day you show the industry of a beaver
> and the harmlessness of a dove,
> while also the wisdom of an owl.
> All this is why I love you so much.

When I had finished reading the last letter, I put them back into the manila envelope they'd been stored in. Dad had tried everything to win Mom back: poetry, pleading, reasoning. And, in the end, he had even tried letting go:

> When It's Over
> Veronica, our love has now come to its end simply because we
> are only friends. Now that our love has ceased to exist, let's try
> to find another means to persist. We were very good for each
> other; now we are somewhat like a sister and a brother. However,

things can never be the same since we have disobeyed the rules of the game. For every move, we make the new year, I want you to give me your ear. For us I pray that it's not really over, my dear.

It was said to me one time that life is something like a dime, for it's never easy to understand how heartaches and despair can take command. However, we both will move further on to new adventures waiting down the line, and perhaps we will find happiness behind with the shadow of Zaire in our mind. But looking back is not the way, for that time has faded with yesterday, there's so much to do today, and unpleasant times will just drift away.
Love, Muhammad
January 8, 1983

I remember sliding down the mahogany stairs on the cardboard boxes that my mother was using to pack the house. Unaware of what they were for, what they symbolized, I had the time of my life soaring down those steps. I would soon discover our days living together as a family were coming to an end.

Dad would visit us at our new house all the time before marrying Lonnie and moving to Michigan. My mom would make him lunch and coffee, and we'd spend the day together doing nothing special, just hanging out and talking. Then, when it was time for him to leave, I would hug him with all of my might. After he walked out the door, Laila carried on with what she was doing. But I stood in the doorway—with my head pressed against the glass, watching him with tears in my eyes, as he slowly walked back down the driveway, got into his car, and drove away.

I'd been worrying about my father since I was about five or six years old. Now I was worrying that he was lonely. I worried that he didn't have food to eat. I worried that he might lose his keys and have to sleep outside. Eventually, I figured that worrying about my father was just a side effect of being his daughter.

There's not much I can share about that time. The pain was so overwhelming, I've blocked much of it from my memory. Like most children, my world was a safe haven, centered around my parents, perfectly formed and protected. A bubble that would never pop. Then one afternoon after school someone asked me how I felt about my parents getting divorced. After that, the bubble exploded and everything went blank.

I don't remember begging my mother to give my father another chance, or promising to be a good little girl. I can't recall the last night I spent in my bed—or moving to our new house. I don't remember the last time I saw Fremont Place, or saying goodbye to my father. From that moment after school, my first clear memory is staring out the window from the living room of our new house, watching my father walk up the driveway to visit us.

"When I married your father, I thought we'd be together for life. Then things gradually changed ... I was not planning on divorcing him, but I went from knowing, to not knowing for sure if it would last forever."

He was standing in the foyer of the Fremont Place house when she'd told him—at the bottom of the stairs next to the grandfather clock. There was a small door in the middle of the clock that I used to hide behind when playing hide-and-seek with my father. At five years old I'd stick my head in the small opening of the clock, thinking I had found the perfect hiding place—unaware my rear end was poking out like a sore thumb in my red pajamas. Dad always pretended not to see me.

"I want a divorce," she'd said.

He said nothing. Tears swelled in his eyes as he stood there. He knew this was coming. They'd been distant for a while, but his fears had become reality when she said it out loud. He stood there motionless, the tears that had been awaiting their release streaming slowly down his face.

"I felt bad," Mom said. "He walked through the house after I told him, crying out loud."

They had spoken to a marriage counselor for four hours the year before. It was a lost cause, probably did more harm than good.

"I can see why you want a divorce," the counselor said to my mother. Hearing my father's views about a woman's role in a marriage bolstered the case against him. But they were just that—views. He couldn't enforce them and he never tried to.

I wonder if Mom told the counselor how much time she spent at the equestrian center, riding her horses Midnight Missy and Sterling around the tracks for ribbons. Running little errands in the day, or practicing opera in her bedroom. How she ate her meals alone, and hired cooks and governesses to take care of us, even when she was at home. I wonder if she told him it wasn't entirely my father's fault—that she, too, was to blame. That she could have done more, tried harder, made it her priority to be a family again. Couldn't she? Knowing Mom, she confessed nothing. In her eyes, it was all my father's doing. But one of his letters told a different story.

To My Veronica
We need today a little more tolerance with each other. We cannot seem to meet on the same ground. I like it when you call me or buzz me before you leave home early in the morning because I may want to tell you something or hug you good-bye or whatever. Us being so different, having such different capacities, states of inhibitions, and tasks in our everyday life ... If Muhammad and Veronica had no tolerance, no desire to keep forgiving, we could never bring harmony into our soul. For you and I live in a world that is not easy and every day demands a victory.

I write to you because you never have much time for me. You are moving at all times. If we don't slow down and talk more, the germs of our actions will spread and bring greater calamities.

In both of us our being is good. Our lack of religion has created a strange way of family life. We, meaning us and the two girls, never pray together. They say the family who prays together stays together. Now, I see that as true. We never worship God together. We never go out together for nothing, not even ice cream for the girls. We never eat any of the three meals together. All these things about natural life our girls will never know when they have children.

We need to find out in what way happiness can be brought about and, in this way, we can realize the peace which is the longing of our soul, and we can impart it to Hana and Laila, thereby attaining our goal, which is the happiness and peace in our lives.
Muhammad Ali

As I said, in the months after the divorce, Dad visited us at our new house often, as he'd promised he would. After he married Lonnie and moved to Michigan, she would pick us up when they were in town while Dad waited in the hotel. Over the years, in between visits, he called us regularly and sent letters and little notes in the mail.

February 23, 1990
Dear Hana and Laila,
I miss you all so much. I pray to Allah all the time. I pray five times a day. I pray that He will help and guide you to the right way of life. One day soon I will see you all. I love you. I hope and pray that I will see you soon. I want you to send me a picture. I will go now. Hope to see you soon.
From your father,
Muhammad Ali
P.S. Serve Allah; He is the Goal.

I used to save my father's telephone messages on our answering service. I'd listen to them repeatedly. I remembered calling him on the intercom from the telephone in my bedroom every morning at Fremont Place. I'd get a kick out of the fact that I could talk to him on the phone, then run down to his office right after and he'd be there, sitting behind his desk.

Listening to his messages on the phone at our new house made me sad. I couldn't run down the steps any more and jump into his arms. There was a whole ocean between us now. But then there were the messages that made me smile—of him making snarling and howling sounds, pretending to be a monster. Before hanging up, he always told us how much he loved us.

387

Knowing my father, I think he was afraid we would forget him, as if that was possible. I remember calling him one afternoon when I was around 12 years old, after I got home from my tennis lessons. I wanted to tell him my mother was getting remarried.

"Is he as pretty as me?" he asked, half-joking.

"No," I said. Which was the truth. Dad chuckled and asked how school was and if I thought any of the boys were cute. As I told him about my latest crush, he softly interrupted.

"Are you going to call him daddy?"

"Never," I said. "You're my only daddy and always will be."

He got off the phone happy.

A couple months later I got into a fight at school. It was a rainy day and I was named as the safety monitor during recess and lunch. My job was to report students who were misusing the playground equipment. A fourth grader was throwing balls at one of the other students, so I reported the incident. After school, the girl walked up to me just as our new governess, Haley, was arriving to pick Laila and me up. It had just started to rain, so Haley was holding an umbrella.

"Hey Hana," said the girl, "you have brain damage just like your dad." Then she smiled and walked away.

After that everything went blank. The next thing I remember was hearing Haley screaming and trying to pull me off the girl. I had grabbed her open umbrella and started beating the girl with it. A few weeks later her mother tried to sue us, but nothing came of it. And whenever she walked past me in the hall she would make faces and turn up her chin, but she never made fun of my father again.

That was the only fight I ever got into. There was another girl at school named Bertha who was in the same grade as me that used to try to stare me down in class and push me while we were standing in the lunch line. She even pushed me on the ground once, when we were playing handball. She continued to bully me for a while, but eventually it stopped and we sort of became friends. I don't know why, but I could never make myself hit Bertha or push her back. But that day when the other girl told me my father had brain damage, I turned into the Tasmanian devil without a second thought.

I brought my father by my mother's house on the Venice Canals once, when he was in Los Angeles with Lonnie on business. It was sometime before he lit the Olympic Torch in 1996. Mom was married to Carl Anderson, her third husband, at the time. When they saw each other, they hugged and my mother's eyes filled with tears. She rushed into her bedroom. She never liked anyone to see her crying. Dad looked at me, confused.

"Why is she crying?"

"I'll go ask her," I said.

Mom was sitting on her bed, wiping her nose with a napkin, when I entered the room.

"Dad wants to know why you're crying. He might think you feel sorry for him or something."

"No, it's not that," she said, tearing up again.

"Then what is it?"

"When I looked in his eyes, I saw God."

I know it sounds improbable, but I knew what she meant. There was a divinity that emanated from him. So many people and reporters have written about it over the years. How, while in his presence, they felt an innocence, a spiritual strength that couldn't be expressed in words. I guess, after all the time that had passed, she had forgotten what it felt like.

When it was time to leave, Dad whispered in her ear, "I still love you." Just as he always had whenever he spoke to her or saw her.

Trying to understand my parents' love story has weighed heavily on my heart, and over the years I've searched the past, revisited days gone by, questioned my mother for a reason why and for answers not even she could give. Only broken fragments of a time long past and haunting reminiscences of a marriage long lost remain.

I wanted to figure out what went wrong with my parents' love story—how the letters ended up in storage. Like with most things we fret over, their misplacement wasn't complicated but the result of a simple, fated occurrence.

Those last few days at Fremont, my grandmother and aunts were helping Mom pack up the house, carefully folding and storing the last of our belongings—my happiest memories—away. Our linens, clothes, dolls, and books. Postcards sent from around the world: Hong Kong, Asia, England. My black fedora hat and sparkling glove, all carefully placed into small cardboard boxes as if to preserve them for another time and home, as if they'd help ease the pain of a ten-year-old girl's broken heart.

Downstairs, my father stood alone in his empty office with nothing tangible left to express his love for my mother but an envelope of hopeful letters it seemed he never gave her. Surely, he must have thought that, if not Marge, Auntie Diane or my grandmother would see them and give them to Mom. Surely, he must have left them there on purpose so that, if nothing else, she'd know he tried. But Marge had put the unaddressed manila envelope into a small box with other random, unpacked items she found around the house and written a short message across the top: *Veronica, Muhammad left this behind, Marge.* If only Mom had been curious and opened it, but she probably assumed it was more of Dad's quotes, notes, and speeches, which he usually wrote on lined yellow paper, and so she might have quickly closed the envelope, if she even saw the box at all, never knowing what the pages contained: my father's bare heart.

I wanted nothing more than to undo Dad's mistakes, clarify the misunderstandings between him and my mother, give life to his unspoken words. I wanted to bring peace to my parents' hearts and heal their wounds, especially my father's. I always thought his heart suffered greatest.

Then, one afternoon in 2014 when I was sitting on the sofa in my father's living room in Scottsdale, Arizona, lost in thoughts about days gone by, I looked at him sitting peacefully in his large leather chair, smiling at the image of his youthful self on the television screen.

"Wasn't I something?" he said, wide-eyed, as he watched himself telling reporters how he'd whooped George Foreman. "*I wrestled with an alligator and tussled with a whale. I handcuffed lightning and threw thunder in jail. Just last week I murdered a rock, injured a stone, and hospitalized a brick! I'm so mean I make medicine sick!*"

"You still are, Daddy," I said. "And you always will be."

He smiled and kept watching with an expression of indescribable peace and satisfaction upon his face. One that a seventy-two-year-old man with Parkinson's wasn't supposed to have. Sitting at home watching himself on television, eating cake and ice cream, entertained by a life well lived.

It was then that I realized it was my heart, not his, that was still fretful with unresolved grief and sorrow about the past. In that moment, I decided I would do as my father had done so many times before, when faced with sorrow, disappointment or loss, in or out of the ring. All I needed to do was *let go and give it to God.* By doing so, I found what I was ultimately looking for, what I'd hoped for all along: peace and acceptance with what was past.

I was always driving past the stone pillars that marked the entrance to Fremont Place, on my way to barbecues at Kim and Karen's, where we reminisced about our childhood over drinks and hot dogs in the same backyard we used to play in when we were little girls. Their mother, Connye, still lived in the same house off Wilshire Blvd. It had become sort of a home-base for me over the years; the only thing left from my childhood that was the same, that I could still visit. Carnation's and Bob's Big Boy were torn down, but the mosque on Vermont, where my father brought me lunch every day, was still there.

I always promised myself I would go back one day and say a proper goodbye to the house on Fremont. I just never got around to it. The closest I had come was on the day I sat in the car with my father, when he was in town to get his star on the Hollywood Walk of Fame, waiting for the red light to change.

"*Daddy, do you want to drive by and see our old house?*" I had asked. "*Another family of four who lives there now ...*"

Me squeezing Dad's arm as he visits us two years after the divorce.

We didn't go that day. But eventually, he went back to Fremont Place. He was with Lonnie. She told me they met the new owners and walked around the house.

I guess he just wasn't in the mood to go that day. Or maybe going back with me—his daughter, with whom he had lived there—was too painful.

***

WITH A HEAVY heart, I put the letters and all the articles and magazines on my nightstand, then I went into the living room to look for Kevin. He had fallen asleep on the sofa. I sat down beside him and gently woke him with a kiss.

"What time is it?" He yawned, stretching his arms and legs.

"Just after four in the morning. I'm just finishing up."

"Is everything okay?"

"Yeah, I found a lot of interesting articles and read some of Dad's letters."

"You sure you're okay?"

"Yeah, I'm just tired."

"Okay, babe," he said. "Let's get some rest."

Then we turned out the lights, climbed into bed, and fell asleep.

38

I WOKE UP the next morning, had breakfast with Kevin, and told him about everything. He listened intently as I explained about the letters, the new tape I had found, and all of the documents and keepsakes I brought home from storage. Then I jumped in the shower, got dressed, kissed Kevin goodbye and drove straight to my mother's house. I was eager to talk to her about it all—especially about my father.

***

"I MET HIM when I was eighteen years old," said Mom. "People think we met in Africa, but we first met in Salt Lake City."

The thought of it made her tearful. She sniffled and swallowed and pushed herself upright in her chair. A hand pressed gently against her mouth and dropped away without comment.

I placed my hand on her shoulder, hoping to comfort her.

"He was tall, handsome, incredibly charismatic, charming, and—to my surprise—terribly shy."

I was thinking, trying to imagine what it must have been like for her. My father always had a sheer physical presence—even as a child. It was quite remarkable, really. He didn't have to do or say anything. He had a magnetic attraction that drew people into the glow of his orbit. Mom never stood a chance, I thought. She would have fallen in love with him just observing him. Like most people did.

"The entire car ride from the airport to his boxing exposition he joked with everyone else and said very little to me," Mom continued.

"He just smiled and pretended not to notice me. He later told me he was afraid of me."

She went on to explain the details behind their courtship. Her condo in Chicago, their trips to the farm in Michigan, where I was born, the stories and details behind their union. All the drama with Belinda— things the world didn't know—why we moved to Los Angeles, their wedding, and their divorce.

I sat there, silently listening to my mom tell her story. It wasn't easy. I wanted to butt in and defend my father. She wasn't speaking badly about him; defending Dad was just something I did naturally.

"That's not fair, Mom," I said when she told me why she divorced him. "You knew he wasn't faithful when you married him." Though she didn't know the extent of it.

I thought about all the things I didn't know—things she *wasn't* telling me. Moments my father's recorder didn't capture and conversations half-finished and abandoned.

Listening to my mother, I felt like a whole new world was revealed to me. There was so much I didn't know—would never have guessed and couldn't remember. But it was a world no longer within my reach. The lost letters, the tape recordings, and the conversations that had become a part of me—they belonged to a long-ago place and time.

So I listened. I listened long and hard, and I asked her hard questions.

"Why did you wait so long to leave ... and how could you not see something was wrong with Daddy?"

There was a pause before she answered.

"Sometime after the Larry Holmes fight we went to the hospital in New York City, where your father was thoroughly evaluated. All they found was that he had a sleep disorder—they said the cause was jet lag."

Even back then the papers were reporting that he was dying and only had months to live. Dad always got a kick out of that. He loved getting the attention.

"Did I make the front page?" he always asked.

Mom didn't know that Dad was having trouble sleeping—until she heard him tell the doctor. They weren't sleeping in separate bedrooms yet. But how would she have known, if he didn't tell her? Unless she had woken up in the middle of the night and found him.

"The truth is," said Mom, "after that I didn't worry because the doctors couldn't find anything wrong with him. A few years later Gene [Dad's long-time friend] took him to the Mayo Clinic. The doctor diagnosed him with Parkinson's syndrome and said it would not progress."

That's when the conversation erupted.

"How could you not know something was wrong with him? I was a little girl and I could see it. The whole world could see it. Why couldn't you?"

"The newspapers were always printing lies when he was fine. Your father was fine."

"He wasn't fine, Mom!" I yelled. "Even I could see that!"

"His speech was slurred at times, but it had been that way for years. We thought he was just tired. All of his medical tests came back fine!" she yelled back at me.

"His hand shook, Mom! Even the newspaper reporters could see it. You still traveled together, Mom! How come you're the only person who couldn't see?"

"I wasn't in his office all the time! I didn't see everything! I wasn't there!" she finally admitted. "I was trying to figure out what to do with my life! His thumb twitched sometimes and his speech was slurred at times, but the doctors said it wouldn't get worse, it wasn't supposed to get worse!"

"But he wasn't fine, Mom! It did get worse and he needed you!"

We were both crying by then. But I had finally asked her the questions. And she had finally admitted that she wasn't around as often as she could have been.

We hugged, wiped each other's tears, and continued our conversation.

"Your father never told me they changed his diagnosis to Parkinson's disease. I found out after we were divorced," said Mom. "He was a decent, loving human being. His biggest fault was fooling around. I didn't always know when he was fooling around," she said, leaning back in her chair. "Sometimes I wouldn't find out until years later. He didn't have affairs—they were mostly one-night stands. But there were too many broken promises. After being hurt so many times my feelings gradually numbed over the years. I couldn't have left him if it weren't for that. Divorce is hard on the person leaving too. I always cared about him, but I had to distance myself somehow."

I realized there was nothing left for me to discover or figure out. This was my parents' love story: their memories, their choices, their sorrows and regrets—*their lessons.*

I told Mom about the tape I found and the Marilyn Funt interview she meant to give me. *"Hana, there was a lot you were too young to remember,"* her note had said. *"Love Mom."*

I told her about the articles, the sales contract of Fremont Place, their prenuptial agreement, and all of the other items I'd found in her storage the day before. Pizza was ordered, coffee was poured. More tears fell and dried. By the end of our conversation, I felt I had healed a little. Ultimately, there was a series of misunderstandings between my parents that led to them sleeping in different bedrooms and eventually their divorce. There was much more to their story than I have shared in this book, but it's not my story to tell. Perhaps one day my mom will tell it.

I finally understood what my mother always hoped I would. I had unfairly appointed her the villain, blaming and punishing her, ever since I was ten, for leaving my beloved father. Dad may have suffered acutely at the end, but my mother's pain was drawn out over many years with each act of betrayal.

Sometimes I still wish I could turn back the hands of time and rewrite the ending of my parents' love story. In my version, my father would have handed her the letters. She would have read them and given him a second chance. I sometimes find myself asking, "What if?"

What if he had stayed retired? What if he was faithful? What if he had given her the letters? Would it have changed things?

Would she have forgiven him? Who can say? But I do know this: even after all of the pain and heartache and sorrow that followed their divorce, I wouldn't change a thing. Everything happens as it's supposed to.

I remember the look in both of their eyes every time they reconnected over the years. And I realize there was no end to their story—not really. Their love will live forever: in my father's letters, through their children's memories, in the photographs on my nightstand, and in this book. Maybe that's enough.

I handed the letters and tape recording to my mother. Finally understanding.

"I always thought he never fought for me," she had said. But after all these years she had found out *he did.*

I hugged her goodbye. "Love you, Mom. See you at Laila's this weekend," I said, walking out the door.

"Okay, love you—drive safe."

***

IN THE EARLY years, Mom had postponed her aspirations to become a medical doctor and dedicated herself totally to their marriage. She even took care of Laila and me in the early years. Life was often idyllic. We traveled everywhere as a family until we started elementary school. Eventually, Mom hired a live-in governess so she could pursue some of her own interests.

She spent a lot of time trying to figure out what she wanted to do. For a while, she turned her hobby of horseback riding into a promising profession. By 1982, she was featured in the September issue of *Jet* magazine, posing with her horses and her countless ribbons and awards. It kept her away from home most of the day, which could be why my father started writing his letters to her. Sometimes he took us to the stables to watch her train, and he occasionally went to her shows. But after a while they both fell into the pattern of living their separate lives. As my father wrote in one of his letters, the relationship between them had become that of a brother and sister.

After the divorce, Mom finally went back to school to earn a doctorate in clinical psychology. She's currently working at one of the best medical centers in the country.

When I think about my childhood, my mother always seemed busy and preoccupied, but at the same time she was always there for me when I needed her most. When I told her I was being bullied by Bertha in the third grade, she came to the school and tracked her down in the playground, holding my hand. Bertha could see us coming and was literally zig-zagging through playing kids and playground equipment trying to avoid us. Mom told her to keep her hands to herself and leave me alone. After that Bertha never bothered me again.

Mom was also great with my schoolwork. She spent hours helping me study for spelling bees and finishing homework. And sometimes she'd stay up until late rolling my hair for me—so I could feel pretty for my school crush. She always came to parents' night and helped me with my class projects.

My mother is a beautiful woman inside and out. She continues to grow and better herself with each passing day. She's a special, classy, intelligent lady, and she has always pushed me to believe in myself. Although I was angry with her for half of my childhood, we've always had a close, open, and honest relationship. I wouldn't trade her for anyone in the world.

Neither of my parents took lessons in child rearing. They were doing the best they could with the weight of the world on their shoulders. And trying to make sense of their own lives in the process. Although they loved each other deeply, their time together had to come to an end.

Like Dad said, *"Life is a fair trade, where all adjusts itself in time ... For all that you take from it, you must pay the price sooner or later."*

***

A FEW MONTHS after I discovered the letters, I arrived at my father's house in Scottsdale, Arizona. Dad was sitting in his usual seat. A large, comfortable armchair that faced his ninety-inch television screen. Centered above it, staring down at him, was a small Neil Leifer portrait of his youthful face. A constant reminder that time waits for no man. His delight was clear in his expression as he watched himself dancing around the ring in the documentary *When We Were Kings*.

His eyes, now sensitive to sunlight, were slightly squinted. I let down the remote-controlled shade behind him, blotting out most of the sun's rays. A few gleams shone through the cracks, casting a soft glow over his serene face. I watched him sitting there for a moment. He looked more at peace with himself than ever.

"I have something for you, Daddy," I said, holding out a color-fully wrapped box. I knew how much he loved opening gifts. His eyes were glued to *himself* on the screen. I waited for the scene to fade—it was him talking about how he planned to destroy George Foreman—then I tried again.

"Daddy, I made you an album of family photos. There are pictures of you, Uncle Rock, Mama Bird, Papa Cash, and all of your children and our mothers."

That got his attention. He loved looking at pictures, especially family photos.

He turned to me and reached for the box. I placed it on the pillow in his lap and helped him open it. His eyes brightened when he saw the first picture: all of his children gathered around him on the front lawn at Fremont Place. I helped him turn the page. He pointed to an old photo of himself standing victorious over Sonny Liston.

"I just turned twenty-two," he said softly. "I predicted I'd be the heavyweight champ by the time I was twenty-one. I missed by one week."

He flipped through the pages and stopped at the picture of himself with Mom, Laila, and me sitting on the steps of Fremont Place.

"Where's your mother?" he asked.

"Home, in Los Angeles."

"Is she still married?"

"No, Carl got leukemia and passed away several years ago, remember? It happened when I was still living in Michigan."

After I came back from the funeral, Dad asked me to call my mother. He wanted me to tell her he still loved her.

"Mom, Daddy wants me to tell you he still loves you."

"Tell him I still love him too ..."

It was a call I'd make many times over the years.

For a moment, I was tempted to tell him about the letters—that Mom had finally read them—but I didn't. His eyes were closed now.

"Daddy," I said softly, "what do you want me to say to the world on your behalf, is there any message you want me to write?" He knew I was planning to write a book featuring some of his recordings. I'd been reading him random pages over the phone.

His eyes opened, as if charged by a divine spark, and they beamed that old familiar twinkle.

"I was a baaaad Nigga! And I'm still 'The Greatest'!"

"Daddy, I can't say that!"

"Yes, you can—they'll laugh. They'll think it's funny."

In the end, I never asked my father about the letters. He had made peace with that time in his life long ago. I didn't want to *stir* his ghosts.

39

MY SIBLINGS ONLY spent three summers at Fremont Place before my parents' divorce. After my father married Lonnie, they both moved to his house in Berrien Springs, Michigan, where Dad continued his tradition of bringing all his children together for summers. The location had changed but the adventures continued. We would swim in the outdoor Olympic-size pool and play tennis. We would roll around in the golf cart, crushing Lonnie's tulips and rose bushes—she was probably sorry she bought it in the first place, after we got ahold of the keys. There was no golf course, but it was needed to get around eighty-eight acres of land.

Sometimes it was Dad who was the ringleader. He'd slam his foot on the gas and shout, "I KILLLLLLLL!" Dashing across the lawn, just as he did when we were little girls sitting in the back of his Rolls with its top down. We all screamed, squeezing the rails beside our seats, even though we were only going ten miles an hour.

Only four of us fit on the cart at once, so we took turns, each ride more exciting than the last. Then we went inside and watched movies. The Lone Ranger, Flashdance, and one of my father's favorites, Blacula, a 1970s incarnation of Dracula. As we watched, and when it was over, Dad always terrorized us, holding out his arms, making faces, and following us around the room, limping and growling as we screamed—making great memories together.

When we argued, he'd sit us all on the sofa and say, "You're sisters, you're supposed to love and protect each other—not fuss and fight . . ."

He was always teaching us about the ways of the world and making sure we learned from mistakes, be they ours or his.

"*Do you remember Elijah Muhammad before he died?*" he asked my sister, Maryum, on one of his recordings when she was a little girl.

"Yes, sir!"

"*He used to teach that white people are devils. Now his son, Wallace Muhammad, teaches that they aren't devils, it's not a person's skin color that makes them a devil ... it's the way they think. You know that, don't you?*"

"Yes, sir," said Maryum. "*I always knew that ...*"

It was my father's dream to have all of his children living under one roof with him.

A couple years after Dad moved to Michigan, I remember visiting one spring when I was twelve or thirteen. Laila usually stayed at the house with Lonnie when Dad and I took long walks up Kephart Lane, the road leading to the main highway from his property. Dad liked to see how far he could walk before getting tired. He never really spoke about his health, other than to say it was a test from God: "*To remind me and the world that I'm just a man like everyone else.*"

As the years passed and his disease progressed, he never let the effects of Parkinson's get the best of him. His mind and spirit remained unaffected.

Several years ago, Lonnie told my father about a friend of theirs who had recently been diagnosed with the disease.

"He isn't taking it well," she said. "What advice can you give him, Muhammad? How do you handle it so well after all these years?"

"I don't know," he said. "I don't think about it. Do people know I have it?"

"Yeah, people know you have it." She laughed.

"Oh," he said, "Do you have anything sweet in the kitchen?"

That was the secret to his success—the essence of his spirit. He kept things simple and never woke up thinking about Parkinson's. The world may have labeled him sick, but he never labeled himself like that. He lived his life one day at a time until, eventually, Parkinson's became an afterthought.

When we reached the end of Kephart Lane, a couple miles outside the gates of my father's farm, we stopped at the corner burger stand and ordered his favorite meal: a cheeseburger with mustard and onions, and a vanilla milkshake.

After eating, he'd call Lonnie on the payphone and have her pick us up. I remember the cool feeling of the air-conditioner on my skin as we entered the gate, passing the large white sign that once read: *Muhammad Ali Farms*. Sometimes we'd get out at the gate and walk back up to the house, admiring the scenery along the way.

As we made the five-minute walk back one day, sipping on our vanilla shakes, Dad stopped and slowly waved his hand across the vast land. "Isn't this beautiful?" he said, his bright eyes blinking rapidly. "I've got eighty-eight acres—eighty-eight acres! I could build a house for each of my children here." His eyes widened, as he visualized his dream. "I'd give each of you five acres; that's a lot of land." He looked at me for approval.

"That's more than enough," I told him.

"We could all live here together," he dreamed.

It was a beautiful idea. But knowing that my father, who had given so much to so many, possessed such a pure and sweet dream, one I knew would not come true, broke my heart.

Several years later, when I was twenty-four, I moved to Michigan to be geographically closer to him. It was a special time. I learned so much about him. I lived with him for a year, then I moved into a house I bought in Saint Joseph—a ten-minute drive away. I had the pleasure of seeing my father's face nearly every day for the six years I lived there.

I cherish the memories we made in that time. We wrote a book, *The Soul of a Butterfly*. We stayed up late watching his old fights and documentaries about him. We watched Elvis Presley and Clint Eastwood movies. *Blue Hawaii, Viva Las Vegas, Pale Rider,* and *The Good, the Bad and the Ugly*. Westerns were always Dad's favorites, but he also loved watching his movie, *The Greatest*.

We took long drives around the neighborhood, and sometimes we drove as far as Chicago to visit my twin sisters, Jamillah and

405

Rasheda, and we'd go to the mosque to pray. As we cruised down the highway, Dad would press his face against the window, waiting for drivers to recognize that it was Muhammad Ali in the car they were passing. When they noticed him, as they always did, he'd smile and wave contentedly. Sometimes he'd gesture for them to pull over on to the side of the road, where he would sign autographs, shake hands, and take pictures.

Some mornings I'd wake up at 5 a.m. and find my father downstairs in the kitchen, looking through the cabinets—searching for sweets. Any cake or pie with vanilla ice cream was his favorite. Mostly I only found the evidence that he'd been there; the trail of cookie crumbs leading from the kitchen over to the couch and back up the stairs. My father's sleeping habits had been the same since his training days. He rose before the sun for prayer, sat up for a while snacking on fruit and watching television, then he headed back upstairs to sleep.

Every morning, Dad would sit at the kitchen island and eat his breakfast, telling jokes to the house and grounds staff: Andy, Mike, Joel, Greg, and Coleen. After eating we'd walk or drive the golf cart up the driveway to his office, where the office staff, Deborah, Kim, Andrea, and David, were always happy to see him. He'd sit at his desk all day working on his papers and fan mail, just as he did when I was a little girl.

Once we drove the golf cart to McDonald's in the middle of the night for ice cream and cheeseburgers. His order was always the same: vanilla ice cream and two quarterpounders with nothing but cheese, mustard, and onions.

I organized his briefcase for his travels and sometimes went with him on trips. One of the most memorable was our visit to Bloomington, Indiana, in September of 2003, for the World Peace Conference. After I read a speech on behalf of my father at the "Let Peace Begin With Me" ceremony, the Dalai Lama gave Dad a scarf symbolizing friendship. Then they planted a peace tree together.

Dad was still traveling the world, but mostly we took trips to Barnes & Noble, bought books, and hung out at home, trading jokes and performing magic tricks for each other. We talked about all sorts of things, from life and death to past wives and family secrets.

Dad liked to go out and just sit and work in his motorhome sometimes. I remember him carrying all of his books and notepads out the back door into the motorhome, which was parked in the driveway. Dad couldn't drive any more. Lonnie bought it to provide a place for him to rest when they traveled to Chicago or Louisville, and for when he attended Asaad's (his son with Lonnie) baseball games—which was often.

Sometimes the old memories came back, of me sitting on his lap, pretending I was driving as we circled the block around Fremont Place. Occasionally honking the horn and speaking into the radio walkie-talkie: "*Clear the roads ... This is the BIG BOPPER!*"

My little hands on top of his, gripping the big steering wheel, thinking I was in control of the vehicle.

"*That's it, Hana,*" he'd say. "*You're a good driver! The best driver in the world ...*" I was five years old at the time.

Of all the precious moments I spent with my father, my most cherished memories of my time living with him in Michigan are simply sitting beside him as he quietly worked at his desk beneath a dim light, helping him organize his papers and religious pamphlets. I'd read him the Quran and repeat his favorite passages to him. "*If all the oceans were ink and all of the trees were pens, it still would not be enough to write the knowledge that God has.*"

I remember sitting with him in complete silence and feeling something divine. He was so peaceful, loving, and forgiving. I could feel a heavenly presence. It made me feel safe, blessed, and grateful for the gift of simply being with him.

My father's farm on Kephart Lane will always hold a special place in my heart. I spent the first few years of my life there—playing in the sun, and running around the open fields where I first learned to walk, fascinated by the butterflies and bees. I loved watching lightning bugs in the night sky and splashing my hands in the pond Dad had built for Mom's white ducks.

We lived in the coach house above the garage and members of my father's entourage occupied the main house. Dad always liked small, cozy spaces. The coach house was like a little oasis that provided privacy for my parents, though Daddy never seemed to need it.

Several farm horses ran freely across the meadow by day, and a herd of black Angus cattle grazed on the vast pastures along the river that circled the property. The geese and ducks my mother raised swam in the ponds searching for food, while the fighting cocks my father admired flew up into the trees and eventually disappeared. I was too young to remember the chicken coop and the rows of hens sitting on their nests laying eggs that rolled down into baskets below, but they're captured in old photographs and my mother's memories.

In those early years, we split our time between the Woodlawn house in Chicago, Dad's training camp in Deer Lake, and the farm in Michigan. By my third birthday, Mom was filling her decorating book with drawings, measurements, and furniture clippings for the house on Fremont Place. She still has the binder today. Among other things, both Mom and Dad had enough of the cold winters and were looking forward to moving to Los Angeles. And for a long while that was the last I had seen of the farm.

My visit to Michigan at twenty-four was a two-week trip that resulted in a six-year stay, and they would be the most cherished and blessed years of my life. The things I witnessed, the adventures Dad and I went on, the lessons learned, the little battles I fought for him, watching him throw punches into the air, probably dreaming he was in the boxing ring, as he napped on the sofa snoring like a grizzly bear. The jokes and laughter. The ups and downs. The changing of the seasons. The bond we shared will always be with me.

But all that's another story.

I only moved back to Los Angeles permanently after Lonnie bought two new houses, one in Scottsdale, Arizona, and the other in my father's hometown, Louisville, Kentucky. They kept the farm, but Lonnie moved my father around according to the weather, so he started to spend less time in Michigan. He ended up spending most of his time at the house in Scottsdale. He said the farm was his favorite property. He missed the green grass and trees and spring flowers. But Arizona grew on him.

"The only thing it's missing is color," he once said.

With Lonnie flying him between his three properties, I saw less and less of my father. So I decided to move back to Los Angeles. At least then I could drive up to Arizona to visit him.

The time of seeing him every day had come to an end. But our private little moments will live in my heart forever.

40

AS MY FATHER put all of the tapes back into his briefcase that afternoon in 1998 in his hotel room, I couldn't shake the feeling that something wonderful was coming.

"These will be yours one day," he had said, placing his attaché case back beside his chair. Ironically, my favorite recording—a modest one that explained why he had made them—was on a tape in that pile before me, but I wouldn't hear it for another five years.

It wasn't until 2003, while we were writing his book *The Soul of a Butterfly*, that I went home with a case full of precious memories, and my life hasn't been the same since.

Summer of 2003

When bedtime stories failed to work their magic, my father often coaxed me to sleep at night by singing a song. A couple of his favorites were Chuck Berry's "School Days" and the Shirelles' "Dedicated to the One I Love". The first time I listened to the tape in question was the day after my father officially gave them to me. I had stayed up all night engrossed in the past—laughing and crying, learning and remembering. The next morning, I grabbed a random cassette to listen to in the car.

I was driving up Hilltop Road, from my house in Saint Joseph, on the way to my father's farm in Berrien Springs. It was 75 degrees in

Michigan that day, and the sky was a perfect, cloudless blue. With the windows rolled down, I put in the tape. As I listened, time rolled back.

All of the feelings I had felt five years earlier, in my father's hotel room, came rushing over me like a tidal wave of love. My mind flooded. I had been met with such memories before, but this was different. There was something special about this recording. He was talking about how beautiful and fleeting life was and explained why he took the time to make all the recordings in the first place. Mostly it felt like a message of love from a father to his daughter, reaching across the barriers of time.

Hearing my father's old familiar voice from the past, speaking to me in the present, as my three-year-old self sat listening beside him, sent chills through me. It wasn't the sound of us singing together that moved me. It was the love in my father's voice when he explained how happy I made him. But most of all, it was his closing words that took my breath away.

"My sweet Hana—my love."

I pulled off the road and listened to the tape again. I treasured this recording for its message and the way my father's words made me feel when he spoke them, but to know that he had recorded it especially for me made it extraordinary. I rushed to my father's house to tell him what I had discovered. I couldn't wait to see him, to kiss him, to hug him—to place his sweet, angelic face in my hands and thank him from the depths of my heart for this immeasurable gift.

When I reached the tall iron gates at the end of Kephart Lane that secured my father's estate, I entered my code, pulled up the flowery driveway, and parked outside his office. The golf cart was there, he had driven up from the house. I walked through the glass doors, down the hall, past the little kitchen and the framed signatures of the supreme court justices who overturned his conviction: *Warren E. Burger, Hugo Black, William O. Douglas, John M. Harlan II, William J. Brennan Jr, Potter Stewart, Byron White, Thurgood Marshall, and Harry Blackmun.*

Dad was sitting behind his desk, just as he had every morning at Fremont Place when I was a little girl. He must have just arrived.

Everything on the table was neatly stacked in front of him. All his notes, pens, markers, and books were just as we had left them the night before. As I walked into the room, he looked up at me with his gentle eyes.

"Maaaaaan!" I shouted, imitating the camaraderie he shared with friends long ago. "Awwww, Maaaaaan! You were a baaaaaad maaaaaaan!"

"Maaaaaan! Maaaan!" he shot back. "Aw, Maaaaaan!"

I laughed out loud as we both chanted back and forth, "Maaaaaan! Awwww, Maaaan!"

His eyes were bright with excitement. "How did you know? Who taught you?" he asked.

"You did," I said. "I learned it from the tape recordings of you talking to your friends." There was a pause, an enduring pause, and I could see in his expression that he was far away and long ago. "Daddy, the recordings brought back so many happy memories. I listened to them all night long."

He smiled, and I did too.

"What's your favorite tape?" he asked.

413

"There are so many, Daddy. I haven't even heard them all yet. But I especially love the recordings of us running around the house with you playing—singing together in the morning—and you reading me bedtime stories at night."

"I remember," he said softly.

"But, Daddy, the tape I just heard today is my favorite."

"Play it," he said. "Let me hear it."

I went to the car to get my purse. When I walked back into the room, I went over to his chair, kneeled down in front of him, and placed his precious round face between my hands. I looked into his eyes and told him everything my heart longed to say: I told him he'd given me the greatest gift; that whatever the future held, his children and posterity would always have this to look back on. I told him I would cherish his recordings and his voice forever. I told him he was the most wonderful father. That he was even greater at being a father than he was at being a world champion. I thanked him for bringing all of his children together so we could grow up together and be friends. I told him that because of his incredible love I'd be able to revisit, time and again, a place my long-ago self had been.

"Thank you, Daddy," I said. "Thank you, thank you, thank you ..."

By the look in his eyes I could see that something deep inside him had stirred to life. Then I sat down in the chair beside him, pulled my Walkman out of my purse, and pushed play. My father leaned back in his chair and listened with his eyes closed, just as I had the first time he let me hear them, flying on the wings of my childhood memories to faraway places and adventures we both lived long ago. Where he would remain forever young. Forever strong. *Forever home.*

***

"HANA, LET'S SING. Time for our singing lessons ... ready?"

"Yeah ..."

We sang together: *"This is dedicated to the one I love, each night before you go to bed, my babeeeee, oooooo ..."*

"Here's another one, Hana." I'm repeating after him, *"Up in the morning off to school / the teachers teach the golden rule / American*

history and practical math, studying real hard and hoping to pass /
working your finger right down to the bone / the guy behind you
won't leave you alone / Ring, ring goes the bell / Cookin" the lunch
and waiting to sell ..." Our voices fade out, laughing together.

After a moment, he speaks back into the recorder. *"Hana, that*
was you singing with your daddy, on December 9, 1979 [three years
old] *in our home on 55 Fremont Place in Los Angeles. You were a*
sweet little girl. You are so beautiful. God blessed us to raise you in
a good way. Your mother, Veronica ... she has the best of manners,
and your father—I do my best. We were so happy with you. I just
kiss your little jaws all the time. I always squeeze you and hug you
..." His voice softened. *"And I love you."*

"These tapes are something I'm making because I am history-con-
scious. We only come through this world once and we're only young
once. We're only babies once, teenagers once, old men and old
women, and then we die. But I knew it would be so beautiful for

415

me to get this—by me being conscious of this—about making tapes and being history-minded.

"I knew that, one day, you would be intelligent enough to appreciate that your daddy made all these tapes so you could hear them someday. Mommy would wake me up in the morning and say; 'Let's make some tapes on Hana.' We both got together and thought of this. We have Laila and Mommy talking to Grandmommy on the telephone, or whomever.

"There's me talking to your other sisters, Maryum, Jamillah, Rasheda, Miya, Khaliah and your brother, Little Muhammad. I did all I could to keep you together and let you know about one another, and mainly to make tapes where you could hear one another in different times in history. So, I love you and may God bless you. I love Hana, I love Laila—all my children.

"So, I want to say to you the Arabic greetings that mean peace be with you. As-Aalaamu Alaykum, my sweet Hana—MY LOVE."

THOSE WERE OUR last days living together as a family. The shattered pieces of my heart remain scattered around the rooms and halls of Fremont Place, deep in the cracks and crevices, embedded in the walls. I don't know if I'll ever recover them, the broken pieces. Or that I even want to. My childhood home has always been a part of me, and I will always be part of it.

The memories long confined to the annals of my mind—old ghosts I have spent my life amongst—have become almost a comfort to me now; something I anticipate and enjoy, like a movie I've watched a hundred times that still moves me to tears of sadness and joy. After reading all the articles, and my father's love letters to my mother, I was inspired. I wanted to bring them all to life again—the ghosts so hauntingly intertwined in my past and present. I wanted to give them a voice, and let them tell their own story.

I wish I could tell you I have forgiven my mother *completely.* I know she's always loved my father. But the truth is, the little girl inside of me still blames her for leaving him. Sometimes I still feel like that five-year-old girl roaming the halls of a mansion, waiting for her daddy to come home.

Dad and me on the front steps of Fremont Place.

THE LAST CHAPTER

ON JUNE 3, 2016, at the age of seventy-four, my father made his ultimate journey. His flight departed at 9:10 p.m. out of Scottsdale, Arizona. I wanted to beg him to stay—beg him to take me with him, like I had when I was a little girl. But I didn't. This time was different. He was going someplace he couldn't take me—on a trip he would never return from.

We were all there to wish him a final farewell—all of his children and grandchildren.

He had prepared me for this since I was a child.

"I'm going to die one day," he said. *"We're all going to die. This life is short. This life is just a test for the eternal life ... God doesn't care that I whooped Joe Frazier. He doesn't care that I knocked out George Foreman. He only cares about how I treated people and how many people I helped ..."*

The week before his great journey, I Facetimed him, blowing kisses as we spoke. *"I love you, Daddy—I miss you—I'm coming to visit you soon ..."*

It was how I opened and closed every conversation, kissing him and telling him how much I loved him. Occasionally he'd ask a question or two; his words a soft whisper, gentle as a feather. But he didn't speak that day—he didn't have to. He had already said it all. His eyes spoke for him; they glistened with love and happiness as he listened to me filling him in on the day-to-day happenings of my life. He always liked hearing about things like that.

"*I love you, Daddy,*" I said, before hanging up. "*See you soon ...*"

A week later the phone rang. It was Laila.

"Daddy's in the hospital, *again* ..."

The following day we landed in Arizona.

Two years earlier, in 2014, I'd received a similar call from my sister. Kevin and I were in Scottsdale to visit my father for the weekend. It was late when we arrived. We checked into a hotel. I was getting dressed the next morning when my cell phone rang. It was Laila.

"Don't freak out, Hana," she said. "Daddy's in the hospital. They had to take him late last night, he was having trouble breathing ... Lonnie didn't want to wake you ..."

Lonnie always called Laila—I think it was too difficult for her to deliver the message to me directly. She knew how I'd react—that my eruption of tears might unleash her own.

Laila gave me the hospital information as my tears fell. I had a feeling this was the beginning—that the end was near.

Kevin and I went straight to the hospital. During Dad's two-week stay, I was there every day—all day and all night. Kevin stayed with me. May May and Laila were there too, but left a couple days later.

"We feel good knowing you're here," they said. "Let us know how he's doing."

His condition was stable. But I couldn't leave. Daddy never left me in the hospital alone. He was there day and night. Now I could do the same for him.

I decorated the walls of his room with photos, flowers and balloons. He slept most of the time but we watched movies on his iPad when he was awake.

Lonnie took the day shift, her sister Marilyn took the night.

I called Dr B, my employer at the time. I had been working with autistic children for ten years by then.

"My father's in the hospital," I said. "I won't be back until he's well ... I don't know when that will be."

I called George Foreman. He and Dad kept in touch over the years.

"Stay strong," he said. "I'm here if you need me." George was a huge help—and support—for me. I'll always be grateful.

Mom called every few days, checking on Dad's progress, relaying messages of love.

"He's asleep most of the day, Mom. I'll tell him when he wakes."

"Whisper in his ear," she said. "His spirit can hear you."

Eventually my father got better—he always bounced back.

"Guess what, Daddy," I would say each time he came home from the hospital. "You were in the newspaper again. The world thinks you're dying ..."

His response was always the same: "Did I make the front page?"

After my father came home from the hospital, I stayed another three weeks. He slept most of the day but within a few weeks he was back to his old routine, watching westerns in the morning. But he wasn't quite the same. I sat beside him all day and night, knitting a scarf for his birthday. It belongs to President Obama now—a gift I would give him at the White House.

"*My father would have wanted you to have this ...*" I wrote in the letter accompanying a photograph of Dad wearing it.

Eventually I went back home and my father regained his strength. But still I had that feeling—the end was coming.

***

I WON'T GO into great detail about my father's passing on June 3, 2016, but I will share this. It was fitting for the loving life he lived. I'd spent my thirty-ninth birthday with him the year before. He celebrated his last birthday with eight of his nine children gathered around him. He laughed and smiled and watched magic tricks being performed. We all cheered at the closing act—a white dove was pulled from a hat and flew around the room above him.

Six months later, he was checked into the hospital.

He wasn't in pain.

At some point, he went to sleep, like he always did during the day, then his organs slowly started to fail and he woke up in heaven.

Before that happened, all of his children and grandchildren had arrived at the hospital in Scottsdale. We were all there with him, telling him how much we loved him—and telling stories and reminiscing about all the fun we had with him over the years.

"Can he hear us?" Jamillah asked.

"Yes," I answered. "His spirit can hear us."

I wasn't ready to say goodbye. But somehow, I found the strength. As we were all gathered around him, memories were shared, tears fell, laughter filled the room as we remembered happier times.

Nurses came and went. Papers were signed ... More tears and more laughter.

At some point a bell started dinging; it was coming from one of the machines.

"DING! DING! DING!"

It sounded like a fighter's bell—like in a boxing ring.

"That's your eight-count, Daddy!" said Rasheda. "Now get your ass up!"

We all laughed—tears followed.

We took turns holding his hand and whispering in his ear.

We kissed him and hugged him. And told him how much we loved him.

When it was my turn, I tried to hold back the tears. I didn't want to make it harder for him. He wasn't conscious, but I believe he could hear.

"You're doing so well, Hana," Lonnie said at one point.

Laila had said the same.

I guess they thought I was going to break down.

He had given so much to us, so much to the world. It was time to let him go.

"I know he loved all of us," said Laila, "but you're the one he really loved ..."

"That's not true," I said. "Don't say that. His spirit can hear you. You're going to make it hard for him to go."

"Okay," she said, and hugged me.

"He really loved you ..." I said again. "He loved us all."

"I know ... I'm here for you, Hana," said Laila. "I'm proud you're doing so well."

421

As the end drew near, Imam Zaid Shakir walked into the room, sat beside my father and read passages from the Quran. We all found a place to be. I stood at the foot of his bed, holding his feet, because I read someplace that the soul leaves through the feet.

We stood there, chanting the words of the Muslim prayer.

One by one, his organs started to fail but his heart kept beating. In the final moments of my father's life I realized how blessed he had been—how peaceful his passing was. His wife and all of his children were there with him, gathered around him, taking turns whispering messages of love in his ear. He had fallen asleep a couple days before and would wake up and meet God.

"It's okay, Daddy," I had whispered. "You can go now—you've done all you can do here. You were the best father. You made me so happy—thank you, Daddy. Go back to God now—we'll be okay. I love you, Daddy. God bless you. Goodbye, Daddy. I'm going to miss you. You'll always be the love of my life. You're free now, Daddy ... You don't have to fight any more."

His body was flown home to Kentucky.

A few days later, on June 10, we took one last drive with our father through the streets of his home town, Louisville. Thousands of people lined the roads and highways. They were on bridges and in building windows, chanting his name and holding up signs:

"We Love You.'"

"Thank You."

"With the Greatest Respect. You Shook up the World in Life and Death. RIP Champ."

For years my father and Lonnie had filled a black binder with details. All his children's mothers were invited. Religious leaders of all faiths were invited. All the world was invited. And everyone showed up.

Our line of black Cadillacs followed the route he planned. Past the house he grew up in on 3302 Grand Avenue. Past the street where his bike was stolen, where he met the officer who introduced him to boxing. Past Central High, where he dreamed of being a world champion and the building where he'd fallen down the stairs after

kissing a pretty girl. As we drove down Broadway—past the cheering crowds of thousands—I realized the recurring dream my father used to have was his vision of this day.

"I used to dream that I was running down Broadway and all of the people were in the street waving at me and cheering me on. I waved back at them, then all of a sudden I took off flying. I dreamed that dream all the time."

***

AFTER MY FATHER passed, I finally went back to Fremont Place. It was a Sunday afternoon, I was alone, driving home from a late lunch with my friend Kenisha Norton. Her father, Ken Norton, had passed a couple years earlier. *"Prepare yourself,"* she said as she hugged me goodbye. *"It gets worse with time."*

I pulled up to the red light on Rossmore, the same light I sat at with my father years before. *"Look, Daddy! It's Fremont Place ... want to go see the old house?"*

I sat there for a moment, staring at the stone pillars, searching my memory for the stories, the dreams, the faded remembrances that seemed so close yet so far away. They felt alive, like a living, breathing entity. The sounds, the songs, the laughter and tears, rich with texture and detail, struggling to break through, to live once more.

"This is Muhammad Ali talking to Hana and Laila at the home on Fremont Place, October the 24th, 1979. Hana and Laila are eating popsicles and I'm home with Veronica. She just turned the television on ..."

Moments passed. I don't know how many.

"HOOOOONK!!!" The sound of the horns pulled me back into the present. The light was green but was now turning yellow again.

"Sorry ..." I waved, as I pulled into the entrance, past the stone pillars, and stopped at the guard house, a tiny white structure with a barn door and window.

"May I help you, mam?"

"Hi, yes, my name is Hana Ali, I lived here at 55 Fremont Place when I was a little girl. I was hoping I could drive by and see the house?"

"I'm sorry, mam, I can't let you in if you aren't a resident."

"Please, sir, I won't bother the tenants. I only need five minutes."

"Mam, I could lose my job."

"Pleeeease, I can give you my license."

"Sorry, mam."

"It's okay. Maybe another time," I said. I could see the house in the distance and imagined my seven-year-old self running buck naked down the street, up to this very window.

"Uncle Steven won't let me watch my cartoons! Come arrest him!"

I started to fumble around with my purse, pretending to be looking for something—stalling for time. I looked at the house again. I could see the palm trees and Laila's balcony.

"Fond memories?" he asked, observing me.

"Oh, you have no idea," I said. Then I put my car in reverse and started to back up. He must have seen or felt something because he motioned for me to come back.

"Okay, mam," he said as my car pulled back up to his window. "But only five minutes. And I'll need to hold on to your license."

"Really? Thank you so much! I can't tell you how much this means to me. Thank you!"

I pulled my license out of my wallet, thanked the man again and drove past the gates onto Fremont Place. When I crossed the threshold, I felt like I was in a dream. The very air seemed to alter. I felt like I had traveled back in time, like I had stepped into one of my father's recordings.

"I'm at 55 Fremont Place, at home with Hana and Laila, and they're eating popsicles. Veronica and me just got in from Las Vegas . . . Lou Rawls was having a concert."

"Daddy, I want to talk to you on that thing."

"Okay, Hana, come talk to Daddy. Say, I like popsicles."

"I like popsicles . . ."

"Say, one day I'll listen to these tapes."

"One day I'll listen to the tapes . . ."

I drove slowly around the corner, past the side lawn, driveway and iron gates, where I used to stand on my tiptoes waiting for my father to come home. I parked across the street, facing the front entrance of the house. I got out of the car and walked over to the curb to the endless row of steps leading up to the mahogany door. I fantasized about walking up to it, knocking on it. I imagined my father answering it. It was as improbable as the hope of his fans—complete strangers who had climbed the steps years ago, hoping and dreaming that he just might answer it, like they had read in so many newspaper articles and magazines about people's dreams being answered when he opened the door.

"We drove all the way from Atlanta," they told reporters. *"We drove up from Washington, Texas, Ohio ... We got his address and just walked up and he answered the door, let us in, fed us and showed us magic tricks. It was unbelievable,"* they said. *"There's no one like him."*

I imagined their eyes widening in disbelief as the door opened and his face appeared.

For those fans, the impossible happened. For me, it could not, and as I stood there remembering I felt the heart-aching nostalgia of never being able to go back again. I was so close, yet so far away. He was gone now—to his forever home.

"We're all going to die one day," his words came back to me. *"I'm going to die; your mother is going to die; and you too will die ... no one lives forever. What we do for God is all that matters—it's all that will last."*

When I miss my father, when I want to hear his voice and the sound of our play and laughter, I put on a recording, close my eyes and travel back to this place—Fremont Place.

"Again, this is October 24, 1979 in the Los Angeles home. I'm taping Hana and Laila for the future. Hana's three years old and Laila will be two in December ... Hana, I'm playing this for you when you get big so you can hear Daddy doing this."

"That's my tape?"

"Yes ..."

"When I get big that won't be yours any more?"

"No, when you get big this will be yours ... Say, I'm going to hear this when I get big."

426

"I'm going to hear it when I get big."
"And I will be glad Daddy did it."
"I'm gonna be glad that Daddy did it ..."

In this house, somewhere in time, I will always be a carefree little girl singing with her father in the morning before school, watching him light the fireplace in his den, begging to sip his coffee ... Eating popsicles for breakfast ... Running through the halls ... Watching his magic shows ... Riding with my father up Wilshire Blvd with the top down, my hair blowing in the wind.

These are my favorite memories. They're frozen in time, in a place where age will never change them, Parkinson's will never shake them, and death will never take them.

"Okay, Hana, now we're going to sign off. Say, I'm a big girl now."
"I'm a BIG girl now!"
"Say, I hope you like the tapes."
"I hope you like the tapes."
"Say, bye Hana."
"Bye Hana ..."
"Signing off ..."

The hair on the back of my neck prickled as I stood there and some small voice inside me gave a warning. I wasn't supposed to be here. I was an unwelcome visitor trying to relive something long past. Something that belonged to another place in time.

It was time to let go and say goodbye.

A black BMW sedan was in front of the house where Dad used to park his Rolls when my mother's Mercedes was too low in the driveway. I wondered if the car belonged to the new owners, the family of four who lived there now, making their own memories. I looked up at the guest bedroom window, the one my father used to sleep in. The sun was out but the light was on. I thought about the songs we used to sing in that room, the bedtime stories he told me. How I used to wake him in the night asking for popsicles and pickles.

I wiped a lone tear, gave one last look at 55 Fremont Place—the steps, the front door, that bedroom window—and as I got back into my car and drove away a poem I once read came to mind.

Though nothing can bring back the hour
Of splendor in the grass, of glory in the flower;
We will grieve not, rather find
Strength in what remains behind.

"Thank you," I said, as the guard handed me back my license.
"Did you get what you came for?" he asked.
"Yes, I did," I said. "It was even more beautiful than I remembered."

EPILOGUE

55 Fremont Place, Los Angeles

I'M STANDING IN front of my childhood home. The sun is shining. My father is calling my name. *This is a dream*, I tell myself. I know this because his voice is loud and clear, the way it sounded when I was a little girl.

"Hana," he calls again. I see him standing at the top of the steps. His face is glowing. He looks strong and healthy—almost ethereal. He calls my name once more.

"I'm coming, Daddy," I shout, but when I run towards him, he disappears. "*Daddy!*" I call out. But he's no longer there. As I stand alone on the steps of Fremont Place, a warm breeze brushes against my cheek, as if to kiss me, and whispers in my ear: *I'm still here.* I wake up in a cold sweat.

The ghosts still stir occasionally. I'd be disappointed if they didn't.

430

APPENDICES

The following are my father's original handwritten notes, letters and drawings revealed in this book, along with other keepsakes shown herein.

O

Dear Veronica

As your Husband, I applaud and affirm all that you are even if not always all that you do, the very idea and core of your existence, your being and the specialness of your unique individuality as just my veronica, as your husband, I am to help you to be the most that you can be, acting, singing or what ever, I want you to have the freedom that you want, I offer you the encouragement of my relatedness to you and of yours to me I do care for you, But I will never possess or use you, I have found that you are your own person, never to be owned or used by anyone else, though you may leave, and others may love you as I do, I am all for you in all ways, and am with you always, living with you are not,

433

(2)

Though We may be Continents
apart, as you put in your
words, about us being two Different
people, Never will I leave you
nor do you in any way, I have
to earn my love for you, You
have that, Everything I have
because you are you, and
because I after living with you
I have found that Veronica is
such a Wonderful special
someone to know.

For what is it is
worth
I still
love
you

March 20-83

April 28-83

Dear Veronica
                    Love always

When I bow before Allah, I think of
Him and His relation to little me, I
become aware of the fact that God has
Created this vast universe for the benefit
of us, My mind is filled with
respect towards the great power that
has been responsible for the universe,

By me now praying every day in devotion
and submission, has developed in me,
and now I am coming closer to Allah,
I am now more Conscious of the fact
that I should not Commit sins. By
Praying 5 times a day. I need this, and it
is helping me, to be a better person, you will
like me, as even love me now, (smile)
If you give me one more Chance, I love
you so much, and it Hurts me so
much now that I Cannot sleep with
you, are have sex with you, I am so
sorry for the way I use to treat you.
If you don't forgive, I pray that Allah
will, I write to you because it is
hard to talk you, I am having a
hard time living without you, I guess
this is the Weakness of the human Mind
I had someone to spell these Big Words
   FOR ME.   OVER

435

The Quran teaches that the Righteous Parents an Children, will be reunited in Heaven, Me, you, Hana & Saela. In the Hereafter I want to Continue to have a good acquaintances with you there, The prayer has been prescribed to keep in Constant Memory of God, that's why I pray 5 times a Day. I wish you would pray with me sometime, before you leave me, allah Can do anything is we ask his help.

1. There is a Creator and Sustainer of this universe
2. Man should live in accordance with the directions of his Lord
3. Those who live accordingly have a bright Future.
4. Those who do not live accordingly will have to face Degradation and ruin.
5. There is a Life after death in which man will have to face the Consequences of the deeds of his previous life.
6. as man's knowledge is limited, the Creator has been sending prophets and Scriptures to guide him. all & Everyone should follow them

[signature]

'Let's try again'

What you wrote in the Poet Book
Made me smile

My days were starting to last for
a long while.

For time has become a long mile
With all its Joys hidden in
a small pile.

Let's try again to Find the
happiness we shared

There is no time like this

moment to Prepare

For tomorrow may be too late
to Care.

Although, We think about We
had no need for despair

Since, We have drifted
away,

We must make the best out
of today

Let's try again before today
becomes yesterday

That Way We Won't regret
the Price We had to Pay.

With love, understanding, and
devotion,

We shall Create a very
special sensation

That Will make each moment
We share an inspiration

Like a quiet summer Breeze Without
ANY FRUSTRATION

438

(3)

Veronica let's try again For
Just th feeling

That one set us Both
Carefree and reeling

And, if by Chance We should
hit the Ceiling

our efforts Will be something
Worthwhile and very
appealing

Yorlanna
Jan 8 83

439

To My Veronica

We need today a little more tolerance with each other, We cannot seem to meet on the same ground, I like it when you call or buzz me before you leave home in the early morning Because I may want to tell or Hug you Goodbye or whatever, us being so different having such different Capacities, states of evalutions, and tasks in our everyday life, If Muhammad and Veronica had no tolerance, No Desire to Keep Forgiveing, We Could never bring harmony into our soul, For you and I live in a world that is not easy and every day demands a Victory I Write to you Because your never have much time for me, you are moving at all times, If We Don't slow Down and talk More, the Germs of our actions will spread and bring greater Calamities,

(2)

she both of us, our being is good, our lack of religon has Created a strange Way of Family life, We meaning us and the two Girls, Never pray togather, they say the Family that prays togather, Stays togather, now I see that this is true, We never Warship God togather, We never go out Togather for nothing, not even ice cream for the Girls, We never eat none of the Three Meals Togather, all these things about materal life our Girls will never no, when they have Children, We need to try and find out in what Way happiness Can be braught about, and in this Way We Can realize that peace which is the longing of our saul, and We can impart it to Hana & Laila. thereby attaing our goal, which is the happiness and peace in our lives.

Muhammad

③ Veronica Oli

I Was thanking of the Way We live
with Hana & Laila. Lets eat Breakfast
Togather and take Pictures of it, So
they can see it When they are older
We can set the table and Bring Sam Can
take the Pictures, you Will be so glad
you did this When you are older and
the girls are Bigger, and lets take them
out for ice Cream and get Bingham
to take pictures of us eating ice Cream
With the girls, Because if We Do Brake
up, the girls will alway have Pictures
of us Togather with them, lets take
them to school one day Just you and
me, and get Pictures in their Class room
with their Teachers, all this Will Be
So Nool, for them in the future, you
will never be sorry if you Do, But you
will if you Dont,

Think about it

I've been so many places
and I've seen so many Faces
until I felt lost in between
Places.

After all the love in my life
after all the Pains in my life.
I think you are going to remain
my Wife.

Where Have you been My Jane
Where Have you been My Dane

I've been searching so long
For Happiness.
Somehow I've never found
tenderness

Where Have you Been My
Lady
Where Have ya Been My
Baby

Now that you've become my
sunshine

There's sweet music on my
Mind

Which makes me Feel very
Divine.

Yes My Love We are one
Hearts
And We Both Knew From the
START

Veronica a Princess of Enchantment *

Your are admired For Many reasons.
For you are a pearl of Wisdom.
that keeps its beauty in all
Seasons.

your smile is beautiful and
Priceless by Far,
Even your eyes sparkle like a
Star *
And your Charm is above Par.

It's easy to see your Passion
There's Very little time For hate
and that's reason enough to
Celebrate

Sometimes you may get
depressed
and Feel the burden of
Stress,
But somehow you Maintain
your ZEST,

your heart is Filled With
allah's Love
and you share that Gift
From above

Veronica My Princess of Enchan
tment you are Rare
Today your golden glow shows
you Care, For allah has made
YOU HARD TO COMPARE

I have found that you have the disposition of an angel. the Way you get around everyday you have the endurance of a Camel, From the First day I saw you, I saw the tenderness of a shepherd, you have always had the devotion of a true Mother. the Way you always see things you have the vision of an Eagle you are a peaceful Person, and have the gentleness of a sheep. Everyday you show the industry of a Beaver, and the Harmlessness of a Dove. also the Wisdom of an owl, all this is why I Love you so Much.

Muhammad

①   When its over.

~~~~~~~~~~~~~~~~~~~~~~~~~~~~~~~

Veronica, our love has now Come
to its end,

Simply because We are only Friends,

~~~~~~~~~~~~~~~~~~~~~~~~~~~~~~~

Now that our love has Ceased
to exist,

Lets try to Find another means
to persist,

~~~~~~~~~~~~~~~~~~~~~~~~~~~~~~~

We Were very good For each other

Now We are somewhat like a sister
and brother

~~~~~~~~~~~~~~~~~~~~~~~~~~~~~~~

However, things Can never be the
Same,

Since We have Disobeyed the
rules of the Game.

~~~~~~~~~~~~~~~~~~~~~~~~~~~~~~~

For every move we make this new
year.

I Want you to give me your ear,

For us I pray that its not really
over my Dear.

Because for me, the meaning of this
thing is not Clear.

~~~~~~~~~~~~~~~~~~~~

It Was said to me one time

That life is something like a
dime.

~~~~~~~~~~~~~~~~~~~~

For it is never easy to

understand

How heartackes and despair

Can take Command.

~~~~~~~~~~~~~~~~~~~~

③

However, We Both Will move
Further on to new adventures
Waiting down the line.

Perhaps, We Will Find Happiness
behind.

In the shadow of ZAIRE Within
our Minds.

~~~~~~~~~~

But looking Back is not the Way,

~~~~~~~~~~

For that time has Faded With
yesterday.

There's So Much to do today

and unpleasent times Will
Just drift away

Terry
McComa

Jun 5 83 :)

450

In Afric
ZAIRE
VERONCA
BY
Muhammad Ali
oct 3-19-74
By Ali
VEROICA
oct 3-74

Dear Hana and Laila, I miss you all so much, I pray to allah all th Time, I pray to allah all th time 5 time, a day, I pray that He will help and guide you to the Right Way of life. One day soon I will see you all, I love you, I Hope and pray allah that I will see you soon, I want you to send me a Picture soon, I will go now, Hope to see you soon

From your Father
Muhammad Ali
2 - 23 - 90

P.S. Serve allah, He is the Goal

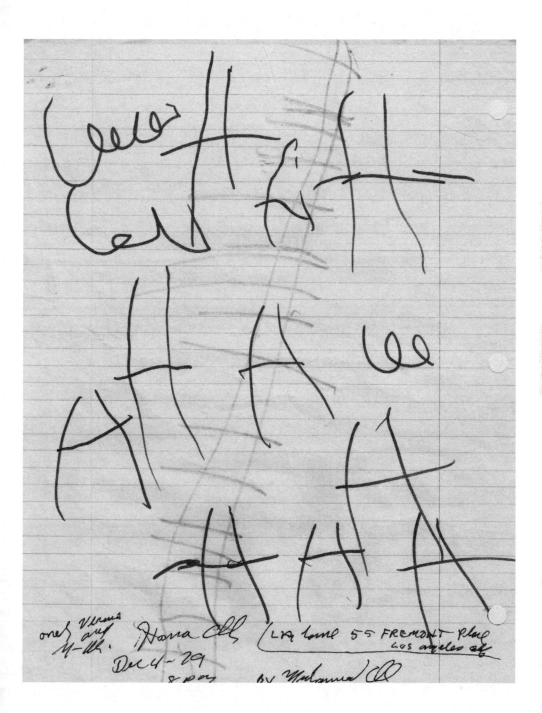

453

the staff and Director
of Pilgrim Foundation are
<u>quite</u> <u>concerned</u> with the
<u>continual</u> <u>misbehavior</u> of
Hana. If improvement does
not take place soon, it
has been suggested that
a different atmosphere
and or school be sought!

Any questions? Please
see Mrs. Beckel.

Thank you for your
cooperation.

— Nursery staff —

454

LOVE IS THE NET
WHERE HEARTS ARE
CAUGHT LIKE FISH

455

ACKNOWLEDGEMENTS

For my father, who has given me the greatest gifts of all. In the words of one of his favorite sayings: If all the trees were pens and all of the oceans were ink, it would still not be enough to write his story of love.

For my beautiful mother, who has always let me express myself freely without judgement. Thank you for teaching me how to be a lady and always setting the highest example of what a lady is: never speaking badly of those who spoke badly of you, always seeing the good, even in those who only sought out the faults in you. And most importantly, for always forgiving those who caused you your greatest pain. It's no wonder Daddy loved you so deeply.

For my husband, Kevin Casey. Thank you for having the utmost patience with me through this long, emotional and liberating process. Your love and support helped me reach my goal.

For Laila's daughter, my six-year-old niece Sydney Conway, who gave me the greatest advice of all. When I told her how hard I had been working on this book, she looked up at me and said, "Auntie Hana, just give it to God."

A VERY SPECIAL thank you for my editor Brenda Kimber at Penguin Random House. Thank you for giving me creative freedom and letting me make so many decisions, from the book cover and the page count to the number of photographs. If this book does not do well, it is certainly not your fault. Thank you for all of your hard work and patience, and for helping me make this book what it is: my own. And for Debs Warner, my copy editor. Thank you for all your hard work and patience. You and Brenda have both gone above and beyond! You have both been absolutely amazing. Thank you. Thank you. Thank you.

For my agent, Jill Marr. I appreciate all of the work that you do. As always, you have been wonderful. Thank you.

For George Foreman, who has been like a second father to me. Thank you for always offering your support in my time of need. You are truly wonderful and I will always be grateful for your presence in my life and that of your beautiful daughter, Georgetta. May God bless you and your beautiful family and grant you endless blessings.

To family friends and photographers who generously let me use some of the photographs in this book. It is such a blessing to have the same generosity which my father bestowed upon the world come full circle to be shared with me.

For Dustin Bingham, who is like a brother to me, and the son of my father's friend, the late Howard Bingham. Thank you for letting me use those wonderful photographs taken by your father over the years. I am forever grateful!

For my father's friends Gene Kilroy and Tim Shanahan, author of *Running with the Champ: My Forty-Year Friendship with Muhammad Ali*. Thank you both for always offering to help me in any way that you can. Gene, the pictures you took of Dad and me at Fighters' Heaven are among my favorites of us together.

For Michael Gaffney, author of *The Champ: My Year with Muhammad Ali*. Thank you for always being so willing to help me. Your photographs have captured so many wonderful memories.

For Bob Rosato, chief operating officer at USA Today Sports Images. Thank you for letting me use one of my all-time favorite photos—me and Dad eating popsicles together in his home office.

For my new friend and very talented poet/writer, Derrick McFadden author of *Prose from a Grandson to a Senior Fellow*. Thank you for all of the long hours you spent proofreading my manuscript and offering your invaluable advice. I hope I can return the favor some day.

For Marnie Summerfield Smith. Although I met you when the book was almost finished, you were a breath of fresh air, who helped me dig deep and bring the suppressed memories to the surface in a couple of the most difficult chapters I had to write. Thank you, Marnie, for all of your efforts and the proofreading and time that you set aside to help me make my deadline.

For Stan Wilson, with PBS, who said to me one day, "You need to write this story in a way that will keep people interested." This inspired me to read a dozen "how to write a memoir" books. Thank you, Stan! Without that simple advice, this book might not have been what it is today.

For Cal Fussman, bestselling author and journalist. Thank you for always being there to give me great advice and offer your insights. Like you said to me long ago in my father's living room in Michigan, I tried to find the little nuggets of gold.

For my friends who read every version as the book metamorphosed over the years.

For my friend Tina Gharavi, a talented screenwriter and director, and my favorite shopping partner. Thank you for all your help and late-night table-reading sessions. Your love, patience and kindness is greatly appreciated.

For my friend Shana Mangatal, author of *Michael and Me*, and her lovely mother, Janice. Thank you both for reading various chapters again and again, and always encouraging me with your positive feedback and fresh enthusiasm. You both read more chapters and versions of this book than anyone else.

For my friend Lauren Ellington. Thank you for always making my father smile and eagerly reading random parts of the manuscript with endless enthusiasm.

For my friend Elizabeth Trumbach. You were there from the very start six years ago when the book was just a pile of transcribed recordings. Thank you for all of your help organizing them.

For my sweet friend Daisy Villa and her husband, Alex. Thank you for always encouraging and uplifting me with your spiritual and loving support. And thank you, Alex, for always being so willing to help me with the book in any way that you could.

For my friend and world-class massage therapist Lama Amin and her friend, Darren. Thank you both for always reading the chapters I emailed you. And thank you, Lama, for those magical massages. They helped me relax, opened my mind and freed my creativity.

For my cousin-in-law Brandy. Thank you for taking the time to read my rough drafts and encourage me.

For my friend Nikki and her father, Neal Kleiner. Thank you both for reading and encouraging me.

For my friend Cia Parker. Thank you for all the nights you spent reading various chapters.

For my friend Valerie Ivette. Thank you for all of the time you put in reading my rough drafts and listening to my ideas.

A very special thank-you to my friend and the director of *I Am Ali*, Clare Lewins. Thank you for all your words of encouragement as you read the early versions of this book.

And last but certainly not least. For my friend Tracy Sherrod, editorial director at Amistad, HarperCollins, who was the editor of my very first book, *More Than a Hero*. Thank you for always being there to advise me and help me over the years. And most importantly, thank you for coming up with the name of this book: *At Home with Muhammad Ali*. In one way or another, you and everyone mentioned here has helped make this book what it is.

I thank you all from the bottom of my heart.

ABOUT THE AUTHOR

Hana Yasmeen Ali was born on 6 August, 1976. She is the third youngest child of Muhammad Ali and was very close to her father. Hana is the author of four books, and worked with autistic children as a behavior specialist for the Center for Behavior, Educational and Social Therapies for ten years. She is now a realtor with Coldwell Banker Residential Brokerage and lives in Los Angeles with her husband, mixed martial arts fighter and professional trainer Kevin Casey.

Instagram: @hanayali
Website: Hanaalirealty.com